BRIT GUIDE

LAS VEGAS

& DAY TRIPS
ARIZONA, UTAH & CALIFORNIA

Karen Marchbank
and Jane Anderson

D0417242

foulsham

Capital Point, 33 Bath Road, Slough, Berkshire, SL1 3UF, England

Foulsham books can be found in all good bookshops and direct from www.
foulsham.com

ISBN: 978-0-572-03915-8

Look out for the latest editions of Foulsham's other travel guides:
Brit Guide to Orlando and Walt Disney World by Simon and Susan Veness
Brit Guide to Disneyland Resort Paris by Simon and Susan Veness
Brit Guide to New York by Amanda Statham

Printed in Dubai by Oriental Press

CONTENTS

Photograph acknowledgements
Arizonaguide.com 233; Caesars Palace 28, 56t, 76, 148, 217b; Cirque du Soleil 60; CityCenter 24, 69, 105, 108, 109, 121, 129; citydata.com 212; Cottonwood Ranch 228; Deer Springs 248; DragonRidge Country Club 208; Fashion Show Mall 73; Fitzgerald's 52; Four Seasons, Larry Hanna 33,; Fremont Casino 157t; Getty Images 1; Goodtimes 172b; Govegas.com 72, 85b; Las Vegas Mini Gran Prix 184t; Las Vegas Natural History Museum 185b; Las Vegas News Bureau 5, 17, 57, 84, 137, 176, 177t, 181, 189, 192, 193, 200, 201, 221, 225b; Las Vegas News Bureau, Darrin Bush 8, 56b; Luxor 13; Tom Mescher 76, 177b; MGM 25, 29, 36, 64, 65, 89, 92, 96, 97, 100, 112, 113, 117, 124, 125, 128, 132, 133, 136, 152, 153, 156, 160, 161, 173, 176, 180, 184b, 216b, 220, 225t; Miracle Mile Shops 80; Mojave Resort Golf Club 209; Old Las Vegas Mormon Fort 186; Paris Las Vegas 224, 249b; Diane Pellegrini 20, 32, 37, 45, 77, 164, 197, 204, 216t, 236, 237; Pioneer Saloon 196; Plaza Hotel 48; Rio Hotel 49; Shapiro-art-studio.com 88t; Shoppes at the Palazzo 81; Skydive Las Vegas 212; Sokolowski.fr 245; Springs Preserve 188; Stratosphere 40, 252; Thirsty Camel 149; Lawrence Tierney 213, 217t; Town Square 95t; Travelutah.gov 240, 241; Treasure Island 12, 41; Tropicana 53, 157b; Venetian 9, 85b, 224; Walkingthroughdreams.com 68, 88b; Wynn Las Vegas 44

A note on the Brit Guides

This *Brit Guide* is one of an innovative series of travel guides that aim to offer practical, user-friendly guidance for the British traveller abroad. Focusing on clear, honest information, it is one British traveller's advice to another – without the jargon or sales pitch of the brochures.

If you would like the chance to see your Las Vegas photos in print, rename up to four high-resolution jpgs with your name and email address (substituting capital A for @) and email them to sales@foulsham.com with a subject line Brit guide to Las Vegas photos. Thank you for supporting the *Brit Guides*.

INTRODUCTION

Sin City continues to grow and remake itself in astonishing ways, and yet it is the same old Las Vegas. Where else can mum relax in the embrace of a world-class spa treatment while dad fires golf balls around a quality nine holes? Then you meet later for a few hours of blackjack, poker or some time pulling on the 'one-armed bandits', before strolling through the fabulous plazas of Caesar's shops. Next, you stop and enjoy a romantic dinner at the two Michelin star Alex at the Wynn before claiming marvellous seats for Elton John or Cirque du Soleil®'s new Elvis Presley show. Then it's drinks and dancing into the small hours at DJ Markus Schulz's session at the hip Marquee nightclub at The Cosmopolitan and before you know it, the sun is peeking over the horizon and you stagger off for a few moments of sleep before rising to do it all over again.

Legions of visitors descend on this isolated city in the desert to spend long, sleepless nights losing their inhibitions in an orgy of memorable good times, best confided with great prudence to family back home! In fact, it is often hard to keep track of everything, from how many glittering resorts are rising on the Strip skyline to which day it is!

Las Vegas is continuing to grow at an astonishing rate, but also in depth and complexity, and – in America at least – there's also been a change in Las Vegas's image. Associated in recent decades with tacky brashness, the city is now being transformed. The monstrous, themed resorts like the Venetian, Caesars Palace, Excalibur, Mandalay Bay and Bellagio have been challenged by new, even more titanic, wantonly decadent creations like Wynn Las Vegas, CityCenter, Trump International Hotel & Tower and The Cosmopolitan. Las Vegas has upped the sophistication with the opening of plush, non-gaming hotels including Mandarin Oriental Las Vegas and Vdara Hotel. The world's first Nobu Hotel is set to open in spring 2012. It will be the city's first boutique hotel and is housed near the Forum Shops at Caesars Palace. Then there's The Linq, a $550m outdoor retail, dining and entertainment district patterned after The Grove in Los Angeles and anchored by the Las Vegas High Roller the world's tallest observation wheel – 107ft/32m taller than the London Eye – which will literally take the mid-strip to new heights in 2013.

Two sides to every adult

After a brief, unsuccessful flirtation with selling itself as a family destination in the 1980s, Las Vegas realised it could never compete with the massive theme parks of Orlando, Florida. Adults were the natural market for Vegas. So, with Circus Circus and Excalibur standing as notable exceptions, Las Vegas has melded itself into an adult playground of such awesome scale and complexity as to be unrivalled by anything on Earth.

Entertainment has topped the list, and Vegas has invested billions of dollars in bringing the finest to its venues. The visually stunning productions of the Canadian troupe Cirque du Soleil® have reigned supreme for many years with hits like Le Rêve, though the new production called Elvis gets mixed reviews. But there are also stunning shows by Elton John, Donny and Marie Osmond, Blue Man Group, Penn & Teller, masked dance troop Jabbawockeez and a legion of others to beguile you, including the risqué Absinthe cabaret show at Caesars Palace. Then there are a constant stream of special concerts, championship boxing matches, Miss Universe pageants and more to draw in the crowds.

Steve Wynn started the Vegas tradition of bringing in greater cultural aspects to Vegas and his Wynn Las Vegas joins Bellagio, Caesars Palace, Venetian and Tropicana with impressive art and museum displays. During a visit to Las Vegas in June 2007, I was able to see gorgeous collections of Matisse at the Venetian, Picasso at Wynn Las Vegas, two impressive museum collections of 'Titanic Artefacts' and 'The Human Body' at the Tropicana and a lovely collection of French Impressionists at Bellagio.

The active crowd also has the attention of the resort moguls. A score of world-class golf courses has turned Las Vegas into a top golfing destination. Meanwhile a host of tour operators now offer rock climbing, horse riding, desert walking, parasailing,

Welcome to Las Vegas

© LVNB

boating, rollercoastering and nearly any other activity one could imagine – all with style and flair.

But the refined end of Las Vegas aside, Sin City has a reputation, well deserved, for sex and titillation. Has Vegas helped engineer the world's embrace of things once considered naughty, or has Sin City simply welcomed the shift in morality? Whichever is true, the number of 'skin' bars has tripled in recent years.

The arrival of the new millennium has ushered in a new age of ever-more-raunchy nightclubs where beds not settees, sofas not chairs give rise to a greater degree of intimacy. A venue's success in the last few years has gone hand in hand with its ability to offer both exclusive facilities for VIPs and saucy settings for a live-hard, work-hard and play-hard clientele.

This has gone hand in hand with Las Vegas touting itself as 'the new Ibiza'. A place to find the hottest DJs and *über* nightclubs, including the new 1OAK nightclub at The Mirage. And the beats don't stop during the day either, with the growing trend for daylight hours pool clubs such as Encore's Beach Club, Venetian's Tao Beach, Hard Rock Hotel's Sunday pool party called Rehab or Nikki Beach at The Tropicana. Here you can dance in the pool, cocktail in hand, to live DJ tunes or rent a cabaña with private Jacuzzi, well-stocked fridge and welcome misters to cool you down in the desert heat.

Where the shopping is easy

If you want it, Vegas has it all – from designer splurges to bargain deals. Everything from colourful souvenir shops to haute couture boutiques can be found, but there has been a definite trend towards high-class shopping outlets. Forum Shops at Caesars Palace led the way with its 3-storey complex of shops and restaurants. The Fashion Show Mall offers 7 fashion department stores in a one-stop destination and the Bellagio, Wynn Las Vegas and the Venetian have whole promenades of designer shopping. Meanwhile, Chelsea Premium Outlets, which specialises in designer outlet stores, similar to the outlet shopping villages in the UK, is now firmly established with 2 large locations in the city. Miracle Mile Shops has over 170 mid-to-high-priced shops. The Esplanade at Encore has a selection of 11 boutiques from Rock & Republic to Chanel; The Shoppes at The Palazzo with its flagship Barneys New

York and the Town Square Las Vegas on the south end of Las Vegas Boulevard with more than 150 shops to spend your dollar, not to mention Crystals, CityCenter's new shopping precinct right on the Strip.

Big is beautiful

None of this has happened by accident. The city has one of the most well co-ordinated and determined marketing strategies of any city in America (if not the world). Galvanised into action in the 1980s and '90s by the growth of Atlantic City, the Las Vegas Convention and Visitors Authority (LVCVA) has overseen marketing strategies that have helped the city reach a figure of 37.3 million visitors in 2010. The worldwide recession has meant that visitor numbers have fallen short of the 5-year plan to attract a phenomenal 43 million visitors per annum by 2009, yet this is a city that will never rest on its laurels.

Las Vegas opened 7,600 new hotel rooms in 2008. Although construction has slowed with the worldwide recession, another 1,265 new rooms were scheduled to open by the end of 2011 and a further 640 in 2012, bringing the total room count to a massive 150,840 rooms to fill.

One of the most significant sources of visitors is the ever-expanding convention industry that ensures those all-important bums are plopped on hotel beds during the week. As the party capital of America, the city has no problem reaching near 100% occupancy at the weekend, but to be truly successful (and provide the expected levels of return on the billion-dollar investments made in resort hotels) the hotels need to reach 80% occupancy all week long, all year round. And they are dazzlingly successful, as in 2010 room occupancy was 80.4%, around 20% above the national average.

Downtown is also becoming a must-see for visitors. Third Street's popularity is quickly growing as a top-notch entertainment district with an impressive list of bars and restaurants including Hogs & Heifers and The Griffin, a new tavern with a movie-set feel, a live music venue. Classic properties such as the Golden Nugget and The Plaza are investing millions in renovations to keep guests coming back.

So the appeal of Las Vegas remains strong and the city continues to grow and grow. A forest of construction cranes reach into the Strip's skyline as the newest creations take shape to shock, inspire and lure us back again and again.

LAS VEGAS TOWN PLAN

Here is a general overview of Las Vegas so you can familiarise yourself with the grid plan. It does not contain all the roads, but does have most of those referred to in this book. Remember Las Vegas Boulevard is the Strip and any roads to the right are East, while any to the left are West. The map in the hotels chapter (see page 21) shows you where the major resort hotels are located.

Top Las Vegas facts and figures (2010)

How many visitors come to Las Vegas each year?	37,335,436
How many convention delegates visit?	4,473,134
How many conventions are held per year?	18,004
What is the Las Vegas Strip's gaming revenue?	$5.8bn
What is the average gambling budget per trip?	$466
How long is the average visitor's stay?	3.6 nights

What to read and watch to get you in the mood

Fear and Loathing in Las Vegas, a novel by Hunter S. Thompson and a film starring Johnny Depp; *The Cold Six Thousand*, a novel by James Ellroy; *Bit the Jackpot* by Erin McCarthy; Elvis: *Viva Las Vegas*; *21* with Kevin Spacey; *Ocean's Eleven, Twelve* and *Thirteen* with Brad Pitt and George Clooney; *The Hangover* with Bradley Cooper; *Leaving Las Vegas* with Nicolas Cage; *What Happens in Vegas* with Ashton Kutcher and Cameron Diaz

ENTERTAINMENT CITY

What the city is all about, when to go and other useful information

Las Vegas as we know it is a little over 150 years young, built in the middle of the desert, and lives like some old American West frontier town. In many ways it is the modern equivalent of an 1880s gold rush town, where thousands of hopeful miners elbowed space on to gaming tables next to Chinese coolies and ranching cowboys. Pianos played loudly, dance hall girls swished their dresses provocatively and the drunken crowds whooped and fired their guns in the air.

Today's Las Vegas is just a bit more modernised, with her casinos, shows, nightclubs and showgirls. Sin City has it all, yet it's not until you see the staggering line-up of monster-sized hotels for yourself that the enormity of it sinks in. In fact, the city never fails to impress. From the revolving restaurants and bars, to the chichi lounges, spectacular thrill rides and state-of-the-art nightclubs, it is such an incredible experience from beginning to end that you'll need to remind yourself to close your mouth on a regular basis!

BRITTIP

Luke, a seasoned high roller, suggested to me that a first visit to Vegas can be so overwhelming that when booking, you should choose the number of days you'd like to stay and halve it!

In this chapter

As you drive up Las Vegas Boulevard South – the Strip, as it is known – from the airport, you'll encounter the triple-pronged Mandalay Bay resort, then the amazing pyramid of the Luxor on your left and the gigantic golden lion of the MGM Grand to your right. Other wondrous sights appear, including the beautiful drawbridge castle of the Excalibur and a complete replica of New York's skyline at the New York-New York resort. And that is before you even reach what used to be the most famous part of the Strip – the old Four Corners that include the Greco-Roman empire of Caesars Palace and the Flamingo. Then it all comes in a rush, with the massive resorts of CityCenter, Planet Hollywood (the old Aladdin), Paris, Mirage, Treasure Island, Venetian, the Wynn and its sister hotel, Encore and many more.

Towering over it all is the Stratosphere, the world's tallest free-standing observation

The Venetian

tower (1,148ft/350m high) at the top end of the Strip on the way to Downtown Las Vegas. Head further down Las Vegas Boulevard and you'll run across the Old Las Vegas. Here you'll find the last vestiges of Las Vegas's former neon culture known as Glitter Gulch in the Fremont Street Experience that totally encloses Fremont Street. Then on your right is the new East Fremont Entertainment District, a 3-block cluster of cool nightclubs, jazz venues and chic eateries, all within walking distance of each other.

What it's all about

Las Vegas is a great source of employment, although prospects weren't looking quite so good in 2011. Up to 6,000 people move into the area every month from southern California, Utah and beyond. In 2010 the US Census Bureau estimated the population of Las Vegas to be 583,756, one of the 10 fastest growing and the 28th most populous cities in the US. The predictions are that the current population of 1.9 million in Clark County, which encompasses Las Vegas, will have increased by over 50% to 2.7 million by the year 2018, after expanding from just 350,000 in 1992. The people came because the jobs were here. Las Vegas area created 47,000 new jobs in 2006, with employment up 5.7% to 875,000. The unemployment rate was a mere 4%. However although a weak dollar means more visitors are flashing their cash in Vegas, a slowdown in construction in response to the worldwide recession saw unemployment creep up to 15% in 2011.

Not all the jobs are in the gambling industry. Many other businesses, especially those in the high-tech industry, are attracted by the low property tax and the lack of income or corporate income taxes. Aggressive advertising campaigns in trade publications such as the *Hollywood Reporter* have played a key part in the expansion of Nevada's film industry, leading to an income state wide of $100m from this source alone.

The golfing industry, too, has had a massive impact, creating 4,500 jobs and bringing $891m to the southern Nevada area, with Las Vegas at its epicentre. All these growth areas were supported by a $91m expansion of the city's airport, McCarran International, and the opening of the $650m Las Vegas Monorail in the summer of 2005. Diversification is the buzz-word today, however – with talk of renewable energy, warehousing and medical tourism as Las Vegas once again reinvents its future.

Developers had been quick to spot the influx of smart, young professionals – lured by wages that vastly outstrip other American cities – and have rushed to provide a wealth of sparkling condos in the heart of the city's most exciting corridor: the Strip. It is these professionals – along with cooler, smarter types of visitor – who have contributed to the explosion of trendy bars, ultra-lounges (see page 135), sophisticated nightclubs and an array of restaurants sporting celebrity chefs. They also played a part in the growth of thrill rides, such as the heartline-twister Manhattan Express™ around New York-New York.

A holiday here can also encompass the fabulous natural sights of the Red Rock Canyon, Valley of Fire, Grand Canyon (by helicopter or plane in a day) and Mount Charleston, not so far away. You can find a venue for nearly every activity you fancy and there are plenty of opportunities to experience the real West. You can go horse riding at any of the national parks, go on a cowboy trail, meet the Native American tribes north and south of the city, go swimming, water-skiing and fishing at Lake Mead and even go skiing in Lee Canyon in winter. If that's not enough action for you, then try skydiving from Boulder City airport near the Hoover Dam.

The power of plastic comes into its own in the myriad shopping centres that have sprung up since Caesars Palace's Forum Shops gave a whole new meaning to the word 'mall'. Now locals and tourists spend even more money flexing their credit-card muscle shopping than they do on gambling, making Las Vegas one of the most successful places for the retail industry in all of America.

History in brief

It's a long way from the days of mobster Bugsy Siegel and, before him, the railroad settlers and Mormons. In fact, the history of southern Nevada reaches back into prehistoric times when it was a marsh full of water and lush vegetation that was home to dinosaurs.

Eventually, as millions of years went by, the marsh receded, rivers disappeared beneath the surface and the wetlands evolved into a parched, arid landscape that can now only support the hardiest of plants and animals. Water trapped underground in the geological formations of the Las Vegas Valley sporadically surfaced to nourish plants and create an oasis in the desert, while life-giving water flowed to the Colorado River.

Hidden for centuries from all but Native Americans, the Las Vegas Valley oasis was protected from discovery by the surrounding harsh and unforgiving Mojave Desert until around 1829 when Mexican trader Antonio Armigo, leading a 60-man party along the Spanish Trail to Los Angeles, veered away from the route and discovered Las Vegas Springs.

On the gold rush trail

The discovery of this oasis shortened the Spanish Trail to Los Angeles and hastened the rush west for the California gold. Between 1830 and 1848, the name Vegas was changed to Las Vegas, which means 'the meadows' in Spanish. In 1844, John C. Fremont camped at the springs while leading an overland expedition west, and his name is immortalised in the downtown Fremont Hotel and Fremont Street.

In 1855, Mormon settlers from Salt Lake City started to build a fort of sun-dried adobe bricks in Las Vegas to protect pioneers travelling between Utah and Los Angeles. They planted fruit trees and vegetables and made bullets from lead mined at Potosi Mountain, 30mls/48km from the fort. With Mormon influence, Las Vegas could have become a conservative, religious oasis in the desert. But it wasn't to be. The Mormons abandoned the settlement in 1858, largely because of Indian raids. The remains of their occupation is the oldest non-Indian structure in Las Vegas and has been designated a historic monument. The new town of Las Vegas had a different future ahead of her.

Working on the railroad

By 1890, railroad developers had chosen the water-rich valley as a prime location for a stop facility and town. When work on the first railroad into Las Vegas began in 1904, a tent-town sprouted, with saloons, stores and boarding houses, and the San Pedro, Los Angeles and Salt Lake Railroad (later absorbed by Union Pacific) made its first run east from California. The advent of the railroad led to the founding of Las Vegas on 15 May 1905. The Union Pacific auctioned off 1,200 lots in a single day in an area that is now known as the Fremont Street Experience.

Gambling got off to a shaky start in the state, which introduced anti-gambling laws in 1910. They were so strict that even the western custom of flipping a coin for a drink was banned. But the locals set up underground gambling dens for their roulette wheels, dice and card games. They stayed illegal but were largely accepted, and flourished until 1931 when the Nevada Legislature, cash starved by the horrific economic depression sweeping America, approved a legalised gambling bill that was designed to generate tax revenue to support local schools. More than 34.1% of Nevada's income comes from gambling tax revenue and the majority of its fund is used to provide state education.

In the same year, construction work began on the Hoover Dam project, which at its peak employed more than 5,000 people. During these economically disastrous years, employment was scarce and money was hard to come by. Yet here were legions of men from the project seeking a break from their 12-hour-a-day, 6-days-a-week work regime. They descended on the town with ample coin in their pocket and normally only 12 to 24 hours to enjoy their riches. After a tour of gambling, drink and women, the men would tumble into the back of a truck and blearily head back to work. Las Vegas traditions of 24-hour fast times and midnight breakfast specials became iconic fixtures. The young town of Las Vegas thrived even during the harsh realities of America's Great Depression.

The Second World War delayed major resort growth, but the seeds for development were sown when Tommy Hull opened the El Rancho Vegas Casino in 1941 on land opposite what used to be the Sahara Hotel. During the Second World War, the nearby Nellis Air Force Base was a key military installation and later became a training ground for American fighter pilots and provided more gamblers to swell the city's halls.

Mob rules

The success of El Rancho Vegas triggered a small building boom in the late 1940s. Capitalising on the expanding traffic from Los Angeles, several hotel-casinos were launched on the 2-lane highway leading into Las Vegas from Los Angeles and these evolved into today's Strip. Early hotels included the Last Frontier, Thunderbird and Club Bingo.

By far the most famous was the Flamingo Hotel, built by mobster Benjamin 'Bugsy' Siegel, a member of the Meyer Lanksy crime family. Complete with a giant pink neon sign, replicas of pink flamingos on the lawn and a bullet-proof, high-security apartment for Bugsy, the hotel opened on New Year's Eve in 1946. Nevertheless, Bugsy was gunned down 6 months later as he sat in the living room of his girlfriend's home in Beverly Hills. After numerous owners, the Flamingo now belongs to the world's largest casino entertainment company, Caesar's Entertainment. Today, only the name remains as the last of the original motel-like buildings were replaced by a $104m tower in 1995.

The early building boom continued and Wilbur Clark, a former hotel bellman, opened the Desert Inn in 1950. Two years later, Milton Prell opened the Sahara Hotel on the site of the old Club Bingo. Despite many changes of ownership, the Sahara survived until 2011, when it closed, taking a bit of history with it. The Desert Inn, underwent a $200m remodelling and construction programme in 1997 and remains as a part of Steve Wynn's new Wynn Las Vegas resort, which opened in March 2005.

The Sands Hotel, a showroom and once the playground for the 'Rat Pack' of Frank Sinatra and his buddies, high-rollers and Hollywood stars, opened in 1952, but was demolished in 1996 to make way for the fabulous Venetian.

In 1976, Atlantic City in New Jersey legalised gambling and so began a new era in Las Vegas's history, as gamblers from the American East Coast were kept away by Atlantic City's proximity. Las Vegas hotel-casinos saw they would need to create a true resort destination to compete. Caesars Palace had been the first hotel on the Strip to create a specific theme for its resort-hotel when it opened in 1966, and 2 years later Circus Circus opened its tent-shaped casino with carnival games and rides. But it was not until the late 1980s and early 1990s that the boom in resort hotels began in earnest.

A new day dawns

In 1989, the $630m upmarket Mirage Hotel opened with a white tiger habitat, dolphin pool, elaborate swimming pool and waterfall and a man-made volcano that belched fire and water. Mirage's owner at the time, Steve Wynn, then built the $430m Treasure Island resort next door, which is now home to the *Sirens of TI* show. Wynn also went into a joint venture with Circus Circus Enterprises to develop another luxury resort hotel – the Monte Carlo, which opened in 1996 – and his next venture – the luxurious Bellagio, styled as an Italian lakeside village – which opened in 1998 on the site of the former Dunes Hotel. Wynn sold all his holdings in these hotels in June 2000 and snapped up the Desert Inn ten days later.

The Excalibur medieval castle opened in 1990 with court jesters and King Arthur's jousting knights entertaining visitors in the massive $290m complex. Circus Circus Enterprises then developed the amazing $375m Luxor next door, opening in 1993.

In the same year, Grand Slam Canyon Adventuredome opened at the Circus Circus hotel, as did Treasure Island and the MGM Grand Hotel and Theme Park. Now one of the world's largest resorts, the MGM Grand has 3 of the largest concert

Treasure Island

and sports venues in Las Vegas, some of the top restaurants and myriad swimming pools and tennis courts.

In 1997, the £460m resort hotel New York-New York that re-creates the Big Apple's skyline added 2,000 rooms. Then came a whole raft of luxury resorts aimed specifically at the sophisticated traveller, including the Mandalay Bay, Paris and Venetian in 1999 – themed as a South Seas island, the French capital and Venice respectively. The Aladdin opened in 2000, almost immediately faced a host of economic problems and descended into bankruptcy. Then the Palms opened in 2001. It all went quiet for a few years until the unveiling of Wynn Las Vegas in 2005, which coincided with a new round of building projects. The Aladdin became Planet Hollywood, and in 2008–2009 the massive constructs of the Cosmopolitan, Trump International and the greatest of them all, CityCenter, opened their doors. The CityCenter Project, built by MGM/Mirage, is the most massive privately financed building project. These new hotels break from the Las Vegas of decadent, themed resorts. Instead, all of them, starting with the Wynn Las Vegas, are not just the last word in luxury, or just magnificent creations on a theme, but have also swelled the cultural and dining coffers of the city.

It seems that after going through all its different marketing ploys – the city that never sleeps, a family town, adults only – Las Vegas has finally become the sophisticated mecca of fun that Bugsy Siegel envisaged so many decades ago. More will follow as Caesar Entertainment break ground to construct the world's largest ferris wheel, The Las Vegas High Roller, in the middle of the strip, due to take its first dizzying spin in 2013. Recent market research has shown that consumers want the familiarity of the Vegas they've always known and loved. People come here to exhale and splurge a little. After a year of flirting with tourism pitches that directly addressed the recession, the city in the desert has resurrected its successful marketing theme: 'What happens in Las Vegas stays in Las Vegas' – unless you've put it on the credit card, of course!

BRITTIP
Don't hire a car from the airport or you'll be charged exorbitant airport 'surcharges'. Take a cheap shuttle to your hotel and sort it out from there.

Getting around

Las Vegas has been growing at such a phenomenal rate in the last 20 years that her roads, especially around the Strip, are hopelessly clogged, especially in the afternoons. In the evenings, it is much faster to walk than to drive along Las Vegas Boulevard, especially if there is a special event happening.

BRITTIP
Make sure you have enough cash in dollars if taking a taxi from the airport as Las Vegas taxis don't accept credit cards.

If you arrive by plane, a taxi ride to a Strip hotel (where most of the major theme resorts are located) will cost around $15, and to a downtown hotel $20–30, depending on the route taken and the time of day. The airport shuttle costs less than $10 to Strip hotels and is excellent value for money. Shuttles can be found immediately on your right as you exit the baggage reclaim area. The ticket office is on your left. In addition, most major hotels run shuttles to and from the airport. If you're a high roller, a limo will no doubt be there to whisk you to your mega suite.

BRITTIP
Many upmarket resorts like the Venetian and Bellagio have counters at the airport where you can check in to your room at the airport. Look into this as you'll save lots of time doing it there!

The pool at the Luxor

Walking

Let's face it, walking is the way most people want to explore the Strip, yet it can be a highly dodgy activity. For one thing, in the summer the heat is suffocating, and while you might see your destination, trust me, it is still a very long way off. Resorts seem so near because they are so massive!

Also, the city – like most of those in America – is mostly geared to cars and is not just pedestrian-unfriendly, but downright dangerous. The construction and heavy traffic make drivers frustrated and hasty: dangerous conditions for pedestrians. In some parts of the Strip, where many of the never-ending construction sites are located, there are no pavements at all. In other parts, where there are pavements and even pedestrian crossings, there is not enough time to get across the road before the lights change. What's worse is that most of the road-users seem to see pedestrians as targets. When the light changes they have the right of way and you'd better dash across.

However, the hotels and city councillors have taken action – footbridges have been built at many of the junctions with more to come. I strongly advise you to use them.

The monorail

Web: www.lvmonorail.com
Prices: Single ride ticket $5; 1-day pass $12, valid for unlimited travel for any 24-hour period; 3-day pass $28, valid for 72 hours from first use. Automated ticket machines can be found at all the stops and some of the resorts.
Hours: 7am–2am Mon–Thurs, 7am–3am Fri–Sun.
The $650m monorail opened in 2004 and is a happy, if somewhat flawed, way to get around. In fact, most times it is by far the fastest way to travel from one part of the Strip to another. The monorail grew from an original transit venture between the MGM Grand and Bally's Hotel in 1993. The Las Vegas Monorail Company, which owns the new transit service, was created in 2000 as a non-profit corporation and now owns the original monorail system.

Monorails come every 4–12 minutes and whisk you along to your destination, avoiding the horrid traffic of the Strip. There are 2 niggles about the monorail service. First, when it opened in 2004 a single fare was only $3, but this was raised in 2007 to $5, which makes it far less of a bargain than originally. Second, all the stops are poorly marked, often difficult to find, and they are also in the very back of each property. This means you must do a lot of walking through these massive resorts to get there, then you face another long walk to get to where you want to be. It may be much faster to simply walk to your destination if it is only one or 2 stops down the line.

The monorail runs on the east side of the Strip, and there are 6 stops, starting here with the southernmost stop:
- MGM Grand main hotel entrance services the Tropicana, Mandalay Bay, Luxor, Excalibur, New York-New York and Monte Carlo
- Bally's and Paris Las Vegas services the Paris, Planet Hollywood, Bellagio, and CityCenter
- Flamingo/Caesars Palace
- Harrah's/Imperial Palace services the Mirage, Treasure Island and Venetian
- Las Vegas Convention Center and Las Vegas Hilton
- Sahara (the station remains although the hotel closed in May 2011) services Circus Circus and Stratosphere

Three other monorails run on the western side of the Strip between Treasure Island and the Mirage; the Bellagio and the Monte Carlo; and the Excalibur, Luxor and Mandalay Bay resorts. These monorails are free. An extension was approved to connect the Sahara to Fremont Street in the downtown area in 2001, but the plan never came to fruition. There are also plans to connect to McCarran International Airport, on hold for the moment.

Buses and taxis

If you're sticking to the main drag, the monorail will be the fastest bet. However, the bus service – Citizens Area Transit (CAT) – has a 24-hour service on the Strip and downtown, plus 40 other routes that operate 5.30am–1.30am daily.
'The Deuce' is the route for Las Vegas Boulevard, sporting double-decker buses that come approximately every 5–10 minutes. Exact change is required, but you can get all-day passes as you board the bus, that are reasonably priced at $4. In the afternoons and evenings the buses can be terribly crowded, with long queues at the (fortunately) shaded bus stops. For information about routes and schedules, call 702 228 7433 or visit www.rtcsouthernnevada.com.

More than 1,100 taxis service the city but costs will mount if you use them all the time. My caveat would be to avoid using taxis where possible and try to

| MONTH | TEMPERATURE °C/°F | | HUMIDITY % | PRECIP. | SUNSHINE |
	MIN	MAX	AM/PM	INCHES	%
January	1/34	13/55	41/30	.50	77
February	3/37	19/66	36/26	.46	80
March	5/41	20/68	30/22	.41	83
April	9/48	25/77	22/15	.22	87
May	15/59	30/86	19/13	.22	88
June	20/68	36/97	15/10	.09	92
July	24/75	40/104	19/15	.45	87
August	22/72	38/100	14/18	.54	88
September	18/64	34/93	23/17	.32	91
October	11/52	27/81	25/19	.25	87
November	5/41	19/66	33/27	.43	80
December	1/34	14/57	41/33	.32	77

use the monorail. A full list of 16 cab companies can be found at taxi.state. nv.us/taxicabinfo.htm. They include Ace Cab Co: 702 888 4888; Checker Cab Co: 702 873 8012; Desert Cab Co: 702 386 4828; Lucky Cab Co: 702 477 7555; Union Cab Co: 702 888 4888; Whittlesea Blue Cab Co: 702 384 6111.

The Nevada Taxicab Authority (www. taxi.state.nv.us) has good taxi information including a chart of simple fares.

BRITTIP
Not only is taking a taxi pricey, but also it is almost impossible to flag one down on the street. You must either pick one up from a hotel (where there's often a queue) or from designated stops.

Car rental

For travelling about the Strip or downtown, you are best off without a car. However, if you want to explore the outlying areas like the Grand Canyon, Hoover Dam and elsewhere a car is a necessity.

Before hiring a car, read Chapter 14 (see page 229) first so you know exactly what you'll have to pay for. Most cars can be hired locally to travel throughout California, Nevada and Arizona. However, if you are travelling outside that area, check with the car hire firm for limitations.

If you do plan to arrange car rental on arrival in Las Vegas, look out for special deals advertised in the local press. The average price for an economy car in Vegas is $25–35 per day, but you might find excellent prices and extras such as free long-distance phone cards. You should also look at the offers with our *Brit Guide* partner, Alamo.

Car rental companies in Las Vegas include: Advantage Rent-A-Car: 702 798 6100; Alamo: 702 263 8411; Allstate: 702 792 5984; Avis: 702 531 1500; Budget: 702 736 1212; Dollar: 702 731 1898; Enterprise: 702 795 8842; Hertz: 702 262 7700; National Car Rental: 702 261 5391; Rent A Vette Sports Cars/Exotics/ Motorcycle Rentals: toll-free 866 871 1893; Thrifty: 702 896 7600.

BRITTIP
Be careful to check what the total cost of car hire will be. Many car hire firms advertise an extremely low rate from the airport, but then you are charged exorbitant airport 'surcharges' that often make the total cost much higher than if you'd rented at your hotel. On the other hand, at relatively quiet times in Vegas, the specials offered at the airport are much cheaper than those in town. Make a few phone calls, asking for the total price 'including all taxes and fees'.

The Strip

Some companies have rental sites at many of the major resort hotels. If booking on site in Las Vegas at a quiet time, you may be offered very cheap upgrades, but beware of hard-sell tactics and if you're certain you don't want or need a bigger car, don't be persuaded.

Limos

It won't cost you an arm and a leg to travel in style in Las Vegas – think tuxedo-ed chauffeurs and neon lighting. You can rent a limo for the ride into town from the airport for as little as $6.50 per person if there are several of you. Check out the deals available on arrival. If you're having a big night out on the town and want to have a drink, at $35 an hour, hiring a limo for the night often works out at about the same price as a taxi.

Limo companies include: Ambassador Limousines: 702 362 6200; Bell Trans/Limousines and Buses: 702 739 7990 or toll-free 1 800 274 7433; Las Vegas Limousine Service Party Bus VIP: 702 448 6789; Las Vegas Limousines: 702 888 4848 or toll-free 1 888 4400; On Demand Sedan-Black Car Service: 702 876 2222; Presidential Limousine: 702 731 5577.

BRITTIP
Some of the smaller rental companies may be cheaper, but always ensure that your rental agreement will allow you to drive outside the state of Nevada.

The best times to go

In 2010, Las Vegas had a staggering 150,840 rooms, but at many times of the year it still gets absolutely packed. A staggering 7,600 new rooms opened in 2008 with 16,000 due to open over the following 3 years. And although construction has slowed due to the worldwide recession, 1,265 new rooms were scheduled to open by the end of 2011 and a further 640 in 2012. The average room price skyrocketed from 'only' $104 in 2005 to a hefty $120 in 2006. Now is as good a time to go as any as room rates have fallen from $97.31 in 2009 to an average $95 as of 2010.

The busiest times are Christmas, June, July, August, Easter and the American bank holidays: President's Day (George Washington's birthday) – the third Monday in February; Memorial Day – the last Monday in May and the official start of the summer season; Independence Day – 4 July (slap bang in the middle of the high season anyway); Labor Day – the first Monday in September and last holiday of summer; and Thanksgiving – always the fourth Thursday in November.

The best times to visit – providing there are no major conferences or boxing matches going on – are from January to the end of April (excluding the bank holidays) and Easter, and October to November. August and September are busier, but are still good times to go, though stiflingly hot.

The weather

One thing you can be sure of – you're not going to freeze! Having said that, in December 2008, Las Vegas experienced as much as 8in/20cm of snow, the most in 30 years.

Generally, Las Vegas has about 300 days of sunshine a year, with an average rainfall of 4.2in/10.2cm throughout the year, making it an arid climate. June to September tends to be the hottest period, with daytime temperatures above 100ºF /38ºC in July and August. So if you're going out for the day, always make sure you put a good sunblock on before you leave your hotel, cover up when necessary and carry water with you.

What to wear

Fortunately, given the climate, the dress code is pretty relaxed in Las Vegas with casual clothes permitted around the clock. But wearing swimming costumes inside a casino or restaurant is not acceptable and it is normal to dress up for a big evening out when you can be as flamboyant as you like and not feel out of place. If you're visiting in early spring or late autumn, take a sweater or light jacket for the evening and something a bit warmer for winter.

BRITTIP

When buying US dollars before your trip, always ask for plenty of $1 bills – known as singles – so you can tip bellboys, porters and taxi drivers on arrival. Also, at many American airports it will cost you $1 to use a baggage trolley.

Tips on tipping

Tipping is not just a way of life in America but a genuine source of income for most employees in the hotel and casino industries and they are even taxed on an expectation of tips received. Sadly, tipping is something that we Brits tend to overlook.

There are some fairly loose customs in Las Vegas, but here is a guide to how much we should tip.

- Bartenders and cocktail waitresses: $1–2 a round of drinks for parties of 1–4 people, more for larger groups.
- Bellboys: $1 per piece of luggage.
- Concierge service: $2-20.
- Food servers and room service: 15–20%.
- Hotel maids: $1–2 a day at the end of a visit.
- Keno runners, slot machine change girls/men and casino dealers: $1–2 for the service and at least a small percentage of any win. Some gamblers who play for long periods tip even if they've lost!
- Maître d': Many showrooms sell assigned seating tickets, which may include the tip. In resort showrooms that have restaurant-style reservations and seating, you can tip the maître d' (Americans don't have head waiters, they have maître d's like the French!) $5–20 to improve your seats.
- Pool attendants: 50 cents–$1 for towels, pads, loungers, etc.
- Showroom servers: $5–10 for a party of 2–4 people at a cocktails-only show, or $10–20 for a dinner show, depending on the service and food quality.

The Monorail

© LVNB

- Taxi drivers: $1–2 per person at the end of the trip, or follow the 15–20% rule, whichever is greater.
- Valet parkers: $2, depending on how quick the service has been.

◀🇬🇧 BRITTIP
Be generous with taxi drivers. Unlike most other cities, it is rare for drivers in Las Vegas to be their own bosses and wages are low, so a decent tip would be appreciated!

You can often get great room upgrades for a $20 tip to the desk clerk when you book in. Take a look at the Brit tip on page 24.

◀🇬🇧 BRITTIP
Most casinos provide free drinks for genuine gamblers, but at busy times the service can become quite slow. One way to receive fast attention is to ask everybody in your party or at your gambling table to offer an additional dollar tip when you first sit down. Give it to the server when you make your first order. Guaranteed, she'll always check your table first and most often!

Medical emergencies

The number for the emergency services is 911.
Medical help: If you need medical help in Las Vegas that does not require an ambulance, there are 3 main options, all of which are open 24 hours a day, 7 days a week: Harmon Medical Center, 150 East Harmon Avenue (702 796 116); Fremont Medical Center, 4880 South Wynn Road (on the corner of Tropicana and Wynn, 702 671 6819); and UMC Hospital, 1800 W Charleston Boulevard (702 383 2000).

Many prescription and over-the-counter drugs are produced under different generic names in America. If you take any kind of regular medication, e.g. for a heart condition or epilepsy, it's a good idea to ask your doctor or pharmacy to find out the American name for your particular prescription drug. Keep this written down with your prescription or put both English and American drug names inside a clear plastic case that is easily accessible for medical crews, in case you are involved in an accident. The American term for paracetamol is acetaminophen.

Useful websites

www.visitlasvegas.com: Run by the city's Convention and Visitors Authority, this website not only supplies information but also carries a preview of good deals.

◀🇬🇧 BRITTIP
The city's Information Center can be found at 3150 Paradise Road. Call 1 877-VISITLV (847 4858) or 702 892 0711. Open Mon–Fri 8am–5pm.

www.ilovevegas.com: Provides current information, supplied by the magazine *What's On, The Las Vegas Guide*, about hotels, casinos, dining, entertainment and recreation. Useful for booking shows and tours online.
www.lasvegasadvisor.com: Run by Huntington Press and Anthony Curtis, a Las Vegas icon for good deals and bargain hunting. Here are rankings of the best deals for gambling, meals, drinks and shows. It also has one of the best web portals for finding cheap Las Vegas hotel rooms.
www.lasvegas.com: Excellent source of detailed information, discounts and booking for hotels, restaurants and clubs.
www.lasvegasgolf.com: First-rate guide for golfers with great deals on packages.
www.lvrj.com: One of the most useful websites with links to entertainment, local news and maps, run by *the Las Vegas Review-Journal*.
www.lasvegasnevada.gov: Government-run site offering a more wholesome view of the city including free family events and the city's green policies. A special 'visitor' section gives useful information on how to get married plus great interactive maps.

◀🇬🇧 BRITTIP
If you run out of cash, you'll find many ATMs (cash machines) in virtually every hotel.

Language in Las Vegas

It has often been said that Brits and Americans are divided by a common language and when you make an unexpected *faux pas* you'll certainly learn how true this is. For instance, never ask for a packet of fags as this is the American slang word for gays and a sense of humour is not their strong point! There are plenty of other differences, so this list should help to avoid confusion. Remember, too, that spellings sometimes vary.

Travelling around

English	American
Aerial	Antenna
Articulated truck	Semi
Bonnet	Hood
Boot	Trunk
Caravan	House trailer
Car park	Parking lot
Car silencer	Muffler
Crossroads/junction	Intersection
Demister	Defogger
Dipswitch	Dimmer
Dual carriageway	4-lane or divided highway
Flyover	Overpass
Give way	Yield
Jump leads	Jumper cables
Lay-by	Turn-out
Lorry	Truck
Manual transmission	Stick shift
Motorway	Superhighway, freeway, expressway
No parking or stopping	No standing
Pavement	Sidewalk
Petrol station	Gas station
Request stop	Flag stop
Ring road	Beltway
Slip road	Ramp
Subway	Pedestrian underpass
Transport	Transportation
Turning	Turnoff
Tyre	Tire
Underground	Subway
Walk	Hike
Wheel clamp	Car boot
Windscreen	Windshield
Wing	Fender

BRITTIP
If you arrive at a hotel by car or taxi, one bellhop (hotel porter) will take your luggage out of the boot (trunk) – for which you have to tip him – then another takes it up to your room – and, yes, he needs a tip, too.

Food and drink

There are plenty of differences in US and UK food terms. For instance, the Americans don't flick fat over the top of an egg when frying it, but turn it over to cook on both sides, so for eggs the way I like them, cooked on both sides but soft, I don't order 'sunny-side up' but 'over easy' and if you like yours well done, then ask for eggs 'over hard'. Many standard American dishes come with a biscuit – which is a corn scone to us! They also have something called

Useful numbers

Airport information:	702 261 5743
Airport parking:	702 261 5121
Citizens Area Transit	702 228 7433
Convention information:	702 892 0711
Directory assistance:	702 555 1212
Emergency Service Dispatch:	911
Highway Patrol:	702 486 4100
Las Vegas Fire Department:	702 383 2888
Las Vegas Transit System:	702 384 3540
Marriage License Bureau:	702 671 0600
Metro Police:	702 828 4348
Road conditions:	702 263 9744
Show Hot Line:	702 258 5188
Tourist information:	702 892 7575
Weather:	702 736 3854

grits, which is a porridge-like breakfast dish made out of ground, boiled corn, plus hash browns – grated, fried potatoes.

English	American
Aubergine	Eggplant
Bill	Check or tab
Biscuit (savoury)	Cracker
Biscuit (sweet)	Cookie
Chickpea	Garbanzo bean
Chips	French fries or fried potatoes
Choux bun	Cream puff
Cling film	Plastic wrap
Coriander	Cilantro
Corn	Wheat
Cornflour	Cornstarch
Courgette	Zucchini
Crayfish	Crawfish
Crisps	Chips
Crystallised	Candied
Cutlery	Silverware or place setting
Demerara sugar	Light-brown sugar
Desiccated coconut	Shredded coconut
Digestive biscuit	Graham cracker
Double cream	Heavy cream
Essence (e.g. vanilla)	Extract
Golden syrup	Corn syrup
Grated, fried potatoes	Hash browns
Grilled	Broiled
Icing sugar	Confectioner's sugar
Jam	Jelly
Ketchup	Catsup
King prawn	Shrimp
Main course	Entree
Measure	Shot
Minced meat	Ground meat
Off-licence	Liquor store

Pastry case	Pie shell
Pips	Seeds (in fruit)
Plain/dark chocolate	Semi-sweet or unsweetened chocolate
Pumpkin	Squash
Scone	Biscuit
Shortcrust pastry	Pie dough
Single cream	Light cream
Soda water	Seltzer
Sorbet	Sherbet
Soya	Soy
Spirits	Liquor
Sponge finger biscuits	Ladyfingers
Spring onion	Scallion
Starter	Appetizer
Stoned (cherries, etc.)	Pitted
Sultana	Golden raisin
Sweet shop	Candy store
Take-away	To go
Tomato purée	Tomato paste
Water biscuit	Cracker

Shopping

English	American
Bumbag	Fanny pack
Chemist	Drug store
Ground floor	First floor
Handbag	Purse
High Street	Main Street
In (Fifth Avenue, etc.)	On
Jumper	Sweater
Muslin	Cheesecloth
Suspenders	Garters
Tights	Pantyhose
Till	Check-out
Trainers	Sneakers
Trousers	Pants
Underpants	Shorts
Vest	Undershirt
Waistcoat	Vest
Zip	Zipper

Money

English	American
Banknote	Bill
Bill	Check
Cheque	Check
1 cent	Penny
5 cents	Nickel
10 cents	Dime
25 cents	Quarter
Dollar	Greenback

General

English	American
Air steward(ess)	Flight attendant
Anti-clockwise	Counter-clockwise
At weekends	On weekends
Autumn	Fall
Behind	In back of
Camp bed	Cot
Cinema	Movie theater
City/town centre	Downtown (not the run-down bit!)
Coach	Bus
Cot	Crib
Diary (appointments)	Calendar
Diary (records)	Journal
Doctor	Physician
From … to …	Through
Lift	Elevator
Long-distance call	Trunk call
Nappy	Diaper
Ordinary	Regular, normal
Paddling pool	Wading pool
Post, postbox	Mail, mailbox
Pram, pushchair	Stroller
Queue	Line, line up
Tap	Faucet
Toilet	Restroom (public) Bathroom (private)

Lake Mead – the perfect place to relax

RESORT HOTELS

The biggest and the best hotels and how to choose the right one for you

Bugsy Siegel started it all and Howard Hughes, the famously reclusive billionaire, lent an air of respectability to the city, but modern Vegas is really a reflection of the dream of one man: Steve Wynn.

Steve Wynn, Las Vegas's modern-day casino mogul, provided the bridge between Mob City and Sin City when he opened the dazzling Mirage Hotel in 1989. It was the first major hotel to be built on the Strip in 16 years. With a $630m price tag, dolphin pool, white tiger habitat, man-made volcano and elaborate swimming pool, it set a new standard and sparked off a massive building rush. Wynn, went on to build the pirate-themed Treasure Island and upmarket Italianate Bellagio before selling out and starting a brand-new project over at the Desert Inn. Between 1989 and 2004 a host of themed resorts, inspired by Wynn's success, erupted along the Strip and turned Las Vegas into a true adult fantasyland.

◀▮▶ BRITTIP

The biggest problem the major resort-hotels have is registering guests – a 30-minute wait is not unusual at busy times! Depending on the room type, you can have access to VIP check-in which will be quicker than standard check-in. Most hotels also offer an express check-out. You register your credit-card details at check-in and then just drop off on check-out.

Historians will no doubt see 2005 as another important year in the city's development. Wynn's first solo project – Wynn Las Vegas – opened to a fanfare of publicity after one of the most tightly guarded developments the city has ever seen. Instead of having an über-fantasy conjuration like Luxor, Excalibur and Circus Circus, or destination fantasies like Mandalay Bay, Paris or Venetian, the Wynn Las Vegas was simple luxury. Its opening also coincided with another hotel 'gold rush' of building after a period of relative dormancy. Just when the whole world is feeling the bite of recession, Las Vegas defiantly declares the show must go on with the opening of MGM/Mirage's

massive CityCenter development housing three resorts: Aria Resort & Casino, Vdara Hotel and the Mandarin Oriental hotel. In addition there's the transformation of the old Aladdin into the uber trendy Planet Hollywood Resort & Casino, the opening of Encore, M Resort and Trump International Hotel & Tower and most recently, the Cosmopolitan. The brand new Plaza Hotel

& Casino has opened on the site of the old Union Plaza Hotel in downtown and the world's first ever Nobu Hotel opens in Caesars Palace in summer 2012. The largest project on the strip since 2007 is the Linq, a $550m retail, dining, entertainment and hospitality district facing Caesars Palace, due to open in 2013. This means a facelift for three strip hotels – The Flamingo, Imperial Palace and Harrah's Las Vegas – in the process.

BRITTIP
There has never been a better time to visit Vegas. Average lodging costs have plummeted in the last few years – from an average $119 in 2008 to $95 in 2010 – as hotels fight a price war to fill over 150,000 rooms.

The magic line-up

To really appreciate the sight of the glittering spectacles that are both resorts and attractions in their own right, it's best to fly into Las Vegas so you can get a bird's eye view as you land at McCarran International airport – either that, or take a fun helicopter flight. However, it's just as fascinating from the seat of a car.

As you come out of the airport you turn right on Las Vegas Boulevard and soon you'll pass the South Seas paradise of Mandalay Bay on your left, before spotting the daunting pyramid of the Luxor and the castle-like vistas of Camelot at Excalibur. At the new Four Corners of Las Vegas on the Strip, you will see the Tropicana to your right. Before you've had time to let out a gasp of amazement, you'll be passing the lion of MGM Grand, opposite the towers of New York-New York and its famous Big Apple landmarks. The Monte Carlo is next on the left, a fine re-creation of the ritzy Place du Monaco, then there is the edifice of CityCenter rising to the skies. Planet Hollywood (originally the Aladdin) is on the right, followed by the Eiffel Tower in Paris – but don't forget to glance left for a swift look at the Italian village setting of the Bellagio.

BRITTIP
2011 kissed goodbye to the Moroccan-style Sahara, and a little bit of Las Vegas history. Opened in 1952, it was the last remaining vintage 'Rat Pack' casino-hotel at the northern end of the Strip.

Now you've reached the old Four Corners, the original section of the Strip that was home to Bugsy Siegel's Flamingo, and here you'll see the majestic Caesars Palace with its Greco-Roman ramparts on the left. Opposite the Forum Shops at Caesars is the modern Flamingo. Then, further north on the right, is the currently Japanese-inspired Imperial Palace opposite the posh Polynesian resort of The Mirage and its erupting volcano. If arriving any time after 4pm, Treasure Island's *Sirens of TI* could well be in action, but don't forget to look right to see the spectacular Venetian with its re-creation of St Mark's Square and the Doge's Palace.

BRITTIP
Internet access through the TV is now available pretty much as standard in the major resort-hotels. Think around $6 for 2 hours or around $10 for 24 hours (plus tax).

Soon, on the left is the circus-dome shape of the Grand Slam Canyon and Circus Circus, a family resort on the theme of a travelling circus. The rose citadel of the Wynn Las Vegas is tantalisingly screened by a large man-made hill and ranks of cool evergreen trees. After that is the spire of the Stratosphere Casino, Hotel & Tower, the tallest free-standing tower in America.

BRITTIP
For a complete list of all dining options – both fine dining and casual – available in each of the resort-hotels see page 93.

Choices, choices! It's an amazing line-up – and it's all thanks to money and the making of it. But where do you choose to stay? There are three schools of thought, depending on your budget and your interests.

BRITTIP
AAA Star Living has come to Las Vegas which has 15 AAA Five Diamond resorts and restaurants – more than any other US city.

Resort-hotels

Undoubtedly, for the best time ever, stay in one of the main resort-hotels – all of which are featured in this chapter. The good part is if you stay and play at the same place you will get the most in convenience (no time-eating drives in Las Vegas traffic),

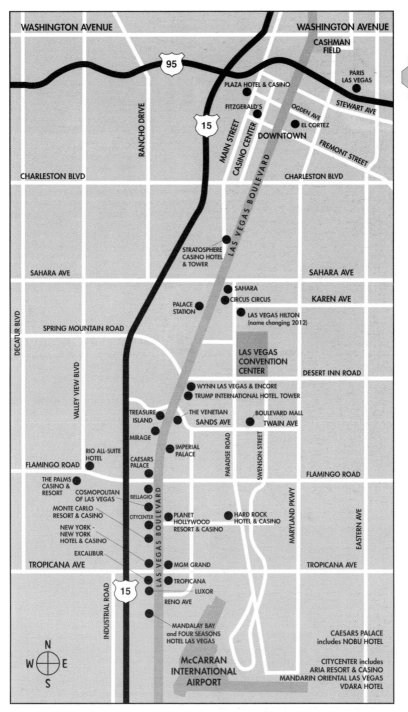

WASHINGTON AVENUE — **WASHINGTON AVENUE**

CASHMAN FIELD

95

15

PARIS LAS VEGAS

PLAZA HOTEL & CASINO

FITZGERALD'S

OGDEN AVE

STEWART AVE

EL CORTEZ

MAIN STREET

CASINO CENTER

DOWNTOWN

FREMONT STREET

RANCHO DRIVE

CHARLESTON BLVD — **CHARLESTON BLVD**

LAS VEGAS BOULEVARD

SAHARA AVE — **SAHARA AVE**

STRATOSPHERE CASINO HOTEL & TOWER

SAHARA

CIRCUS CIRCUS

KAREN AVE

PALACE STATION

LAS VEGAS HILTON (name changing 2012)

DECATUR BLVD

SPRING MOUNTAIN ROAD

LAS VEGAS CONVENTION CENTER

DESERT INN ROAD

VALLEY VIEW BLVD

WYNN LAS VEGAS & ENCORE

TRUMP INTERNATIONAL HOTEL TOWER

TREASURE ISLAND

THE VENETIAN

SANDS AVE

BOULEVARD MALL

TWAIN AVE

MIRAGE

RIO ALL-SUITE HOTEL

IMPERIAL PALACE

PARADISE ROAD

SWENSON STREET

FLAMINGO ROAD

CAESARS PALACE

THE PALMS CASINO & RESORT

COSMOPOLITAN OF LAS VEGAS

BELLAGIO

MONTE CARLO RESORT & CASINO

CITYCENTER

PLANET HOLLYWOOD RESORT & CASINO

HARD ROCK HOTEL & CASINO

FLAMINGO ROAD

NEW YORK - NEW YORK HOTEL & CASINO

MARYLAND PKWY

EASTERN AVE

EXCALIBUR

TROPICANA AVE

MGM GRAND

TROPICANA

TROPICANA AVE

15

LUXOR

RENO AVE

INDUSTRIAL ROAD

MANDALAY BAY and FOUR SEASONS HOTEL LAS VEGAS

CAESARS PALACE includes NOBU HOTEL

CITYCENTER includes ARIA RESORT & CASINO MANDARIN ORIENTAL LAS VEGAS VDARA HOTEL

McCARRAN INTERNATIONAL AIRPORT

N
W E
S

2

attractions and night-time thrills. However, these places are pricey. For instance, rooms can be had at Caesars Palace for $99 midweek, and at Circus Circus, Excalibur and Luxor an incredible $20–50 a night, but on a busy convention day the *minimum* room price can soar to $750/night! Then the gambling minimums and odds are also more expensive in these posh surroundings. Still, for many, being able to have the ultimate experience makes the budget less important, especially since the resorts do have a number of different price ranges.

BRITTIP

Staying at a resort-hotel may be more pricey but you might get better value for money as rates often include gaming, entertainment and dining credits and airport limousine transportation, which are sometimes worth more than the room price itself. If the hotel is part of a group – for example MGM Mirage includes the Bellagio, the MGM Grand and The Mirage – you will get preferred seating across all their entertainment venues and restaurants.

On a budget on the Strip

For the budget conscious, a great option is to stay at one of the many budget establishments on the Strip, downtown or on the locals' Boulder Highway Strip area where budget casinos offer clean and cheap rooms with great gambling odds. Then make the trip into the Strip area to enjoy the attractions and shows along the expensive real estate. While cheaper, the hotels are definitely **not** memorable and be aware that you will spend a lot of time travelling back and forth.

Aria Resort and Casino

© CityCenter

BRITTIP

The term 'the Strip' was coined by a former Los Angeles police captain in 1938. Guy McAfee said the stretch of road with its brightly lit hotels and casinos reminded him of Hollywood's Sunset Strip, another mecca for night owls!

Strip resorts

A third option is to stay in Strip resorts for delightful accommodation and for the attractions. Then for those intent gamblers, take a trip down to Fremont Street where the loose slots and advantageous gambling odds give you much longer play on your gambling budget.

Making your choices

To try to make your life easier – for both choosing a hotel and for seeing them as the attractions they are – I've given a full run-down of their facilities and roughly how much it costs for a room with two people sharing.

BRITTIP

One tradition left over from the old mob-run casino days is the '$20 room upgrade'. When you check in, you'll need to show the desk clerk your passport and a credit card. When you do, add a $20 bill (as a tip) and say 'Am I eligible for any complimentary room upgrades?' If there are any better rooms available, be they larger or perhaps with a lovely view of the Strip, the desk clerk will book you into one at the cost of your original reservation. If they can't, because the hotel is fully booked or for some other reason, the desk clerk will apologise and return the $20 to you. It usually works, and I've often been able to stay in rooms costing several hundred dollars more than I paid for!

I have not given the major resorts a rating for the simple reason that they are aimed at different types of people, so a comparison would not really be appropriate. Also, do remember that in Las Vegas, as in no other city on earth, supply and demand vary greatly and the differences are reflected in hugely fluctuating room prices. My notes on booking your hotel room in Chapter 13 give a more detailed picture of how to find a room not only at the inn of your choice, but also at the right price.

Major resorts on the Strip

Aria Resort & Casino

If you want to be part of the in-crowd, book into this flagship CityCenter gem.
Location: Part of the CityCenter development on the Strip between Bellagio and Monte Carlo resorts
Grand opening: 16 December 2009
Theme: Breathless avant garde
Cost: Part of the $8.5b CityCenter development
Web: www.arialasvegas.com
Reservations: 866 359 7757
Rooms: 4,004
Room rates: From $159 for guestrooms and from $400 for suites
Restaurants: 13 restaurants of incredible diversity. Making his Las Vegas debut, Chef Masayoshi Takayama's BARMASA has a ceiling that soars 35ft/10.6m above diners' heads as he serves up modern Japanese food. In Sage, chef Shawn McClain named Best Chef Midwest offers farm-to-table produce, artisan meats and sustainable seafood. American Fish draws inspiration from America's lakes, rivers and coasts. Then there's a whole array of steakhouses, Italian, patisseries, Chinese, Thai and cafés. Put it this way, you won't be going hungry here.
Nightlife: 9 bars and lounges and a spectacular nightclub.
Show: Resident Cirque du Soleil production, Viva Elvis, celebrating the musical legacy of Elvis Presley.
Attractions: At reception, guests are wowed by artist Maya Lin's 84ft/26m silver cast of the Colorado River, which is made from reclaimed silver and represents Nevada's standing as the 'Silver State'.
Gambling: More than 160,000ft^2/15,000m^2 of gaming.
Chilling out: 3 swimming pools, 50 cabañas and a huge tropical oasis pool deck, plus 2 European pools at the adults-only Liquid Pool Lounge.
Shopping: Just outside Aria is Crystals, CityCenter's retail and entertainment district with more than 500,000ft^2/46,450m^2 of shopping including Louis Vuitton, Hermes, Prada, Dior, Tiffany & Co. And new to Vegas are Tom Ford, Miu Miu and Marni amongst others.
Other amenities: 2-storey spa and salon with 62 treatment rooms – its only place in the country offering Ganbanyoku

(Japanese heated stone beds) – and 3 spa suites for couples or hen parties; championship golf nearby.

BRITTIP
'European', when applied to swimming pools, means topless.

Aria is a spectacular new gaming resort and part of CityCenter, the dazzling new vertical city on the Las Vegas Strip, which secured a AAA Five Diamond Award in its debut year. Designed by the world-renowned firm Pelli Clarke Pelli, it's high tech meets arty with an exterior of elegantly sweeping ripples of steel and glass with lavish natural elements indoors including plants, wood and stone. Guestrooms are bursting with technology. When guests enter they are greeted by lights filling the room, curtains parting to show the view and a TV asking for your preferences. Every time you return to your room, your preferences are remembered. Guests can wake up gradually through controlled temperature, lighting, curtain opening and choice of music. If you're feeling a bit green, you can opt for low lighting.

There are some of the most innovative restaurants in town, the most exciting show to hit the Strip for years and properly cool places to hang out. Definitely on the hip list.

Bellagio

Based on an entire village in northern Italy, this truly is a treat for romantics!
Location: The Strip at the corner of West Flamingo
Theme: Upmarket, romantic Italian lakeside village
Cost: $1.6bn, plus $375m in 2005 for the new Spa Tower and $70m in 2011 for room redesign
Web: www.bellagio.com

Bellagio

© MGM

Reservations: 888 987 6667
Fax: 702 693 8546
Rooms: 3,933
Room rates: From $169
Restaurants: 7 fine dining options including the award-winning Picasso, Le Cirque and Michael Mina Bellagio and 12 casual eateries including FIX for Classic American food and Jean Philippe Patisserie for fabulous cakes.
Nightlife: The Bank nightclub plus 7 bars and lounges.
Show: Cirque du Soleil® theatrical circus spectacular, O.

◀🇬🇧▶ **BRITTIP**

Room rates are a rough guide only as they can vary wildly. If there's a large convention booked to stay at the hotel of your choice, rates can easily rise by $200 or more. Do your homework before booking your flights – see page 18 for details of good websites to check.

Attractions: The Fountains of Bellagio, the Conservatory and Botanical Gardens and the Bellagio Gallery of Fine Art (BGFA), Jeff Mitchum Gallery displaying fine art photography and artefacts such as Ansel Adams' desert hiking boots.
Gambling: Blackjack, craps, mini-baccarat, roulette, European roulette, baccarat, pai gow poker, pai gow, big 6, Caribbean stud poker, let it ride, war, three card poker, sic bo, poker room, 2,400 slot machines, video poker and the race & sports book.
Chilling out: 5 outdoor pools; 4 whirlpools; 52 private cabañas in a Mediterranean courtyard setting.
Shopping: Via Bellagio filled with designer shops including Prada, Chanel, Giorgio Armani, Tiffany & Co., Gucci, Fendi and Louis Vuitton; Via Fiore with Giardini Garden Store and many other outlets.
Other amenities: 2 wedding chapels and Terrace of Dreams; a salon for facials, manicures and pedicures, barber room; Zen-influenced Spa Bellagio has 56 treatment rooms including 4 couple's rooms, meditation room and men's spa areas for 'shy guys' and Jukari Fit to Flex workouts by Reebok and Cirque du Soleil; Shadow Creek Golf Course.

One of Las Vegas's largest luxury mega-resorts, its 'signature' show is the free Fountains of Bellagio – a $30m aquatic spectacle created by colourful, soaring fountains in a synchronised water ballet accompanied by lights and soaring music by Copland and Strauss, and famous renditions by Celine Dion and Elton John. Another enjoyable freebie is the Conservatory and Botanical Gardens. The Conservatory is a 55ft/17m high, glass-ceilinged edifice with floral displays that reflect the seasons and major American holidays. Each display is planned a year in advance to ensure the necessary flowers, plants and trees are available. The Bellagio is also home to its own art gallery, which houses travelling exhibitions of exceptional art. 2011 featured 'A Sense of Place: Landscapes from Monet to Hockney' encompassing a wide range of landscape styles.

The real crowd-puller of the hotel is O, the show by the world-famous Cirque du Soleil®. A special $70m theatre, modelled on the Paris Opera House, was built as a permanent home for the theatrical acrobatics and breathtaking stunts that make Cirque shows so amazing. The Bank nightclub is sought after and has a glass encased dance floor and elegant VIP booths. The Hyde Lounge, designed by Philippe Starck and launched on New Years Eve 2011, is the first indoor-outdoor nightclub, with a terrace overlooking the Bellagio fountains. For daytime lounging, the Pool Bar serves great Bellagio Mojitos with fresh blueberries.

◀🇬🇧▶ **BRITTIP**

If you want to experience the vibes of the Bellagio without paying to stay, check out the sophisticated Caramel Lounge. Have a drink, take the weight off your slingbacks and just watch the beautiful people while the band plays in the background. You may even spot the odd celeb!

From each of the many rooms are panoramic views of the 8.5acre/3.4ha lake, classical gardens, elegant pools and landscaped grounds filled with fountains, waterfalls and pools. The 512 suites and a new Executive Suite Lounge opened in January 2009 and the $70m room redesign in 2011 has given main tower rooms vibrant, warm colours with botanical images and enhanced functionality such as brighter lighting and bigger and better mod cons including a 40in/1.6m mounted flat-screen TV.

The restaurants range from casual bistros to the gourmet restaurants Le Cirque and Picasso, which are among the most successful and popular in Las Vegas. When you have a spare moment (and a spare million), try browsing round the esplanade lined with Chanel, Armani, Prada and Tiffany boutiques, before taking afternoon tea – one of the more affordable pleasures at the Bellagio!

Caesars Palace

Originally designed for high rollers, it's still posh but is now accessible to all and should at least be on your must-see list.
Location: On the Strip at the famous Four Corners with Flamingo
Theme: Greco-Roman empire
Web: www.caesarspalace.com
Reservations: 702 731 7110
Fax: 702 946 4925
Rooms: 3,300 in 5 towers: Augustus, Centurian, Forum, Roman and Palace
Room rates: From $99
Restaurants: 16 in total from contemporary French dining to a casual 24-hour café. Top of the list are the fine-dining establishments of Guy Savoy (with Krug Champagne Room), Rao's and celebrity chef Bobby Flay's new Mesa Grill and Central by Michel Richard which takes 24/7 dining to a new level. Across from Rao's is Payard Patisserie & Bistro, one of the most luxurious pastry shops in the country. Serendipity 3 is one of New York's most beloved eateries and replacing beloved Neros is NYC's Old Homestead Steakhouse. One of the greatest budget eateries you'll find on the Strip is the Cypress Street Marketplace, just outside the Colosseum's ticket office.
Nightlife: Cleopatra's Barge and Pure, which has become hot with the young Hollywood crowd, and Shadow Bar live music lounge.

BRITTIP
If you want to smoke in your hotel room, you must specify you want a smoking room, both when you book and when you check in. Even if you do get a smoking room, the ashtray may be hidden away in a drawer.

Shows: Its 4,100-seat Colosseum has showcased world-class entertainers like Bette Midler, Cher and Jerry Seinfeld. 2011 saw the arrival of Celine Dion, Shania Twain, Elton John and Rod Stewart. It also hosts outdoor events in the Roman Forum, the latest, carnival spectacle Absinthe.
Gambling: Blackjack, craps, roulette, baccarat, pai gow poker, pai gow tiles,

slots, poker, race and sports book and keno.
Chilling out: Garden of the Gods pools and gardens featuring the Venus Pool Club.
Shopping: Appian Way in the hotel, plus the fabulous Forum Shops.
Other amenities: Spanish Steps, 4 wedding chapels, 3 late-night lounges with live music, plus an outdoor amphitheatre, Qua Baths & Spa, salon and golf through Cascata and Rio Secco Golf Courses; PetStay programme.

BRITTIP
Dog-friendly hotels are expanding for those who, like Paris Hilton, would like to bring their pooch. PetStay Las Vegas launched in October 2010, has expanded with dogs now receiving 'VID' treatment at Caesars' 8 resorts. The programme offers treats, a mat, dog-walking routes and walking, sitting and grooming services.

The first-ever hotel of Las Vegas to be entirely based on a theme, Caesars Palace opened in 1966, specifically aiming at big-money gamblers. Although it allows more ordinary mortals to enter its palatial doors these days, the emphasis is still very much on luxury and opulence. The Palace underwent a $600m expansion at the turn of this century, which included building the 17-storey Palace Tower, a Garden of the Gods outdoor area, with pools and landscaped gardens, and a wedding chapel.

Throughout the 85acre/34ha resort are spectacular fountains, majestic cypress trees, gleaming marble statues and beautiful landscaping. The Garden of the Gods area has 6 outdoor swimming pools inlaid with marble and granite, adjoined by 2 whirlpool spas and rimmed by lush gardens and over 40 new cabañas. There are also 3 floodlit tennis courts and an intimate outdoor amphitheatre.

BRITTIP
Be warned – there are no mini bars in your rooms – the hotels want you drinking downstairs where you can gamble too! Nor are there any tea- or coffee-making facilities, so remember to buy water or orange juice for yourself in the morning.

The massive Colosseum quickly became a Strip landmark when it opened. Specifically built to house Celine Dion's A New Day one-woman show, the 4,100-seat, state-of-the-art venue can also be adapted to accommodate headliners and host major boxing events.

The hotel has joined the ranks of other major Strip properties in providing more adult-orientated entertainment and its Shadow Bar – right in the centre of the casino – is one of the places to visit during a stay in Vegas. A relaxed, comfy lounge by day, by night it is home to topless dancers who perform sexy routines behind backlit screens. There is also a secluded adult area for 'European sunbathing' for those who wish to go topless.

All of the rooms have Jacuzzi tubs and the latest fax/phone gadgetry, while the fabulous Forum Shops are also known as the Shopping Wonder of the World (see page 74). If you want to see how the other half lives, take a wiggle on down to the posh baccarat and VIP high-roller areas. You never know, you may just get a proposal of sorts!

Circus Circus

A great-value, family-fun destination with some surprisingly good restaurants.
Location: The Strip between West Sahara and the Convention Center
Theme: Circus carnival featuring the world's largest permanent circus
Web: www.circuscircus.com
Reservations: 702 734 0410
Rooms: 3,770 plus KOA Circusland Recreational Vehicle Park with 399 spaces
Room rates: From $20
Restaurants: Despite its emphasis on good prices, Circus Circus has 8 good eating outlets and The Steak House consistently wins awards for great food. For more casual dining there's Blue Iguana Mexican

Express, The Garden Grill, West Side Deli and Rock & Ritas.
Attractions: Free circus acts, carnival games, IMAX® theatre and Adventuredome indoor theme park.
Gambling: Blackjack, craps, roulette, big six, pai gow poker, let it ride, Caribbean stud, casino war, poker, over 2,250 slots, video poker, video keno machines and the race and sports book. Complimentary gaming lessons.
Chilling out: 2 pools and one at the RV park.
Shopping: 40,000ft^2/3,720m^2 promenade with fun shops like Criss Angel – MINDFREAK Superstore.
Other amenities: The surprisingly stunning Chapel of the Fountain wedding chapel; Année of Paris Beauty Salon (702 731 3201 for appointments); Walters Golf Course.

The owners of Circus Circus were the second operators to build a theme casino on the Strip. It originally opened in 1968 as the world's largest permanent circus tent plus casino but without any hotel rooms. Now it has 3 towers housing nearly 3,800 rooms and an RV park, 3 major gambling areas, a whole raft of shops and some major family attractions. Inspired by the turn-of-the-century circuses that used to visit towns throughout America, it aims its services directly at the cost-conscious family market.

During the 1990s, Circus Circus had started to become seriously worn from years of gamblers and herds of kids. However, recently MGM Mirage has invested untold millions into the property and today it is a comfortable place. Part circus tent and part renaissance fair, it can also be a quirky place.

Caesars Palace

BRITTIP

Circus Circus is so popular with families that it can seem that you're surrounded by wall-to-wall kids!

The Circus Arena appears in the *Guinness Book of Records* as the world's largest permanent circus and covers 120,000ft²/11,160m² with a 90ft/27m high tent-shaped roof. The Carnival Midway is a circus-themed amusement arcade and its centre stage is where free half-hourly shows are presented at 11am by top circus acts, from high-wire daredevils to flying trapeze artists, acrobats, magicians and jugglers.

BRITTIP

Circus Circus provides rooms with roll-in showers that have been designed for the disabled. It also has its own phone line for the hearing impaired: 1 800 638 8595.

The Circus Circus theme park – the Adventuredome – is a fully enclosed 5acre/2ha elevated theme park, which is climate-controlled to provide temperatures of 72ºF/21ºC all the year round. This first-ever Las Vegas amusement park has been improved over the years and now has thrilling rides in a canyon-like setting (see Chapter 10).

BRITTIP

Las Vegas hotels are not known for their fantastic rooms. Unless you're paying top dollar for rooms at The Venetian, Wynn, Four Seasons, Bellagio or a suite at one of the new hotels at CityCenter, they are fairly plain affairs with few facilities.

If you're a novice and fancy a flutter on the Strip, this is the place to try out your luck on the roulette wheels as it has four areas (Main Casino, West Casino, Skyrise Casino and Slots of Fun) offering 100,000ft²/9.3m² of gaming. You can then move on to a high-stakes poker game elsewhere (we can dream, can't we?).

The Cosmopolitan of Las Vegas

Modern, funky five-star style bang on the Strip.
Location: Mid-Strip next to Bellagio and opposite Planet Hollywood

Grand opening: December 2010
Web: www.cosmopolitanlasvegas.com
Reservations: 702 698 7575
Rooms: 2,995 luxury rooms, suites and condo-hotel residences
Room rates: From $160
Restaurants: A dizzying delectable range of 13 restaurants, including Estiatorio Mills – the only Greek restaurant on The Strip and Italian restaurant Scarpetta from award winning chef Scott Constant.
Nightlife: The Chandelier cocktail bar and The Marquee luxury nightclub.
Shows: 1,800-seat theatre, 500-seat cabaret.
Gambling: 100,000ft²/9.3m² casino offering table games: blackjack, roulette, craps, baccarat, pai gow poker, 3-card poker, Texas hold'em, crazy 4 poker and Spanish 21; slots; a new race and sports book at 43 plush 'trading' stations.
Chilling out: The hotel has 3 swimming pools at The Pool District, The Cosmo Beach Club, with its 5acre/2ha pool deck overlooking the Strip; 50,000ft²/4.6m² Sahra Spa and Hammam, salon and fitness centre.
Shopping: Shopping mall with new to market retailers including AllSaints, Spitalfields, Beckley, CRSVR Sneaker Boutique, DNA2050, Droog, Molly Brown's Swimwear, Retrospecs and Co, Skins 6/2 Cosmetics and STITCHED.

The Grand Hyatt Corporation made its Las Vegas debut in late 2010, as one of the few independently owned, operated and privately financed developments on the Strip to fast become one of Sin City's hottest addresses. The Cosmopolitan features two 50-storey towers on 8.7 acres/3.5ha of land, each featuring oversized residential space and expansive one-of-a-kind private terraces – it's the only hotel on The Strip where the rooms have balconies.

Circus Circus

© MGM

Splash down

Cool down from Las Vegas' dry heat with a dip in one of its ultra hip pools.

Fashionistas head to **Bare** at The Mirage (www.mirage.com), whose pool lounge offers the ultimate pampering with private daybeds and cabanas, 2 saltwater dipping pools, ultra VIP service and a DJ to get the party started. The adventurous may prefer **The Tank** at the Golden Nugget (www.goldennugget.com), where a 3-storey chute takes you straight through some of the sea's deadliest creatures, including sharks and rays. If that's too scary, try the 2acre/0.8ha adult playground with 2 waterfalls, 3 pools and 4 bars at **The Palms** (www.thepalmslasvegas.com), Vegas' most lavish, lush and stylish watering hole, it has **The Glass Bar** under a glass-bottomed pool, and a pool deck which can hold 3,000 people for its The Sunday Scene pool party. **Voodoo Beach**, the gorgeous adults-only European-style pool at The Rio (www.riolasvegas.com) comes complete with a sand beach, waterfalls, 3 pools, 4 swimming pools and 5 Jacuzzi-style spas – with DJ and indulgent poolside massages.

Other European-style pools include the **GO Pool** at the Flamingo Las Vegas (www.flamingo.com) and the 'toptional' **Moorea Beach Club** at Mandalay Bay (www.mandalaybay.com) overlooking the 11acre/4.5ha Mandalay Bay Beach with DJ sets at weekends and pampering in the form of poolside massage and even chilled towel service. Spa services, fashion shows on Sundays and a new hookah lounge in the rotunda overlooking the Strip are found at **AZURE** at the Palazzo (www.palazzo.com). M Resort (www.themresort.com) adults-only **Daydream** has a sleek infinity pool with an iced-railing bar and **The Pool District** at The Cosmopolitan (www.cosmopolitanlasvegas.com) has three distinct vibes: surfer dude, chic lounge and relaxing spa.

You can even continue gambling poolside with blackjack and craps at the **Encore Beach Club** at Encore (www.wynnlasvegas.com/encore), with DJ and weekly night-time pool parties, or with bikini blackjack Fridays to Sundays in the **Stratosphere Hotel & Casino** (www.stratospherehotel.com). Sip wine and nibble at hors d'oeuvres on the sleek loungers, opium beds or in the cabanas at **Nikki Beach** at the Tropicana (www.troplv.com) by day – with swim-up blackjack, and a private island in the centre of the tropical pool – and glamorous ultra-lounge and dance floor in Club Nikki by night. Recover with Rockstar Lemonades and dance to world-famous DJs at **Rehab** every Sunday at the Hard Rock Hotel and Casino (www.hardrockhotel.com). Other top pool parties in town include **Wet Republic** at MGM Grand (www.mgmgrand.com), **The Venus Pool**, Caesars Palace (www.caesarspalace.com) and **TAO Beach** at The Venetian (www.venetian.com).

Deutsche Bank, owners of the Cosmopolitan, which is superbly located in the mid-Strip, have taken more than a leaf or two out of the very successful Palm's book and are clearly focusing on attracting a youthful, celeb-driven clientele. It's bang on trend being modern and funky, with no gambling in the lobby. Its restaurants are part of the new-style gourmet flair to hit Las Vegas with celebrity chefs at the ready and gimmicks galore such as liquid nitrogen, bubblegum flavoured meringues at Holstein's Shakes and Buns restaurant. The Cosmo Beach Club, with its 5acre/2ha pool deck, not only overlooks the Strip, but has activities from dawn until dusk. The Chandelier cocktail bar stretches over 3 floors part bar, part casino and part art exhibit and The Marquee luxury nightclub has become quickly established as a place to be seen with high profile DJs including Markus Schultz.

Encore

More of the Wynn-ing formula is rolled out in this upscale hotel.
Location: Next door to the flagship Wynn Las Vegas property on the Strip
Grand opening: December 2008
Theme: Tasteful extravagance with European touches
Cost: $2.3bn
Web: www.wynnlasvegas.com
Reservations: 877 321 9966
Rooms: 2,034
Room rates: From $229
Restaurants: In keeping with the culinary standards set by Wynn Las Vegas, Encore introduces a new all-star team of chefs, each of whom is in their kitchens cooking dinner every night. Sinatra is a salute to Ol' Blue Eyes. Chef Theo Schoenegger's modern Italian cuisine riffs with Sinatra tunes. At Switch, chef Marc Poidevin's French-inspired seafood and steakhouse is a surprise. Diners can appreciate the art collection by

CityCenter

Located between the Bellagio and Monte Carlo resorts, CityCenter (www.citycenter.com) features Aria Resort & Casino, Vdara Hotel, Mandarin Oriental hotel, the residential Veers Towers, a fine art collection and Crystals retail and entertainment district where *Desperate Housewives* star, Eva Longoria Parker has opened Beso restaurant. For more information on each hotel, see them listed alphabetically in this chapter.

CityCenter is the new address to have on the Strip and the place to be seen, having received the AAA Five Diamond Award for Aria Resort & Casino and the Mandarin Oriental in its debut year. We're talking not millions, but billions – $8.5bn to be exact. MGM Mirage is making what's being billed as the single largest private investment in US history. Opened at the end of 2009, CityCenter signals the move away from themes and into dreams of sophisticated living with fine art and sustainability at its still hedonistic heart. It brings a new level of environmental consciousness to the world famous Strip as 8 renowned architects including Studio Daniel Libeskind and Foster + Partners, have created the largest sustainable development in the world. The project is designed to achieve more than 30% improvement in energy efficiency.

Columbian artist Fernando Botero at Botero Steak while sampling chef Mark LoRusso's modern cuisine. Society Café Encore was designed with the whimsical era of Oscar Wilde in mind, to match the imaginative cooking of chef Kim Canteenwalla. Turn a corner in the casino and come face to face with a 27ft/8m crystal dragon, mounted at Wazuzu, where rising star chef Jet Tila serves up pan-Asian cuisine.

Nightlife: XS nightclub and the more bijou Surrender nightclub where Cirque de Soleil® dancers twirl from poles.

Show: Attracts the likes of Beyonce. *Le Rêve* at Wynn Las Vegas.

Gambling: A new softer, intimate approach to casino life with columned pavilions and draped private chambers with garden or pool views.

Shopping: The Esplanade at Encore has 11 boutiques including the edgy Rock & Republic, Hermes, Chanel and an array of clothing, shoe, jewellery, home décor and accessory stores.

Other amenities: Spa and salon and über popular daytime pool party at Encore's stunning beach club.

Steve Wynn is back for more with Encore, sister resort to Wynn Las Vegas offering the same high levels of service and style. Central to Encore's fanciful and intimate feel are sunlit corridors with flowering atria and sprawling pools visible from throughout the property. Natural light floods the resort to reveal gardens, vibrant butterflies and signature mosaics.

Encore has 2,034 spacious suites that offer casual elegance in a comfortable, residential setting. The Resort Suites span up to 700ft²/65m² and Tower Suites measure up to 5,800ft²/540m². Two

separate arrival and check-in areas pamper guests and showcase the textured details of Roger Thomas' interior design.

Todd-Avery Lenahan designed The Spa and The Salon at Encore. Upon arrival in the grand Spa Court, guests are welcomed into a vaulted, softly-lit and glass-enclosed courtyard. The Salon is full-service and The Spa contains 37 treatment rooms, 14 naturally lit garden rooms and 4 oversized couples' suites for massage, body treatments and facials.

A top attraction is XS, the nightclub where exclusive DJs The Manufactured Superstars and Afrojack spin their magic in an outdoor pool environment with a sizzling club atmosphere. The club's design is inspired by the sexy curves of the human body, while the dance floor has 10ft/3m rotating chandeliers!

Excalibur Hotel & Casino

Great for family fun at reasonable prices, it should also be on your must-visit list.

Location: The Strip at West Tropicana
Theme: King Arthur and the Knights of the Round Table
Cost: $290m
Web: www.excalibur.com
Reservations: 702 597 7777
Rooms: 4,000
Room rates: From $32

BRITTIP

Beat the queues! You can fast track your check-in by filling out the King's Express form in advance or by going to one of the self check-in kiosks on arrival to get your keys instantly.

Restaurants: 6 restaurants including an all-you-can-eat Excalibur Buffet; the Steakhouse at Camelot, the lively Dick's Last Resort and the new concept restaurant Lynyrd Skynyrd BBQ & Beer.

Nightlife: Octane – a Vegas take on a classic biker bar.

Attractions: *Tournament of Kings* dinner show; comedy show *Defending the Caveman*; Bee Gees tribute band; live music in Octane Lounge; free fire-breathing dragon show; strolling entertainers; 2 magic-motion cinemas include a Spongebob Squarepants 4D ride; Australia's *Thunder from Down Under*, definitely one of the hottest male strip shows in town and every Thursday to Sunday pole and burlesque dancing at Night School 4 Girls, run by ex-Playboy playmate, E!'s Laura Croft.

> ### 🇬🇧 BRITTIP
> Don't miss the medieval-costumed staff at the Excalibur, where entertainers wander around playing medieval trumpets!

Gambling: Slot and table games, poker room, full-service race and sports book and live keno round the clock.

Chilling out: New pool area with 4 pools, cabañas, a fire pit, sundecks and a water slide, a 25-seat spa, snack bar and cocktail bar, open 9am–7pm daily (subject to seasonal change).

Shopping: Castle Walk Shops

Other amenities: The Royal Treatment Spa and Fitness Center; links to 6 challenging golf courses including Bali Hai, Resort Pines, Royal Links and Stallion Mountain

Golf Club; 2 wedding chapels on a light and airy medieval theme (truly not an oxymoron in this case!).

The beautiful spires of the Camelot-style entrance building are set between two huge castle-like towers that house the 4,000-odd rooms at this family-orientated resort. Make no mistake, though, the free Dragon Battle that takes place every hour on the hour 10am–10pm to draw the crowds has the sole purpose of inviting you in to part with your cash in the casino as do the dancers in the party pit within. But there are plenty of other free entertainments to keep you amused as you wander round the Castle Walk shops and restaurants, from the strolling entertainers to the free variety acts on the Court Jester's Stage from 10am every day.

You can eat dinner and see the *Tournament of Kings* at either 6pm or 8.30pm most days of the week, or dance to live music at the Minstrel's Lounge. The house of fun also has 6 restaurants and parking is free and relatively accessible by Las Vegas standards.

Excalibur

Four Seasons Hotel Las Vegas

Provides an oasis of elegance – predominantly for business people – as the original non-gambling hotel-cum-retreat on the Strip.

Location: The Strip, just south of the Mandalay Bay

Theme: Understated luxury

Web: www.fourseasons.com/lasvegas

Reservations: 702 632 5000

Rooms: 424 including 86 suites

Room rates: From $179

Restaurants: 3 restaurants and lounges including the Verandah Bar and Lounge, which has introduced a new modern Italian concept, Charlie Palmer Steak Lounge and Pool Bar.

Chilling out: Pool and health and fitness club (and the *only* hotel in Las Vegas to provide those facilities free and exclusively to guests).

Other amenities: The opportunity to wed in 3 of the most amazing suites in Las Vegas.

Although the guestrooms of the hotel are located on floors 35 to 39 of the Mandalay Bay, the Four Seasons is a separately functioning hotel. The first hotel in recent history to open on the Strip without massive theming, it is also the only one without a casino and one of 10 with an AAA Five Diamond rating in Las Vegas.

The real beauty of the hotel comes in its divine suites, where spaciousness, supreme elegance and to-die-for views reign supreme. The Four Seasons is most famous for its Specialty Suites with 180-degree views of the glistening Strip and glistening desert. With the added bonus of separate lounge and dining areas filled with sumptuous furnishings, these suites were designed to provide the ultimate safe haven from the never-ending ker-chink, ker-chink of Las Vegas's casinos!

Ostensibly geared up for business people – it is the only hotel in Las Vegas to have a corporate rate – it still attracts tourists, many of whom are dedicated followers of the Four Seasons brand. While guests have access to all the facilities of the Mandalay Bay, they have their own exclusive facilities, too, starting with the private drive and entrance, and the casino-free, super-cool, gleaming lobby plus the lavishly landscaped private pool (where attentive staff are on hand to give you a cooling Evian spritz!), 2 whirlpools and an exclusive health and fitness club.

BRITTIP

You've got more chance of getting a room – and cheaply – at the resort-hotels if you go between Sunday and Thursday.

The restaurants – including celebrity chef Charlie Palmer's Steak Lounge – have been building up a regular band of loyal locals as well as guests of the hotel. Nor are they overpriced. At the Four Seasons it's all about understated elegance, darlink!

The Spa at Four Seasons is open 8am–8pm and features result-orientated treatments conceived to hydrate the skin, promote anti-aging and elevate the art of relaxation. There are 16 elegant treatment rooms and a large steam room. It's signature Four Seasons Desert Oasis Treatment begins with a brisk full-body, salt exfoliation followed by a massage with the essential oil of your choice. A warm blanket wrap during a relaxing scalp, shoulder and facial massage completes the treatment. Can you think of any reason why you would ever want to leave this paradise?

BRITTIP

The Spa at the Four Seasons ranked 4th on Conde Nast Traveler's list of the Top 100 Resort Spas in the US 2011 and Number 1 Spa in Vegas.

Luxor

Ancient Egyptian theme resort at good-value prices.
Location: The Strip between Tropicana and Reno
Theme: Ancient Egypt
Cost: $375m, plus a $240m expansion
Web: www.luxor.com
Reservations: 702 262 4444
Rooms: 4,887
Room rates: From $50
Restaurants: 9 dining options include Rice & Company, an Asian Bistro from restauranteur David Wu at the entrance to The Shoppes at Mandalay Bay; Tender steak & seafood; Pyramid Café and Ri Ra Irish Pub at Mandalay Place.
Nightlife: LAX Nightclub, a range of bars and a made to measure experience at Savile Row.
Shows: *Criss Angel Believe* with Cirque du Soleil, Comedian Carrot Top, the adult revue *Fantasy* (formerly *Midnight Fantasy*) and *Menopause the Musical*.
Attractions: Bodies ...The Exhibition and Titanic: The Artifact Exhibition.
Gambling: Slots, tables, poker room, high limit area, race and sports book.
Chilling out: 4 swimming pools and relaxing Jacuzzis in a luxurious oasis setting; the Oasis Spa; access to golf at 4 different courses; it is host to LBGT pool party Temptation Sundays at Luxor, voted the 2010 Best Gay Event by *Q Vegas*.
Shopping: Luxor Galleria Stores.
Other amenities: Nuture, the Spa at Luxor; wedding chapel.

For us Brits, this is the hotel that is synonymous with Las Vegas extravagance, and staying in the fabulous replica of a pyramid is up there on many people's must-do list. With its trademark beacon of light that can now be seen from outer space (along with the Great Wall of China), the hotel is one of the most tastefully executed

The lobby at the Four Seasons

theme resorts in the middle-market sector. You enter the beautiful structure through a life-size replica of the great Temple of Rameses II, which takes you directly into the casino (funny that!) where there's 120,000ft²/11,150m² of gambling space.

BRITTIP
One company now owns the Mandalay Bay, Luxor and Excalibur and has built a monorail linking them to supplement the well-signposted walkways between them. The walkway from the Excalibur to its neighbouring rival, New York-New York, is **not** signposted but can be found just outside the main entrance.

On the show front, Carrot Top, a wacky entertainer who delights crowds with his idiosyncratic gadgets and sometimes coarse humour, draws great crowds, while the adult topless revue, *Fantasy*, keeps people out late. Perhaps the most popular though is the award-winning magical *Criss Angel's Believe* by Cirque du Soleil®. Criss actually lives in a suite atop the pyramid.

To get to your room, you'll travel on the elevator at a bizarre 39-degree angle, while there are shops selling Egyptian antiquities, gemstones, charms and limited-edition art.

BRITTIP
Make sure you have lip balm with you all the time as the constant air conditioning in the hotels really dries out your lips.

Chill out in one of the attractive swimming pool areas or pay $20 ($25 to non-hotel guests) for a day Spa Pass, which includes use of the hot and cold whirlpools, steam bath, dry sauna, fitness centre and a complimentary fruit juice or mineral water.

Mandalay Bay

A luxury resort filled with must-see shows, must-eat-at restaurants and some of the coolest nightlife venues in town.
Location: The Strip, just south of West Tropicana Avenue (entrance off Hacienda Drive)
Theme: South Sea Islands
Cost: $950m
Web: www.mandalaybay.com
Reservations: 702 632 7777
Rooms: 3,724
Room rates: From $90
Restaurants: 13 signature restaurants

including Aureole with its very own Wine Angel stewards who gracefully ascend the tower to retrieve wine, 8 casual restaurants and 6 quick eats.
Nightlife: 7 full on bars and nightclubs including the House of Blues.

BRITTIP
The Mandalay Bay hotel's wave pool is generally closed for maintenance from around the end of October to March.

Shows: Ongoing calendar of concerts and shows and the first venue to host the new *Michael Jackson: The Immortal World Tour* by Cirque du Soleil®.
Attractions: Shark Reef Aquarium
Gambling: Slots, tables, blackjack and poker in lush surroundings; race and sports book.

BRITTIP
Never use the phone in your hotel room – you'll be charged a small fortune. Get an international phone card before you go instead, if you prefer not to use your mobile.

Chilling out: Sand-and-surf beach and the lazy river ride; Moorea Beach Club, a 'toptional' adult pool.
Shopping: Selection of shops on the South Seas theme, selling everything from cigars to Bali treasures.
Other amenities: Spa Mandalay, 2 wedding chapels.

Aimed at a slightly more sophisticated traveller than its sister property, the Luxor, Mandalay Bay is still excellent value for money and well worth forking out that bit extra for.

For starters, it's one of the few hotels on the Strip where you don't have to walk through the casino to get to your room and, secondly, many of the rooms have massive soaking/Jacuzzi tubs plus a separate shower. A large number also have fabulous views down the entire Strip and, despite being the nearest hotel to the airport, you don't hear a peep out of those planes thanks to some pretty nifty double glazing.

Dan Aykroyd's House of Blues, the first of which opened on Sunset Strip in Los Angeles, has a home here. The live music venue is drawing such crowds that you need to book at least four weeks in advance. And if you just can't get enough of the blues, then ask for a room on the 34th floor of the hotel – it's filled with House of Blues-themed guestrooms.

Among the numerous upmarket restaurants are celebrity-chef hot spots: Charlie Palmer's Aureole, Trattoria del Lupo, owned by Wolfgang Puck, one of the most influential chefs in the US as well as Hubert Keller's Fleur and Rick Moonen's RM Seafood. The Mix offers amazing views of the Strip from its lofty spot, while it also has a wonderful chill-out lounge. In addition, there's Red Square, the Russian-inspired homage to vodka and caviar. Celebrities have their own vodka lockers, but the less well-to-do can try the frozen ice bar where there are more than 100 frozen vodkas and infusions, Martinis and Russian-inspired cocktails. You can also dine on an extensive selection of caviars or Russian classics.

It's not all fast-paced at the Mandalay, though, as there are plenty of ways to unwind in the 11acre/4.5ha tropical water environment. Try out the city's first sand-and-surf beach at Moorea Beach Club, a 'toptional' adult pool experience overlooking the 11acre/4.5ha beach which offers everything from chilled beach towels to live DJ sets at weekends or just go for a lazy river ride. You can now also get a day pass to the spa or opt for one of the many excellent massages, body treatments or facials. For something more thrilling, try diving with sharks at the Shark Reef Aquarium or petting Zebra Shark pups – the newest addition to the Touch Pool.

◀▷ **BRITTIP**

While most fine dining establishments close around 10pm or 10.30pm, all the major resort-hotels have at least one café that's open round the clock (24/7) and many others that stay open late.

On the site of the Mandalay Bay is its cousin property, THEhotel, which has an additional 1,117 suites in 43 storeys of upscale and secluded sanctuaries. Amenities here include dog-friendly suites which offer everything from pet treats and special meal options on the in-house menu to walks down 'Barking Lot Lane'.

Mandarin Oriental Las Vegas

Location: At the entrance to CityCenter on the Strip between Bellagio and Monte Carlo.
Grand opening: December 2009
Theme: Holistic Eastern luxury
Cost: Part of the $8.5bn CityCenter development
Web: www.mandarinoriental.com/lasvegas/

Reservations: 800 2828 3838 or 702 590 8888
Rooms: 392
Room rates: $229
Restaurants: An all-day dining establishment called MOzen Bistro serves Asian and multi-national cuisine; Signature fine-dining restaurant Twist by Pierre Gagnaire on 23rd floor. Mandarin Bar; Tea Lounge; Poolside Café and Amore Patisserie on Las Vegas Boulevard – an adaptation of the Mandarin Cake Shop at the Hong Kong Mandarin Oriental – offers gourmet foods, homemade breads and pastries.
Attractions: Some of the finest inroom entertainment and technology systems. Top concierge. On its exterior, Typewriter Eraser, Scale X, 1998–1999, a legendary sculpture by Claes Oldenburg and Coosie van Bruggen – basically a 4 tonne, 19ft/5.8m stainless steel and fibreglass typewriter eraser.
Chilling out: 2 outdoor swimming pools – one on the rooftop – Jacuzzi, deck and 20 cabañas.
Shopping: Close to Crystals, CityCenter's retail and entertainment district.
Other amenities: Mandarin Spa including 17 treatment rooms, 3 VIP suites, 3 couples suites, rasul and hamam. Fitness centre, Pilates, spinning and yoga studios; stay more than 5 nights to get the complimentary Jet Lag Recovery Experience.

The arrival of the prestigious Mandarin Oriental chain is another indication that Vegas courts sophistication and it attracted a AAA Five Diamond Award in its debut year. With its 47-storey glass facade, this 5-star resort that brings Eastern chic to the Strip is connected to the rest of CityCenter with glass-enclosed sky bridges. Unlike most hotels, guests will check in on the 23rd floor at the Sky Lobby with dramatic views of the Las Vegas skyline through a wall of glass. This hotel is all about luxury and service and doesn't pander to any of the gaudy excesses of the town it's in, though it will help you to access them!

MGM Grand

Massive resort-hotel that is good fun for the whole family, yet provides plenty of adult entertainment.
Location: The Strip at Four Corners with East Tropicana
Theme: The City of Entertainment
Cost: Originally $1bn, plus a $950m expansion and theme transformation
Web: www.mgmgrand.com
Reservations: 702 891 7777

Rooms: 5,780
Room rates: From $60
Restaurants: Michelin-starred chef Joël Robuchon has created Joël Robuchon at the Mansion, while other fine dining highlights (10 in all) include the Japanese Shibuya. Other stalwarts remain, including Nobhill Tavern and Craftsteak; and 9 casual outlets including the Rainforest Café.
Nightlife: Studio 54 nightclub, Tabu Ultra Lounge, Centrifuge, Rouge and Zuri bars.
Shows: *Kà* by Cirque du Soleil®; sporting events and major concerts in the Grand Garden Arena (seats 16,325); smaller gigs in the 650-seat Hollywood Theatre; plus the *Crazy Horse Paris* adult show.
Attractions: CSI: The Experience interactive exhibit; Arcade centre with high-tech virtual reality games; the free Lion Habitat; the Youth Activity Center.
Gambling: Poker, blackjack, slot machines, VIP lounge and 104-seat race and sports book.
Chilling out: Wet Republic Ultra Pool and Grand Pool Complex.
Other amenities: 2 wedding chapels; MGM Grand Spa & Health Club; Christophe Salon; access to golf at Shadow Creek.

BRITTIP
If you're staying at the MGM Grand or New York-New York, then head to the south baggage area at McCarran airport to check in while waiting for your luggage to come off the plane. For an extra fee you can even take the direct shuttle to your hotel.

The MGM Grand is so huge it can be all things to all people. It is easy to get lost in the array of opportunities to eat, drink and generally be merry. In recent years, there has been a shift away from the old-style family-orientated entertainments to a more adult-based scene.

The hotel is famous for staging headliner shows and big fights in its Grand Garden Arena and Hollywood Theatre.

In an effort to cater to the adult market, the hotel opened Tabu Ultra Lounge, while the Studio 54 nightclub has a more raunchy twist, Zuri supplies a 24-hour drinking spot and Rouge is the latest seductive addition.

Many rate MGM Grand's pool offerings as the best in Vegas and the South Beach ambience of Wet Republic Ultra Pool is certainly lively. Meanwhile you can check out your cardiovascular rating in the state-of-the-art fitness centre at the spa. Afterwards, there are seemingly no end of eating choices available and if you wish you can even pop out to the neighbouring United Artists Showcase cinema.

BRITTIP
Speed up your check-out times by taking advantage of the check-out systems available on many of the hotel's TVs. DO check the bill thoroughly, though, before paying, as mistakes can occur, and always resolve any queries before leaving the hotel.

The rooms, especially the suites, are very good for the price, with each one having artwork of Hollywood movies and celebrities of the past. A great game is to walk down your hallway trying to put names to the famous faces mounted on the walls.

The 'cousin' towers – the Signature at MGM Grand and Skylofts – offer another 1,441 luxury suites for those looking for the most pampered of settings.

Mirage

An elegant taste of paradise, yet within reach of most budgets.
Location: The Strip, between Flamingo and Spring Mountain
Theme: Polynesian, South Seas oasis
Cost: $730m
Web: www.mirage.com
Reservations: 702 791 7111
Rooms: 3,044
Room rates: From $89
Restaurants: 6 fine dining experiences including the award-winning Onda and Fin restaurants, plus 9 casual options.
Nightlife: The hopping JET nightclub, plus a superb lounge scene for live music at the Japonais Lounge, the Onda lounge, Caribbean Rhumbar and the Beatles

MGM Grand

© MGM

Revolution lounge and live music at BB Kings Blues Club.

Shows: Cirque du Soleil's® Beatles tribute, Love™; America's Got Talent winner Terry Fator with his amazing impressions and ventriloquism; plus a roster of visiting acts.

Attractions: Siegfreid & Roy's Secret Garden & Dolphin Habitat, Volcano show and aquarium.

Gambling: Extensive casino

Chilling out: 2 pools and cabañas in a lush, tropical setting; the Bare pool area allows 'European-style' sunbathing.

Shopping: The Street of Shops promenade. Don't miss the couture lollipops at the Sugar Factory – a hit with celebrities including Britney Spears and the Pussycat Dolls.

Other amenities: Mirage Spa and Kim Vo Salon – spa access is free when you book a treatment, otherwise $20; the hotel has a link with Shadow Creek Golf Course.

BRITTIP

One of the most unusual experiences Las Vegas has to offer is available at the Dolphin Habitat, where you can learn the art of being a dolphin trainer.

The entrance garden surrounds you with a mass of foliage and waterfalls that cascade over 50ft/15m rocks to the lagoon below before you reach the Mirage signature volcano. This erupts every 15 minutes from dawn till dusk, spewing smoke and fire 100ft/30m above the water. The Mirage has just joined forces with legendary Grateful Dead drummer Mickey Hart, Indian music sensation Zakir Hussain, and the Fountains of Bellagio design firm WET to create an all-new audio-visual spectacle for its famous volcano attraction with massive fireballs that shoot more than 12ft/3.7m into the air. The reception area is a tropical rainforest, filled with 60ft/18m high palm trees, more waterfalls, banana trees and tropical orchids, kept in perfect condition with natural sunlight and a computerised misting system. Behind the check-in desk is a massive coral reef aquarium that is home to sharks, puffer fish and angel fish, swimming among the buildings of a sunken city. The forest provides the delightfully exotic setting for Kokomo's, one of the Mirage's top-notch restaurants, serving steaks and seafood.

The Mirage joined the rank of Las Vegas resorts which host a Cirque du Soleil® fantasy, when in 2007 it opened Love™. The Beatles' old studios, Abbey Road, provided the digital recording masters to make the music as real as possible.

When it opened in 1989, the Mirage's theme of a Polynesian island oasis was a taste of the big things to come in Las Vegas, and it has stood the test of time. Once host to the famous Siegfried & Roy magical show of illusions featuring tigers, lions, leopards and other animals, the habitat for the dolphins remains. It has become an educational and research facility and it is possible to spend a day with a trainer. The Secret Garden, where you can see white lions, and the vast Dolphin Habitat were built to create public awareness of the plight of endangered animals.

Accommodation ranges from luxurious standard rooms to opulent bungalows with their own private garden and pools, and eight 2- and 3-bedroom private residences. Admission to the luxurious day spa and fitness centre costs $25, but is free if you book any one of the pampering treatments.

Monte Carlo Resort & Casino

Posh-but-worth-it hotel with great chilling-out facilities.

Location: The Strip just north of West Tropicana

Theme: Re-creation of the Place du Casino in Monte Carlo

Cost: $344m

Web: www.montecarlo.com

Reservations: 702 730 7777 at Monte Carlo 877 576 3232 at Hotel 32 Monte Carlo

Rooms: 2,900

Room rates: From $70 at Monte Carlo and from $170 at HOTEL32 Monte Carlo

Restaurants: 9 places to dine including the famous André's and the sinfully seductive Diablo's Cantina on The Strip. There's also a Brand Steakhouse, Buffet and Monte Carlo Brew Pub. Dragon Noodle and d.vino Italian restaurant are the most recent openings.

New York-New York

Nightlife: Monte Carlo Brew Pub nightclub
Shows: *Jabbawockeez*, the award-winning all male dance troupe.
Gambling: Table games, slots, poker room, race and sports book and players club.
Chilling out: 21,000ft²/1,950m² pool area with waterfalls, spa, children's pool, wave pool and rafting down the Easy River.
Shopping: Street of Dreams promenade.
Other amenities: A wedding chapel; spa and exercise room.

◀🇬🇧▶**BRITTIP**
Skip the expensive buffet at the Monte Carlo and go for one of the gourmet restaurants instead.

This elegant, upmarket resort-hotel is so popular that it is hard for British travel agents to find you a room here. Modelled on the famous Place du Casino in Monaco, the emphasis is definitely on providing an elegant and refined atmosphere in which to part with wads of cash in the casino. Massive chandeliers, marble flooring, ornate fountains and gas-lit promenades all go towards setting the elegant tone. After a hard day seeing the sights, make sure you get back in time to make full use of the water facilities, which include a heated spa, children's pool and wave pool that re-creates both the sound and feel of ocean surf waves.

New show *Jabbawockeez* has changed the way dance is seen in America. The Monte Carlo Brew Pub not only offers an excellent selection of beers, but also offers live music and dancing with a DJ and live music from a band kicking off around 9pm most nights.

If you're feeling particularly flush, book into HOTEL32 at Monte Carlo which opened August 2009. Located on the top floor of the Monte Carlo, things go up a notch in this exclusive boutique hotel with flash interiors, limousine transfer to and from the airport, a dedicated 'suite assistant', 12 pillow types, a private Lounge 32 for cocktails and preferred reservations at MGM Mirage restaurants and shows.

New York-New York Hotel & Casino

The most electrifying club scene in Vegas!
Location: The Strip at West Tropicana
Theme: The Big Apple – doh!
Cost: $460m
Web: www.nynyhotelcasino.com
Reservations: 866 815 4365
Rooms: 3,490

Room rates: From $70
Restaurants: 9 choices from fine dining to casual including Gonzalez Y Gonzalez and Gallagher's Steakhouse and Chin Chin Cafe or under a huge map of iconic landmarks in America.
Nightlife: Rok Vegas nightclub. Dulce Latin Night at Gonzalez Y Gonzalez. Great range of bars including Coyote Ugly, Nine Fine Irishmen, the Bar at Times Square and the Big Chill.
Shows: *Zumanity*, the adult-themed Cirque du Soleil® extravaganza.
Attractions: Manhattan Express™ roller-coaster ride.
Gambling: Slots, table games, race and sports book.
Chilling out: Outdoor pool with 3 relaxing whirlpools.
Shopping: Numerous gift shops in the Central Park area.
Other amenities: Wedding chapel; spa and fitness centre; golf.

◀🇬🇧▶**BRITTIP**
It's a good 10-minute walk through shops and casinos to get to the New York-New York's roller-coaster ride, but it's well worth the trek!

Dubbed the 'greatest city in Las Vegas', the resort's façade re-creates the Manhattan skyline with 12 of its most famous skyscrapers from the Empire State Building to the Statue of Liberty, along with a 300ft/90m long replica of Brooklyn Bridge and a Coney Island-style roller-coaster called Manhattan Express™. From the food and the architecture, to the sights and sounds of America's famous city, this Las Vegas resort re-creates the energy and vibrancy of New York – then adds the Central Park casino!

The resort is part of the MGM Mirage – whose empire includes the MGM Grand, Mirage, Bellagio and Treasure Island – and entertainment is an important facet of the experience. Cirque du Soleil's® *Zumanity* has turned into a long-running success.

The Sporting House offers classic casual American grub in a sports-themed environment, The Screening Room provides multi-game viewing, direct audio control for all televised games around two 14ft/4m screens and a dozen 36in/90cm video monitors with tiered seating, while the Sports Arena has more than 10,000ft²/930m² of interactive games.

However, it is the bar scene with its fun entertainment and live music that puts the 'party, party, party' atmosphere into New York-New York. Top of the pile is Coyote Ugly, which is based on a Southern-style bar, complete with gyrating female bartenders atop the bar. No fancy drinks here, just shots and beer. Anyone who asks for a water or soda is given a shower of water that is sprayed over the entire crowd! Then there is the Big Chill, serving frozen cocktails, and the Bar at Times Square, where you can sing along to tunes played by two pianists. The party-style ambiance is continued into the dining area Gonzalez Y Gonzalez, a New York Mexican-style café famous for its tequilas. The addition of the Rok Vegas nightclub provides a sexy late night edge to proceedings.

Chilling-out facilities include a pool area with patio chairs for the cool cabañas. The new restaurant sets a lively vibe, while other fun elements include volleyball, poolside chair massages and a sound system. The spa is open daily 6.30am–7pm, and golf is at a choice of 3 courses: Desert Pines, Bali Hai and Royal Links.

Paris Las Vegas

A tribute to the French capital, from the undersized Eiffel Tower to the Arc de Triomphe.
Location: The Strip, south of East Flamingo
Theme: Capital of France!
Cost: $785m
Web: www.parislasvegas.com
Reservations: 702 946 7000
Rooms: 2,900
Room rates: From $60
Restaurants: 11 dining establishments include the popular Eiffel Tower Restaurant, the wonderful Mon Ami Gabi, with outside dining right on the Strip, the poolside Le Café du Parc.
Nightlife: Napoleon's dueling piano bar; live music at Le Cabaret show lounge and dancing under the stars on the rooftop at Chateau Nightclub & Gardens.
Attractions: Observation deck on the Eiffel Tower; the Le Rendez-Vous Lounge on the 31st floor offers drinks with a fab view of the Strip. Paris has developed itself into one of the finest adult entertainment stops in Las Vegas: Stephane Vanel's Magic of Paris and Barry Manilow are resident entertainers.
Gambling: The usual rundown of gaming in an extraordinary setting in the base of the Eiffel Tower!
Chilling out: Roof-top swimming pool in a manicured French garden setting; tennis courts.

BRITTIP

For a complete low-down on getting married in Las Vegas, see Chapter 8, Going to the Chapel.

Shopping: French shops in the resort's Le Boulevard District made its highly anticipated debut at Paris Las Vegas in 2011 as well as at Bally's Paris Promenade.
Amenities: 2 wedding chapels; Paris Spa by Mandara; golf is offered at the Cascata Golf Club.

Bringing to life the ambience and spirit of the French capital, this theme resort opened in the autumn of 1999 with replicas of the Eiffel Tower, Arc de Triomphe, Paris Opera House and the Louvre. The 34-storey hotel tower is fashioned after the famous Hôtel de Ville. Like the Mandalay Bay and Venetian, the Paris is aimed at the more sophisticated traveller, with prices – by Las Vegas standards, at least – to match.

The hotel is home to Napoleon's, a gorgeous Champagne and jazz bar and Las Vegas' newest lavish nightlife venue with a view, the 2-storey high-energy Chateau Nightclub & Gardens, with a 10,000ft²/930m² balcony and Parisian gardens with a rooftop dance floor, 4 bars and VIP seating encircled by an 8ft/2.3m glass wall.

All the restaurants – in true French fashion – provide wonderful food and the new 30,000ft²/2788m² shopping district in the west wing houses the Sugar Factory's largest store yet with an American Brasserie with 200 items on the menu and decadent Chocolate Lounge open 24 hours a day, 7 days a week, and serving up Sin City's biggest sugar rush.

There is a caveat, though. While so many aspects of this resort are wonderful, the service can be poor and prices are on the expensive side. It can feel as though you really are in Paris! Well, maybe not. Look out for signs such as L'Hôtel Elevators and Le Service Captain. On top of this, all the staff have been trained to say 'bonjour' and 'merci' but can't actually understand a word of French. Of all the resorts, this is the one that comes off with the thinnest veneer.

Planet Hollywood Resort & Casino

A well-priced mega resort now home to some of the most adult-orientated entertainments on the Strip.
Location: The Strip on the corner of Harmon Avenue, south of the Paris resort

and almost directly opposite the Bellagio
Theme: The outrageously popular Planet Hollywood formula of film styling and memorabilia
Cost: $1.4bn in 2000, plus $100m in 2006–2007
Web: www.planethollywoodresort.com
Reservations: 702 785 5555
Rooms: 2,567
Room rates: From $109
Restaurants: 9, headlined by the Japanese offerings of Koi and the popular Chinese-fusion food of PF Changs. The lone holdover from the Aladdin days is the Spice Market Buffet, one of the best value buffets in Vegas. Plus the Miracle Mile shopping area has more great dining with 15 restaurants including the rocking Cabo Wabo Cantina. Pink's Hot Dogs opened its first location in Vegas here in August 2009.
Nightclubs: The Playing Field Lounge, Extra Lounge, the Heart Bar, Koi Lounge and new Gallery Nightclub fusing vintage gothic with the contemporary, such as sexy voyeuristic photography.
Shows: Peepshow with dancers and performers from the world of pop music, film, television and Broadway, Ke$ha Get $leazy Tour, *Tony 'n' Tina's Wedding,* the second longest running show in Off-Broadway history and Ryan Ahern's high energy *Piano! Las Vegas* in the V theatre.
Gambling: Nearly 3acres/1.2ha of casino, including the Pleasure Pit which features blackjack and roulette dealt by scantily clad women as go-go dancers do their thing.
Chilling out: The Pleasure Pool's a 26th-floor outdoor terrace and swimming pool area overlooking the Strip with pool decks and cabañas.
Shopping: The Miracle Mile – once The Desert Passage at the Aladdin – is a massive shopping area with more than 170 shops including H&M and Urban Outfitters

and 15 restaurants from fine dining to casual eateries (see page 79).
Other amenities: Spa by Mandara; wedding chapel.

Seemingly born under an unlucky star, Planet Hollywood is hoping that her original (and unlucky) life as the Aladdin is behind her and she can look forward to a profitable future by mixing Hollywood Glamour with Vegas Sin.

Having opened in 2000, the Aladdin had one of the bumpiest rides of any of the major resort-hotels in recent time. Of course, it didn't help that the project went massively over budget, nor that the opening was postponed for 5 months, nor that when it did finally open there weren't enough hotel rooms ready for all the reservations taken. So much for a 'grand' opening!

BRITTIP
If you don't want to walk miles to your hotel room, request one near to the lifts. These hotels are massive and rooms can be a considerable distance from the lifts!

The Aladdin was bought by Planet Hollywood, Starwood Hotels and Bay Harbor in the bankruptcy courts for $637m in 2004. A further $100m was spent on renovations that changed the facade, improved the casino and added restaurants, a 1,300-seat showroom and a 500-seat TV studio.

Planet Hollywood has also worked on her contacts in the entertainment industry to attract crowds of celebrities on a daily basis. *Extra* is a popular television show of big-name interviews and gossip mongering, and it has set up its headquarters in the Extra Lounge. They bring in a daily influx of beautiful well-known people who willingly glad hand and pose for photos with their adoring fans.

A programme to improve guest facilities means that rooms now come with marble bathrooms with oversized bathtubs, and in-room personal computers.

Stratosphere Casino, Hotel & Tower

Extremely good-value hotel with some of the best gambling odds on the Strip.
Location: At the northern end of the Strip
Theme: Tallest building west of the Mississippi
Cost: $550m and a £12m refurb in 2011
Web: www.stratospherehotel.com
Reservations: 702 380 7777

Stratosphere

Rooms: 2,577
Room rates: From $35
Restaurants: 2 fine-dining experiences including the revolving Top of the World Restaurant on the 106th floor and Fellini's Ristorante, plus 4 casual dining outlets.
Nightlife: Romance at The Top of the World, Back Alley Bar, Images Lounge, Air Lounge with live DJ and the upmarket Level 107 Lounge.
Shows: *Bite* topless revue.
Attractions: Highest observation tower in America at 1,149ft^2/350.2m^2, world's highest roller-coaster and world's highest thrill rides, Big Shot! SkyJump too for those who dare.
Gambling: 80,000 ft^2/7432m^2 casino; bikini-clad blackjack dealers poolside each Friday, Saturday and Sunday in the summer and there's a poker room.
Chilling out: Level 8 pool and recreation deck; Roni Josef Salon and Spa.
Shopping: The Tower Shops.
Other amenities: Wedding chapel; state-of-the-art video arcade.

Stratosphere has paid the price for being located at the most northern point of the Strip – just that little bit too far from the rest of the action and in a little seedier part of town. Having faced bankruptcy, then received an injection of capital to provide a raft of new amenities, the Stratosphere underwent a £12m makeover in 2011 in order to bring the hotel back to its iconic glory. This meant the redesign of 909 rooms – with flat screen TVs and up-to-date bathrooms with granite countertops and a sweeping marble tile ramp leading guests to a new VIP lounge, the hotel lobby and a newly carpeted casino.

Some real crowd-pleasers include XScream, Big Shot! and other rides which attract the thrill seekers. Those with a less robust constitution can enjoy the observation deck in the tallest building in the city and enjoy a drink as the bar gently circles so you can see every dramatic view.

The restaurant scene is one of the hotel's biggest hits. Its Top of the World Restaurant provides great food and an incomparable view of the Strip.

Beach Club 25 was the first of the 'European-style' sunbathing facilities in Las Vegas. It is a popular, secluded adult environment with table tennis, fitness equipment, water volleyball and fun parties, with fantastic views of the Strip from its 25th-floor location although it was closed indefinitely for renovations at the time of going to press. It was incredibly popular with cast members of the topless *Bite* show

who frequent the facilities to perfect their tans and allow the males to drool.

Another chill-out zone is provided at Level 8 Pool – on the 8th floor of the tower block. The 67,000ft^2/6,224m^2 pool and recreation deck offers a huge pool, oversize spa, waterfall and private cabañas.

The competitively priced rooms are among the cheapest on the Strip, especially so now they've been given a facelift, although they aren't quite as good value as at first blush. The otherwise budget-priced hotel charges a sometimes pricey 'resort fee' on top of your hotel bill, which makes the value go from amazingly cheap to merely very good. But odds in the casino make it the best place to try out your new found skills on the tables (see Chapter 7)!

Treasure Island

It's kept the family-style brand, but is now offering a more adult package of entertainments.
Location: The Strip at Spring Mountain Road
Theme: Robert Louis Stevenson's novel *Treasure Island*, as only Vegas can do
Web: www.treasureisland.com
Reservations: 702 894 7111
Rooms: 2,885
Room rates: From $64
Restaurants: 2 fine-dining including Phil's Steak House and Isla Mexican Kitchen plus 7 casual eateries plus the newest, Señor Frog's opening in 2012.
Nightlife: Siren's Sip, Isla Tequila Bar, Margarita Bar, Breeze Bar and Kahunaville Party Bar with live entertainment; Gilley's Saloon with Texan food and bull riding contests by day.
Shows: Cirque du Soleil's® *Mystère* and the *Sirens of TI* sea show.
Gambling: All the usual suspects.

Treasure Island

Chilling out: Tropical paradise pool with private cabañas and a 25-person hot tub.
Shopping: The Pirate's Walk shopping promenade.
Other amenities: 2 wedding chapels; spa and beauty salon.

Built by Steve Wynn, who was also responsible for the Mirage and the Bellagio (before selling up to create Wynn Las Vegas and Encore), the owners MGM Mirage have gradually steered the resort away from families to provide a more adult-orientated destination.

BRITTIP

If you plan to see the **Sirens of TI** show at Treasure Island, arrive early to grab a prime spot as crowds build quickly.

The free *Sirens of TI* show is a steamy affair, with wanton sirens tempting buccaneers in a wild, outdoor sea battle 4 times nightly every 90 minutes starting at 7.30pm. While you can see it from Las Vegas Boulevard, you can also watch it from the outdoor patio of Gilley's Saloon. And while Cirque's *Mystère* show continues to wow audiences twice nightly, there is a much more adult selection of bars. The Kahunaville Party Bar is a tropical hotspot with eclectic music and flair bartenders that turn the venue from restaurant to party central until 3am every morning.

Trump International Hotel & Tower

Aside from its flashy exterior, this is one of Vegas's more reserved hotels.
Location: Where the Strip meets Fashion Show Drive near Wynn Las Vegas
Grand opening: 31 March 2008
Theme: Luxury
Cost: $2.1bn
Web: www.trumplasvegashotel.com
Reservations: 866 939 8786
Rooms: 1,282
Room rates: From $152
Restaurants: DJT
Chilling out: The Spa at Trump, heated outdoor pool and fitness center and salon
Shopping: Across the street from the Fashion Show Mall.

Another non-gaming hotel to open on the Strip, true to Donald J. Trump's ostentatious style, Trump International Hotel Las Vegas resembles a shot of gold bullion, its 64-storey tower encased in 24-carat gold glass. There's nothing so humble as a guestroom here, rather studio suites

rising to ten 3-bedroom penthouse suites. There are white-gloved doormen and the signature services of a Trump Attaché to help your stay run smoothly and noting all your preferences. The Spa at Trump has some great treatments to ease yourself through a hectic stay including the Sun-Worshipper Body Wrap, the Royal Flush Facial and the Morning-After Eye Cure, a New Mom package, offering 'me time' and post-baby rejuvenation and even a Paws Massage Package as part of the Trump Pet Programme.

Vdara Hotel

One of a new line of tasteful non-gaming hotels.
Location: Part of the CityCenter development on the Strip attached to the Bellagio
Grand opening: October 2009
Theme: Sophisticated non-gaming retreat
Cost: Part of the $8.5bn CityCenter development
Web: www.vdara.com
Reservations: 866 745 7767
Rooms: 1,495 suites
Room rates: From $139
Restaurants: Grab-and-go Market Cafe Vdara reminiscent of a California coastal café; Bar Vdara is an eclectic lobby lounge that works for morning espressos or late-night cocktails; Aria, Bellagio and Crystals offer plenty of dining options nearby
Nightlife: Bar Vdara connects to an intimate outdoor space with a garden-oasis feel where guests can lounge on spacious swings.
Attractions: Nancy Rubins' immense installation, Big Pleasure Point, made up of numerous row boats, kayaks, canoes, small sailboats and so on – in gravity defying form.
Chilling out: The Sky Pool & Lounge has spa cabanas, semi-secluded plunge pools, a high-energy bar and lounge open day and evening.
Shopping: Crystals is CityCenter's retail and entertainment district with more than 500,000ft²/46,450m² of shopping including Louis Vuitton, Hermes, Prada, Dior, Tiffany & Co. And new to Vegas are Tom Ford, Miu Miu and Marni amongst other famous brands.
Other amenities: Vdara Health & Beauty is a 2-level spa, salon and advanced fitness area focusing on holistic health.

Soaring 57 storeys above the Strip, Vdara Hotel is an all-suite and spa hotel with exclusivity at its heart. There are all the vices of Vegas out there waiting to be discovered, but here you have a non-gaming, smoke-free and sustainable retreat to take a breath from the madness. Vdara's distinctive crescent shape and skin of patterned glass is one of the biggest design statements in the city. Corner view suites are sought after with expansive views of the city and mountains beyond. Each has a gourmet kitchen. The spa is a focus of the hotel's holistic approach with a Champagne and smoothie bar. Green credentials Vegas-style mean the world's first fleet of stretch limos powered by compressed natural gas.

The Venetian

Luxurious recreation of the romantic city of Venice, and a favourite with celebrities and CEOs alike.
Location: The Strip at East Spring Mountain Road
Theme: Renaissance Venice
Cost: $1.2bn, plus $275m Venezia Tower
Web: www.venetian.com
Reservations: 702 414 1000
Rooms: 4,000 suites, plus another 3,025 in the familial Palazzo next door
Room rates: From $159
Restaurants: 16 fine-dining establishments throughout the hotel and Grand Canal Shoppes, including AquaKnox, Bouchon and Tao, plus 19 casual dining outlets.
Nightlife: TAO nightclub, LAVO nightclub, Tao Beach, V Bar and La Scena Lounge and new Double Helix Wine & Whiskey Bar.
Shows: Joan Rivers at The Venetian Showroom, Andrew Lloyd Webber's *Phantom of the Opera*, Blue Man Group and *Jersey Boys*, comedians David Spade and Rita Rudner.
Attractions: Madame Tussauds and gondola rides.
Chilling out: Pool deck with private cabañas, Tao Beach for 'European-style' sunbathing.
Gambling: The Venetian House Casino has state of the art video poker and slot games under hand-painted frescoed ceilings. Surreal and totally Vegas!
Shopping: Grand Canal Shoppes and the new Shoppes at The Palazzo.
Other amenities: A massive wedding chapel, which can be divided up into 3; and Canyon Ranch SpaClub – one of the most luxurious on the Strip; golf.
 Here you will find replicas of everything that Venice stands for, from the Doge's Palace to St Mark's Square, the Grand Canal and Rialto Bridge, all re-created in the finest detail by sculptors with the help of two Italian historians to 'ensure the integrity of the design and architecture'. In fact, its beauty and style is only matched by its service, which has firmly established the Venetian as one of the most successful resorts on the Strip.
 For many years the one thing missing at the Venetian was first-rate entertainment, but no more. The Venetian spent a raft of money to develop a dazzling theatre for a lavish production of Andrew Lloyd Webber's *Phantom of the Opera*. Then they wooed the staggeringly popular Blue Man Group from the Luxor and have popular comedians David Spade and Rita Rudner – the longest-running, most successful one person comedy show in Vegas.

> ◀◆▶ **BRITTIP**
> For a truly romantic wedding, you can get married on the Ponte al di Piazza bridge overlooking the Venetian's St Mark's Square.

 The Venetian has a host of bars, lounges and restaurants that will help make your nights memorable. The flagship is Tao, both a fabulous Asian restaurant and a nightclub, with a 40ft/12m long outside terrace, giving spectacular views of the Strip, and go-go dancers. The swanky V Bar, based on LA's sophisticated Sunset Room, continues to be popular, as does La Scena Lounge. The Venetian is the king of upscale Las Vegas dining with more celebrity chefs than you can shake a spatula at, starting with Emeril Legasse's Delmonico's Steakhouse.
 The pool deck is based on a Venetian garden and includes a swimming pool, 3 spa pools and ornate gazebos. It is highly prized as a remarkable location for wedding receptions.
 If you need refreshing, try the Canyon Ranch SpaClub, next to the 5acre/2ha pool deck, which has private cabañas and is modelled on a Venetian-style garden. The state-of-the-art spa, beyond a shadow of a doubt the best in Las Vegas, features massage and treatments, a 40ft/12m rock-climbing wall, Pilates studio, spinning gym, therapeutic Watsu pools and Canyon Ranch Café.
 The centrepiece of the main shopping mall, known as the Grand Canal Shoppes (see page 87), is the reproduction of Venice's majestic Grand Canal and St Mark's Square and for a price you can even take a romantic gondola ride. There are actually two places you can take a gondola ride – along the Grand Canal

but also outside the main entrance by the massive edifice of the Doge's Palace. The ride in front is special, as all the gondoliers are accomplished singers who sing romantic Italian songs while they take you through the tunnels of the front waterways. Our boatman confided he was from Italy, studied at Juilliard and was working until he could find a job at one of Las Vegas's shows. Also, there are a number of eateries along St Mark's, making it a great place to have a coffee or lunch, and watch Las Vegas-Venice pass by.

Another in the line of 'cousin' properties, the Palazzo opened in 2007 next door to the Venetian to add another 3,025 luxury suites spread over 50 floors to the mix.

Wynn Las Vegas

The last word in luxury, glamour and elegance.
Location: The Strip at Spring Mountain Road
Theme: Understated glamour
Cost: $2.7bn
Web: www.wynnlasvegas.com
Reservations: 877 321 9966
Rooms: 2,359 rooms, 270 parlour and salon suites, 45 executive suites, 36 1- and 2-bedroom fairway villas, 6 private-entry villas
Room rates: From $179
Restaurants: 15 including Okado, The Buffet and the newest, La Cave Wine and Food Hideaway, open until 3am.
Nightlife: Tryst and a selection of bars.
Shows: The $13m *Le Rêve*.
Gambling: Extensive casino.
Shopping: Wynn Esplanade with high-scale promenade with designers such as Chanel, Manolo Blahnik, Dior, Louis Vuitton, Cartier, Gaultier, Oscar de al Renta, Jo Malone and Graff.
Chilling out: European-style pool and 2 Jacuzzis.

Wynn Las Vegas

Other amenities: 3 wedding chapels; spa and salon.
Golf: The only hotel on the Strip with its own golf course; the 18-hole course has been designed by Tom Fazio.

Steve Wynn decided on a complete change of tack with his new resort. He snapped up the elegant but failing Desert Inn and its 215acre/87ha site for a mere $275m. He then went back to the drawing board for 18 months before announcing plans for the *Le Rêve* (the dream) in 2002. Eventually, it evolved into Wynn Las Vegas, hands-down the provider of the finest, most elegant, most luxurious service in a hotel casino. And the proof is that the Wynn Las Vegas is the only hotel-casino in the world to have been awarded both Mobil 5-star and AAA Five Diamond ratings.

A budget of $13m alone was given for the fantastic new *Le Rêve* production (all that remains of the original name for the hotel), which was created by Franco Dragone, the man behind so many Cirque du Soleil® spectaculars. *Le Rêve* is now unquestionably the swankiest show currently showing in Sin City.

And golfers will be delighted by the 18-hole golf course designed by Tom Fazio, in conjunction with Wynn himself, that requires no trip out of town, only a greens fee of $500 per round.

While there is no theme to this resort, it is inspired by Steve Wynn's love of the Impressionist painters. The original name, *Le Rêve*, comes from a well-loved Picasso painting, while much of the decoration of the hotel lobby and casino are based on Matisse colours and themes. None of the resort's facilities can be seen from the Strip and only those who journey up the long driveway will get to see the 50-storey, curved tower covered in bronze glass.

BRITTIP
Steve Wynn has brought another first to the city: the hotel's Oscar de la Renta store is the only Oscar boutique in the world.

Guestrooms provide a jaw-dropping spectacle in themselves. Executive suites come with floor-to-ceiling glass that spans the entire room from wall to wall, over 26ft/8m, to give breathtaking views of the Strip and the mountains surrounding the desert heart of the city. These vast suites include separate bathrooms for him and her – his with glass-enclosed shower, hers with soaking tub, and both equipped with LCD TVs and over-sized Turkish towels.

The living area is home to a sofa, console, coffee table, plus dining room table and chairs. And as you jump into the king-size bed you can snuggle into 320-count European linens before picking up the controls for the curtains and TV. In-room services include massage, manicure, pedicure and hair styling.

If you ever wish to leave your suite, then the resort's buffet is one of the best in town – with 17 live-action exhibition cooking stations and a sumptuous array of dishes, redefining the notion of buffet dining. As you would guess, food is toe-curlingly excellent with places like Okada.

Start the weekend with *Nightlife Starter Kit* every Friday and Saturday night after 9pm, which eases guests into the evening with a 200ml bottle of tequila, a 375ml bottle of vodka, Red Bull and Fiji water then head to Tryst where the dance floor extends into a breathtaking 90ft/27m waterfall that cascades into a secluded lagoon.

The following morning allow your body a chance to recover in the spa, which offers 45 treatment rooms for massage, body treatments, facials and hydrotherapy. There are also separate his and hers facilities with showers, steam room, sauna and whirlpool for ultra comfort and privacy.

Resort-hotels off the Strip

Hard Rock Hotel & Casino

A big hit with models and celebrities, plus trendy young things.
Location: 4455 Paradise Road; one mile east of the Strip at the corner of Harmon Ave and Paradise Road
Theme: Rock 'n' roll
Web: www.hardrockhotel.com
Reservations: 702 693 5000
Rooms: 670
Room rates: From $79
Restaurants: 3 fine-dining experiences, including the famous Nobu, and 3 casual establishments, including the Mexican Pink Taco, which is great for outdoor seating and the Tuscan-style Ago.
Nightlife: The Joint live gig venue, Center Bar, Rehab pool party, Vanity, Poolside shows and Pink Taco Bar.
Gambling: Poker Lounge Hell's Belles where blackjack meets go-go dancers, table games, slots and race and sports book.
Shopping: Hard Rock Store, Rocks jewellery and Love Jones lingerie.
Chilling out: Beach Club and Reliquary Spa.
Other amenities: Golf is offered through Walters Golf. Hart & Huntington Tattoo Company.

A truly trendy hangout and an instant hit when it opened at the end of the 1990s, it has remained a mecca for celebs and the beautiful people despite new competition in the guise of The Palms. A $750m expansion project included another 950 guest rooms, more casino space, more food outlets, a larger pool, new shops and spa. A new Paradise Tower is an 18-floor tower with 490 guest rooms designed with the Hard Rock's signature party attitude in mind but with a jolt of luxury and sophistication. There's a mega penthouse and 10 pool suites, 2 of which have their own cabaña or pool deck and glass balconies.

Its restaurants are some of the best in town and in 2005 three won a total of 4 Epicurean Awards, including Best Japanese Restaurant for Nobu, Best New Restaurant off the Strip for Simon Kitchen & Bar (now closed), and Best Mexican Restaurant for Pink Taco.

Definitely not for the faint-hearted, there is a strong adult vibe at this resort. In addition to the very raunchy nightlife scene, the Beach Club (open to hotel guests only) has become a haven for 'some of the most beautiful bodies in Las Vegas'. With palm-shaded sandy beaches and blue water lagoons, the grass-shack cabañas (with phone, fridge and misting system!) are highly sought after. Every Sunday is Rehab, a hard-partying, adults-only pool party which has become a Las Vegas tradition. After a hard day by the pool, if you need a little more R&R, try the Reliquary Spa to prepare you for a night of partying. You can even get your gaming and pool lounging at the same time, with Hard Rock Café's Poolside Blackjack.

Hard Rock Café

M Resort Spa Casino

Modern and fresh with fabulous city views, you can't go wrong here.

Location: Approximately 10mls/16km to the south of the Strip on Las Vegas Boulevard South, just minutes from the airport
Theme: Modern with warm touches
Grand opening: 1 March 2009
Cost: $1bn
Web: www.themresort.com
Reservations: 702 797 1000
Rooms: 390
Room rates: From $75
Restaurants: 7 eateries including Studio B, the resort's show kitchen buffet with a live-action cooking studio. At Marinelli's guests can enjoy authentic Italian dishes. Anthonys combines great charcoal-grilled steak and seafood with a buzzy social scene. Gracing the summit of the M Resort, Veloce Cibo has an extensive menu of appetizers, entrées, sushi, sashimi and nigiri. Hash House A Go Go is a 1920s art-deco inspired 24-hour gathering spot and the place for hand-prepared American classics.
Nightlife: Ravello entertainment lounge for live bands; Hostile Grape Wine Cellar and Tasting Room.
Gambling: Casino floor with tables games, poker room and slots.
Chilling out: Phenomenal pool with infinity feature in the piazza area and 20 VIP cabañas. A more private pool, Daydream, is a bit hipper and more locals oriented.
Shopping: Vice shop and convenience store. Up to 1 million ft^2/92,900m^2 of retail in the planning.
Amenities: Spa Mio has 16 treatment rooms, Jacuzzi and sauna.

Set at an elevation of 400ft/122m higher than most other properties around, M Resort has fantastic views of the city and the mountains from its lobby, restaurant and most guestrooms. This classy modern hangout was built by Anthony Marnell, III, son of casino-building pioneer Tony Marnell, who has built much of Las Vegas including the Mirage, Caesars Palace, Wynn and much more – a family hotel so to speak. And it shows. The Marnell family, for example, owns and operates all the restaurants so nothing is leased out. The concepts are all their own and everything is made fresh daily. Dining selections at the M Resort include recipes from the Marnell family recipe book and a reserve list of American-raised Wagyu Kobe Beef from the Marnell family ranch. Guests can also taste wines from the Marnell family private

label. Each room offers a living space that includes high-technology amenities such as a Bose® Wave sound system, iPod® docking station and 42in HD LCD flat screen television. The spa-like bathrooms offer guests a marble vanity with double sinks, inlaid mirror television and separate bathtub and shower. All resort rooms and suites feature automatic lighting controls for energy efficiency and floor to ceiling windows with unrivalled views of the Las Vegas Strip or mountains. Uniquely designed, the M Resort does not feature reflective glass and includes skylights on the casino floor allowing natural light in – a rare feature in the casino industry.

Las Vegas Hilton

Filled with conventioners, it now has a lively night scene. However, as we went to press, the Las Vegas Hilton was looking for a new management contract and expecting to change its name before the end of 2011.

Location: Paradise Road and Karen Avenue (behind the Strip)
Web: www.lvhilton.com
Reservations: 702 732 5111
Rooms: 3,261 including 305 suites
Room rates: From $45.95
Restaurants: 4 fine-dining restaurants including the delightfully Mediterranean Casa Nicola and the Japanese Benihana, plus 9 casual eateries including classic Vegas Buffet.
Nightlife: 8 popular bars from Tempo lounge bar to SpaceQuest Bar set in the 24th century.
Gambling: At 74,000 ft^2/6487 m^2, one of the largest off-strip casinos with everything from state of the art slots to classic table games.
Shows: Liza Minelli; Impressionist Greg London; an Elvis tribute and various other performers.
Chilling out: Pool, spa, tennis courts.
Shopping: 2 promenades.

⚜ BRITTIP

When Elvis first appeared in Las Vegas at the Last Frontier Hotel on the Strip in 1956 he was a flop. He didn't return until 1969 when he mostly appeared – to great acclaim, of course – at the brand new Las Vegas Hilton where he kept a residence until 1976. Barry Manilow was here for 5 years, finishing his run in 2010.

Built on the site of the Las Vegas Park Speedway, a horse and auto racing facility, an understated elegance pervades what is ostensibly an upmarket hotel resort for business people attending one of the over 20,000 annual conventions held in Las Vegas. For them, its location near the Convention Center is perfect, but it's about a 12-minute walk to the Strip, so it's a little off the beaten track for real tourists. Fortunately, the tram has a stop right outside the Convention Center to whisk you away to the wilder parts of Sin City. The hotel looks set to change its name once again – rumour has it that it will go back to its original opening name International Hotel – in 2012.

The Palms

A sultry boutique resort, which has rapidly established itself as the city's top place to party, attracting both the hip and the famous, in part due to its top-notch recording studio.
Location: Flamingo Road, west of the Strip, close to the Rio All-Suite Hotel
Theme: Sophisticated adult playground
Cost: $265m, plus $600m
Web: www.palms.com
Reservations: 702 942 7777
Room rates: From $89
Rooms: 455 deluxe rooms
Restaurants: Include N9NE Steakhouse from Chicago, Little Buddha Café from Paris, the upmarket Alizé, Garduños Mexican restaurant, Blue Agave Oyster and Chile Bar and new Simon Restaurant & Lounge.
Nightlife: This is club city, a long list of popular hotspots including the Playboy Club, Rain in the Desert Nightclub, Moon Nightclub and Ghost Bar, an indoor-outdoor lounge.
Attractions: The Brenden Theater Complex, a state-of-the-art 14-screen cinema complex; new state of the art concert venue The Pearl, a drive-in betting shop; and 2 Bachelor Suites for stag parties and hen nights including The Barbie Suite. Sophisticated recording studio where everyone from Lady Gaga to Celine Dion has cut a record.
Gambling: No casino. But gamers fear not. Just a short stroll through a SkyTube is the adjacent Palms Casino Resort.
Chilling out: Palms Pool Lounge.
Other amenities: 20,000ft²/1,860m², 3-storey spa featuring candlelit yoga classes and fun and fruity body treatments.

The hotel opened to a fanfare of glory in 2001, and from the outset the Texas-based Malouf family targeted celebrities, making

this the home of the Cine Vegas Film Festival (now closed) and thus ensuring its status as one of the most star-laden hotels in Las Vegas.

BRITTIP
Just to give you an insight into VIP prices: a private room at The Palm's Rain Nightclub costs $300–1,000 a night!

The original 455 rooms – a mere drop in the ocean for this city – has been increased with a whopping $600m expansion programme that includes a 347-room Fantasy Tower, 2,200-seat showroom, 50-storey condo hotel and spa and a new pool. The Hardwood Suite is clearly targeted at the money-is-no-object end of the market with its own indoor basketball court (the new must-have!), scoreboard, pool table, poker table and dance floor, among many other facilities. As it is, revellers can choose between bungalows, Playpen Suites or 'Hugh Hefner's Skyloft for ultimate party hospitality where the likes of Kanye West hold court.

The Palms quickly became one of the most coveted private party spots in Las Vegas and its Real World Suite has already been used to host events for Leonardo DiCaprio, Avril Lavigne and Mark Wahlberg. Ordinary mortals need not miss out on the fun as the hotel also has two Bachelor Suites, fitted out with dance poles (think Jamie Lee Curtis in *True Lies!*), a wooden dance floor and sophisticated sound system. The ultimate playrooms, perfect for both stag parties and hen nights, they're decked out in 1960s retro colour patterns, a mirror wall made up of fragmented squares of glass to create the effect of a disco ball, the same type of mirror above the bed, an LED lighting system and plasma TV screens.

BRITTIP
If good service is important, then The Palms could be the place for you as the Malouf family is famous for excellent hospitality.

In the meantime, punters flock to what is still just a bijou gem due to its huge array of entertainment amenities.

The award-winning Rain Nightclub located on the casino level, is a multi-storey, multi-environment nightclub and concert. It combines performances by international headliners, such as Britney Spears, with an ultra-cool dance club (see page 139) with top DJs in residence including Pauly D and private event facility, and comes with some amazing special effects including fog, haze, 16ft/5m fire plumes and 3ft/1m fireballs, while the bamboo dance floor is surrounded by a computer-programmed river of water with dancing jets and fountains. Ghostbar is a vibrant open-hour lounge on top of the 42-storey hotel tower, which has already won plaudits as a hot nightspot.

◀▌▶ BRITTIP

Single girls looking for the ultimate girly party venue, should head to the Barbie Suite at The Palms.

This resort-hotel also has a fantastic line-up of restaurants that cover upmarket, steaks, casual and bistro-style dining. Top of the pile is the Alizé, the latest and probably swankiest offering from Las Vegan gourmet masterchef and restaurateur André Rochat. Named after the gentle wind that runs along the Mediterranean, it offers a French Riviera-style dining experience in an amazing glass atrium with aquamarine glass walls that provides spectacular views of the city. VIP tables are in front of the windows and secluded from the rest of the dining room by a curved glass partition. Rochat has won a clutch of awards for his distinctive restaurants. The latest opening is the Signature Simons Restaurant & Lounge from celebrity chef Kerry Simon.

The Palms Pool Lounge set a new trend in exotic oasis indulgence with relaxation pools, chaise longues, 4 bars, billiard tables, outdoor swings, poolside blackjack and trampolines. You can even hire one of the private cabañas that come with TVs, fridges, telephones and VIP amenities, while DJs spin tunes day and night and food can be ordered from the Nine Steakhouse. The whole area is only open to hotel guests during the day, but is turned into a voyeuristic club at night (see page 141).

Plaza Hotel

Plaza Hotel & Casino

A modern classic in an original Las Vegas great.
Location: At the western end of the Fremont Street Experience in Downtown.
Grand opening: Original Union Plaza 1971; re-opening 1st Sept 2011
Web: www.plazahotelcasino.com
Reservations: 702 386 2110
Rooms: 1,037
Room rates: From $44–109
Restaurants: Casual dining includes Zaba's Mexican Grill, branches of Island Sushi, Hawaiian Grill, Radio City Pizzeria and home-grown Las Vegas Hash House A Go Go, which describes itself as 'twisted farm food'. Those with a sweet tooth can get their fix at Gigi's Cupcakes, with 30 mouthwatering varieties. Oscar's steakhouse in the iconic dome, boasts the best view in town of Fremont Street's famous neon canopy with historic Vegas memorabilia celebrating Oscar Goodman's time as mayor.
Nightlife: The historic 600-seat retro Vegas showroom, with cocktail tables and chairs, features afternoon and late-night entertainment, mingling and singalongs around 2 pianos, along with rounds of mini golf at the Swingers Club.
Shows: Nightly productions by Insurgo Theater Movement in the Theater on the third floor.
Gambling: The all new 80,000ft²/7,400m² casino floor has 28 table games, 800 slot and video poker machines, race and sports book and bingo room on the third floor.
Other amenities: Exposed hair salon.

On the site of the first train depot in Las Vegas, the Union Pacific Railroad depot, the Union Plaza made its debut in 1971. With 22 stories and 504 rooms, and a 66,000ft²/6132m² casino – twice the size of the Las Vegas Hilton, the next largest at the time – it was the largest property downtown, and with the station and ticket windows directly connected to the hotel, the only US train station located in a casino. It took the highly controversial step of hiring women dealers, banned at the time, who quickly became popular. It also introduced plays that featured sexy themes and top Hollywood names.

Sold to the Tamares group in 2004 by Jackie Gaughan, a Las Vegas gaming pioneer, it reopened its doors in summer 2011 – after an extensive almost year-long renovation – sporting brand new guestrooms and suites, a redesigned casino and lobby and all new restaurants, bars and entertainment. Set in 2 towers on 16.5acres/6.68ha of land, it is still one of the largest hotel-casinos in downtown Las Vegas.

It continues to be a pioneer with the debut of award-winning Insurgo Theater Movement which includes members of Cirque Du Soleil®, *Le Rêve*, Blue Man Group and other famous groups, marking the first time a local repertory theatre has been given a residency at a major hotel/casino in Las Vegas.

It's also still a bit risqué, with the cheekily named 'Swinger's Club' and Exposed hair salon, aimed at men, where cocktail waitresses strut around in bikinis and lingerie.

Future plans include refurbishing the rooftop pool and outdoor recreational areas, including basketball and tennis courts and an outdoor amphitheatre.

Rio All-Suite Hotel & Casino

Proving there is life beyond the Strip, the Rio is an entertainment city in its own right.
Location: 3700 West Flamingo
Theme: Tropical paradise
Cost: $200m expansion
Web: www.riolasvegas.com
Reservations: 866 746 7671
Rooms: 2,563 suites
Room rates: From $59
Restaurants: 14 eateries in all including fine-dining, city favourite Buzios Seafood Restaurant plus the Gaylord India Restaurant. More casual places include the funky VooDoo Steak Lounge.
Nightlife: Great spots include the Flirt lounge, Voodoo Rooftop Nightclub and I-Bar ultra-lounge.

⚡ BRITTIP
The Rio may be off the beaten track of the Strip, but if you're near Harrah's, take the free shuttle bus between the two hotels – you don't have to be a guest of either to get a ride.

Shows: The amazing Penn & Teller and Chippendales.
Attractions: *Show in the Sky* (free); Lucky Strike Bowling Alley.
Gambling: State of the art slots, video poker, 80 gaming tables, keno lounge and race and sports book.
Chilling out: Voodoo sand beach and outdoor recreational area, plus Rio Spa and Salon.
Shopping: Masquerade Village.

Other amenities: 3 wedding chapels; golf is available at the Rio Secco or Cascata Golf Course.

The Rio is consistently voted the best-value hotel in America and has some of the finest restaurants in Las Vegas including Gaylord India Restaurant. Its buffet is second to none. It is also home to the city's first Wine Cellar Tasting Room, which has the world's largest collection of fine and rare wines, along with an array of tasting accessories.

The *Show in the Sky*, one of Vegas's best free shows, allows guests to ride aboard fantasy floats that glide above the crowds in a Mardi Gras-style fiesta of music and dance. This is an adult-orientated show with topless girls for the evening performances, while the hotel has generally shifted in a more raunchy direction with two chi-chi lounges for grown-ups: Flirt and the ever-popular VooDoo Rooftop Nightclub.

During June and July it is impossible to get a room here, as it hosts the annual World Series of Poker (see page 146) and poker pros and addicts descend on it in droves.

Outside, the Voodoo Beach comes with real sand beaches at the edge of a tropical lagoon, complete with waterfalls, plus 4 nautical-shaped swimming pools and 5 Jacuzzi-style spas. Here you can bask in the sun or order a variety of services including personal massages, poolside cocktails and food. European-Style pool, The Voo, has live DJs and go-go dancers.

When it comes to weddings, the Rio does it in style. An entire floor of the Masquerade Tower has been given over to wedding facilities, including 1 chapel and 1 themed, 1,200ft²/111m² honeymoon suites and reception areas.

Queen suite at the Rio

Other resort-hotels

The following hotels still have their place in the city's hall of fame, but cannot compete with the big shots!

Imperial Palace Hotel & Casino

Friendly, reasonably priced hotel in prime location.
Location: 3535 Las Vegas Boulevard South; The Strip at West Flamingo
Theme: Japanese
Web: www.imperialpalace.com
Reservations: 702 731 3311
Rooms: 2,700
Room rates: From $22
Restaurants: 7 including the Emperor's Buffet.
Show: Frank Marino's Divas Las Vegas, Smokey Robinson's Human Nature.
Attractions: A collection of over 250 antique and collectible cars and access to 3 golf courses.
Gambling: Straightforward casino with Dealertainers Pit who impersonate and perform hits from the likes of Michael Jackson, Cher, Dolly Parton, Stevie Wonder and Elvis nightly.
Chilling out: Olympic-size swimming pool with waterfall and Jacuzzi, heated Zen-inspired spa and salon and 7 bars, including the Sake Bar.
Other facilities: 2 wedding chapels; the only 24-hour medical facility on the Strip (phone direct on 702 735 3600) and a PetStay programme.

When the reviews of Las Vegas accommodation are given, the Imperial Palace has hardly taken centre stage, yet it has reasonable prices and good gambling odds. However, that was before The Linq, which will completely transform the facade, porte cochere, casino and hotel reception to polish it up for the limelight in 2013. The resort is home to a collection of vintage and special-interest cars and has a good-value full-service spa. It holds a Hawaiian-style Imperial Luau complete with Polynesian fire dancers, roast pig and unlimited piña coladas and mai tais!

Tropicana Las Vegas

Exotic chilling-out environment for grown-ups.
Location: The Strip at Tropicana
Theme: Tropical paradise island
Web: www.troplv.com
Reservations: 702 739 2222
Rooms: 1,875
Room rates: From $109.99
Restaurants: 5, including Biscayne Steakhouse and the new Cafe Nikki.
Nightlife: Ambhar Lounge with live DJs and Club Nikki.
Shows: *Gladys Knight*; comedian Brad Garrett.
Attractions: Interactive exhibit Las Vegas Mob Experience; Nikki Beach.
Gambling: Some of the loosest slots and video poker on the Strip.
Chilling out: Tropical Pool and Nikki Beach Las Vegas; Glow Mandara Spa.
Other amenities: A wedding chapel; barbers shop and salon.
Shopping: Trop Shops – specialty shops.

The Tropicana has a Caribbean Village façade, while its 'signature' is a spectacular laser light show on its Outer Island.

The 12,000ft^2/1,115m^2 main pool is the centre of the summer action with its bar and swim-up blackjack games. There's also a swim-up bar, next to which sliding glass doors partition off a 1,500ft^2/139m^2 heated indoor pool, one of the only indoor pools in Vegas, surrounded by lush tropical garden views. There is also an adults-only lagoon pool and a garden pool, while over 60 varieties of trees, ground cover, foliage and flowers create explosions of colour. In 2011, the Tropicana upped its chill out cool with the arrival of Miami's sexy Nikki Beach. Set in over 4acres/1.6ha of lush natural pool landscape, the beach club has sleek loungers, opium beds and cabañas as well as a restaurant, outdoor café and bar, swim-up blackjack, and a private island in the middle of the Tropical Pool. Night time cool is in the form of the 15,000ft^2/1,395m^2 Club Nikki, with a glamorous ultra-lounge and dance floor.

Staying in Henderson

Just a 17ml/27km drive from the Strip, Henderson is a small but important location overlooking the brilliant blue waters of the 320acre/130ha manmade Lake Las Vegas. Ultra-romantic settings with wonderful water-based amenities, they're a great place to base yourself if you want to escape the maddening kerchink, kerchink of slot machines yet be within easy reach of the city's fun-filled attractions.

Ravella at Lake Las Vegas

An ultra-romantic, deluxe desert retreat-style resort that is still conveniently close to the hustle and bustle of Las Vegas.
Location: MonteLago Village, 1610 Lake Las Vegas Parkway, Lake Las Vegas Resort, Henderson

Theme: Classic, Tuscan-inspired elegance
Web: www.ravellavegas.com
Reservations: 888 810 0440
Rooms: 349
Room rates: From $129
Restaurants: Medici Café and Terrace, Firenze Lobby Lounge, Lagoon Bar and Grill and Dining at the Village.
Nightlife: Firenze Lobby Lounge with live music.
Chilling out: Pool with cabañas for hire and gardens, lagoon with white sand beach and water activities.
Other amenities: Spa; access to 2 golf courses; fly fishing; kayaking; gondola rides; 3 wedding chapels; nature hikes, free bike rental; exclusive access to Jack Nicklaus' SouthShore Golf Club.

Previously the upper-crust Ritz-Carlton, this hotel now under the management of Dolce Hotels & Resorts opened in February 2011, with a redesigned contemporary lobby. This hotel is about location and the sandy shores of the beautiful Lake Las Vegas don't disappoint, especially if you're looking for an oasis of calm that's just a short ride from the Las Vegas Strip and the delights of Sin City.

Guests can stroll from their rooms over a quaint stone bridge, fashioned after Florence's Ponte Vecchio, to find themselves in an olde worlde area filled with shops, restaurants and the neighbouring Casino Monte Lago. The landscaped grounds provide a series of scenic walkways and cycling trails around the lake's shoreline, or guests can take to the waters in canopied water taxis, sailing boats or kayaks.

◀️🇬🇧 **BRITTIP**

The Ravella at Lake Las Vegas now offers the best of both worlds: a gambling-free environment but with adjoining casino. The separately run Casino Monte Lago sits next to the hotel, adjacent to The Village at Monte Lago, an upscale shopping complex.

A relaxed but elegant Mediterranean ambience is reflected in the arched doorways, clay tile roofs, interior courtyards and the palette of sun-washed colours that are reflective of European waterside towns and lakeside villas. The rooms come with top-notch Frette bed linen, oversized marble bathrooms and a casual yet classy decor. Many of the rooms also have balconies that look over the vine-covered trellises, shaded loggias, water features, white sand beach and heated swimming pool. There are also 35 suites and 2 whopping 2,400ft^2/223m^2 suites.

The fabulous Medici Café and Terrace is set in an incredibly romantic courtyard with pretty Florentine gardens for outdoor dining and views over the lake. Elegant yet relaxed, you can have breakfast and lunch here, while it turns into a fine-dining experience for dinner.

The luxurious, 30,000ft^2/2,790m^2 spa is the first in America to offer desert- and Tuscan-inspired treatments. It's particularly good for couples, with Massage Mentoring which teaches couples how to massage one another.

Henderson and nearby Boulder City, Nevada are home to several world-class golf clubs and courses, all within just a few minutes of Lake Las Vegas. Highlights include the renowned Cascata, Revere at Anthem and Rio Secco.

Top budget hotels

There are also a host of inexpensive hotels that follow the Las Vegas tradition of cheap hotels, food and drinks to draw the budget-conscious gambler. You will never gush about the rooms, but many have an engaging character sometimes missed in the massive resorts. If you want to experience Las Vegas and want to spend less money on your hotel room and more on the sights and fun, then here are some good places to consider.

El Cortez Hotel & Casino

Mobbed-up hotel getting a new life.
Location: Fremont Street and North Sixth, one block from Las Vegas Boulevard
Web: www.elcortezhotelcasino.com
Reservations: 702 385-5200
Rooms: 250
Room rates: From $30
Restaurants: 4 including 2 awesome value options, The Flame Steakhouse and Café Cortez.

Many experienced Las Vegas travellers might raise their eyebrows at the inclusion of El Cortez. This was one of Bugsy Siegel's first properties and was long known for its great promotions, cheap lodging and fantastic gambling odds as well as mouldy carpets, smoky and dilapidated rooms and a clientele of wheelchair-bound octogenarians spending their pension cheques. That time is history. A $12m renovation in 2007 to go along with the development of the East Freemont Street Entertainment District has made the old girl into a freshly scrubbed belle of the ball.

The room rates are still wonderfully

low, but the rooms are astonishingly comfortable. The Flame Steakhouse and Café Cortez also put out the best cheap food you will ever find anywhere.

The best part is getting rooms in the oldest part of El Cortez. There are no lifts to these rooms, only narrow stairs, but here Bugsy Siegel lorded over his early Las Vegas empire, and it has been said that more than one card shark had his hands broken, or some mob swindler met a bloody end here.

Fitzgerald's Casino & Hotel

Friendly, reasonably priced hotel in downtown Las Vegas.
Location: Fremont Street
Web: www.fitzgeraldslasvegas.com
Reservations: 702 388 2400
Rooms: 638
Room rates: From $29
Restaurants: 4 including Krispy Kreme Doughnuts.
Show: Kevin Burke – *Fitz of Laughter*; *Marriage can be Murder*.

In the centre of the Fremont Street Experience, 'the Fitz' is the tallest building downtown, and if you get the right room you can have a dazzling view of the best of Las Vegas. Try the '$20 upgrade' (see page 24) to get a south-facing corner room on an upper floor.

It has its own 40,000ft²/3,716m² casino, is easy walking to all the downtown activities, is just 2 blocks from 'the Deuce' bus to the Strip, and 3 blocks to the East Fremont Street Entertainment District. Rooms are clean and comfortable, if nothing special. This is also a place very popular with Brit and Aussie tour groups, and after a few days listening to the Yanks mangle the language, you'll be happy to hear a familiar accent.

Fitzgerald's

Palace Station Hotel Casino

One of the best-value hotels in Las Vegas.
Location: 115 at West Sahara
Web: www.palacestation.com
Reservations: 702 367 2411
Rooms: 1,000
Room rates: From $29.99
Restaurants: 8 including a raw Oyster Bar.
Attractions: Live Las Vegas Music at Jack's Irish Pub and Louie LOL at the Louie Anderson Theater.
Chilling out: 2 pools and a Jacuzzi.
Other facilities: Free shuttle to the airport and the Strip for guests with room keys.

Station Casinos own 8 'locals' casinos in the Las Vegas area. They don't particularly cater to tourists, but to local gamblers. This means they offer great deals, and you can get a room at an unbelievable price, plus the brand offers an aggressive marketing campaign of special freebies for customers. I've often stayed for free here; in fact, the most I've ever paid is $12 a night for 2 people. Again, the rooms are nothing to write home about, but the free shuttle to the Strip is a huge boon.

Coming soon

The world's first ever Nobu Hotel, Restaurant and Lounge opens in the Centurion Tower at Caesars Palace on the Strip in summer 2012 after a multi-million dollar refurbishment to house the exclusive 180-room five-star boutique hotel. The stylish interior of its 16 suites and a penthouse is designed by David Rockwell and showcases natural materials fused with Nobu's signature Japanese elegance. With, of course, private check-in and room service from Nobu's acclaimed culinary team.

At the heart of the hotel is the 9,500ft²/882.6m² Nobu restaurant and lounge, at the base of the Nobu Tower, which will offer teppanyaki tables, a sushi bar and private dining on cuisine by celebrated Chef Nobu Matsuhisa. Definitely the new place to see and be seen.

BRITTIP
You cannot register at any hotel with a casino if you are under the age of 21 – nor can you gamble if you are under 21.

The urban myth that Vegas is the 'brightest place on earth' is certainly continuing with its many new resorts. The home of safe excess marches on.

SHOWTIME

3

All the best shows from major productions to adults only

It has long been a Las Vegas basic that if you keep the customers entertained they will happily slap money on to the gaming tables. As the years have passed, the entertainment offerings have grown from scantily clad show girls to headliners like Elvis Presley and Frank Sinatra, and to a modern entertainment scene that rivals, and often surpasses, anything you might find in London, New York or even Los Angeles.

The top shows here are the incredible, mind-boggling, gravity-defying multi-million-dollar Cirque du Soleil® extravaganzas for which auditoriums have been purpose built up and down the Strip. Adding to the already hugely successful *Mystère, O, Zumanity, Kà, Le Rêve* and *Love* the opening of CityCenter heralded the arrival of a new show, *VIVA Elvis*, based on the life and music of Elvis Presley. Housed at Aria Resort & Casino, it features state-of-the-art technology and captivating visuals. What, after all, could be more Vegas than the King? A contemporary contender is Michael Jackson whose estate has teamed up with Cirque du Soleil® to produce *Michael Jackson – The World Immortal Tour*, which opened in December 2011 at Mandalay Bay. The second show will find a permanent home in a yet to be determined Las Vegas location in 2013.

🇬🇧 BRITTIP

Want to know why you pay so much to see some of these Las Vegas shows? It's reported that Cher, the 65-year old singer who claimed she would never perform live again, signed a deal worth more than £100 million for a 3-year residency at Caesars Palace hotel from 2008 to 2011. And you don't get the likes of replacements Celine Dion, Rod Stewart or Elton John on the cheap...

Stage plays are also the rage in Las Vegas these days. Many resorts have spent lavish amounts on Broadway hits like Andrew Lloyd Webber's *Phantom of the Opera, Jersey Boys, The Producers* and *Mamma Mia!* and others that play to packed houses. The latest to appear is *The Lion King* at the Mandalay Bay.

In this chapter

This is Vegas, though, so there are changes. Most of the plays offered are a shorter version than the originals, in fact *Phantom – The Las Vegas Spectacular* is only 95 minutes long and full of jaw-dropping special effects. Keep them happy but out there gambling, right?

There is a glut of high-profile magicians – think Penn & Teller. Cirque du Soleil® has teamed up with master illusionist Criss Angel to present *Believe* at the Luxor,

Las Vegas showgirls at the Tropicana

which reinvents the traditional magic show. There are more intellectually challenging stand-up acts such as the irrepressible Rita Rudner and the city has hosted a raft of rip-roaringly funny impersonators like Danny Gans who does everyone from Al Pacino to Kermit the Frog. Terry Fator, winner of NBC's *America's Got Talent* signed a 5-year deal with The Mirage to perform his ventriloquism and impressions of everyone from James Blunt to Marvin Gaye.

BRITTIP

If you are flexible and don't mind waiting until the last minute, you can save lots of money on show tickets. There are many half-price ticket stands along the Strip and Fremont Street and shows that aren't overbooked will sell tickets through these dealers at cut rates to put bums on the seats. You can often get tickets at 50% off by buying on the day of the performance from one of these shops. But sorry, this won't do for hard-to-find tickets, so Cirque extravaganzas are rarely available this way.

Of course, where Las Vegas sets itself apart from the rest is with its entertainment blockbusters. Celine Dion returning for a three year residency from 2011, packs them in at The Colosseum, Caesars Palace along with headline shows from Elton John's *The Million Dollar Piano* to Rod Stewart and Barry Manilow and from December 2012, Shania Twain.

If there is a downside to the spectacles and headliners, it is undoubtedly the ticket prices. They have skyrocketed during the last decade with a single ticket quickly hitting the $100 mark and rising steeply to more than $200. But, the good news is, ticket prices, like room rates, have come down and are now a bit of a bargain, with top shows from $60/70. But, for something a little kinder on the pocket, make the most of the lounge music scene. Nowhere does it better than Las Vegas. And when you've done all that there is, there are those adult revues. As the city's motto goes: 'What happens in Las Vegas stays in Las Vegas' – unless, of course, you take the video camera!

In previous years, some prices were inclusive of sales tax. Alas, as part of the rise in costs almost all tickets prices now require you to add 7%.

There are other acts that are booked on a 1- or 2-night basis and you can check these out before you go at: visitlasvegas.

com (the city's official website with details of all current shows), lasvegas. com (a comprehensive section on shows, comedians, regular local acts and live music venues) and vegas.com (a great place for show tickets). Also bear in mind you can visit ticketmaster.com to book more mainstream events.

Guide to ratings: ***** pure brilliance; **** fantastic; *** a great show; ** poor value for money.

Major productions

Absinthe

Roman Plaza at Caesars Palace, 800 745 3000, www.caesars.com
The crown jewel of the Spiegelworld experience, *Absinthe* is an over-the-top, circus-style show or adult carnival, for those who want something a little edgier, a little more absurd and a lot less censored than a Cirque du Soleil show. Expect a woman wearing pasties who gets inside a balloon and an outrageous cast of characters who were likely plucked from places just as exotic as the African outback. As nightfall approaches, performances take place in the Spiegeltent, a wooden show tent from Europe opulently decorated with mirrors, stained glass and velvet.
Rating: **** An imaginative show in a unique venue
Shows: 8pm and 10pm
Tickets: $79–$109

Barry Manilow

Le Theater des Arts, Paris Las Vegas, 702 492 3960, www.parislasvegas.com and www.manilowparis.com
After *Mandy* shot him to fame in 1975, Barry Manilow hasn't looked back. Moving here from a five year spell at the Las Vegas Hilton, with a new album *The Greatest Love Songs of All Time* released in 2010, expect a sentimental evening with this legendary singer-songwriter in a romantic new venue.
Rating: *****His show is, in a word, gorgeous
Shows: Every day except Mon and Thurs, 8pm
Tickets: $95–$299 plus tax

Celine Dion

Colosseum at Caesars Palace, 1-877 423 5463, www.caesarspalace.com and www.celineinvegas.com
Much-loved Celine Dion has returned with

Something for nothing

Don't miss the amazing – and free – Fremont Street Experience in downtown Las Vegas. In addition to the multi-million dollar electronic light and sound show, which takes place in the enclosed, traffic-free pedestrian mall, the city also provides five blocks of street performers and live music. Street performers abound. Live bands usually perform at stages on First Street and Third Street Tues–Sat and the Fremont Street Experience takes place every hour on the hour 6pm–midnight. Call 702 678 5600 for information, visit vegasexperience.com or just head downtown in the evening.

Most spectacular new entrant in the category of free shows is *Azure* at the Mermaid Restaurant & Lounge at the Silverton Hotel & Casino, 702 263 7777, silvertoncasino.com. An underwater fantasy show, all the action takes place inside a 120,000gall/545,530l saltwater aquarium as mermen and mermaids execute innovative choreography among the 4,000 fish and stunning coral. Shows run hourly on the hour Thurs–Sun 5–11pm. You will of course have to pay for dinner or at least have drinks at the bar!

You can get into the carnival spirit at the Rio All-Suite Hotel by either watching or taking part in the newly reinvented *Show in the Sky* which features dancers in costumes on floats suspended above the crowd. Three different performances include sexy and seductive scenes co-ordinated to popular hits. Free shows hourly 6–11pm, Thurs–Sat or you can pay $12.95 to don an exotic costume and ride on one of the main floats. You have to buy the costumes in person at least 1 hour before the show and they do sell out! Call the Rio for more information on 702 252 7777.

Treasure Island's free show is also worth a mention. The *Sirens of TI* re-creates the age-old battle of the sexes between mermaids and pirates nightly at 5.30pm (autumn/winter) and 7, 8.30, 10 and 11.30pm (spring/summer). Viewing is on a first-come, first-served basis, but guests at the hotel get exclusive VIP viewing access.

Other free shows include Fall of Atlantis at the Forum Shops at Caesars Palace and free circus acts in the Main Arena of Circus Circus every 30 minutes 11am–midnight every day. At Planet Hollywood's Miracle Mile shops don't miss the free laser and fountain shows, and there's even a rainstorm outside the Merchants Harbor Coffee House. Then there's the famous volcano at The Mirage which erupts every 15 minutes from dusk to midnight, the famous Bellagio fountain shows plus its conservatory and botanical gardens and finally, the Lion Habitat at the MGM Grand.

a brand new show centered on classic Hollywood movies and stunning visuals and featuring 31 musicians, including a full orchestra and band. Continuing her record of creating groundbreaking concert performances, it promises to be her best spectacle yet. It premiered in March 2011 at the beginning of her three year residency at the Colosseum, so there's plenty of time to see it.
Rating: *****It's a sell out – book early
Shows: Every day except Mon and Thurs, 7.30pm
Tickets: $55–250 plus tax

Donny & Marie

Flamingo Showroom, Flamingo Las Vegas, 702 733 3333, www.flamingolasvegas.com
The Osmond family flame still burns bright with this brother and sister act. This energetic 90-minute variety show includes singing (hits such as *Paper Roses* and *Puppy Love*), dancing, comedy and the stars' signature sibling banter.
Rating: *** A must for anyone who grew up with The Osmonds
Shows: Daily except Sun, 7.30pm
Tickets: $95, $109, $125, $260 plus tax

Elton John

Colosseum at Caesars Palace, 1-877 423 5463, www.caesarspalace.com
The Rocket Man returned to Vegas with a new show Million Dollar Piano in late 2011, as part of a three year residency, his second as a headliner at Caesars Palace. The 90-minute show includes old favourites *The Bitch is Back, Bennie and the Jets* and of course, *Rocket Man*.
Rating: ***** A gargantuan feast of music and imagery
Shows: Days vary, 7.30pm
Tickets: From $155 plus tax

Gladys Knight

Gladys Knight Theater, Tropicana Las Vegas, 702 739 2411, www.troplv.com
7-time Grammy Award winning performer Gladys Knight brings a new show *A Mic & A Light* to the theatre named in

her honour backed by an 11-piece band including Merald 'Bubba' Knight, an original member of the Pips. Expect old favourites *Midnight Train to Georgia, The Best Thing that Ever Happened to Me* and *I Heard it Through the Grapevine* as well as her 2010 hit single *Settle*.
Rating: ***** Good music never dies
Shows: Tues–Sat 8pm
Tickets: $40, $75, $85, VIP $105 plus tax

Jabbawockeez

Monte Carlo Theatre, 702 730 7160, www.montecarlo.com
The famous all male dance troupe combine hip hop swagger and picture mimes in white masks and gloves in their show MUS.I.C. (pronounced Muse I See). Fresh from their Philippines tour, these boys won MTV's America's Best Dance Crew, so expect a high energy, contemporary performance.
Rating: **** Laugh. Cheer. Move
Shows: Sun–Tues 7.30pm, Thurs–Fri 9.30pm; Sat 7pm and 9.30pm
Tickets: From $52.45 without tax

Kà by Cirque du Soleil®

Kà Theater, MGM Grand, 702 531 3826 or 866 740 7711, www.ka.com
The circus-based Canadian performance company Cirque du Soleil® is noted for making visually stunning productions. Las Vegas is its playground and the magnificent *Kà* is the standard bearer for the MGM Grand. Each show has a theme, *Kà* has fire. The main subplot revolves around fire's dual powers both to destroy and create.

Essentially a tale of duality, *Kà* tells the epic story of separated twins who set out on a perilous journey through challenging landscapes, such as a mysterious sea

Donny and Marie Osmond at the Flamingo

Celine Dion at Caesars Palace

shore, menacing mountains and foreboding forests, to fulfil their shared destinies. What makes it different from all the astonishing acrobatic performances available in other Cirque shows is that this production (a mere snip at $165m!) also incorporates the thrills and action of different martial arts forms from all over the world, plus amazing innovations in puppetry, multimedia and pyrotechnics.
Rating: ***** Breathtaking stunts that dazzle to the max
Shows: Tues–Sat, 7pm and 9.30pm
Tickets: $69, $99, $130 and $150, all plus tax

LOVE

The Beatles LOVE Theater, Mirage, 702 792 7777, www.mirage.com
Unveiled in 2007, The Beatles *LOVE* grew out of a mutual admiration between the late George Harrison and Cirque founder Guy Laliberté. This is a different Cirque show compared to the others in Vegas. Here they have taken the original master recordings from the Abbey Road Studios and, instead of the traditional Cirque acrobatic wonders, have melded a celebration of modern marvels as rollerbladers and skateboarders fly and twist in youthful energy. There are still the dazzling sound and visual effects you would expect of a Cirque display, but mixed with a rawer emotion.
Rating: **** A Beatles love-fest only Cirque du Soleil® and X-Games could produce
Shows: Thurs–Mon 7pm and 9.30pm
Tickets: $79, $93.50, $99, $130 and $155 plus tax

Mystère

Treasure Island, 702 894 7722, www.treasureisland.com

The first of the Cirque du Soleil's® Las Vegas marvels, *Mystère* takes you on a journey through time that allows the supreme athletes to show off their strength and extraordinary flexibility with a mesmerising aerial bungee ballet, a precision performance based around Chinese poles and an awe-inspiring trapeze act. This is the most acrobatic of all the Cirque shows, and the most circus-like. It is also truly state-of-the-art theatre. The show originally cost $20m to stage and should definitely be on your must-see list.

Rating: ***** You'll want to go back again and again

Shows: Sat–Wed 7pm and 9.30pm

Tickets: $69, $79, $95, $99, $109 plus tax

BRITTIP

If you're trying to decide between **Mystère** and **O**, most people find **Mystère** more accessible. **O**, although brilliant, is more ethereal.

O

Bellagio, 702 693 7722, www.bellagio.com

If you've ever been lucky enough to see the Cirque du Soleil® troupe in action, you'll know what makes these artists so special. The 70-odd cast of dancers, acrobats, actors, clowns, comedians and musicians may represent age-old talents of an old-style circus (without the animals), but that is where any similarities with the past come to an end. *O*, like all the shows performed by the troupe, is a surrealist celebration of trapeze, dance, high-flying acrobatics and humour. In this case though, every act is performed in, on and above water in a $70m theatre that was developed specifically for the Bellagio resort and Cirque du Soleil®.

O takes its title from the phonetic spelling of the French word for water – *eau*. The story takes you on a 90-minute voyage through the history of theatre in the trademark Cirque style with daring displays of aerial gymnastics, high-flying trapeze numbers, synchronised swimming, fire-eating, mind-boggling contortions, clowns and high-diving stunts.

Rating: ***** Breathtaking

Shows: Wed–Sun 7.30pm and 10pm

Tickets: $93.50, $104, $130 and $155 all plus tax

Piano! Las Vegas

V Theater at Miracle Mile at Planet Hollywood Hotel & Casino, 702 932 1818, www.pianolasvegas.com

World champion pianist Ryan Ahern mesmerises audiences with his hand speed as he plays music genres from Broadway to rock 'n' roll to boogie woogie, backed by six Las Vegas musicians. Expect favourite hits like Jerry Lee Lewis's *Great Balls of Fire* to movie themes such as Bette Midler's *Wind Beneath My Wings* and classics including the *Flight of the Bumblebee Boogie*.

Rating: **** Masterful showcase

Shows: Sat–Thurs 2.30pm

Tickets: $29.99; VIP $39.99 plus tax

Le Rêve

Wynn Theater, Wynn Las Vegas, 702 770 7000, www.wynnlasvegas.com

Franco Dragone, former creative collaborator with Cirque du Soleil® – responsible for top-selling shows such as *Saltimbaco*, *Mystère* and *La Nouba* – set up his own production company Dragone in 2000.

BRITTIP

At all of the Cirque shows, including Dragone's **Le Rêve**, try to be in your seats by 20 minutes before curtain up. There is always a comedic pre-show show as cast members go out into the audience and do humorous bits with unsuspecting victims. Maybe you!

Now he has returned to Las Vegas to create a world of dreams for another epic at Steve Wynn's Wynn Resort. What sets this work apart is not only the visually

Africa from **O**

© LVNB

stunning performances themselves, but also the design of the theatre, which means that no one sits more than 42ft/13m from the main stage.

The main aim was to allow people to forget the world as they entered the dream-like realm of the theatre and this is achieved through a set that seems to owe more to the form of a temple than a stage. The dream-like quality is enhanced by a bank of digital windows that change displays from statues to clouds to birds as effortlessly as the performers execute feats of impossibility (to the ordinary mortal) in front of you. This is, without doubt, the most visually stunning show in Las Vegas.

Rating: ***** Thrilling perfection
Shows: Sun, Mon, Tues, Fri, Sat 7pm and 9.30pm
Tickets: $99, $119 and $179 for the true luxury of seating in overstuffed chairs with chocolate-dipped strawberries and a bottle of Champagne for two, plus tax of course

BRITTIP
Most big shows have a dinner and show package on offer. For example, Le Rêve Buffet Package includes show tickets to Le Rêve and a meal at a choice of 16 live action cooking stations from $160 per person (888 320 7110, http://boxoffice.wynnlasvegas.com/packages.html). Check details at the time of booking.

Rod Stewart

Colosseum at Caesars Palace, 1-877 423 5463, www.caesarspalace.com
Legendary rock icon Rod Stewart kicked off his two year Vegas residency at the Colosseum in August 2011. *Rod Stewart: The Hits* will feature the songs that have made him famous during a career that has spanned five decades.
Rating: ***** A rock legend
Shows: Days vary, 7.30pm
Tickets: $49–$250 plus tax

Shania Twain

Colosseum at Caesars Palace, 1-877 423 5463, www.caesarspalace.com and www.shaniainvegas.com
International superstar and the world's best selling female country artist of all time comes to Vegas on 1st December 2012 with her best hits packed into a brand new show *Still the One*.
Rating: Not available yet

Shows: Every Sat, Sun, Tues and Wed, with extra days thrown in
Tickets: $55–250 plus tax

BRITTIP
To get a better deal on the major shows, pick up as many of the visitor magazines as you can and look through for discount coupons and 2-for-1 specials.

Toni Braxton Revealed

Flamingo, 702 733 3333, www.harrahs.com
International singing sensation and 8-time Grammy winner Toni Braxton exploded on to the Vegas scene with her steamy extravaganza. The music is hot, the dance and choreography sizzling, the wardrobe steaming and her unique voice dazzling in a superb production.
Rating: ***** Hot, hot, hot!
Shows: Every day except Mon and Sun, 7.30pm
Tickets: $69, $89, $109 plus tax

V – The Ultimate Variety Show

V Theater at Miracle Mile at Planet Hollywood Hotel & Casino, 702 932 1818, www.vtheshow.com
This is traditional old Las Vegas entertainment, harking back to the days when Dean Martin would be performing and suddenly Sammy Davis Jr would show up and perform a few numbers. There is a core of show entertainers plus a plethora of talented acts who perform elsewhere on the Strip through the week, so no two shows are the same. When it first started, the acts were sometimes a hodgepodge, and you could get some real rotten tomatoes in the mix, but over the years the booking has improved so every show includes a combination of magic, special effects, death-defying stunts and wild comedy. *V* has become a Las Vegas icon.
Rating: ***** Top-notch entertainment
Shows: Nightly at 7.30 and 8.30pm
Tickets: From $59.95; $20 extra for dinner package

Viva Elvis

Aria Resort at CityCenter, 702 590 7757 or 877 253 5847, www.cirquedusoleil.com/en/shows/elvis/show.aspx
This Cirque du Soleil production pays tribute to Elvis's music and life, fusing dance and acrobatics, live music and iconic tracks, nostalgia and modernity,

Booking tickets in advance

By and large you should have no problem getting tickets to see most of the shows, and you can usually buy them in advance by phone or in person at the hotel's theatre box office. Just bear in mind that getting show tickets in Las Vegas depends on the time of year, the day of the week and whether there is a huge convention in town. For details of the best times to visit see The best times to go (page 18). In all cases, phone ahead to confirm show times, dates and prices as these are subject to change without notice. You can find out exactly who will be performing – including the big top-billing stars – during your visit to Las Vegas by visiting the Las Vegas Convention and Visitors' Authority's official website at visitlasvegas.com or the useful vegas.com to book online. Many of the major tour operators will also be able to book tickets in advance for the major shows or you can try attraction specialists Keith Prowse (0203 1377420, keithprowse.com). Most shows are now available through Ticketmaster – just visit www.ticketmaster.com.

high technology and raw emotion. In short, the show is in Elvis's image: powerful, sexy, whimsical and truly unique. The creative combination of live musicians and singers, projections, dance and the latest multimedia sound and lighting technology stimulate the senses. If you're a die-hard Elvis fan, you might have to hold back the tears of emotion.
Rating: ***** No tribute show can touch this one in its level of sophistication and its power of evocation
Shows: Tues–Sat 7.30pm and 9.30pm
Tickets: $69, $99, $125, $150, $175

Zumanity

New York New York, 866 606 7111, www.nynyhotelcasino.com and www.zumanity.com
Billed as the provocative, erotic, adult side of the Cirque du Soleil®, this show combines the usual amazing Cirque stunts, acrobatics and high-flying – only this time with a sensual, passionate and sometimes raunchy twist. There is also a feel of an old Parisian cabaret here. The cast of 50 performers and musicians blend erotic rhythm with dance with ribald comedy to create a world in which inhibitions are discarded.
Rating: ***** Sensual and stunning
Shows: Mon, Tues and Fri–Sun 7.30pm and 10pm
Tickets: $69, $79, $105 and $129 (per person on a duo sofa) plus tax

BRITTIP
Love birds wanting a romantic night out will adore the love seats and duo sofas that have been specially created in New York-New York's new theatre – custom-built for Cirque's over-18s-only **Zumanity**.

Other productions

Blue Man Group

Blue Man Group Theater, Venetian, 702 414 9000, www.blueman.com
This off-the-wall, off-off-Broadway production, which has been surprising, terrifying and entertaining theatre-goers in New York, Boston and Chicago, has become a Las Vegas staple. Mainstream this isn't. Throughout the black stage the three 'blue men' explore the world with both child-like innocence and social incompetence. Here, plastic pipes and breakfast cereal are musical instruments and toilet paper is a signal for a riotous party. Children delight in it, even though it is not a 'children's show'. As an adult, you either love this show or hate it; there is no in between.
Rating: **** Delightfully kooky
Shows: 7pm and 10pm nightly
Tickets: $74.90, $101.85 and $147.50 plus tax

Charo

Riviera Hotel & Casino, 702 794 9433, www.rivierahotel.com
Larger than life Latino singer Charo returns to the Las Vegas Strip in her new show, *Charo in Concert: A Music Sensation*, debuting at the Riviera Hotel & Casino. The musical variety show features Charo's virtuoso flamenco guitar accompanied by a full orchestra performing her biggest hits and a cast of world-famous Spanish flamenco dancers.
Rating: *** Loud and very Vegas!
Shows: Wed–Mon 7.30pm
Tickets: $49.95, $59.95, $69.95 plus tax

Human Nature

Imperial Theater, Imperial Palace, 888 777 7664, www.imperialpalace.com
Smokey Robinson presents Australian quartet Human Nature who offer *The Ultimate Celebration of Motown* with their distinctive harmonies.
Rating: *** * If you love Motown, you'll be in heaven
Shows: Daily except Fri, 7.30pm
Tickets: $49.95, $59.95 plus tax

Master magicians

Criss Angel Believe & Cirque du Soleil

Luxor 702 352 0197, www.luxor.com
Hearthrob Angel re-invents the traditional magic show and adds a big helping of gothic fantasy in this partnership with Cirque du Soleil. Fusing together revolutionary illusions and mystical artistry with acrobatics, dance, puppetry, music and poetry, you'll be riveted.
Rating: **** Something for the rebels out there
Shows: Tues–Sat 7pm and Tues, Fri, Sat 7pm and 9.30pm
Tickets: $59, $89, $109, $130, $160

Dirk Arthur's Wild Magic

O'Shea's Showroom, 702 733 3333, www.harrahs.com/osheas
With the departure of Siegfried & Roy, it was only a matter of time before someone else mixed big cats with magical illusion. In this mesmerising show, beautiful blue-eyed Bengals, African black leopards and a pure white snow tiger appear out of nowhere.
Rating: **** Truly entertaining
Shows: Mon–Sat 7pm
Tickets: $29.95, VIP $39.95 plus tax and surcharge

Jan Rouven

Fame Theater, Clarion Hotel & Casino, 702 800 5888, www.clarionhotelvegas.com
Direct from Europe, master illusionist Jan Rouven's new hair-raising, death-defying show *Illusions* combines heart-thumping music with uniquely-styled costumes. Having won accolades such as Musician of the Year, his edgy shows have earned him the nickname 'The Man With Nine Lives'.
Rating: **** Death-defying edgy show by a master
Shows: Thurs–Tues 7pm
Tickets: From $57.85 plus tax

Provocative and erotic Zumanity

Scarlett

Mardi Gras Plaza on the third floor of the
Riviera, 702 794 9433, www.rivierahotel.com
Scarlett, accompanied by her Seductive
Ladies of Magic, has carved a niche for
herself in the male-dominated business of
magic. She has mastered some of the most
difficult feats performed by Harry Houdini.
Rating: *** Good to see her breaking
through the glass ceiling of magic.
Shows: Nightly except Fri 10pm
Tickets: $44.55, $53.64 plus tax

Magical comedy

The Amazing Jonathan

The Harmon Theatre inside Miracle Mile
Shops at Planet Hollywood Hotel & Casino,
702 836 0836, www.harmontheater.com
Two-time winner of the Best Comic
Magician of the Year by the World Magic
Awards, Jonathan may not be well known
to British audiences, but he is famous in
America for his razor-sharp wit and bizarre
illusions. Dubbed the Freddy Krueger of
Comedy, he has his own TV show and has
a long string of TV appearances.
Rating: ***** Crazy, wild, hilarious –
don't miss it!
Shows: Tues–Sat 9pm
Tickets: $49.95, VIP $59.95 plus tax

The Mac King Comedy Magic Show

Comedy Cabaret, Clint Holmes' Theatre,
Harrah's Las Vegas, 702 369 5222,
www.harrahs.com
Mac King spent his summer holidays doing
a 2-person magic act with fellow college
student, the now legendary Lance Burton,
before taking his show on the road. Along
the way he has made a name for himself
as a talented magician with an off-beat,
witty twist, and has appeared on shows
such as *The World's Wildest Magic, An
Evening at the Improv, Penn & Teller's Sin
City Spectacular* and *Comic Strip Live.*
Surprisingly, discounted tickets are regularly
available for his show, and he is a fixture
on the *Las Vegas Adviser's* list of Top Ten
Las Vegas Values.
Rating: ***** Great fun and excellent-
value entertainment
Shows: Tues–Sat 1pm and 3pm
Tickets: $32.95 plus tax

Penn & Teller

Calypso Showroom, Rio All-Suite Hotel,
702 777 7776, www.riolasvegas.com
The famous duo have one of the funniest
and most tantalising shows around. They
are defiantly proud as they take many
traditional magic tricks and expose their
secrets to the audience. Then they stun you
with a dazzling magical extravaganza, all
the while making you hold your sides in
pain from the laughter.
Rating: ***** Both riveting and funny
Shows: Sat–Wed 9pm
Tickets: $75.95, $85, $95 plus tax

◀▮▶ **BRITTIP**
Shows generally last 90 minutes
and there are no intervals. You
can take drinks in plastic containers.

Stand-up comedy

Carrot Top

Luxor, 702 262 4400, www.luxor.com
Standing up for redheads everywhere,
Carrot Top (Scott Thompson) offers a young
and energised comedy set using very, very
silly visual props.
Rating: **** Loveable!
Shows: Mon, Wed-Sun 8.30pm
Tickets: $49.95 plus tax

Penn & Teller

Afternoon shows

Defending the Caveman: relationship comedy. See review and details below.
The Mac King: Comedy magic show. See review and details on page 61.
Dirk Arthur's Wild Magic: See review and details on page 60.

David Spade Live

The Venetian Showroom, The Venetian, 702 414 9000, www.venetian.com
With success on tough shows like *Saturday Night Live*, Spade is best known for his sarcastic sense of humour and cutting one-liners. The performance runs for 75 minutes and features real-life situations that only he can turn into laughs.
Rating: **** A regular guy who'll make you laugh out loud – a lot
Shows: 9pm. Check scheduled dates
Tickets: $65.75, $85.75, $105.75 including tax. A limited number of VIP front row tickets cost $175.75 with an opportunity to meet Spade after the show

Defending the Caveman

The Improv at Harrah's Las Vegas, 702 369 5111, www.harrahslasvegas.com
The longest running solo play in Broadway history, this show about the differences between the sexes originally opened at the San Francisco Improv in 1991, so is

Hot venues

Here are some other venues worth checking out for their edgier vibe.
House of Blues: Mandalay Bay Resort, 702 632 7600, ticketmaster.com
A massive array of acts such as Norah Jones covering everything from gospel to blues, jazz and even country.
The Joint: Hard Rock Hotel, 702 693 5066, hardrockhotel.com
Attracts the likes of Aerosmith, Blondie, Lenny Kravitz and No Doubt. Legendary guitarist Carlos Santana is its first rock and roll resident artist.
Mandalay Bay Beach: Mandalay Bay Resort, 702 632 7580, ticketmaster.com
A great location for enjoying acts such as the Doobie Brothers.
The Pearl: The Palms, 866 942 7777, palmspearl.com
The Palms new concert hall which seats 2,400 and has state-of-the-art technology for recording live albums. Depeche Mode, Mariah Carey and Kylie Minogue have all played.

now coming home to its roots. Comedian Kevin Burke, recently named 'Las Vegas Entertainer of the Year', has couples nudging each other in the ribs he explores the gender gap hilariously.
Rating: **** Relationships are funny!
Shows: Nightly 7pm, Sun–Mon 3pm
Tickets: $39.95–65.95 plus tax

Rita Rudner

The Venetian Showroom, The Venetian, 702 414 9000, www.venetian.com and www.ritafunny.com
It's rare that a woman makes it to the top in Las Vegas without taking her clothes off, yet the multi-talented Rita has done just that. She stands on the stage in a long, classically leggy dress making wry, quirky comments on everything from relationships to family and cleaning women. She was named Las Vegas Comedian of the Year 5 years running. She's been at New York-New York and Harrah's Las Vegas, and she keeps selling out.
Rating: ***** Comedic genius
Shows: Mon–Wed 8.30pm
Tickets: $49 and $69 plus tax

George Wallace

Flamingo Showroom, Flamingo Las Vegas, 702 733 3333, www.flamingolasvegas.com
Wallace began his career as a comedy writer for *The Redd Foxx Show* and made a big splash on *The Big Laugh Off*, one of America's top stand-up competitions. His humour is based on making observations about everyday life – a type of comedy that had been selling out venues all over North America before he arrived in Las Vegas.
Rating: *** Great fun
Shows: Tues–Sat 10pm
Tickets: $49.95, $59.95, VIP $75 plus tax and fees

Impressionists

La Cage

Four Queens Hotel & Casino, 702 492 3960, www.fourqueens.com
Having entertained in Vegas for 20 years, this glamorous extravaganza has been reborn with a new host – internationally known comedian and impressionist Jimmy Emerson – new location and a new cast of characters. Top-notch female impersonators in the guise of Madonna, Lady Gaga, Liza Minelli, Bette Midler, J Lo and more, plus a man as an excellent Michael Jackson. The La Cage dancers are 100% Las Vegas showgirl with plenty of feathers and Rhinestones.

Headliner showrooms

Celebrity Room: Bally's, 877 603 4390, www.ballyslasvegas.com for information, times and reservations. Headliners have included Liza Minnelli and Penn & Teller.

Circus Maximus: Caesars Palace, 702 731 7333, www.caesarspalace.com. Recent acts include Huey Lewis and the News, Earth, Wind and Fire and Tony Bennett.

Circus Maximus Showroom: Caesars Palace, 702 731 7333, www.caesarspalace.com. Judy Garland, Frank Sinatra, Diana Ross and Liberace have all headlined here since the gala opening in 1966. More recent stars include David Copperfield, Liza Minnelli, Julio Iglesias and Celine Dion.

The Colosseum at Caesars Palace: Caesars Palace, 1 888 702 3544, www.caesars palace.com. When Celine is not in action, the massive auditorium is used for major shows. Elton John and Rod Stewart are recent headliners and Shania Twain is soon to come.

Crown Theater: Rio All-Suite & Casino www.riolasvegas.com. Created by Darin Feinstein of Hollywood's famous Viper Room has a 900 seat capacity in the round design and features both big and up and coming names in music.

Grand Garden Arena: MGM Grand on the Strip, 702 891 1111, www.ticketmaster. com. The biggest venue in Las Vegas regularly hosts major concerts and sporting events. This is where Holyfield met Tyson for their heavyweight champion title clash and where top-notch performers like Sting, Elton John, Bette Midler, Gloria Estefan and Phil Collins play when they're in town. The 16,325-seat venue has also hosted the Professional Bull Riders Championships and national league hockey. The headliner in 2011 was *Crazy Horse Paris* cabaret. Tickets are likely to cost anything from $50.

Hilton Theater: Las Vegas Hilton, 702 732 5755, www.lvhilton.com. Headliners include Johnny Mathis and Barry Manilow.

Hollywood Theater: MGM Grand, 866 740 7711, www.mgmgrand.com. The MGM's more intimate venue (a mere 740 seats) is still big enough to attract such names as Tom Jones, David Copperfield and Howie Mandel.

Mandalay Bay Events Center: Mandalay Bay, 702 632 7580, www.mandalaybay.com. A 12,000-seater which has seen the likes of Beyonce, Bob Dylan and B.B. King perform.

Orleans Showroom: The Orleans, 702 365 7075, www.orleanscasino.com. Recent headliners include KC and The Sunshine Band and Alice Cooper.

Theater for the Performing Arts: Planet Hollywood Resort and Casino www.planet hollywoodresort.com is a 7000 seat venue suitable for anything from a Broadway play to a concert.

Rating: **** Returns to the delight of audiences
Shows: Wed–Sun 9pm
Tickets: $34.98 plus taxes

Terry Fator

Terry Fator Theater, The Mirage, **702 792 7777**, www.mirage.com
Terry Fator, winner of NBC's *America's Got Talent* and The Mirage signed a 5-year deal from March 2009, with an option for an additional 5 years. Talk about rags to riches! The comic impersonator, along with his cast of 7 puppets, combines the art of ventriloquism with celebrity impressions. Fator and his puppets, Cowboy Walter, Emma Taylor and Winston the Impersonating Turtle, effortlessly perform the singing styles of an eclectic group of stars including Elvis, Maroon Five, Nat King Cole, James Blunt and Marvin Gaye.
Rating: ***** See it to believe it!
Shows: Tues–Sat, 7.30pm
Tickets: $59, $79, $99, $129, $149

Comedy clubs

Improv Comedy Club

The Improv, Harrah's Las Vegas, **702 369 5223**, www.harrahslasvegas.com
Recently voted Best Comedy Club in the *Las Vegas Review Journal* by readers and critics for its stand-up routines by up-and-coming stars of comedy.
Shows: Tues–Sun 8.30pm and 10.30pm
Tickets: $29.05, $44.95 plus tax

Riviera Comedy Club

Mardi Gras Plaza on the first floor of the Riviera , **702 794 9433**, www.rivierahotel.com
A nightly line-up of top stand-up comedians and comedy acts, many of whom have appeared on American TV, in an intimate nightclub setting.
Shows: Nightly 9pm
Tickets: $24.99, VIP $34.99 plus tax

The Venetian after dark

Dinner shows

Tony 'n' Tina's Wedding

V Theater, Planet Hollywood Resort & Casino, 702 949 6450, www.tonyandtina vegas.com

Having moved from the Rio to Planet Hollywood, a new lease of life has been given to this comedy dinner show which takes you on a romp through a classic American-Italian wedding as Anthony Nunzio Jr marries Valentina Lynne Vitale. The satire begins with the announcement of the wedding, then members of the audience join in the entire event from wedding ceremony to rowdy reception complete with Italian buffet dinner – allowing for plenty of improvisation along the way!
Rating: **** Great fun
Shows: Nightly except Sun,7.30pm
Tickets: $69.99, $99.99 including tax and an Italian buffet dinner

Dragon Knight at the Tournament of Kings

Tournament of Kings

King Arthur's Arena at the Excalibur, 702 597 7600, www.excalibur.com

Central to this re-creation of a knights' battle are the laser lights, fireworks and clouds of billowing water vapour that give the production an air of mystery and magic. The musical begins when Merlin grants a young boy's wish to be a knight by transporting him back to the Middle Ages and transforming him into the White Knight of Kent. Along the way he meets King Arthur and Queen Guinevere and battles with the treacherous Dark Knight to win a princess's hand in marriage. The trick to seeing this show is to finish off your dinner before you become engulfed in water vapour!
Rating: **** One of the top shows – good for horses, feasts and magic!
Shows: Nightly except Tues, 6pm and 8.30pm; Mon 6pm only
Price: $59 plus tax; $44.35 without three course dinner

Adults only on the Strip

Watch out if you go down to the big theme resorts today, for you're more and more likely to find topless shows in what were once considered family-friendly hotels. Of course, adult shows have always been a facet of Las Vegas entertainment, but never quite so blatantly on the Strip. Is it a reflection of waning interest in traditional shows – unlikely – or just another cleverly disguised attempt to get punters into gambling dens? Your guess is as good as mine, but either way, here they are.

🇬🇧 BRITTIP
You must be over 18 and sometimes over 21 to see any of these adult show. Check when booking.

Bite

Theater of the Stars, Stratosphere, 702 380 7711, www.stratospherehotel.com
A topless revue loosely based around a vampire 'story' of sin, sex and seduction. The Lord Vampire, aided by a coven of sultry dancers, goes on a search for the perfect female specimen to make the queen of the night. The story is told through the classic rock songs of the '70s, '80s and '90s. Best shock/surprise of all: members of the audience are chosen to become part of the erotic adventure.
Rating: **** Once bitten, you'll be going back for more!
Shows: Daily except Thurs, 10.30pm
Tickets: $49.95 including tax and tip

Jubilee!

Jubilee Theater, Bally's, 1-800 237 7469, www.ballyslv.com
A lavish, 7-act tribute to American music, with topless showgirls and scantily clad guys. From the roaring twenties to the rock 'n' roll era of Elvis, it also features a seductive Samson and Delilah sequence, a master magician who makes a 26-ft/8-m long helicopter appear, and a

spectacular sinking of the *Titanic* in which 2,000galls/9,000l of water flood on to the stage. Just to give you some idea of the scale of its lavishness, more than 1,000 costumes are worn by the cast of 100 dancers and singers, while 70 different sets and backdrops and about 100,000 light bulbs are required to create the enchanting spectacles.
Rating: **** Lavish, wonderful over-the-top production numbers
Shows: Sat–Sun and Tues–Thurs 7.30pm and 10.30pm; Mon and Wed 7.30pm
Tickets: $57.50, $77.50, $97.50, $117.50

🇬🇧 BRITTIP
You can now get a behind the scenes look at the world of Jubilee! Showgirls conduct tours every Mon, Wed and Sat at 11am. Tickets $12 if bought with a show ticket, or $17.

Peepshow

CHI Showroom at Planet Hollywood Las Vegas, 1 800 745 3000, www.lasvegaspeepshow.com
Peepshow is one of the hottest adult shows in Vegas. A full-throttle production, there are 25 sizzling dancers and performers from the world of pop music, film, television and Broadway. Holly Madison from *E!'s The Girls Next Door* stars, and former Spice Girl Mel B, was once in the line-up.

Fantasy at the Luxor

© MGM

Rating: **** A sexy modern take on showgirls
Shows: Fri–Sat 8pm and 10.30pm; Sun, Mon, Tues and Thurs 9pm
Tickets: $66, $76, $101, $126 plus tax

X Burlesque

Bugsys Cabaret, Flamingo, 702 733 3333, www.flamingolasvegas.com
Heralded as the 'steamiest show on the Strip', X Burlesque topless review has sexy dancers who hotfoot their way through popular songs like Jessica Simpson's 'Boots' and Aerosmith's 'Pink' in barely-there costumes. The 90-minute, high energy show has won numerous accolades and after four years at The Flamingo has extended until 2013.
Rating: **** Artful titillation
Shows: Nightly 10pm
Tickets: $44.95, $55.95 plus tax

BRITTIP
Release your inner bombshell at **Night School 4 Girls** at the Excalibur Hotel & Casino, where E's Laura Croft teaches the art of seduction, pole and burlesque dancing (tickets $39–$99). Otherwise try **Stripper 101**, daily at the V Theater, Planet Hollywood Resort & Casino (tickets $39.99–$125) or X-Burlesque University daily at 3pm in the showroom at Flamingo ($34.95).

Showgirls

Crazy Girls Sexiest Topless Revue

The Mardi Gras Pavilion, Riviera Hotel, 702 794 9433, www.rivierahotel.com
Updated version of the classic topless revue with music, dance, song and comedian Stuart May.
Rating: *** Enjoyable
Shows: Nightly except Tues 9.30pm
Tickets: $44.95, VIP from $60 plus tax

Fantasy

Pharaoh's Theater, Luxor, 702 262 4400, www.luxor.com
Featuring singing, dancing and a lot more besides in an outrageous and provocative topless revue.
Rating: **** Filled with sexy ladies
Shows: Nightly 10.30pm
Tickets: $39 plus tax

MGM Grand's Crazy Horse Paris

Crazy Horse Paris Theater, MGM Grand, 866 740 7711, www.mgmgrand.com
Billing itself as a show that 'celebrates beautiful women and the art of the nude', all the 12 dancers are members of the original Crazy Horse dance troupe from one of the hottest popular nightspots in Paris. This is the same show that used to be called La Femme. It has just reverted to the same name used in Paris.
Rating: *** Classy nudes!
Shows: Wed–Mon 8pm and 10.30pm
Tickets: $50.50, $60.50 including tax and programme

Girls' night out

American Storm

Variety Theater, Planet Hollywood Hotel & Casino, 702 260 7200 or 800 932 1818, www.varietytheater.com
A lot of muscle is on show at this sexy male revue, voted 'Best Male Strip Show of 2008' by the Las Vegas Review Journal. Many of the cast members are winners of VH1's Strip Search reality show and several have appeared on the cover of Playgirl.
Rating: *** Good unclean fun
Shows: Fri 10pm and Sat 11.30pm
Tickets: From $49.99 plus tax

Chippendales – The Show

Club Rio, Rio All-Suite Hotel, 702 777 7776, www.riolasvegas.com
One of the loudest of the all-male revue shows, which leaves very little – a floss-thin G-string – to the imagination. Think motorcycles, beds and a giant computer monitor and imagine 12 über-fit men writhing all over them and you'll build up a good picture of what's in store. Prepare to get your best screaming voice ready!
Rating: **** Polished perfection
Shows: Daily 8pm; Fri and Sat also 10.30pm
Tickets: $39.95, $49.95, $59.95 plus tax

BRITTIP
Most shows offers special rates for group bookings.

Thunder from Down Under

Merlin Theater, Excalibur, 702 597 7600, www.excalibur.com
Once a trio of Aussie beefcakes, this troupe

has expanded to a cast of 8 breathtaking hard bodies. However, the troupe remains one of the best all-male entertainers in town – largely because they don't take themselves seriously and because they like to include members of the audience in the show. Watch out if you get pulled on stage, you could find yourself murmuring 'Oh baby' into a microphone in your best Meg Ryan-faking-it voice!

Rating: ***** Just ... WOW!
Shows: Sun–Thurs 9pm; Fri–Sat 9pm and 11pm
Tickets: $40.95 or $50.95 VIP plus tax

Cinemas

Brenden Theaters

The Palms, 4321 West Flamingo Road, 702 507 4849, www.brendentheaters.com
A state-of-the-art, 14-theatre cinema complex at this ultra-hip hotel resort including the largest IMAX in Vegas. The brainchild of Johnny Brenden, grandson of the legendary Mann's Chinese Theater developer in Hollywood, LA, it has wall-to-wall curved screens, THX digital sound and stadium seating with comfortable, high-backed rocking chairs, plus love seats. Brenden Theaters has fast become the hottest Cineplex in town and now hosts many film premières with post-première parties at The Palms' Little Buddha restaurant. Tickets $10.50 adult, $7 child (3-12). $8 matinees.

Rave Motion Pictures

Town Square 18 Las Vegas, 6587 Las Vegas Boulevard South, 702 362 RAVE, www.mytownsquarelasvegas.com
A great choice of popular movies if you need a respite from shopping. Typically over-the-top choice of screens, popcorn and comfort!

BRITTIP
The Las Vegas Film Festival each July is now in its fourth year and for the last two years has been held at the Las Vegas Hilton. It has taken over after the demise of CineVegas and combines the excitement of red carpet premieres with the glitz and glamour of Vegas. The Festival annually presents the best new independent films, documentaries and shorts, as well as parties up and down the famed Las Vegas strip. Great for celeb spotting!

United Artists Showcase

Showcase Mall, 3785 Las Vegas Boulevard South, 702 597 3117
Still the only cinema on the Strip, you may have a hard time finding it as it's tucked down the side of the MGM Grand complex next to the parking garage – behind the giant coke bottle! Parking is free if you keep your cinema ticket for validation.

 BRITTIP
With so much to see and do, it's unlikely you'll have time to go to the movies, but there are 2 advantages to doing so: you get to see a film before it hits our shores and you can guarantee not to hear the sound of slot machines! Tickets cost around $10.

Bonanza of musicals and plays

There's a growing trend for Broadway shows to be staged at some of the classier theatres. Of course, we get them all in London as well now, but there's a big difference between something being available on our own doorstep and actually seeing it. Here is a selection of the venues and their offerings at the time of going to press.

Jersey Boys

The Palazzo, The Venetian, 702414 9000, www.jerseyboysvegas.com
This blockbuster musical takes you inside the lives and music of Frankie Valli and The Four Seasons from the streets of Newark to the Rock and Roll Hall of Fame. Hits include 'Big Girls Don't Cry' and 'Can't Take My Eyes Off You'.

Menopause the Musical (MTM)

Luxor, 702 262 4400 or 800 557 7428, www.luxor.com and www.menopausethemusical.com
An international sensation that has landed in Las Vegas. A musical comedy inspired by 'a hot flush and a bottle of wine', it is a celebration of all women over 40 who have survived life.

Phantom – The Las Vegas Spectacular

Paris Opera House, Venetian, 702 414 9000, www.venetian.com
A lavish production of Andrew Lloyd Webber's classic Phantom of the Opera in

a dazzling recreation of the Paris Opera House. Tickets from $59.

The Smith Center for the Performing Arts

702 614 0109 info 702 982 7805 tickets, www.thesmithcenter.com
Boosting Las Vegas's bid for sophistication is the groundbreaking opening of The Smith Center for the Performing Arts. Scheduled to open in March 2012, this 4.75-acre/2-ha complex in the Union Park in downtown Vegas, houses the Nevada Ballet Theater and the Las Vegas Philharmonic and will become the city's cultural hub. It will foster local talent and feature music, theatre and dance companies from all over the world. Broadway Las Vegas in 2012 will feature *The Color Purple*, *Mary Poppins*, *Million Dollar Quartet* and *Memphis*. *Wicked* will be the first full-length season show, in August 2012.

Coming soon

Michael Jackson: The Immortal World Tour

Cirque du Soleil®, www.cirquedusoleil.com
After debuting at the Mandalay, this tour based on the music and songs of legendary Michael Jackson will find a permanent home in Vegas in 2013, developed along with lifestyle projects such as a nightclub. Watch this space...

Phantom is showing at the Venetian

4 SHOPPING

Everything from top designer malls to discount shopping outlets

The wild success of the opening of the Forum Shops in 1992 gave the business community an epiphany. People come to Las Vegas to spend money – and not just on gambling! Since then, Sin City merchants have outdone themselves in piling on one new shopping experience after another, each new mall and store more wildly successful than the last! In fact, Las Vegas is now an international mecca for high-end merchandise. In past eras, a hot producer would first think about opening a new store in London, or Paris, New York or Los Angeles. No more – it's on to Vegas!

So shopping addicts beware: Las Vegas can do serious damage to your credit cards! According to a Las Vegas Visitor Profile Study, Las Vegas shoppers spent an average of $122.80 per trip, more than twice as much as on sightseeing and show tickets combined. But then the Las Vegas malls do it in such style and with so much 'free entertainment' attached, it's hardly surprising we can't resist. The trend for providing more and more shopping continues and over the last few years so many major American department stores have opened in the city that it now rivals, and perhaps surpasses, New York and San Francisco for upscale shops.

The explosion of more sophisticated hotels has brought with it even more high end shopping choice – think Chloe, Dolce & Gabbana and Prada with the opening of the Esplanade at Encore, The Shoppes at The Palazzo, The Shops at Cosmopolitan, Town Square Las Vegas and the incredible array of shopping at CityCenter's Crystals which opened in December 2009.

Major shopping malls: At the top of the pile is the **Fashion Show Mall**, which spent $1bn to turn itself into the largest shopping destination on the Strip attracting more than 10 million visitors every year. In keeping with its name, Fashion Show includes an elevated runway for staging events such as fashion shows and special promotions. The title of biggest and best used to belong to the **Forum Shops at Caesars**, which set new standards for shopping malls when it opened in 1992. It's still an excellent shopping destination and remains an attraction in its own right with its Roman

décor and wide range of restaurants including Wolfgang Puck's Spago. Other high-end shopping malls can be found at the **Grand Canal Shoppes** at the Venetian. Apart from the Fashion Show Mall, best by far for a rounded shopping experience, with more mid-range shopping, is the **Miracle Mile Shops** at Planet Hollywood Resort & Casino. There's also the **Hawaiian Marketplace**.

BRITTIP

The Las Vegas Convention and Visitors Authority offers visitors a Shop Las Vegas Passport, a collection of vouchers and discounts at major shopping centres and outlets around the city. Download from www.visitlasvegas.com or call 020 7367 0979.

Discount shopping: Designer junkies got a great shot in the arm with the opening in August 2003 of the **Las Vegas Premium Outlets** right in the heart of downtown. There are many other discount outlet shopping malls, too, including the **factory**

Crystals at CityCenter

outlet district, so it really is possible to leave Las Vegas with your overdraft intact! **Hotel shopping:** Each of the major resort-hotels has its own range of shopping opportunities, topped by **Le Boulevard** at Paris Las Vegas, **Mandalay Place** at Mandalay Bay and **Via Bellagio** at the Bellagio.

Off-Strip shopping: If you want to shop like the locals you can find plenty of shops off the Strip too at **The Boulevard Mall, The District at Green Valley Ranch, The Fashion Outlets of Vegas, Galleria Mall, Las Vegas Premium Outlets** and the **Meadows Mall.**

Crystals at CityCenter

Location: 3720 Las Vegas Boulevard South, between Excalibur and The Bellagio
Tel: 702 590 9299
Web: www.crystalsatcitycenter.com
Open: Sun–Thurs 10am–11pm and Fri–Sat 10am–midnight

Opened 3 December 2009, CityCenter resort has brought an architectural edge to shopping in Las Vegas. Crystals, a high-end shopping precinct designed by Studio Daniel Libeskind, offers luxury brands under a crystalline canopy. Inside, David Rockwell has created an abstract 21st-century park with changing artwork celebrating the seasons and landmarks such as an 80ft/24.4m soaring 3-storey sculptural tree house, a staircase inspired by Rome's Spanish Steps and ice and water sculptures, Glacia and Halo. Crystals covers 500,000ft^2/46,450m^2 and features Prada, Christian Dior, Louis Vuitton, Gucci, Fendi, Versace, Bulgari, Cartier, Harry Winston, Yves St Laurent, Hermes, Tiffany, Balenciaga, de Grisogono jewellery and watches, Van Cleef & Arpels' largest US boutique, Roberto Cavalli, Mikimoto pearls, Bally, Emilio Pucci, Ilori. Many are choosing CityCenter to make their Las Vegas debut, including Tom Ford, Mui Mui, Kiki De Montparnasse, Nanette Lepore, Kiton, Brunello Cucinelli, Paul Smith, Marni, Lanvin, Stella McCartney, Donna Karan, Porsche Design, H Stern jewellery, Boutique Tourbillon with an exclusive range of Swatch watches, Tag Heuer timepieces and Assouline publishing. On the eating and drinking side, there is groundbreaking pub by Todd English and two new dining concepts by Las Vegas old hand, Wolfgang Puck. The first, opened in June 2010, is Pizzeria & Cucina serving his famous pizzas and the second, known as the Wolfgang Puck 'Pods', will be centrally located on the iconic Crystals staircase with

dramatic views and serving high-quality, light American and Mediterranean cuisine. Innovative sushi restaurant, The Social House, was created by chef Joe Elevado who trained under Nobuyuki 'Nobu' Matsuhisa. Actress Eva Longoria Parker opened her Beso Steakhouse and Mastro's Ocean Club with its signature seafood towers, melt-in-your-mouth warm butter cake over daily live piano music, opened inside the tree house in February 2010. The Cup, is a 'green' coffee shop serving Fair Trade teas and coffees. It's definitely the place to hang out.

Fashion Show Mall

Location: 3200 Las Vegas Boulevard South, at Spring Mountain Road, just north of Treasure Island and opposite the site of the Wynn Resort
Tel: 702 784 7000 (information) or 702 369 8382 (concierge desk)
Web: www.thefashionshow.com
Open: Mon–Sat 10am–9pm and Sun 11am–7pm
Parking: Underground car park is accessible via Spring Mountain Road and Fashion Show Drive North, then take the escalators to the shopping level, or use the North and South parking decks accessible from Industrial Road West, then follow the signs; there is also complimentary valet parking available at 3 points around the mall.
Attractions: The only mall in America with 7 major US department stores under one roof: Neiman Marcus, Saks Fifth Avenue, Macy's, Dillard's, Bloomingdale's Home, Nordstrum and Forever 21, plus a further 250 shops; plus a live fashion show runway.
Cafés and restaurants: The main restaurants include the Capital Grille Steakhouse, Maggiano's Little Italy and RA Sushi Bar Restaurant; plus a raft of casual dining options including California Pizza Kitchen, NM Café at Nieman Marcus and Johnny Rockets.

◀🏴 BRITTIP ———————
Maggiano's Little Italy restaurant is a dazzling dining room on the second floor of the Fashion Show Mall, with great views of Wynn Las Vegas across the Strip. It also has a pianist in its lounge during dinner.

Services: Cashpoints (ATMs), postage service, the Concierge Desk can supply directions, concert tickets and show reservations, multilingual brochures, golf

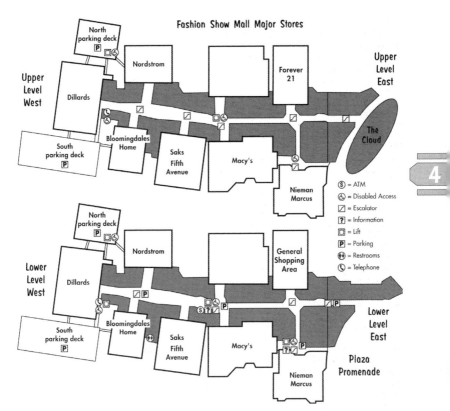

Fashion Show Mall Major Stores

North parking deck
P
Nordstrom
Upper Level West
Dillards
Bloomingdales Home
South parking deck
P
Saks Fifth Avenue
Macy's
Forever 21
Upper Level East
The Cloud
Nieman Marcus

(S) = ATM
(&) = Disabled Access
[/] = Escalator
[?] = Information
[ ] = Lift
[P] = Parking
(††) = Restrooms
(C) = Telephone

North parking deck
P
Nordstrom
Lower Level West
Dillards
Bloomingdales Home
South parking deck
P
Saks Fifth Avenue
Macy's
General Shopping Area
Lower Level East
Nieman Marcus
Plaza Promenade

tee times and special event information. Wheelchairs are also available.

For those who are serious about shopping, this is the place to come. Following a massive renovation and expansion programme, the Fashion Show Mall doubled in size within a few short years of opening and in the process turned itself into an entertainment experience as well.

Hard to miss is the Cloud structure, which rises 20 storeys above the Strip, and is nearly 500ft/152m long, providing a much-needed shaded area during the day and a giant image projection surface at night. Below it is the 330ft/100m long Media Bank with 4 extraordinarily sized LED screens that are used to broadcast videos and events inside the mall and around the city.

The Great Hall, a 72,000ft²/6,689m² pedestrian plaza, is home to both the elevated Food Court overlooking the plaza and the Strip, and the 28ft²/2.6m² stage and 80ft/24m retractable runway, which is used for fashion shows and other events.

Save as you go

Before you start to browse around the shops, join the Premier Shopper Club by going to the Customer Service Center and filling out the form or using the Smart Shopper Pavilion touch screen. Once you have been accepted, you can browse through the website and pick up a startling array of money-saving coupons from the stores. You can also find out about all the latest promotions and activities going on at each of the stores. As a club member, you will automatically be entered into free prize draws simply by swiping your card at the Smart Shopper Pavilion! There are many other bonuses, but most are really aimed at people living in America.

BRITTIP
While Fashion Show Mall closes at 9pm, the main restaurants stay open until around 11pm or midnight.

The show must go on!

There are now 6 major anchors to the mall – the most in any American mall and the only one to have all the main department store brands in one location: Macy's, Dillard's, Nieman Marcus, Nordstrum, Bloomingdale's Home and Saks Fifth Avenue. There are over 250 other shops, too. Here is a rundown of the main beauty boutiques, women's stores, men's stores, shoe shops and electronic outlets.

BRITTIP
Always take a bottle of water with you on a shopping trip – the air con will have you dropping before you finish shopping!

Accessories

Bally of Switzerland: 702 737 1968, www.bally.com
Banana Republic: 702 697 2011, www.bananarepublic.gap.com
BCBG Max Azria: 702 737 0681, www.bcbg.com
Claire's Boutique: 702 650 9006, www.claires.com
Cole Haan: 702 731 3522, www.colehaan.com
Swarovski: 702 732 8161, www.swarovski.com

Clothes for women

A Pea in the Pod: 702 732 2022, www.apeainthepod.com
Abercrombie & Fitch: 702 650 6509, www.abercrombie.co.uk
Abercrombie Kids: 702 369 0653, www.abercrombiekids.com
Ann Taylor: 702 734 8614, www.anntaylor.com

Fashion Show Mall

Arden B: 702 735 0090, www.intl.ardenb.com
Banana Republic: 702 697 2011, www.bananarepublic.gap.com
BCBG Max Azria: 702 737 0681, www.bcbg.com
bebe: 702 892 8083, www.bebe.com
Betsey Johnson: 702 735 3338, www.betseyjohnson.com
Billabong: 702 737 6930, www.billabong.com
Caché: 702 731 5548, www.cache.com
Chico's: 702 791 3661, www.chicos.com
Cotton On: 702 433 0864, www.shop.cottonon.com
Diesel: 702 696 1055, www.diesel.com

BRITTIP
One of the things the American clothes stores do brilliantly is smart-yet-casual outfits at great prices for career women.

Everything But Water: 702 734 7946, www.everythingbutwater.com
Express: 702 737 8999, www.expressfashion.com
Fossil: 702 369 3986, www.fossil.com
Fredericks of Hollywood: 702 893 9001, www.fredericks.com
French Connection: 702 369 0852, www.frenchconnection.com
GAP: 702 796 0010, www.gap.com
Guess: 702 691 2541, www.guess.com
Hot Topic: 702 650 9710, www.hottopic.com
J Jill: 702 769 6014, www.jjill.com
Kate Spade: 702 691 9968, www.katespade.com.
Lacoste: 702 796 6676, www.lacoste.com
LOFT: 702 731 0351, www.loft.com
Lucky Brand: 702 369 4116, www.luckybrand.com
Paul Frank: 702 369 2010, www.paulfrank.com
SoHo Collections: 702 732 0430
Talulah G: 702 387 2303
Tommy Bahama's: 702 731 6868, www.tommybahama.com
Victoria's Secret: 702 737 1313, www.victoriassecret.com
Wet Seal: 702 796 0344, www.wetseal.com
White House: 702 697 0247, www.whitehouse.com
Zara: 702 733 1113, www.zara.com

Clothes for men

Abercrombie & Fitch: 702 650 6509, www.abercrombie.co.uk

After Hours Clubwear: 702 792 2700
Bally of Switzerland: 702 737 1968,
www.bally.com
Banana Republic: 702 697 2011,
www.bananarepublic.gap.com
Billabong: 702 737 6930,
www.billabong.com
Buckle: 702 650 5348, www.buckle.com
The Coach Store: 702 759 3451,
www.thecoachstore.com
Cole Haan: 702 731 3522,
www.colehaan.com
Cotton On: 702 433 0864,
www.shop.cottonon.com
Desigual: 702 696 9027,
www.desigual.com
Diesel: 702 696 1055, www.diesel.com
Ed Hardy: 702 784 0501,
www.edhardyshop.com
Express Men: 702 737 8999,
www.expressfashion.com
Fossil: 702 369 3986, www.fossil.com
French Connection: 702 369 0852,
www.frenchconnection.com
GAP: 702 796 0010, www.gap.com
Guess: 702 691 2541, www.guess.com
Harris & Frank: 702 737 7545
Hollister: 702 696 0480
www.hollisterco.com
Hot Topic: 702 650 9710,
www.hottopic.com
Johnston & Murphy: 702 737 0114,
www.johnstonmurphy.com
Lacoste: 702 796 6676, www.lacoste.com
Levi's: 702 731 1866, www.eu.levi.com
Lucky Brand Jeans: 702 369 4116,
www.luckybrandjeans.com
Oakley: 702 366 7080, www.oakley.com
Paul Frank: 702 369 2010,
www.paulfrank.com
pull in: 700 286 2422
Tommy Bahama's: 702 731 6868,
www.tommybahama.com
Zara: 702 733 1113, www.zara.com

Health and beauty

Aveda: 702 733 6660, www.aveda.com
Bare Escentuals: 702 369 1556,
www.bareescentuals.com
Bath & Body Works: 702 784 0183,
www.bathandbodyworks.com
The Body Shop: 702 737 1198,
www.thebodyshop.com
GNC: 702 651 9090, www.gnc.com
H2O Plus: 702 893 1332,
www.h2oplus.com
L'Occitane En Provence: 702 369 1286,
www.loccitaine.com
Regis Salon: 702 733 1400,
www.regishairstylists.com One of the

largest and most experienced hair salons in
the world.
Victoria's Secret Beauty: 702 796 0110,
www2.victoriassecret.com/beauty

BRITTIP
The Fashion Show Mall's Capital
Grille restaurants became an
instant hit when they opened in
2005. See Chapter 5 for full reviews.

Music and electronics

Brookstone: 702 650 2048,
www.brookstone.com
EB Games: 702 731 1733,
www.ebgames.com
Futuretronics: 702 387 1818,
www.futuretronics.com

BRITTIP
Just remember that American
DVDs are only compatible with
UK players if you have a multi-region
DVD player. US blu-rays are not usually
compatible with UK players.

Shoes

Aerosoles: 702 796 4144,
www.aerosoles.com
Aldo: 702 735 5590, www.aldoshoes.com
Bakers: 702 737 0108,
www.bakersshoes.com
Bally of Switzerland: 702 737 1968,
www.bally.com
Banana Republic: 702 697 2011,
www.bananarepublic.gap.com
BCBG Max Azria: 702 737 0681,
www.bcbg.com
Boot Star: 702 682-0848,
www.boot-star.com

Evening at the Fashion Show Mall

Champs Sports: 702 893 7745,
www.champssports.com
Clarks England/Bostonian: 702 732 1801,
www.clarks.com
Cole Haan: 702 731 3522,
www.colehaan.com
Crocs: 702 737 8092, www.crocs.com
Diesel: 702 696 1055, www.diesel.com
Easy Spirit: 702 693 4732,
www.easyspirit.com
Ecco: 702 733 6453, www.ecco.com
Flip Flop Shop: 702 207 1953,
www.flipflopshop.com
Footlocker: 702 369 0401,
www.footlocker.com
Johnston & Murphy: 702 737 0114,
www.johnstonmurphy.com
Journeys: 702 732 0130,
www.journeys.com
Lady Foot Locker: 702 735 7030,
www.ladyfootlocker.com
Nine West: 702 693 4128,
www.ninewest.com
Payless Shoe Source: 702 697 0280,
www.payless.com
Pinto Ranch: 702 228 3400,
www.pintoranch.com
Puma: 702 892 9988, www.puma.com
Shiekh Shoes: 702 369 5881,
www.shiekhshoes.com
Skechers: 702 696 9905,
www.skechers.com
Steve Madden: 702 733 2904,
www.stevemadden.com
Vans: 702 369 0352, www.vans.com
Walking Company, The: 702 369 0048,
www.thewalkingcompany.com

Cafés

NM Café: 702 697 7340 Contemporary-
style lunch and dinner cuisine in a
fashionable yet casual setting where you
can watch chefs at work. Located on the
second level of Neiman Marcus. Open
Mon–Sat 11am–6pm and Sun 12pm–5pm.

◀▓▶ BRITTIP
The NM Café has a brilliant
Happy Hour for Martinis and
food, such as the Mezze Sampler,
served nightly on the outdoor terrace
overlooking the Strip.

Nordstrum Marketplace Café: 702 862
2525. Salads, sandwiches, pastas, pizzas
and an assortment of daily specials, plus a
wide variety of drinks. On the third level of
Nordstrum, you can even order food and
drinks to take away.

Restaurants

California Pizza Kitchen: 702 893 1370,
www.cpk.com Part of one of America's
leading casual dining chains, it features
a wide variety of pizzas, pastas, salads,
soups, sarnies, starters and desserts and
has *Small Cravings* and *Wine Cravings*
taster menus. Located on the first floor next
to Bloomies.
Maggiano's Little Italy: 702 732 2550,
www.maggianos.com Lavish portions of
southern Italian cuisine are served in a
vibrant dining environment. Dishes range
from homemade pastas to salads, prime
steaks, fish and chicken. Located on the
second level, corner of Las Vegas Blvd and
Fashion Show Drive.
Capital Grille: 702 932 6631. A fine-
dining establishment on the third level at
the corner of Las Vegas Blvd and Fashion
Show Drive. Serving dry aged steaks, fresh
seafood, chops and irresistible desserts in a
relaxed ambiance. Open for lunch Mon–Fri
11am–3pm, Sat noon–3pm and for dinner
nightly Mon–Sat 5–11pm, Sun 4–10pm.
RA Sushi: 702 696 0008, www.rasushi.
com An upbeat, lively restaurant where
the music and the food are as hot as a
dollop of wasabi. Japanese fusion cuisine
is served here in a sleek and contemporary
environment. Additions include a sushi bar,
cocktail bar and lounge and upbeat music,
with a weekend DJ spinning hot tunes and
fresh mixes. The bar is open until 2am. First
level, corner of Las Vegas Blvd and Fashion
Show Drive.
Luciano: 702 732 1266. Italian restaurant
serving fresh baked bread, pizzas and al
dente pastas prepared from scratch in a
rustic ambiance of inviting warm colours,
hand painted tiles and open brick oven.
Lower level, between Saks Fifth Avenue and
Bloomingdales.

◀▓▶ BRITTIP
Download the free Simon Malls
iPhone app to help you find
your favourite shops, dinner and
entertainment as well as get the latest
deals and events at Forum Shops at
Caesars.

Forum Shops at Caesars

Location: Right next to Caesars Palace
Tel: 702 893 4800
Web: www.simon.com/mall/landing/224/
Open: Sun–Thurs 10am–11pm, Fri and Sat
10am–midnight; most of the restaurants are
open throughout
Parking: Either in the Caesars Palace free

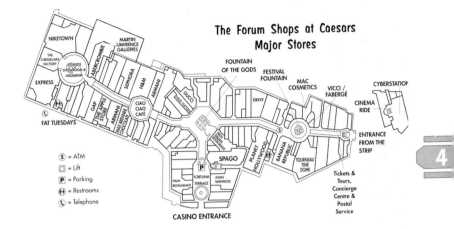

The Forum Shops at Caesars
Major Stores

covered car park or make use of the valet parking in the underground traffic tunnel at Caesars Boulevard

Attractions: Festival Fountain, Atlantis and the Great Hall shows, plus the aquarium

Cafés and restaurants: 13 restaurants and speciality food shops including fine-dining outlets the Palm, Wolfgang Puck's Spago, BOA Steakhouse and Joe's Stone Crab; casual outlets include the Cheesecake Factory, La Salsa, Planet Hollywood, Sushi Roku, Il Mulino and PJ Clarke's.

Services: Concierge services provided by Tickets & Tours include wheelchair and buggy rentals as well as tickets, tours, golf and dining reservations.

BRITTIP

All cafés and food outlets are open at the same time as the mall unless otherwise stated.

More than 22 million people – including 6.9 million non-Americans – visited the Forum Shops in 2006. Annual sales average more than $1,600 per ft² of retail space, far exceeding America's national average of $300–400.

Heralded as the 'Shopping Wonder of the World', the Forum Shops are so amazing they should be on your must-visit list, even in the unlikely event you don't plan to do any shopping (yeah, right!). It was deliberately built as an entertainment mall and transports people back in time to the great Roman Empire era with architecture, materials and street lighting to match. Even the piazzas and streets are laid out in the traditional format of a Roman town. The entire mall is enclosed,

temperature-controlled and covered with a 'sky' that changes throughout the day from a rosy-mauve dawn to high noon, the fading gold of the afternoon, twilight and finally night-time with twinkling stars.

The original $110m complex, which opened in 1992, proved so successful that it was expanded and a further 35 stores and entertainment outlets opened in 1997. A second extension opened in the summer of 2000, adding another 240,000ft²/ 22,297m² to the existing 533,000ft²/49,517m². In 2004, a $139m expansion added 175,000 ft²/53,340 m² and boutiques such as Harry Winston, Ted Baker, Thomas Pink, Nanette Lepore and Vosges Haut Chocolats arrived in Vegas. There are now more than 160 stores – continuing its expansion, the world's largest H&M opened here in 2011. Popular shops here include Kate Spade, Louis Vuitton, Escada, Gucci, Guess, Christian Dior, NikeTown, Fendi, Polo/Ralph Lauren and Hugo Boss.

Fabulous features include a sweeping plaza with replicas of the fountains of Treviano Triton, a massive reflecting pool, dazzling skylight and amazing spiral escalator.

The Festival Fountain undertakes a 7-minute Tale of the Roman Gods show using music, sound effects, animatronics and special scenic projections every 90 minutes from 10am.

At the Great Roman Hall, Atlantis comes to life hourly 10am–11pm in a spectacle that has the gods unleashing their wrath on the ancient city. Fire, water, smoke and special effects are used to create a show in which the animatronic characters of Atlas,

Gadrius and Alia struggle to rule Atlantis.

Surrounded by a massive saltwater aquarium, the mythical sunken continent rises and falls before your eyes. The Great Hall is surrounded by giant projection screens which, together with lasers and other special effects, help create the illusion that you are genuinely part of the action.

Another free show is the aquarium maintenance and feeding time, which takes place several times a day. Inside are sharks and schools of coral-reef fish.

Visit the website for all the latest details of the stores.

Accessories

Anthropologie: 702 650 0466, www.anthropologie.com
Balenciaga: 702 732 1660, www.balenciaga.com
BCBGMAXAZRIA: 702 699 5498, www.bcbg.com
Brighton Collectibles: 702 933 1330, www.brighton.com
Christian Lacroix: 702 731 0990, www.christian-lacroix.com
Coach: 702 651 0363, www.coach.com
Davante: 702 737 8585, www.davante.com
GUESS by Marciano: 702 369 0322, www.marciano.com
Intermix: 702 731 1922, www.intermixonline.com
Juicy Confidential: 702 369 3684, www.juicycouture.com
Judith Leiber: 702 792 0661, www.judithleiber.com
Louis Vuitton: 702 732 1227, www.vuitton.com

Montblanc: 702 732 0569, www.juicy confidentialmontblanc.com
Swatch: 702 734 1904, www.swatch.com
Tumi: 0800 783 6570, www.tumi.com
Vilebrequin: 702 894 9460, www.vilebrequin.com

Clothes for men

7 For All Mankind: www.7forallmankind.com
Abercrombie & Fitch: 702 731 0712, www.abercrombie.com
AIX Armani Exchange: 702 733 1666, www.armaniexchange.com
Banana Republic: 702 650 5623, www.banarepublic.gap.com
BOSS Hugo Boss: 702 696 9444, www.hugoboss.com
Brooks Brothers: 702 380 3081, www.brooksbrothers.com
Diesel: 702 791 5927, www.diesel.com
DKNY: 702 650 9670, www.dkny.com
Dolce & Gabbana: 702 892 0880, www.dolcegabbana.com
Elie Tahari: 702 732 2454, www.elietahari.com

> ### BRITTIP
> Most restaurants have long wait times to be seated, so make a reservation. Or better still, place your name with the maitre d' and go shopping for an hour!

Emporio Armani: 702 650 5200, www.emporioarmani.com
Ermengildo Zegna: 702 650 2312, www.zegna.com
Express: 702 892 0424, www.express.com
GAP: 702 737 1550, www.gap.com

The entrance to the Forum Shops

Guess: 702 727 1816, www.guess.com
H&M: 702 207 0167, www.hm.com

BRITTIP
Arrive early for the Atlantis shows as the crowds build up early and you'll want a good view of the sunken city.

Lacoste: 702 791 7616, www.lacoste.com
Lucky Brand Jeans: 702 369 2536, www.luckybrandjeans.com
Marc Jacobs: 702 369 2007, www.marcjacobs.com
Stash: 702 382 0006, www.stashclothing.com
Ted Baker: 702 369 4755, www.tedbaker.com
Thomas Pink: 702 696 1713, www.thomaspink.com
Tommy Bahama's: 702 731 6868, www.tommybahama.com
Versace: 702 932 5757, www.versace.com
Vilebrequin: 702 894 9460, www.vilebrequin.com
Weft Denim: 702 650 5492, http://weftdenim.com

Clothes for women

7 For All Mankind: 7forallmankind.com, www.7forallmankind.com
Abercrombie & Fitch: 702 731 0712, www.abercrombie.com
Agent Provocateur: 702 696 7174, www.agentprovocateur.com
AIX Armani Exchange: 702 733 1666, www.armaniexchange.com
Ann Taylor: 702 794 0494, www.anntaylor.com
Anne Fontaine: 702 733 6205, www.annefontaine.com
Anthropologie: 702 650 0466, www.anthropologie.com
Banana Republic: 702 650 5623, www.bananarepublic.gap.com
bebe: 702 735 8885, www.bebe.com
Bettie Page: 702 369 8277 www.bettiepageclothing.com
BOSS Hugo Boss: 702 696 9444, www.hugoboss.com
CH Carolina Herrera: 702 894 5242, www.carolinaherrera.com
Christian Dior: 702 737 9777, www.dior.com
D & G: 702 732 9292, www.dolcegabbana.com
Diesel: 702 791 5927, www.diesel.com
DKNY: 702 650 9670, www.dkny.com

Dolce & Gabbana: 702 892 0880, www.dolcegabbana.com
Emporio Armani: 702 650 5200, www.emporioarmani.com
Ermengildo Zegna: 702 369 5458, www.zegna.com
Escada: 702 791 2300, www.escada.com
GAP: 702 737 1550, www.gap.com
H&M: 702 207 0167, www.hm.com
Intermix: 702 731 1922, www.intermixonline.com
Juicy Couture: 702 365 5600, www.juicycouture.com
Lacoste: 702 791 7616, www.lacoste.com
Lucky Brand Jeans: 702 369 2536, www.luckybrandjeans.com
Marc Jacobs: 702 369 2007, www.marcjacobs.com
Marciano: 702 369 0322, www.marciano.com
Shanghai Tang: 702 255 9090, www.shanghaitang.com
St John: 702 893 0044, www.stjohnknits.com
Tadashi: 702 733 6071, www.tadashicollection.com
Ted Baker: 702 369 4755, www.tedbakercollection.com
Thomas Pink: 702 696 1713, www.thomaspink.com
Tommy Bahama's: 702 731 6868, www.tommybahama.com
Valentino: 702 737 7603, www.valentino.com
Versace: 702 932 5757, www.versace.com
Victoria's Secret: 702 765 5425, www.victoriassecret.com

4

Fountain at the Forum Shops

Health and beauty

Anthropologie: 702 650 0466,
www.anthropologie.com
Bath & Body Works: 702 796 4902,
www.bathandbodyworks.com
Dior Beauty: 702 369 6072,
www.dior.com
Fresh: 702 631 5000, www.fresh.com
Inglot Cosmetics: 702 735 9064,
www.inglotcosmetics.com
Kiehl's: 702 784 0025, www.kiehls.com
MAC Cosmetics: 702 369 8770,
www.maccosmetics.com
Oro Gold: 702 369 0752,
www.orogoldcosmetics.com
Victoria's Secret: 702 765 5435,
www.victoriassecret.com

Jewellery

Cartier: 702 418 3904, www.cartier.com
Chopard: 702 862 4440,
www.chopard.com
David Yurman: 702 862 4440,
www.davidyurman.com
De Beers: 702 650 9559,
www.debeers.com
Harry Winston: 702 933 7370,
www.harrywinston.com
Hyde Park: 702 794 3541,
www.hydeparkjewelers.com
Intermix: 702 731 1922,
www.intermixonline.com
Judith Ripka: 702 792 5900,
www.judithripka.com
Montblanc: 702 732 0569,
www.montblanc.com
Pandora: 702 489 2674,
www.pandoralv.com
Swarovski Crystal: www.swarovski.com
Swatch: 702 734 1093, www.swatch.com
Tiffany & Co: 702 644 3065,
www.tiffany.com
Tourneau: 702 732 8463,
www.tourneau.com
Vicci: 702 734 3008, www.vicci.com

Music and electronics

Apple Computer: 702 684 8800,
www.store.apple.com
Sony Style: 702 697 5420,
www.store.sony.com

Shoes

Bally: 702 893 7718, www.bally.com
BCBGMAXAZRIA: 702 699 5498,
www.bcbg.com
Christian Louboutin: 702 818 8444,
www.us.christianlouboutin.com
Donald J Pliner: 702 796 0900,
www.donaldjpliner.com
Giuseppe Zanotti: 702 866 0055,
www.giuseppezanotti.com
Jimmy Choo: 702 691 2097,
www.jimmychoo.com
Louis Vuitton: 702 732 1227,
www.vuitton.com
Shoooz at the Forum: 702 734 7600,
www.shoooz.com
Skechers Shape Ups: 702 433 0560,
www.skechers.com
Stuart Weitzman: 702 369 9222,
www.stuartweitzman.com
The Walking Company: 702 792 8400,
www.thewalkingcompany.com
UGG Australia: 702 430 7250

Stationery, cards, books and gifts

Anthropologie: 702 650 0466,
www.anthropologie.com
Essentials at The Forum: 702 866 1207
Forum Gifts & Sundries: 702 734 0678
Magnet Maximus: 702 369 0195
Montblanc: 702 732 0569,
www.montblanc.com

Speciality shops

Antiquities: 702 792 2274,
www.antiquities.com
The Art of Peter Max: 702 644 7070,
www.petermax.com
Burberry: 702 731 0650,
www.burberry.com
Caesars: 702 731 7851
Christian Dior: 702 737 9777,
www.dior.com
Chrome Hearts: 702 893 9959,
www.chromehearts.com
Coach: 702 651 0363, www.coach.com
Custo Barcelona: 702 893 0015,
www.custo-barcelona.com
Davante: 702 737 8585,
www.davante.com
Elie Tahari: 702 732 2454,
www.elietahari.com
Emilio Pucci: 702 735 7731,
www.emiliopucci.com
Fabergé: www.faberge.com
Fendi: 702 893 2616, www.eluxury.com
Field of Dreams: 702 792 8233,
www.fieldofdreams.com
Galleria di Sorrento: 702 369 2085,
www.gdsorrento.com
Georg Jensen: 702 369 2424,
www.georgjensen.com
Gucci: 702 369 7333, www.gucci.com
Houdini's Magic Shop: 702 866 0010,
www.houdini.com
Ice Accessories: 702 696 9700,

www.iceaccessories.com
Jay Strongwater: 702 732 4448,
www.jaystrongwater.com
Judith Leiber: 702 792 0661,
www.judithleiber.com
La Perla: 702 732 9820, www.laperla.com
Longchamp: www.longchamp.com
Louis Vuitton: 702 732 1227,
www.vuitton.com
Montblanc: 702 732 0569,
www.montblanc.com
Niketown: 702 650 8888, www.nike.com
Planet Hollywood Superstore: 702 369
6001, www.planethollywood.com
Playboy: 702 851 7470,
www.playboy.com
Roman Times: 702 733 8687
Saint Andrews Golf Shop: 702 837 1234,
www.saintandrewsgolfshop.com
Scoop NYC: 702 734 0026,
www.scoopnyc.com
Tod's: 702 792 1422, www.tods.com
Tumi: 0800 783 6570, www.tumi.com
West of Santa Fe: 702 737 1993,
www.westofsantafe.com

Toys and games

FAO Schwarz: 702 796 6500,
www.faoschwarz.com

Cafés

Cafe Della Spiga: 702 731 7110
Café Expresso: 702 893 4045

Restaurants

BOA Prime Grill: 702 733 7373,
www.boasteak.com
Cheesecake Factory: 702 792 6888,
www.cheesecake-factory.net
Il Mulino New York: 702 492 6000,
www.ilmulinonewyork.com
Joe's Seafood, Prime Steak & Stone Crab:
702 792 9222, www.joes.net
La Salsa: 702 735 8226, www.lasalsa.com
The Palm Las Vegas: 702 732 7256,
www.thepalm.com
Planet Hollywood: 702 791 7827,
www.planethollywood.com
Spago: 702 369 6300,
www.wolfgangpuck.com
Sushi Roku: 702 733 7373,
www.sushiroku.com
Trevi Italian Restaurant: 702 735 4663,
www.trevi-italian.com

Miracle Mile Shops

Location: Wrapped around Planet
Hollywood Resort & Casino with entrances
on the Strip and Harmon Avenue
Tel: 702 866 0703
Web: www.miraclemileshopslv.com
Open: Sun–Thurs 10am–11pm; Fri and Sat
10am–midnight
Parking: Free valet and parking available at
Planet Hollywood.
Attractions: Rainstorm in Merchants'
Harbor every hour on the hour Mon–Thurs
and every half hour on Fri and Sat; plus
live entertainment from musicians and
comedians in the courtyards.
Cafés and restaurants: Fine-dining outlets
include Lombardi's Romagna Mia and
Pampas Churrascaria Brazilian Grill; the
casual options are Aroma D'Italia, Blondies
Sports Bar & Grill, La Salsa Cantina,
Merchants and Todai Sushi Bar. Trader
Vics has now been replaced by the rockin'
Cabo Wabo Cantina restaurant and
nightclub, owned by rock legend Sammy
Hagar – all very in keeping with the Planet
Hollywood ethos. Think tacos, tequila and
tunes and the end of 2011 saw the launch
of New England-style Lobster ME, with the
world's best lobster roll.

 BRITTIP

If you're serious about your
shopping, check out Miracle Mile's
VIP Shopper packages at http://
miraclemileshopslv.com/vip.php, which
include discounts on meals, makeovers,
spa treatments and gifts.

Miracle Mile invites you to 'shop the
planet'. And with an incredible array of
shops, you do feel like you're on some
incredible shopping planet. Another
50,000ft²/4,645m² of shops including
Guess, popular jeweller Pandora,
trendsetter Chinese Laundry, Basin White
and jeweller Kafri de Mexico were added
and others redesigned in 2011. You'd
never know this was once the Desert
Passage under the old Aladdin. What was
once a façade of a Moroccan shopping
fantasy has been completely ripped away
as part of a $100m make-over to the
Miracle Mile Shops. The exterior 1001
Arabian Nights theme was taken down in
2007, replaced by the new, Rodeo Drive
hipness of the Miracle Mile Shops. Now it's
all tall windows and floor-to-ceiling heavy
glass doors with brushed steel accents,
and flat-screen monitors offering directions
and advertisements. Don't miss the free
laser show and fountain show at the
heart of Miracle Mile shops with its water
effects, colour-changing fog and dramatic

soundtrack. There's even a rainstorm too outside Merchants Harbor Coffee House!

This is the place that's seen shop after trendy shop opening in true Vegas style. Chester Bennington, co-owner of the new Club Tatoo and Linkin Park band member, held an autograph-signing session plus an acoustic performance with his new side project Dead by Sunrise, and hosted a terrifying 'Death Drop' escape performed by Daredevil Magician Steve Wyrick. Just your average shop launch in Sin City!

Clothes and accessories for women

Alpaca Imports: 702 862 8297, www.alpacapetes.com
American Apparel: 702 691 2506, www.americanapparel.net
BCBG Max Azria: 702 735 2947, www.bcbg.com
bebe: 702 892 0406, www.bebe.com
Betsey Johnson: 702 731 0286, www.betseyjohnson.com
Bettie Page: 702 636 1100, www.bettiepage.com
Bikini Bay: 702 699 5597, www.bikinibay.com
Billabong: 702 454 7143, www.billabong.com
Caché: 702 699 5448, www.cache.com
Carlo Ferre Leather Collection: 702 450 9777
Champs Sports: 702 693 6996, www.champssports.com
Chico's: 702 732 2816, www.chicos.com
Club Tattoo: 702 363 2582, www.clubtattoo.com Tattoo and body piercing.
Crazy Shirts: 702 893 7780, www.crazyshirts.com
DC Shoes: 702 369 2730, www.dcshoes.com
Foot Locker: 702 733 4942, www.footlocker.com

Miracle Mile shops

Frederick's of Hollywood: 702 731 9360, www.fredericks.com
French Connection: 702 733 6420, www.frenchconnection.com
Front Row Sports: 702 369 8158, www.frsstore.com
GAP: 702 862 4042, www.gap.com
GapBody: 702 862 4042, www.gap.com
Guess by Marciano: 702 650 9928, www.marciano.com
H&M: 702 369 1195, www.hm.com
Herve Leger: 702 732 4529, www.herveleger.com
LOFT: 702 732 3348, www.loftonline.com
Lucky Brand Jeans: 702 733 6613, www.luckiebrandjeans.com
Marshall Rousso: 702 733 0611, www.marshallretailgroup.com
Mimi Mango: 702 650 2295, www.bikini-bay.com/mimimango
Napoleon: 702 733 6005, www.napoleonfashions.com
Original Penguin: 702 734 0089, www.originalpenguin.com
Parallel: 702 732 4489, www.bdbg.com
Rock & Religion: 702 836 9990
Roxy: 702 731 1521, www.quiksilver.com
Scat: 702 734 7228
Sisley: 702 733 3083, www.sisley.com
Stash Womens: 702 794 0003, www.stashclothing.com
Tommy Bahama: 702 731 3988, www.tommybahama.com
True Religion Brand Jeans: 702 893 2340, www.truereligionbrandjeans.com
United Colors of Benetton: 702 731 2317, www.benetton.com
Urban Outfitters: 702 733 0058, www.urbanoutfitters.com
Vegas Royalty: 702 731 1956, www.vegasroyaltylv.com
Victoria's Secret: 702 735 3174, www.victoriassecret.com
Volcom: 702 369 2340, www.volcom.com
West Coast Wraps: 702 731 1805
White House/Black Market: 702 732 2562, www.whiteandblack.com

Clothes and accessories for men

Alpaca Imports: 702 862 8297 www.alpacapetes.com
American Apparel: 702 691 2506, www.americanapparel.net
Ben Sherman: 702 688 4227, www.bensherman.com
Bikini Bay: 702 699 5597, www.bikinibay.com
Billabong: 702 454 7143, www.billabong.com

Carlo Ferre Leather Collection: 702 450 9777

Champs Sports: 702 693 6996, www.champssports.com

Club Tattoo: 702 363 2582, www.clubtattoo.com Tattoo and body piercing

Crazy Shirts: 702 893 7780, www.crazyshirts.com

DC Shoes: 702 369 2730, www.dcshoes.com

Foot Locker: 702 733 4942, www.footlocker.com

French Connection: 702 733 6420, www.frenchconnection.com

Front Row Sports: 702 369 8158, www.frsstore.com

GAP: 702 862 4042, www.gap.com

GapBody: 702 862 4042, www.gap.com

H&M: 702 369 1195, www.hm.com

Lucky Brand Jeans: 702 733 6613, www.luckiebrandjeans.com

Metropark: 702 650 7200, www.metroparkusa.com

Napoleon: 702 733-6005, www.napoleonfashions .com

Original Penguin: 702 734 0089, www.originalpenguin.com

Quiksilver: 702 731 1521, www.quiksilver.com

Rock & Religion: 702 836 9990

Scat: 702 734 7228

Shaunz: 702 792 5255, www.shaunz.com

Sisley: 702 733 3083, www.sisley.com

Stash Men's: 702 893 0010, www.stashclothing.com

Tommy Bahama: 702 731 3988. www.tommybahama.com

True Religion Brand Jeans: 702 893 2340, www.truereligionbrandjeans.com

United Colors of Benetton: 702 731 2317, www.benetton.com

Urban Outfitters: 702 733 0058, www.urbanoutfitters.com

Vegas Royalty: 702 731 1956

Volcom: 702 369 2340, www.volcom.com

Besides shopping, Miracle Mile is host to the Variety Theater, which means it is one of Las Vegas's entertainment hot spots. The performance line-up is tantalising, including *After the Show*, where artists try out their material from comedy to acrobatic, *Amazed* magic show, *American Storm* strip show, *Fab Four Live* Beatles act, *Marc Savard's Mesmerized*, *Popovich Comedy Pet Theater*, *Sin City Comedy*, *Stripper 101*, *The Mentalist* and *V – The Ultimate Variety Show*.

Just a few steps away are the entertainment options of Planet Hollywood, which includes *Amazing Jonathan*,

Hitzville and *Tickled Pink*. This makes Miracle Mile a great way to spend a day shopping, eating, taking in a show followed by some late-night dancing or gambling.

BRITTIP

Ticketed shows at Miracle Mile Shops include beatleshow! in the Saxe Theater 5.30pm nightly, naughty boys hypnosis show in the Harmon Theater 9pm nightly and Stripper 101 at the Variety Theater – where women over 18 can learn sexy stripping complete with feather boas, chairs and poles.

The Shoppes at The Palazzo

Location: 3325 Las Vegas Boulevard, South
Tel: 702 414 4525
Web: www.theshoppesatthepalazzo.com
Open: Sun–Thurs 10am–11pm; Fri–Sat 10am–midnight
Parking: An underground self-parking site is available under the Palazzo with elevators and escalators that arrive at the centre of the casino. Alternatively, you can use the 24-hour complimentary valet parking available at the front of the Palazzo Hotel Casino.
Cafés and restaurants: Restaurants are headed up by some of the world's most famous celebrity chefs and include Wolfgang Puck's Cut, Shimon Bokava's SUSHISAMBA and Emeril Lagasse's Table 10 and casual eateries include i love burgers.

Anchored by a flagship, 85,000ft²/ 7,897m² Barneys New York, The Shoppes at The Palazzo offers more than 60 luxury boutiques. In addition to Barneys

The Shoppes at the Palazzo

Off-Strip shopping

If you want to shop like the locals, you can find plenty of shopping excitement off the Strip, too.

The Boulevard Mall: www.boulevardmall.com. One of Nevada's largest shopping centres with more than 1 million ft²/92,903m² of retail space, features anchor department stores J.C. Penney, Sears and Macy's. The Boulevard Mall also offers specialty shops such as Yankee Candle Co., Charlotte Russe and a Footlocker Triplex.

The District at Green Valley Ranch: www.thedistrictatgvr.com. This is one of the more unique shopping experiences in Las Vegas, with more than 40 shops and restaurants situated along a tree-lined street adjacent to Green Valley Ranch Resort & Spa. The anchors at The District include Williams-Sonoma and Pottery Barn, with other stores being firsts to Las Vegas, such as REI, Coldwater Creek and Anthropologie. The District features cobblestone sidewalks, park benches and even pet-friendly areas,

The Fashion Outlets of Las Vegas: www.fashionoutletlasvegas.com. This shopping mall in Primm, Nevada, offers savings up to 75 per cent off more than 100 brand names such as Ann Taylor, DKNY, Kenneth Cole, Banana Republic, Williams-Sonoma, Hugo Boss, Hollister, Bath & Body Works, Tommy Bahama and Wilson's Leather. It is located at the Southern Nevada–California border, 35mls/56km south of Las Vegas off Interstate 15. A shuttle bus service is available from the Las Vegas Strip as well as from New York-New York Hotel & Casino and MGM Grand.

Galleria Mall: www.galleriaatsunset.com. Southwestern-themed, this is located at Sunset Road and Stephanie Street in Henderson, Nev., about 12mls/19km east of Las Vegas. Galleria tenants include J.C. Penney – check out the new Sephora, Macy's, Dillard's, MAC Cosmetics, American Eagle, Cache, Champs Sports, Victoria's Secrets, Tivoli Jewelers and a 600-seat food court.

The Meadows Mall: www.meadowsmall.com. Exemplifying the ease of one-stop, convenient shopping in a multilevel centre, this is located near the US 95 Expressway at Valley View Boulevard. The Meadows Mall provides its own downtown trolley that travels to and from the Downtown Transportation Center in less than 8 minutes. The mall has 2 levels of speciality stores and 5 courtyards. Anchor stores include Dillard's, Macy's, J.C. Penney and Sears.

New York, 20 stores and luxury brands have made their Las Vegas debuts at The Palazzo. They include Chloe, Tory Burch, Christian Louboutin, Diane Von Furstenberg, Van Cleef & Arpels, Catherine Malandrino, Anya Hindmarch, Michael Kors, Ralph Lauren, Jimmy Choo, Piaget, Burberry, Salvatore Ferragamo, Fendi, Bottega Veneta and Montblanc. Elton's men's store is a previous winner of 2008 Best Retailer of the Year for Best Contemporary Store in the United States by *MR Magazine*, the industry's leading publication for men's retail. Worth checking out!

Accessories for men and women

7 For All Mankind: 702 369 0570, www.7forallmankind.com
Bellusso: 702 650 2988, www.rolexreferencepage.com/travel/25_files/vegas1.html
Bottega Veneta: 702 369 0747, www.bottegaveneta.com
Burberry: 702 382 1911, www.burberry.com

Canali: 702 862 4447, www.canali.it
Canturi Jewels: 702 851 1555, www.canturi.com
Catherine Malandrino: 702 369 7300, www.catherinemalandrino.com
Chloé: 702 266 8122, www.chloe.com
Christian Louboutin: 702 818 1650, www.christianlouboutin.com
Coach: 702 547 1772, www.coach.com
Cole Haan: 702 369 2381, www.colehaan.com
Diane von Furstenberg: 702 818 2294, www.dvf.com
Fendi: 702 369 0587, www.fendi.com
Gal: 702 792 9005
Links of London: 702 733 4065, www.linksoflondon.com
Mezlan: 702 893 6116, www.mezlanshoes.com
Michael Kors: 702 731 2510, www.michaelkors.com
Montblanc: 702 696 0185, www.montblanc.com
Optica: 702 699 9678, www.optica.co.nz
Piaget: 702 418 3033, www.piaget.com
Piazza Sempione: 702 650 3137, www.piazzasempione.com

Shopping hints and tips

Duty free: Buy your booze from US liquor stores – they're better value than airports, but remember your allowance is 1 litre of spirits and 2 bottles of wine. And always take ID – the USA is very stringent on age checks.

Measurements: The Americans still work in feet and inches, which is great for anyone over the age of 40!

Sizes: Clothes sizes are one size smaller in America, so a dress size 10 in the US is a size 12 in the UK. It means you can travel out in a size 12 and come back in a size 10! It is the same for men: a jacket size 42 is the English size 44. But it's the opposite with shoes: an American size 10 is our size 9.

Taxes: In all cases you will have to add local taxes on to the cost of your goods. In Nevada this adds 7.5% on to the final price.

UK shopping allowances: Revenue and Customs set the rules for duty free and currently state that from outside the EU you can bring in goods up to £390 without paying tax or duty. If you arrive by private plane or boat, there's a limit of £270. It is worth noting that if one item is worth more than the total (for example, you bring in a £400 item), you have to pay tax on the full item value, not just the value above £390. It is always advisable to check with Revenue and Customs as the limits do change. More info including limits on alcohol and cigarettes can be found at: www.hmrc.gov.uk/customs/arriving/arrivingnoneu.htm

4

Poleci: 702 835 1246, www.poleci.com
Prosecco: 702 607 3956, www.lvtsg.com/news/publish/Fashion/article_24195.shtml
Ralph Lauren: 702 650 5656, www.ralphlauren.com
Salvatore Ferragamo: 702 369 0251, www.salvatoreferragamo.com
Scene: 702 696 9528
Splendida: 702 836 2001
Tory Burch: 702 369 0541, www.toryburch.com
Van Cleef & Arpels: 702 696 7139, www.vancleefarpels.com
Venetzia Fine Jewelry: 702 734 5100
Victoria's Secret: 702 696 0110, www.victoriassecret.com

Clothes for women

7 For All Mankind: 702 369 0570, www.7forallmankind.com
Annie Creamcheese Designer Vintage: 702 452 9600, www.anniecreamcheese.com
Bottega Veneta: 702 369 0747, www.bottegaveneta.com
Burberry: 702 382 1911, www.burberry.com
Catherine Malandrino: 702 369 7300, www.catherinemalandrino.com
Chloé: 702 266 8122, www.chloe.com
Cole Haan: 702 369 2381, www.colehaan.com
Diane von Furstenberg: 702 818 2294, www.dvf.com
Fendi: 702 369 0587, www.fendi.com
Gal: 702 792 9005
Michael Kors: 702 731 2510, www.michaelkors.com

Piazza Sempione: 702 650 3137, www.piazzasempione.com
Poleci: 702 835 1246, www.poleci.com
Ralph Lauren: 702 650 5656, www.ralphlauren.com
Salvatore Ferragamo: 702 369 0251, www.salvatoreferragamo.com
Thomas Pink: 702 369 2469, www.thomaspink.com
Tory Burch: 702 369 0541, www.tonyburch.com
Victoria's Secret: 702 696 0110, www.victoriassecret.com

Clothes for men

7 For All Mankind: 702 369 0570, www.7forallmankind.com
Andrew's Ties: 702 242 4506, www.andrewstiesusa.com
Billionaire Italian Couture: 702 765 5551, www.billionairecouture.com
Bottega Veneta: 702 369 0747, www.bottegaveneta.com
Burberry: 702 382 1911, www.burberry.com
Canali: 702 862 4447, www.canali.it
Catherine Malandrino: 702 369 7300, www.catherinemalandrino.com
Cole Haan: 702 369 2381, www.colehaan.com
Elton's: 702 853 0571, www.eltonslasvegas.com
Fendi: 702 369 0587, www.fendi.com
Gal: 702 792 9005
Mezlan: 702 893 6116, www.mezlanshoes.com

Town Square

Ralph Lauren: 702 650 5656,
www.ralphlauren.com
Salvatore Ferragamo: 702 369 0251,
www.salvatoreferragamo.com
Thomas Pink: 702 369 2469,
www.thomaspink.com

Clothes for kids

7 For All Mankind: 702 369 0570,
www.7forallmankind.com
Burberry: 702 382 1911,
www.burberry.com
Cole Haan: 702 369 2381,
www.colehaan.com
Ralph Lauren: 702 650 5656,
www.ralphlauren.com

Shoes

Bottega Veneta: 702 369 0747,
www.bottegaveneta.com
Burberry: 702 382 1911,
www.burberry.com
Catherine Malandrino: 702 369 7300,
www.catherinemalandrino.com
Christian Louboutin: 702 818 1650,
www.christianlouboutin.com
Coach: 702 547 1772, www.coach.com
Cole Haan: 702 369 2381,
www.colehaan.com
Jimmy Choo: 702 733 1802,
www.jimmychoo.com
Mezlan: 702 893 6116,
www.mezlanshoes.com
Michael Kors: 702 731 2510,
www.michaelkors.com

Department

Barneys New York: 702 629 4200,
www.barneys.com

Homewares and home

Catherine Malandrino: 702 369 7300,
www.catherinemalandrino.com

Cafés and restaurants

Café Presse: 702 607 0730
CUT by Wolfgang Puck: 702 607 6300,
www.wolfgangpuck.com
Double Helix Bar: 702 735 9463,
www.doublehelixwine.com
Expressamente illy: 702 869 2233,
www.lapalazzo.com
FIRST Food Bar: 702 607 3478,
www.www.palazzolasvegas.com/first.aspx
i love burgers: 702 242 2747,
www.iloveburgers.com
Lavo Italian restaurant and nightclub: 702
791 1800, www.lavolv.com
SUSHI SAMBA by chef Jose Mendin: 702
607 0700, www.sushisamba.com
Table 10 by Emeril Lagasse: 702 607
6363, www.emerils.com

Town Square Las Vegas

Location: 6605 Las Vegas Boulevard, South
Tel: 702 269 5000
Web: www.mytownsquarelasvegas.com
Open: Mon–Thurs 10am–9.30pm; Fri and
Sat 10am–10pm; Sun 11am–8pm
Parking: Town Square has 5,800 parking
spaces available in 3 different parking
garages or sidewalk parking. It also offers
valet parking.
Attractions: Rave Motion Pictures Cinema,
Children's Park at Town Square, Town
Square Park
Cafés and restaurants: 13 great places to
drink, snack or dine

This is definitely a place where you'll
rub shoulders with Las Vegans and their
kids. Town Square Las Vegas is an open-air
centre featuring 22 buildings detailing a
collage of Old World and contemporary
architectural styles, along with pedestrian-
friendly streets and lushly landscaped
walkways. As well as having a great
range of shops, unusually it has a fabulous

Children's Park with superb attractions like a 42ft/13m tree house in a live oak tree that features a rock wall and a fort. There's a Princess Tower, a Bakery Café Playhouse, Hedge Maze, merry go round and even a children's theatre. A rare find, in a city now geared mostly for adults. Next door, is the equally family-friendly Town Square Park with a picnic area, bridge and water fountain and pavilion for concerts and fashion shows. As for the shopping, there are more than 150 retail stores including H&M, Abercrombie & Fitch, Juicy Couture, Lucky Brand Jeans, bebe, Robb & Stucky and more, plus a great range of kids' clothes shops.

Town Square

Clothes and accessories for women

Abercrombie & Fitch: 702 270 2889, www.abercrombie.com
Aeropostale: 702 914 9311, www.aeropostale.com
American Eagle Outfitters: 702 260 0486, www.ae.com
Ann Taylor: 702 270 0692, www.anntaylor.com
Ann Taylor Loft: 702 407 0469, www.loft.com
AX Armani Exchange: 702 263 3393, www.armaniexchange.com
Banana Republic: 702 260 0551, www.bananarepublic.gap.com
BCBGMAXAZRIA: 702 616 2249, www.bcbg.com

bebe: 702 260 6274, www.bebe.com
Brighton Collectibles: 702 369 4904, www.brighton.com
Cache: 702 256 0100, www.cache.com
Chico's: 702 361 4904, www.chicos.com
ECCOCI: 702 361 4904, www.eccoccionline.com
English Laundry: 702 263 9100, www.englishlaundry.com
Ever: 702 407 2900
Express: 702 270 6479, www.expressfashion.com
Finish Line: 702 263 6023, www.finishline.com
GAP: 702 361 2447, www.gap.com
GUESS: 702 617 3489, www.guess.com
GUESS by Marciano: 702 269 8601, www.marciano.com
H&M: 702 260 1481, www.hm.com
Hollister Co.: 702 260 4591, www.hollisterco.com
J. Crew: 702 263 8950, www.jcrew.com
Juicy Couture: 702 269 3199, www.juicycouture.com
Lucky Brand Jeans: 702 614 5260, www.lucybrandjeans.com
Michael Stars: 702 851 0511, www.michaelstars.com
New York & Company: 702 260 0532, www.nyandcompany.com
Old Navy: 702 361 7479, www.oldnavy.gap.com
Pacsun: 702 260 8237, www.shop.pacsun.com
Puma: 702 759 0435, www.puma.com
Rock & Roll Religion: 702 263 6493
Roxy: 702 260 1741, www.roxy.com
Soma Intimates: 702 270 0168, www.soma.com

Grand Canal Shops

4

Tommy Bahama Store: 702 948 6828,
www.tommybahama.com
Victoria's Secret: 702 270 0088,
www.victoriassecret.com
White House/Black Market: 702 269 3043,
www.whitehouseblackmarket.com
Zumiez: 702 260 1887, www.zumiez.com

Clothes for men

Abercrombie & Fitch: 702 270 2889,
www.abercrombie.com
Aeropostale: 702 914 9311,
www.aeropostale.com
American Eagle Outfitters: 702 260 0486,
www.ae.com
AX Armani Exchange: 702 2633393,
www.armaniexchange.com
Banana Republic: 702 260 0551,
www.bananarepublic.gap.com
Eddie Bauer: 702 492 4791,
www.eddiebauer.com
English Laundry: 702 263 9100,
www.englishlaundry.com
Express: 702 270 6479,
www.expressfashion.com
Finish Line: 702 263 6023,
www.finishline.com
GAP: 702 361 2447, www.gap.com
GUESS: 702 617 3489, www.guess.com
H&M: 702 260 1481, www.hm.com
Hollister Co.: 702 260 4591,
www.hollisterco.com
J. Crew: 702 263 8950, www.jcrew.com
Lucky Brand Jeans: 702 614 5260,
www.lucybrandjeans.com
Old Navy: 702 361 7479,
www.oldnavy.gap.com
Pacsun: 702 260 8237,
www.shop.pacsun.com
Phenom: 702 570 6627
Puma: 702 759 0435, www.puma.com
Quiksilver: 702 260 8773,
www.quiksilver.com
Rock & Roll Religion: 702 263 6493
Tommy Bahama Store: 702 948 6828,
www.tommybahama.com
Zumiez: 702 260 1887, www.zumiez.com

Clothes for kids

abercrombie: 702 260 7693,
www.abercrombiekids.com
Finish Line: 702 263 6023,
www.finishline.com
GAP: 702 361 2447, www.gap.com
Gymboree: 702 740 7000,
www.gymboree.com
H&M: 702 260 1481, www.hm.com
Juicy Couture: 702 269 3199,
www.juicycouture.com
Justice: 702 263 3860,

www.justiceclothing.com
Old Navy: 702 361 7479,
www.oldnavy.gap.com
Quiksilver: 702 260 8773,
www.quiksilver.com
Roxy: 702 260 1741, www.roxy.com
Sanrio: 702 279 0161, www.sanrio.com
Tommy Hilfiger Childrenswear: 702 361
3773, www.tommyhilfiger.com

Shoes

ALDO: 702 269 6173,
www.aldoshoes.com
Barefoot Don: 702 361 3615
Brighton Collectibles: 702 369 4904,
www.brighton.com
Clarks: 702 617 4674,
www.clarksoriginals.com
Crocs: 702 263 2199, www.crocs.com
Finish Line: 702 263 6023,
www.finishline.com
Journeys: 702 269 7236,
www.journeys.com
Pacsun: 702 260 8237,
www.shop.pacsun.com
Puma: 702 759 0435, www.puma.com
Skechers: 702 361 8958,
www.skechers.com
Steve Madden: 702 361 2871,
www.stevemadden.com
Zumiez: 702 260 1887, www.zumiez.com

Health and beauty

Bath & Body Works: 702 263 3559,
www.bathandbodyworks.com
The Body Shop: 702 269 0273,
www.thebodyshop.co.uk
MAC: 702 492 1173,
www.maccosmetics.com
Origins: 702 407 8955, www.origins.com
Perfumania: 702 269 9208,
www.perfumania.com
Sephora: 702 361 3727,
www.sephora.com
Victoria's Secret: 702 270 0088,
www.victoriassecret.com

Music and electronics

Apple: 702 221 8826, www.apple.com
Fry's Electronics: 702 932 1400,
www.frys.com
Guitar Center: 702 450 2260,
www.guitarcenter.com
Verizon/Diamond Wireless: 702 896 0468,
www.verizonwireless.com

Cafés and restaurants

Blue Martini bar and tapas: 702 949 2583,
www.bluemartinilounge.com

Brio Tuscan Grille: 702 914 9145, www.brioitalian.com
California Pizza Kitchen: 702 896 5154, www.cpk.com
Claim Jumper classic American cuisine: 702 270 2509, www.claimjumper.com
english's: 702 478 8080, www.englishstownsquare.com
Johnny McGuire's: 702 982 0002, www.johnnymcguires.com
Kabuki Japanese Restaurant: 702 896 7440, www.kabukirestaurants.com
Nu Sanctuary Lodge: 702 527 7851, www.nulounge.com
Texas de Brazil: 702 614 0080, www.texasdebrazil.com
Tommy Bahama's Restaurant & Bar: 702 948 8006, www.tommybahama.com
Yard House: 702 734 9273, www.yardhouse.com

Grand Canal Shoppes

Location: The Venetian, 3377 Las Vegas Boulevard South Suite 2600
Tel: 702 414 4500
Web: www.thegrandcanalshoppes.com
Open: Sun–Thurs 10am–11pm; Fri and Sat 10am–midnight
Parking: Parking at the Venetian; valet parking available.
Attractions: Streetsmosphere at St Mark's Square, hourly noon to 6pm.
Cafés and restaurants: Fine dining is unparalleled here with one fantastic place after another. There's the Delmonico Steakhouse, Pinot Brasserie and Wolfgang Puck's Postrio to name just a few, while you can listen to live music at Tao.

This is another luxurious shopping environment with over 80 shops and restaurants that has been specifically created to provide entertainment as well as retail outlets. As you enter from the Strip, you are greeted by extravagant vaulted ceilings adorned with images reminiscent of Italy's great pointed palazzos.

Along the streets of this recreated 15th-century Venice are high-fashion luxury boutiques, national branded stores of America and entertainment retailers. After wandering past some of these shops you arrive at the huge space called St Mark's Square from where you can take a gondola ride – just like those on Venice's fabled canals – and enjoy the illusion created by decorated second-storey balconies.

Posh stores include Dooney & Bourke, Davidoff and Kenneth Cole. Other retailers include Ann Taylor, Banana Republic and bébé. Interesting one-off shops include Il Prato, which sells authentic Venetian masks, Ripa di Monti for Venetian glass and collectibles, and Sephora beauty emporium.

The whole process of browsing or parting with your cash is made sweeter by the entertainments, with jugglers showcasing their talents along the cobblestone walkways and the glass blowers demonstrating their craft in St Mark's Square.

Hawaiian Marketplace

Location: 3743 South Las Vegas Boulevard, just south of Harmon Avenue and in front of the Polo Towers
Tel: 702 795 2247
Web: www.vegas.com/shopping/hawaiian.html
Open: Hours vary, but generally 10am–10pm daily
Parking: A small car park is available next to the market or you can try the Polo Towers public car park.
Attractions: Show by an animatronic bird show in the Enchanted Forest on Fri, Sat and Sun 1–3pm; and Thurs–Sat Team Aloha puts on extended shows that include singing, dancing, fire-knife dancers and live bird shows.
Cafés and restaurants: Indian Tamba, Zinger's hamburger joint, China Star Buffet and Filipino fast food at Kapit Bahay

While the outdoor market is still popular, with several dozen thatch huts and carts from which you can buy a wide range of shirts, mobile phone accessories and tourist memorabilia, the interior of this $175m centre is dead, including most of the restaurants. The story goes that one group of investors bought out almost all of the interior stores, then promptly went bankrupt. A shame, as this was a pleasant shopping experience. It still is, but on a much smaller scale. Until the owners get the problems sorted out, there is little reason for a special trip, but if you are near the MGM Grand/Planet Hollywood area, it is worth stopping by.

BRITTIP

If you are having trouble finding a parking spot, try the valet parking at the side entrance of Polo Towers and you'll be just steps away from the Hawaiian Marketplace.

4

Hawaiian Marketplace

Las Vegas Premium Outlets – North

Location: 875 South Grand Central Parkway, downtown Las Vegas, just off Interstate 15
Tel: 702 474 7500
Web: www.premiumoutlets.com/lasvegas
Open: Mon–Sat 10am–9pm; Sun 10am–8pm
Parking: Free and immediately outside the village.
Cafés and restaurants: Auntie Anne's Soft Pretzels, China Pantry, Dairy Queen/ Orange Julius, The Fudgery, The Great Steak & Potato Co., Italia Express, Japan Café Grill, Makino's Seafood & Sushi Buffet, Starbucks Coffee and Subway.

Grand Canal Shoppes

Services: Download a map from the website to see the full layout or pick one up from the management office in Suite 1690; there you can also rent a pushchair, wheelchair, get a trolley, arrange for international shipping and buy international phone cards; 3 sets of WCs; 3 cashpoints (ATMs), foreign currency exchange; telephones.
Additional services: Attraction tickets, dinner and show reservations and sightseeing tours available through the Allstate Ticketing (Showtickets.com) located in the kiosk in front of Timberland at suite 1901.

Discount shopping in Las Vegas took a turn for the better with the arrival of Chelsea Premium Outlets' latest village – the $95m Las Vegas Premium Outlets with 150 stores. Run by the same people who run Woodbury Common in New York, this is one of the best discount outfits in America. Each of their village-style settings is picturesque, well laid out and fully serviced by food and drink outlets and plenty of toilets.

On top of that, it provides high-end designer gear such as AIX Armani Exchange, Burberry, Calvin Klein, Dolce & Gabbana and Ralph Lauren at 25–65% of the original price on a year-round basis, while also running fabulous sales with even cheaper prices – generally held on the major American holidays and over Christmas.

However, with its open design, and paucity of shade, it can be an uncomfortable experience trudging around on very hot or very windy days.

To get to Premium Outlets by car, take Interstate 15 northbound, then take Exit 41B Charleston Boulevard, southbound, and exit at Charleston Boulevard. This will take you on to Martin Luther King Boulevard. Turn left into Charleston Boulevard and left again into Grand Central Parkway. If you are going by taxi, there's a pick up behind Ann Taylor at Suite 1201 and a drop off between Adidas and Brooks Brothers, suite 1701.

If more convenient, a second outlet Las Vegas Premium Outlets – South, with 140 stores, is located at 74000 Las Vegas Boulevard South (702 896 5599), a short cab or Citizens Area Transit (CAT) bus ride from the Strip.

Hotel shopping

In addition to the major shopping parades featured at different hotels, earlier in this chapter, here is a full guide to the shops available in each of the major resort-hotels. Some offer high-end items – such as the Paris Resort – while many provide shopping that fits in with the theme of the hotel.

Bally's Hotel

Bally's Avenue Shops, 877 603 4390, www.ballyslasvegas.com
More than 20 stores from jewellery to fashion, plus men's and women's hair salons and an ice-cream parlour.

Open 7 days a week. Most shops open at 9am; closing times vary.

The Bellagio

Via Bellagio, 702 693 7111, www.bellagio.com
The tenants of the Bellagio's shopping 'mall' – a street Via Bellagio which winds its way from the hotel down to the Strip – fit in perfectly with the elegant surroundings. Prada, Georgio Armani and Chanel cater to the Bellagio's well-heeled clientele, as does Tiffany & Co, the epitome of subdued shopping style. Bellagio Exclusive shops such as artist Dale Chihuly, are found on Via Fiore.

Open 7 days a week. Most stores open 10am–midnight.

Via Bellagio

© MGM

Appian Way Shops

Appian Way, 702 731 7110,
www.caesarspalace.com
Despite its proximity to the Forum Shops at Caesars, Appian Way is a fair-sized corridor winding through the hotel and connecting the Roman, Palace and Centurion Towers, which is filled with some of the most exclusive shops and finest salons in the world and graced by a life-size replica of Michaelangelo's David.

Shops include Ancient Creations, filled with high-quality jewellery and rare coins and artefacts; Cartier; Le Paradis jewellery store; Venus Salon for hair, nail, make-up and skin services; Cottura for hand-painted ceramics; Galerie Michelangelo filled with fine art; Emperors Essentials for Caesars logo merchandise; Piazzas Del Mercato for sportswear, perfumes, golf collections and spa products; Godiva Chocolatier; Colosseum Cigars, Bernini Couture; Cuzzens for men's clothing; Paul and Shark for men's sportswear; Carina for women's designer clothes, shoes and accessories; and Paradiso for swimwear.

Open 7 days a week from 10am; closing times vary.

Circus Circus

Circus Circus Shops, 702 734 0410,
www.circuscircus.com
Want a break from high-falutin', designer-by-the-dozen, serious shop-till-you-drop malls? Then, head to the hotel's 40,000ft^2/3,716m^2 shopping promenade. You won't find Dior's latest must-have sunglasses, but you will find a whole lot of laughs in shops such as Criss Angel Mindfreak, Nothing But Clowns (yup – they come in all shapes and sizes!), Houdini's Magic Shop, Circus Kids and LYSONSPL8 for fun licence plates. Also pretty handy are the off-licence, newsagent and gift shop. Circus Circus also is a frequent host of liquidation sales, where overstock jeans and other merchandise from national chains are heaped in massive boxes and sold at pennies on the retail dollar.

Open 7 days a week from 10am; closing times vary.

✚ BRITTIP
Bag a half price ticket to over 75 fabulous Las Vegas shows at Tix4Tonight at Circus Circus Shops – even those that are 'always sold out'.

The Cosmopolitan of Las Vegas

The Shops at Cosmopolitan, 702 698 7575,
www.cosmopolitanlasvegas.com
The Shops at Cosmopolitan take Las Vegas shopping up a few levels with an eclectic line up of new-to-market shops including AllSaints Spitalfields, clothing designs by emerging talent Beckley, limited editions at CRSVR Sneaker Boutique, DNA2050, Amsterdam's Droog, Molly Brown's Swimwear, Retrospecs and Co, Skins 6/2 Cosmetics and STITCHED menswear.
Open 7 days a week from 10am; closing times vary.

Encore

The Esplanade at Encore, 702 770 8000,
www.wynnlasvegas.com/amenities/
shopping
Definitely one for fashionistas! All 11 shops are delicious and a little bit edgy. There's Rock & Republic, the distinguished Hermes and the eternally classic Chanel, along with Ensemble, Homestore, In Step, Nite Life Shop, Shades, Swim and Wynn & Company. An additional store featuring cooking products designed by and used by the Wynn Las Vegas and Encore Las Vegas chefs is due to open. The Spa Shop is located upstairs inside the Encore Spa. The Esplanade has the Botero Restaurant and is adjacent to the XS nightclub if you're late night shopping and fancy a boogie!
Open daily 10am–11pm.

Excalibur Hotel

Castle Walk Shops, 702 597 7850,
www.excalibur.com
This is as much a show as a shopping experience, with live jousting in King Arthur's Tournament between stores. Fantasy shops on the medieval theme include the Excalibur Edge, Castle Keepsakes, Kids of the Kingdom, Spirit Shop, Dragon's Lair. Lids Hats have a wide range and Marshall Rousso clothes for every occasion.
Open 7 days a week from 9am; closing times vary.

Las Vegas Hilton

Las Vegas Hilton Shops, 702 732 5111,
www.lvhilton.com
This area is about to change its name as we go to press.
Don't forget to pick up Elvis souvenirs

and other goodies at The Strip Store at the Hilton shops.

Open 7 days a week from 9am; closing times vary.

The Luxor

Luxor Galleria Stores, 702 262 4444, www.luxor.com

The Galleria contains 10 shops selling everything from King Tut's souvenirs to ice cream and sweets. Other shops include Relics for hieroglyphic T-shirts and sweatshirts and handcrafted souvenirs from Egypt, and the Logo Shop selling everything from Luxor key chains to stuffed animals and glassware and Criss Angel Mindfreak. Exclusive is LX Fashions the exciting women's clothing store that has everything from business outfits to cutting-edge designer gear.

Open 7 days a week from 10am; closing times vary.

Mandalay Bay

Mandalay Bay Shops, 702 632 7777, www.mandalaybay.com

A selection of tropically themed shops to match the hotel, Mandalay Place is 100,000ft²/9,290m² and connects Mandalay Bay and the Luxor via a 310ft/95m retail sky bridge. The Shoppes at Mandalay Place 41 retailers include Urban Outfitters, The Art of Shaving, Elton's men's store, Nora Blue, Shoe Obsession, Fashion 101, LUSH, the world's first Nike Golf store and the First GUINNESS® Store in the US.

Open 7 days a week from 10am–11pm; closing times vary.

MGM Grand

MGM Grand Avenue, 702 891 3300, www.mgmgrand.com

The City of Entertainment has fun and exclusive shops that provide something for everyone from fine jewellery to men's, women's and children's fashions. You can browse through the luxurious shops along Studio Walk, visit Star Lane Shops on the lower level of the main lobby, or explore the shopping outlets located throughout MGM Grand. Studio Walk is a magnificent 115,000ft²/10,684m² shopping promenade located between the casino and the gardens and is designed to look like a Hollywood sound stage, while each of the shops and restaurants has been inspired by some of Hollywood's legendary buildings and landmarks. Star Lane Shops has a variety of outlets in a fun and colourful shopping arcade.

Open 7 days a week from 10am; closing times vary.

The Mirage

The Street of Shops, 702 791 7111, www.mirage.com

An exclusive collection of designer boutiques offering everything from unique gifts to beautiful jewellery and designer clothes in a sophisticated Parisian/Italian boulevard setting. Designers include DKNY, Moschino and La Perla and there's Misura for men while there are also souvenir shops for Siegfried and Roy's and Terry Fator.

Open 7 days a week; Sun–Thurs 10am–11pm; Fri and Sat until midnight.

Monte Carlo

Monte Carlo Shops, Street of Dreams, 702 730 7777, www.montecarlo.com

Boutiques include a convenience store, sweet shop, style at Juicy Couture, Marshall Rousso and Misura for men and speciality shops such as Casino Royale for gaming merchandise.

Open 7 days a week from 10am; closing times vary.

M Resort

M Resort shopping, 702 797 1000, www.themresort.com

Within this hotel is the Vice Shop and convenience store but a 1 million ft²/92,903m² area of retail and shops is planned.

New York-New York

Soho Village, 866 767 3757, www.newyorknewyork.com

Provides a limited number of stores but still a fun experience. The village is set against a background of New York landmarks and includes both Greenwich Village and Times Square.

Open 7 days. Most Stores open at 10am–10pm.

Paris Las Vegas

Le Boulevard, 702 946 7000, www.parislasvegas.com

Paris Las Vegas features upscale French retail shopping, located within the resort's quaint Le Boulevard District. The interior buildings are covered with façades representative of real Parisian districts. Picturesque cobblestone streets and winding alleyways take guests on a

European shopping spree. Le Boulevard features a wide array of authentic French boutiques, such as Le Cave, where you can sample premier French wines and private labels; Les Enfants, a purveyor of French children's toys and games; Lunettes designer eyewear; Le Paradis fine jewellery and crystal; and La Boutique by Yokohama de Paris.

Open 7 days a week 10am–10pm.

Rio All-Suite Hotel

Masquerade Village Shops, 866 746 7671, www.riolasvegas.com
The $200m Masquerade Village is actually a combination of shopping, dining, entertainment and gaming woven together by the ongoing carnival atmosphere of the hotel's *Show in the Sky* (see page 49). Here you can stroll down 200-year-old Tuscan-tiled streets filled with eclectic boutiques selling everything from Harley Davidson clothing to Field of Dreams sports memorabilia.

Open 7 days a week from 10am; closing times vary.

Stratosphere Hotel

Tower Shops, 702 380 7777, www.stratospherehotel.com
Visitors pass through a variety of shops on themed street scenes reminiscent of Paris, Hong Kong and New York on their way to the Broadway Showroom and lifts to the Observation Deck.

Open Sun–Thurs 10am–11pm; Fri and Sat until midnight.

Wynn Las Vegas

Wynn Esplanade, 702 770 7100, www.wynnlasvegas.com
In April 2005, the much-anticipated opening of Wynn Las Vegas brought one of the more high-end shopping experiences to the Las Vegas Strip. Wynn Esplanade features the first Oscar de la Renta boutique fashion store and the first Jean Paul Gaultier designer store in the country. Among the big-name shops in the Wynn Esplanade are Manolo Blahnik, Cartier, Louis Vuitton and Christian Dior. Also among the top brands is the Penske-Wynn showroom, home to the hotel's Ferrari-Maserati dealership.

Open 7 days from 10am; check website for closing times as they do vary.

The shops at Mandalay Bay

© MGM

RESTAURANTS

Your choice of the best restaurants and eating places in town

Food, glorious food abounds in Las Vegas from the classiest gourmet restaurants to the cheap and cheerful diner and from relaxed lounge-style settings to trendy bistros. Not so long ago, the city was most famous for its $1.99-cent shrimp (giant prawn) cocktails and the amazing all-you-can-eat buffets and not a lot else in the dining department. But, like every other aspect of Las Vegas, things have changed as a result of the massive influx of bright young professionals from California and a surge in sophisticated visitors looking for something more than a bit of casino action.

The resorts have gone far afield to woo top chefs from every country and discipline to open dazzling eateries. While most resorts or hotels worldwide are happy if they have one, or perhaps two, world-class restaurants, the Las Vegas resorts collect them like some do postage stamps. The Venetian is proud to boast of having 16 4- or 5-star eating houses of distinction on their property. Most of the other grand resorts have half a dozen each. The king of Las Vegas food must be the iconic celebrity chef Wolfgang Puck, who has no less than 6 restaurants covering Sin City and 2 more opening in the new Crystals Center at CityCenter, plus a Wolfgang Puck Gourmet Express at McCarran airport!

 **BRITTIP**

If you're here to spend, spend, spend, blow the budget at restaurants Guy Savoy at Caesars Palace, Joel Robuchon at MGM Grand, or Picasso and Le Cirque at Bellagio.

Vegas has more Master Sommeliers than any other city in the world and more wine sold per capita than any other destination. Las Vegas's credibility as one of the globe's centres for fine dining grew even more when, in 2008, it became the fourth US city to be profiled by the authors of the *Michelin Guide*. In 2009, Alex at Wynn Las Vegas (now closed) and Joel Robuchon at The Mansion at MGM Grand were honoured with a 5-star rating by the *Mobil Travel Guide*. *Bon Appetit* magazine, a leading authority in the culinary world, cemented

In this chapter

Vegas's place among US dining capitals by declaring it as one of the nation's top 5 restaurant cities. In 2011, Alex at Wynn Las Vegas, Guy Savoy at Caesars Palace, Joel Robuchon at MGM Grand and Picasso and Le Cirque at Bellagio were repeat winners of AAA Five Diamond awards.

◄ ≋ BRITTIP

Do not assume that because you can smoke anywhere you like in gaming areas of casinos (though many now offer smoke-free areas) that the same goes for the restaurants. All hotel restaurants are completely non-smoking.

But while the classy restaurants have taken over the headlines, with $777 Kobe beef hamburgers and $421 white truffle lobsters, there are still quality cheap eats if you know where to look. You can get a huge presentation of shrimp downtown at Golden Gate Hotel & Casino for a mere $1.99, while the Rio All-Suites Hotel & Casino's Carnival World buffet has more than 300 mains and 70 desserts. If you're a fry-up kind of person, a massive steak and eggs breakfast can be had for a snip 24-hours a day on Boulder Highway's Arizona Charlie's. Many places retain the 'Midnight Menu' for late revellers and gamblers where filling breakfasts and sandwiches can be had for a pittance after midnight.

Obviously, space dictates that I cannot list all the restaurants on offer, so I have provided information on what are considered to be the finest restaurants in each category. They're all popular, though, so book a table in advance. I have also included a good smattering of extremely well-priced cafés – some of which are open 24/7 – and plenty of non-resort restaurants with enduring appeal. As the celebrity chef culture is so strong here, I've begun with a quick rundown of every high profile restaurant with a big name at the helm.

Celebrity chef restaurants

Historically, major hotel-casinos featured 'gourmet rooms' in order to cater to high rollers' tastes. Each restaurant created an ambience designed to transport diners to a world far away from the action of the casinos. However, by the late '90s, high-end eateries became the rage with their appeal extending beyond just high rollers. Las Vegas hotels recruited some of the top chefs in the world to open and run

restaurants inside their properties. Today, Las Vegas has the most comprehensive collection of the world's top chefs and television icons. If you like to namedrop about your food, these are the eateries for you – just make sure your bank balance is up to the challenge!

- Paul Bartolotta (Bartolotta Ristorante di Mare at Wynn Las Vegas/Encore)
- Mario Batali (B & B Ristorante and Enoteca Otto Pizzeria at The Venetian)
- Kim Canteenwalla (Society Café at Encore)
- Tom Colicchio (Craftsteak at MGM Grand)
- Alain Ducasse (Mix at Mandalay Bay's THEhotel)
- Todd English (Olives at Bellagio, Todd English PUB at Crystals)
- Susan Feniger and Mary Sue Milliken (Border Grill at Mandalay Bay)
- Bobby Flay (Mesa Grill at Caesars Palace)
- Jean-Marie Josselin (8-0-8 at Caesars Palace)
- Hubert Keller (Fleur at Mandalay Bay)
- Thomas Keller (Bouchon at The Venetian)
- Emeril Lagasse (Emeril's New Orleans Fish House at MGM Grand and Delmonico Steakhouse at The Venetian)
- Mark LoRusso (Botero Steak at Encore)
- Sirio Maccioni (Le Cirque at Bellagio and Sirio at ARIA)
- Steve Martorano (Martorano's at Rio All-Suite Hotel and Casino)
- Nobu Matsuhisa (Nobu at Hard Rock Hotel & Casino and the new Nobu Hotel)
- Jean-Philippe Maury (Jean Philippe Patisserie at Bellagio and JP Patisserie at ARIA)
- Maurizio Mazzon (Canaletto at the Venetian and Il Fornaio at the New York-New York and Green Valley Ranch)
- Shawn McClain (Sage at Aria)
- Michael Mina (Nobhill Tavern and Seablue at MGM Grand, Michael Mina at Bellagio and Strip Steak at Mandalay Bay and American Fish at Aria)
- Tom Moloney (AquaKnox at The Venetian)
- Rick Moonen (RM Seafood at Mandalay Place)
- Charlie Palmer (Aureole at Mandalay Bay and Charlie Palmer Steak at The Four Seasons)
- Francois Payard (Payard Patisserie at Caesars Palace)
- Marc Poidevin (Switch at Encore)
- Wolfgang Puck (Spago and Chinois at The Forum Shops at Caesars, Postrio at

The Venetian, CUT at The Palazzo, Lupo at Mandalay Bay and Wolfgang Puck Bar & Grill at MGM Grand)
- Joël Robuchon (L'Atelier de Joël Robuchon and Joël Robuchon at The Mansion at MGM Grand)
- André Rochat (Alizé at The Palms, Andre's Monte Carlo)
- Guy Savoy (Restaurant Guy Savoy at Caesars Palace)
- Theo Schoenegger (Sinatra at Encore)
- Piero Selvaggio (Valentino at The Venetian)
- Zack Allen (B&B Ristorante at The Venetian/The Palazzo)
- Julian Serrano (Picasso at Bellagio and Julian Serrano at ARIA)
- Kerry Simon (Simon at Palms Place)
- Joachim Splichal (Pinot Brasserie at The Venetian)
- Masayoshi Takayama (BARMASA and Shaboo at ARIA)
- Jet Tila (Wazuzu at Encore)
- Jean-Georges Vongerichten (Prime Steakhouse at Bellagio and Jean Georges Steakhouse at ARIA)
- Michael White (Fiamma at MGM Grand)
- Devin Hashimoto (Okada at Wynn Las Vegas)
- Jose Andres (China Poblano at The Cosmopolitan)
- Bruce and Eric Bromberg (Blue Ribbon Sushi Bar & Grill at The Cosmopolitan)
- Scott Conant (Scarpetta at The Cosmopolitan)
- Stephen Hopcraft (STK Las Vegas at The Cosmopolitan)
- Akira Back (Yellowtail Japanese Restaurant at Bellagio)
- Stephane Chevet (Shibuya at MGM Grand)
- Pierre Gagnaire (Twist at Mandarin Oriental)
- Martin Heierling (Sensi at Bellagio and Executive Chef at Vdara Hotel & Spa)

BRITTIP

If you're a total foodie, head to Vegas in May when the city hosts its annual epicurean event called Vegas Uncork'd (www.vegasuncorked.com). Four days of grand chefs and grand tastings!

We have included as many websites as possible. In some cases, you can go direct to the restaurant's web page. In other cases, it is quicker to go to the main resort-hotel page, then select the dining option, rather than key in a long URL.

BRITTIP

Time your visit with Restaurant Week each autumn where 80 fine dining restaurants offer prix fixe menus – proceeds benefit charity Three Square Food Bank, working to end hunger.

Price codes
Per head for a 3-course meal and 1 drink:
$ = under $40
$$ = up to $80
$$$ = $81 and over!

American restaurants

Addiction Restaurant
Rumor, 455 East Harmon Ave, www.rumorvegas.com/addiction/
This sleek modern venue with notorious chef Vic Vegas at the helm, serves classic dishes with a twist for breakfast, lunch and dinner. Dine indoors or out on signature dishes like the Cuban Reuben, sea bass satay or Kurobutakarmal pork. A big hit with the gay community. Open daily 6am–11pm. **$$**

Alexis Gardens Restaurant
Alexis Park Hotel, 375 East Harmon Ave, 702 796 3300, www.alexispark.com
Pegasus offers gourmet dining in a classy environment. Dishes include freshly-made pastas, steaks and fresh fish that come with delicious vegetables. Open daily 6am–10pm. **$$**

All-American Bar & Grille
Rio All-Suite Hotel & Casino, 702 777 7923, www.riolasvegas.com
The newish All-American Bar & Grille is the place to come for Brits looking for hearty American meals. Think 'Rio Dry Aged' in-house steaks famous for their taste and sizzle. Tuck into mammoth salads, fresh seafood and burgers prepared in an open mesquite wood grill. Make sure you come with an appetite. Afternoon margaritas here are good. Open daily 11am–6am. **$**

Aureole
Mandalay Bay, 702 632 7401, www.mandalaybay.com/dining/signature-restaurants/aureole.aspx
Charlie Palmer, famous for his New York Aureole, opened his second outlet, this time in Las Vegas, which now has a Michelin

5

star. The New York restaurant is consistently voted number one for American cuisine by the Zagat survey and Charlie was awarded Best Chef by the James Beard Foundation. Aureole features seasonal dishes including artisan dry-aged beef and fresh seafood that reflect Palmer's progressive American cuisine. For this restaurant, a 4-storey wine tower has been created and wine stewards strap on harnesses to be hoisted up the tower to make their wine selections. Open daily 5.30pm–10.30pm. **$$$**

◀✠▶ **BRITTIP**
For the ultimate fast fix of American food, head to Pink's Hot Dogs at Planet Hollywood Resort & Casino with 14 varieties of hot dog!

Binion's Ranch Steak House

24th fl, West Tower, Binions Gambling Hall, 702 382-1600, www.binions.com
Vegas's best-kept local secret, at the top of the famous Binion's Gambling Hall is a romantic gourmet penthouse restaurant with spectacular views of the Las Vegas valley. Dine on Creekstone Farm's Midwestern, corn-fed, certified Black Angus beef aged a minimum of 28 days and prepared to order, filet mignon, Australian lobster tail, prime rib of beef, 21oz Porterhouse steaks, salmon, and its signature chicken fried lobster in vintage Vegas décor with soft romantic lighting. It's best reached

Fix at the Bellagio

© MGM

by taking the glass lift suspended on the outside of the tower. Open daily 5.30–10.30pm **$$**

◀✠▶ **BRITTIP**
For a bird's eye view of the pirate ship action outside Treasure Island, book yourself a window seat at the Buccaneer Bay Club.

Biscayne Steak, Sea & Wine

Tropicana, 800 462 8767, www.troplv.com
This tropical South Beach-style steak and seafood restaurant serves prime cuts of beef, Safe Harbor certified fresh seafood along with a 200-bottle wine list and signature cocktails. Treat yourself to the 4-course tasting menu for $39.99. Open Sun, Mon, Thurs 5–10pm; Fri–Sat 5–11pm. **$$–$$$**

Central

Caesars Palace, 702 650 5921, www.centrallv.com
James Beard Award-winning chef Michel Richard has brought a version of his popular 24/7 dining experience from Washington DC to Las Vegas. Adjacent to the Caesars Palace hotel lobby, Richard's style marries whimsy with mouthwatering food meaning signature dishes such as 72-hour short ribs, razor clam chowder, fried chicken and his celebrated burger are served in a 9,600ft²/891m² space which seats around 300, with an outdoor patio terrace and large lounge bar for beers on tap and cocktails. Open daily 24 hours. **$**

Cheesecake Factory

Forum Shops at Caesars Palace, 702 792 6888, www.thecheesecakefactory.com
Famous for its extensive menu – there are more than 200 items plus nearly 50 cheesecakes – this is more of a place to people-watch than expect gourmet cuisine, yet the food is delicious too. Portions are huge, but please find some room at the end for a serving of their excellent, and imaginative, desserts. Open Mon–Thurs 11.10am–11.30pm; Fri 11.10am–12.30am; Sat 10.10am–12.30am and Sunday brunch 10.10am–11.30pm. **$**

FIX

Bellagio, 702 693 8865, www.bellagio.com/restaurants/fix.aspx
The menu, designed to offer the best in classic American fare, focuses on simply

© MGM

Shanghai Lilly

prepared, top-quality fish, meat and poultry, cooked to order on a wood-burning grill. The longer-than-usual opening hours allow for both pre-show and après-show dining, while the bar and lounge offer a full menu of speciality cocktails. Open Sun–Thurs 5pm–11pm; Fri and Sat 5pm–1am. **$–$$**

Holsteins Shakes and Buns

The Cosmopolitan, 702 698 7940, www.holsteinslv.com
An exciting place for anything from a quick gourmet burger with friends to a wacky wedding meal (trust me, it happens in Vegas). A vast menu of Tiny Buns and Big Buns but your waitress will tell you that you can have any combination of what you see on the menu. There are also salads listed under 'Graze' and plenty of hearty 'Snacks' from Fried Pickles to Artichoke Guacamole. Desserts are over-the-top creations which have to be seen to be believed. Good fun. **$$**

i love burgers

Second level, Shoppes at The Palazzo, 702 242 2747, www.iloveburgers.com or www.theshoppesatthepalazzo.com
A modern take on the classic American burger joint serving premium gourmet burgers with creative toppings and sides. Choose from signature burgers with toppings including farm-fresh vegetables, smoked meats and an array of cheeses. Open Sun–Thurs 10am–11pm; Fri–Sat 10am–midnight.

Old Homestead Steakhouse

Caesars Palace, 866 227 5938, www.caesarspalace.com and www. theoldhomesteadsteakhouse.com
The Meatpacking District's Old Homestead Steakhouse is the latest NYC eatery to head to Vegas and replacing the much-loved Nero's restaurant at Caesars Palace. It's large at 16,000ft^2/149m^2 with 250 seats in the dining room, lounge and bar and a 'temple for carnivores' according to Zagat, signature dishes from the classic NYC menu include the popular colossal crab cake, 32oz Gotham rib eye steak and the old homestead New York-style cheesecake, to name a few. Opening hours not yet available. **$$–$$$**

P.J. Clarke's

Forum Shops, Caesar's Palace, 702 434 7900, www.pjclarkes.com/Vegas
Established in 1884 in New York, P.J. Clarke's traditional saloon has entertained the famous, the infamous and everyone else in its colourful history. Open daily 11am–1am. **$$**

Society Café Encore

Encore Las Vegas, 702 248 3463, www.wynnlasvegas.com
Society Café Encore was designed with the whimsical era of Oscar Wilde in mind, to match Chef Kim Canteenwalla's (yes, that's really his name!) wildly imaginative American cooking. The hip place to come

5

Best views in the valley

Alizé at The Palms (page 102)

Binions Ranch Steak House: Binions Gambling Hall (page 96)

Cabo Wabo Cantina: Miracle Mile Shops (page 110)

Eiffel Tower Restaurant: Paris Las Vegas (page 102)

Firenze Lobby Lounge: Ravella at Lake Las Vegas (page 118)

Mix: Mandalay Bay (page 104)

Mon Ami Gabi: Paris Las Vegas (page 103)

Olives: Bellagio (page 110)

Tao: The Venetian (page 99)

The Top of the World: Stratosphere (page 115)

Twist: Mandarin Oriental (page 104)

Yellowtail Sushi Restaurant & Bar: Bellagio (page 109)

VooDoo Steak: Rio All-Suite Hotel (page 101)

with glorious decor. Go for the pink sofa alone! Open Sun–Thurs 7am–11pm; Fri and Sat 7am–1am. **$–$$**

Tableau

Wynn Las Vegas, 702 248 3463, www.wynnlasvegas.com
Open for breakfast, lunch and Sunday brunch, Wynn's signature restaurant, Tableau is to be found in a light, airy atrium setting with poolside views. Rising star chef David Spero showcases American ingredients prepared with French flair. Mon–Fri breakfast 7–10.30am; lunch 11.30am–2.30pm. Brunch on Sat and Sun 7am–2.30pm. **$**

Tommy Rocker's Cantina & Grill

4275 Dean Martin Drive, 702 261 6688, www.tommyrocker.com
It's unlikely you'll be visiting Tommy's unless you're coming here for the music, as it's a little off the beaten track. What will surprise you though, will be the half-decent, well-priced, largely American grub that allows you to enjoy the live music and DJ well into the night. **$**

Union Restaurant and Lounge

Aria Resort & Casino, 877 230 2742, www.arialasvegas/dining/union.aspx
Chef Brian Massie has introduced an edgy American dim sum style concept at Aria, featuring unique interpretations of American favourites made from the finest quality ingredients. Small, sharable plates supplement the menu and offer diners a variety of dishes to excite the palate. Open Sun–Wed 5pm–10pm, Thurs–Sat 5pm–11pm. **$$**

Asian restaurants

Bamboo Garden

4850 West Flamingo Road, 702 871 3262
Popular spot for locals who love the delicious range of unusual dishes at the very reasonable prices. It looks modest enough, but the friendly staff provide excellent service and dishes include: cream of seafood soup; Mongolian lamb; firecracker beef; emerald shrimp; and Peking duck with Mandarin pancakes. Open Mon–Sat 11am–10.30pm. **$$**

Chin Chin

New York-New York Hotel, 702 740 6300, www.nynyhotelcasino.com/restaurants/ chin-chin-cafe.aspx
In a restoration of New York Chinatown, you'll find everything from the Pacific Rim to Szechuan and Cantonese food in a bright and colourful setting. Open Mon–Fri 7.30am–11pm; Sat–Sun 8am–11pm. **$$**

Pearl

MGM Grand, freephone 702 891 7380, www.mgmgrand.com/restaurants
A stylish, upmarket Chinese-meets-Western restaurant based on Cantonese and Shanghai specialities. The largely seafood dishes include both Maine and Australian lobsters, shark fin and lobster spring rolls and Sian bouillabaisse. An added bonus is the trolley with a range of fine Chinese teas – for a good pick-me-up, try green tea. Open Sun–Thurs 5.30–10pm; Fri and Sat 5.30–10.30pm. **$$–$$$**

Shanghai Lilly

Mandalay Bay, 702 632 7409, www.mandalaybay.com/dining/ signature-restaurants/shanghai-lilly.aspx
Classic Cantonese and Szechuan dishes using only the finest ingredients make this one of the best places to enjoy Eastern

Most romantic spots

Alizé: The Palms (page 102)
André's: South 6th Street (page 102)
Aureole: Mandalay Bay (page 95)
Eiffel Tower Restaurant: Paris Las Vegas (page 102)
Gaylord India Restaurant: Rio All-Suite Hotel (page 105)
Jasmine: Bellagio (page 101)
Le Cirque: Bellagio (page 103)
Mon Ami Gabi: Paris Las Vegas (page 103)
Picasso: Bellagio (page 110)
Postrio: The Venetian (page 100)
Sage: ARIA Resort & Casino (page 102)
Valentino: The Venetian (page 126)

cuisine. Open Tues–Thurs 5.30–10.30pm, Fri–Sat 5.30-11pm. $$$

Tao

The Great Hall, Grand Canal Shoppes at the Venetian, 702 388 8338, www.taolasvegas.com
This amazing $20m complex of nightclub and restaurant specialises in Hong Kong Chinese, Japanese and Thai cuisines. Chef Ralph Scarmadella's creations include everything from Kobe beef to traditional Peking duck, all prepared by master chefs from across Asia. How popular is it? It is by far the most successful privately owned restaurant in the USA, having twice the revenue of the second ranked (Tavern on the Green in New York City). Open Sun–Thurs 5pm–midnight; Fri and Sat 5pm–1am. $$–$$$

Thai Spice

4433 West Flamingo Road, 702 362 5308
A friendly restaurant that attracts a lot of the local Asians and tourists alike. Tuck into traditional Thai food from fish cakes to Pad Thai noodles, Thai-spiced beef and pepper-garlic pork. Open Mon–Sat 11am–10pm. $

Todai Seafood & Sushi Buffet

Miracle Mile Shops, 702 892 0021, www.todai.com
More than a sushi buffet, Todai offers Japanese, Chinese and Korean cuisine alongside salads, rice and noodle dishes and, of course, a full range of fresh sushi. Open daily for lunch 11.30am–2.30pm and for dinner Sun–Thurs 5.30–9.30pm; Fri and Sat 5.30–10pm. $–$$

Wazuzu

Encore Las Vegas, 702 248 3463, www.wynnlasvegas.com
Turn a corner in the Encore casino and come face to face with a 27ft/8m crystal dragon, mounted at Wazuzu, where rising star Chef Jet Tila serves up innovative pan Asian delights. This dramatic café-style restaurant showcases his deft touch with Chinese, Japanese, Indian, Singaporean and Thai cuisines. Open Sun–Thurs 11.30am–10.30pm; Fri and Sat 11.30am–1am. $–$$

Bistros and brasseries

Bouchon

The Venetian, 702 414 6200, www.bouchonbistro.com
World-renowned chef Thomas Keller, named America's best chef by *Time* magazine, is the sole recipient of consecutive Best Chef awards from the prestigious James Beard Foundation. Bouchon opened in 2004 in the beautiful Venezia Tower and is one of the finest restaurants in Las Vegas.

An extensive selection of bistro classics is added to by raw seafood and seafood platters, including lobster, oyster, shrimp, mussels and crab. Fabulous main courses include roasted leg of lamb with flageolet beans in a thyme jus, pan-seared prime flatiron served with maître d'hôtel butter and French fries and roasted chicken with garlic-braised Swiss chard and pommes sarladaises. Salivating stuff! Open for breakfast Mon–Fri 7–10.30am and dinner 5pm–10pm; Sat and Sun for brunch 8am–2pm; nightly 5–10pm for dinner. $$–$$$

Pinot Brasserie

Venetian, 702 414 8888, www.venetian.com/Las-Vegas-Restaurants/Fine-Dining/Pinot-Brasserie/
Famous Los Angeles chef Joachim Splichal brings his Pinot concept to the city. The food is delightful and service is spot on. It looks out over the Venetian gardens and the Venezia Tower's pool area, giving the lunch crowd a lovely view. Open for lunch daily 11.30am–3pm; for dinner Sun–Thurs 5.30–10pm; Fri and Sat 5.30–10.30pm. $$

5

Postrio Bar & Grill

Venetian, 702 796 1110,
www.venetian.com/Las-Vegas-Restaurants/
Fine-Dining/Postrio/
Based on Wolfgang Puck's San Francisco
bistro, which serves up American food
with Asian and Mediterranean influences,
Postrio is looking fresher than ever after
a recent change of menu and décor.
House specialities include wood-baked
pizzas, handmade pastas and signature
dishes, lobster club sandwich with apple
wood smoked bacon and truffled potato
chips with blue cheese sauce. By the
way, Postrio has been named one of
the 10 best restaurants in the world by
Hotels magazine. Open Sun–Thurs 11am–
10.30pm, Fri and Sat 11am–11pm. **$$**

⚜ BRITTIP
If you love people-watching, then
make the most of Postrio's patio
dining area which gives a great view
of the beautiful people who flock to
the Venetian.

Sensi

Bellagio, 702 693 8865,
www.bellagio.com/restaurants/sensi.aspx
With carved stone, earthy hues, mirrored
chrome and waterfalls, Sensi offers a
delightful environment in which to discover
delicious dishes based around Italian,
Asian, seafood and American grill all
created by executive chef Martin Heierling,
using quality fresh ingredients. Open Mon–
Thurs 5–9.45pm; Fri–Sun 5–10.15pm. **$$**

Emeril's New Orleans Fish House

© MGM

Brazilian restaurant

Texas de Brazil

Town Square Las Vegas, 702 614 0080,
www.mytownsquarelasvegas.com and
www.texasdebrazil.com
Combining the bold flavours of southern
Brazil with the generous spirit of Texas,
Texas de Brazil at Town Square Las Vegas
marks the restaurant's 14th worldwide
location. Guests can enjoy tantalising cuts
of meats, appetisers, soups, a 60-item
salad bar with cheeses and vegetables and
a variety of sides. Texas de Brazil offers
guests a truly unique Brazilian experience,
complete with sword carrying gauchos
(a.k.a. Brazilian cowboys), who roam the
dining area serving various delectable
cuts and types of meat. Complementing
the meal, Texas de Brazil also offers an
extensive wine list, signature cocktails,
an assortment of desserts and hand-rolled
cigars. Open for lunch and dinner. **$**

Cajun/Creole restaurants

Big Al's Oyster Bar

New Orleans Hotel, 702 365 7111,
www.orleanscasino.com
Get a flavour of New Orleans-style dining
with this Cajun/Creole restaurant with
a Bayou oyster bar. Opt for oysters and
clams on the half-shell with various oyster
shooters from the bar, or choose from
a range of southern specials including
gumbo, Jambalaya pasta, steamed clams,
bouillabaisse and Voodoo mussels. Open
Sun–Thurs 11am–10pm; Fri and Sat 11am–
midnight. **$**

Big Mama's Soul Food Kitchen

2230 West Bonanza, 702 597 1616,
www.bigmamaslasvegas.com
Good, honest food at rock-bottom prices.
Known for its gumbo, fried catfish and
barbecue dishes. For a slice of real New
Orleans food, try a piece of pecan pie.
Open Mon–Sat 11am–9pm; Sun
12 noon–8pm. **$**

Emeril's New Orleans Fish House

MGM Grand, 702 891 7374,
www.mgmgrand.com/dining
A real must-visit restaurant if you want to
experience celebrity chef Emeril Lagasse's
New Orleans blend of modern Cajun/

Creole cooking. Tuck into seared Atlantic salmon served on a wild mushroom potato hash with herb meat juices and a spicy onion crust or grilled fillet of beef with Creole oyster dressing and homemade hollandaise sauce. Open daily lunch 11.30am–2.30pm, dinner 5pm–10pm. Next door is the seafood bar, a walk-up style of eatery featuring fresh shellfish and seafood specials. **$$**

VooDoo Steak

Rio All-Suite Hotel, 702 777 7923, www.riolasvegas.com
Premium quality beef with a French-Creole flair in an elegant New Orleans setting, and the view of the Strip is one of the best in town. Specials include Bayou seafood platter for starters, Ménage à trois of filet mignon, lobster and prawns for main course and bananas Foster for dessert. Open 5–11pm. Lounge 7pm–3am. **$$**

Caribbean restaurant

Florida Cafe

Howard Johnson Hotel, 1401 Las Vegas Boulevard South, 702 385 3013, www.floridacafecuban.com
Native Cuban chef Sergio Perez makes a fantastic Cuban sandwich and Cuban coffee and, of course, authentic Mojito, at this Cuban Bar and Grill in downtown, near the Fremont Street Experience. The walls are a showcase for local Cuban art. Open daily 7am–10pm. **$**

Caviar restaurants

The Petrossian Bar

Bellagio, 702 693 7111, www.bellagio.com
A lavish bar next to the resort's dramatic entrance with its walkway overhung by beautiful cypress trees. It specialises in everything from afternoon tea to caviar, Champagne and smoked salmon. Open Sun–Thurs midday–midnight; Fri and Sat midday–1am. **$$$**

Red Square

Mandalay Bay, 702 632 7407, www.mandalaybay.com/dining/ signature-restaurants/red-square.aspx
Check out the extensive caviar selection or try out the menu of updated Russian classics at the frozen ice bar, where you can choose from a selection of more than 100 frozen vodkas and infusions, Martinis and Russian-inspired cocktails. Open Sun–Thurs 4pm–1am; Fri and Sat 4pm–2am. **$$$**

Chinese restaurants

Beijing Noodle No. 9

Caesars Palace, 877 346 4642, www.caesarspalaace.com
Beijing Noodle No.9 has a watery theme with a large, salt-water aquarium at the entrance to reflect the waters of its cuisine – from the bustling streets of Shanghai, Hong Kong and Beijing. Open daily 11am–10.30pm. **$**

Cathay House

The Palms, 702 990 8888, www.palms.com
The second Las Vegas location, Cathay House at the Palms offers authentic and reasonably priced Chinese and dim sum. Delicious and healthy favourites include orange chicken, lettuce wraps and beef broccoli to jelly fish and salt and pepper pork chops washed down with hot teas – jasmine, pur erh, oolong and chrysanthemum – or a bottle of Tsingtao beer. Open Sun–Wed 10am–2am, Thurs–Sat 10am–4am. **$$**

Fin

Mirage, 866 339 4566, www.mirage.com
Sophisticated contemporary Chinese cuisine tempered with an eclectic blend of international dishes. Prix-fixe menu $49.99. Open Thurs–Mon 5–11pm. **$$**

Jasmine

Bellagio, 702 693 8865, www.bellagio.com
Chef Philip Lo, an originator of nouvelle Hong Kong cuisine, creates contemporary and classic Cantonese, Szechuan and Hunan dishes in a delightfully romantic setting overlooking the Bellagio lake and gardens. Dishes include Maine lobster dumplings with ginger sauce, minced squab in lettuce petals, crystal Florida stone crab claws, garlic beef tenderloin and imperial Peking duck. Open daily 5.30–10pm. **$$**

Lillie's Asian Cuisine

Golden Nugget Hotel, 129 Fremont Street, 702 385 7111, www.goldennugget.com/LasVegas
Provides downtown gamblers with delicious and exotic Cantonese dishes in a serene eastern setting with great service. The Great Combination Plate is a favourite starter, before moving on to black pepper steak,

5

Entertainment dining

Dining and entertainment go hand-in-hand at several locations throughout southern Nevada. Dinner theatre options include the *Tournament of Kings* at Excalibur where guests are transported to the feasts of the Renaissance while watching a knightly battle. If you're in the mood for love, how about *Tony 'n' Tina's Wedding* at Planet Hollywood? Be a special guest of Anthony Nunzio, Jr. and Valentina Lynne Vitale, an Italian–American couple who come from two slightly dysfunctional families. The wedding is complete with drunken guests, a pregnant maid-of-honour, an impromptu 'YMCA' dance and, of course, family bickering. Guests can either participate in the wedding with actors who never step out of character or they can simply watch the family drama unfold!

stir-fried shrimp or lemon chicken. Open daily 5pm–midnight. **$**

Wing Lei

Wynn Las Vegas, 702 248 3463, www.wynnlasvegas.com
This Asian delight is an elegantly casual Chinese restaurant with a dramatic yet sumptuous décor that owes much to the colour schemes of French-influenced Shanghai. Executive chef Richard Chen oversees the masterful mix of refined Cantonese, Shanghai and Szechuan cooking styles that feature wok-fried Szechuan Kobe beef, Peking duck for two (served tableside), Mongolian lamb and beef chow fun with abalone fried rice. Open nightly 5.30–10pm. **$$**

Farm-to-table restaurant

Sage

Aria Resort & Casino, 877 230 2742, www.arialasvegas
His first restaurant outside of Chicago, chef Shawn McClain – named Best Chef Midwest by the James Beard Foundation – spotlights farm-to-table produce, artisan meats and sustainable seafood. Designed by Jacques Garcia Decoration, the restaurant will envelop guests in a sophisticated yet comfortable atmosphere. Open Mon–Sat 5pm–11pm, closed Sun. **$$**

French restaurants

Alizé

The Palms, 702 951 7000, www.andrelv.com/alize
Las Vegas's very own celebrity chef and restaurateur André Rochat, who also owns his own restaurant called André's, has created a gourmet dining experience at the top of the very trendy Palms hotel. Breathtaking views accompany dishes such as sautéed Muscovy duck breast and market-fresh seafood. This is a top-of-the-pile dining experience, which includes the classic French sorbet between courses for cleansing the palate, a cheese trolley and an extensive wine list. Open nightly from 5.30pm–late. **$$–$$$**

André's

Monte Carlo, 702 798 7151, www.andrelv.com/montecarlo
André's has been serving up delicious gourmet food to locals and tourists alike for nearly 2 decades and although his original restaurant has now closed, it has found a new, sexy, urban and luxurious home, in the Monte Carlo on the Strip. The menu changes all the time, but mouth-watering offerings include chartreuse of Muscovy duck, stewed in Merlot with portabello mushrooms and spring vegetables, sautéed prime fillet of beef with green peppercorn and cognac cream sauce, baked zucchini, gratin dauphinoise and baby carrots anglaise and Maine lobster. Open Tues–Sun from 5.30pm. **$$$**

Eiffel Tower Restaurant

Paris, 702 948 6937, www.parislasvegas.com
The signature dining experience of this playful resort hotel is set 17 storeys up on the Eiffel Tower replica and has stunning views of Las Vegas's glittering golden mile. The softly lit ambience includes a romantic piano bar where you can enjoy a glass of Champagne or an entire meal while absorbing the views, or try the full gourmet experience in the restaurant owned by celebrity chef Jean Joho. Open for lunch daily 11.30am–2.30pm; for dinner Sun–Thurs 5–10.15pm, Fri and Sat 5–10.45pm. **$$$**

Fleur

Mandalay Bay, 702 632 9400,
www.mandalaybay.com/dining/ signature-
restaurants/fleur.aspx
A beautiful offering at the Mandalay Bay
gives Hubert Keller the chance to show off
his signature French cuisine in Las Vegas.
Starters include ocean baeckeoffe with
Maine lobster, crab cake, lobster bisque,
leeks and wild mushrooms and smoked
salmon ravioli with guacamole. Mains
include slow-roasted Alaskan king salmon
with hazelnut crust, leeks, duck comfit and
black Perigord truffle vinaigrette, roasted
sea bass with chicken jus flavoured with
passion fruit and filet mignon with braised
oxtail tortellini. Open daily 11am–
10.30pm. $$$

Joël Robuchon at the Mansion

MGM Grand, 702 891 7925,
www.mgmgrand.com/dining
Named France's Chef of the Century, and
the first and only chef to win 3 consecutive
Michelin stars, Joël Robuchon has been
lured to the MGM Grand, providing a
counter service setting in which you can
watch your dinner being prepared before
your eyes. Tapas and entrées include
fresh tomato and king crab, asparagus
with Oscetra caviar, fresh scallop with
lemon and seaweed butter, pan-fried sea
bass with lemongrass foam and stewed
baby leeks and sautéed veal chop with
vegetable taglierini flavoured with pesto.
Open Sun–Thurs 5.30–10pm; Fri and Sat
5.30–10.30pm. $$$

Le Cirque

Bellagio, 702 693 8865, www.bellagio.com
Elizabeth Blau, who had been with
the Maccioni family's famous flagship
restaurant in New York for more than a
decade, re-created its gourmet French
dishes with great aplomb here before
moving on. An AAA Five Diamond award
for nine consecutive years speaks for the
food, while the views of the Bellagio's
spectacular fountain show lend it more
than a touch of elegance. Open Tues–Sun
5.30–10pm. $$$

Les Artistes Steakhouse

Paris, 702 862 5138,
www.parislasvegas.com
A wide choice of gourmet dishes include
the signature Scottish pheasant brushed
with tarragon mustard sauce and served
with red-bliss potatoes, and lime oil-

Restaurants with live music

Cabo Wabo Cantina: Miracle Mile Shops
at Planet Hollywood Resort & Casino (see
page 110)
Eiffel Tower Restaurant: Paris Resort (see
page 102)
Crossroads at House of Blues: Mandalay
Bay (see page 115)
Harley Davidson Café: Southern end of
Strip (see page 117)
Kahunaville: Treasure Island
(see page 105)
N9ne Steakhouse: The Palms
(see page 113)
Rí Rá Irish Pub: Mandalay Bay
(see page 105)
Tommy Rocker's Cantina & Grill: 4275
Dean Martin Drive (see page 98)
VooDoo Steak: Rio All-Suite Hotel (see
page 101)

brushed swordfish with basil garlic mashed
potatoes. Desserts include classics such as
crème brûlée and raspberry clafoutis. Open
nightly 5.30–10.30pm. $$$

Mon Ami Gabi

Paris, 702 944 4224,
www.parislasvegas.com
A Parisian-style café set in the Louvre
façade of the Paris hotel. It is on the
Strip and you can even opt to sit outside.
Open for breakfast 7–11am; for brunch
11am–3pm Sat and Sun; for lunch
11.30am–3.45pm Mon–Fri; for dinner
4–11pm Sun–Thurs, 4pm–midnight Fri and
Sat. $$

Pamplemousse

400 East Sahara Avenue, 702 733 2066,
www.pamplemousserestaurant.com
Like all the top French restaurants, this small
but elegant establishment can be pricey –
but it's worth it. House specialities include
roast duckling in red wine and banana rum
sauce and veal medallions in cream sauce,
plus a huge selection of fresh seafood
according to the season from mussels to
monkfish and salmon. Open daily 6–11pm.
$$–$$$

Restaurant Guy Savoy

Caesars Palace, 877 346 4642,
www.caesarspalace.com
The famous French restaurateur, Guy
Savoy, winner of 3 Michelin stars and

Chef of the Year, France in 2002, opened his first restaurant in America in Caesars Palace. Run by his son and protégé Franck Savoy, the new restaurant takes pride of place on the second floor of the hotel's Augustus Tower, offering delightful views of the Roman Plaza. Open Wed–Sun 5.30–10.30pm. **$$$**

✠ BRITTIP —————
As in every other American city, top-notch, gourmet restaurants have prices to match, particularly with bottles of wine that can easily cost $200 each, so take care when making your choice!

Stratta

Wynn Las Vegas, 702 248 3463,
www.wynnlasvegas.com
Chef Alessandro Stratta, winner of the James Beard Foundation's Best American Chef, South-west, brings a taste of the French Riviera to the desert oasis of Las Vegas although his restaurant is now run by his assistant executive chef, Joseph Leibowitz. And what better setting in which to tuck into roasted monkfish or Tuscan-style pork with stewed tomatoes than in the outdoor seating area? Hard to make a choice? Go for the 'tasting menu' and tuck into tiny courses of carpaccio of red prawns, sea scallops with white asparagus and foie gras ravioli. Open nightly 5.30–10.30pm. Starlight menu 10.30pm–6am. Sat–Sun lunch 12–3.30pm, lounge menu 3.30–5pm. **$$$**

Switch Steak

Encore Las Vegas, 702 248 3463,
www.wynnlasvegas.com
A surprise awaits at Switch as chef René Lenger's French-inspired seafood and steakhouse fare is served in a dramatic space with an ambience that shifts throughout the evening. Go see! Open Sun–Thurs 5.30–10.30pm; Fri–Sat 5.30–11pm. **$$**

Fusion restaurants

Little Buddha

The Palms, 702 942 7778,
www.littlebuddhalasvegas.com
Based on the award-winning Buddha Bar and restaurant in Paris, this stylish eatery serves up both Pacific Rim and Chinese dishes with a French twist. There are 3 dining areas, all decorated in an opulent

East-meets-West style, plus a sushi bar. Open Sun, Wed, Thurs 5.30–10.30pm; Fri and Sat until 11.30pm. **$$**

✠ BRITTIP —————
Little Buddha offers poolside dining during the summer season and is one of the best places in town to spot a celeb or two.

Mix

Mandalay Bay, 702 632 9500,
www.mandalaybay.com/dining/ signature-restaurants/mix.aspx
With its cutting-edge interior and fab views, Mix at the Mandalay Bay hotel is the perfect place to enjoy wonderful fusion cuisine. Think roasted Maine lobster, curried, with coconut basmati rice, bison tenderloin with sauce au poivre, seared rare tuna with prosciutto shavings and Colorado rack of lamb with Mediterranean condiment. Open 6–11pm. **$$**

Roy's

620 East Flamingo Road, 702 691 2053,
www.roysrestaurant.com
Hawaiian fusion is the name of the game in a restaurant that serves up European-style dishes with an Asian and Pacific flavour. Prix-fixe menu. Open Mon–Thurs 5.30–9.30pm; Fri 5.30–10pm and Sat 5–10pm, Sun 5–9.30pm. **$**

Twist

Mandarin Oriental, Las Vegas, 1-888 881 9367, www.mandarinoriental.com/lasvegas/ dining
Situated on the 23rd floor. Twist is the only restaurant in the US where you can experience the cuisine of 3-star Michelin chef Pierre Gagnaire, who is celebrated as a pioneer of the fusion movement. Here he introduces another entirely new concept combining flavours and textures in the most unexpected way. Each dish delights the senses with the familiarity of classic French cuisine and the modern twist. The interior is designed by Adam D. Tihany. It is a match for the Las Vegas skyline with 300 illuminated gold globes seeming to float across the ceiling and a dramatic suspended wine loft, reached by a glass staircase. Platforms throughout the restaurant ensure each guest enjoys these rare views of the glittering city heights through 20ft/6m high windows. Open Tues–Thurs 6–10pm; Fri–Sat 6–10.30pm. **$$$**

Greek restaurant

Estiatorio Mills

**The Cosmopolitan, 877 893 2003,
www.cosmopolitanlasvegas.com**
The only Greek restaurant on the Strip, is
also one of North America's finest with
restaurateur Costas Spiliadis at the helm.
Enjoy fresh seafood, Greek-style on the
terrace overlooking the Vegas Skyline or
inside the glass-enclosed restaurant with
elegant lanterns. Open daily lunch Sun–Sat
noon–2.30pm; dinner Sun–Thurs 5.30–
11pm; Fri–Sat 5.30pm–midnight.

Hawaiian restaurant

Kahunaville

**Treasure Island, 702 894 7390,
www.kahunaville.com**
A lively (too much so for some) tropical
restaurant setting complete with tiki torches
and plants, this features Hawaiian dishes
such as teriyaki ginger steak, Hawaiian
pork tenderloin and coconut shrimp. It
also doubles as a supper club with live
entertainment and a 'Rock the Mic' live
karaoke every Thurs, Fri and Sat, and there
is a great choice of margaritas, coladas,
beers and wine. Open daily 7am–10pm.
The bar is open 11am–3am. **$**

Indian restaurant

Gaylord India Restaurant

**Rio All-Suite Hotel, 1-800 752 9746,
www.riolasvegas.com**
A romantic setting with authentic Indian
artefacts in which to enjoy tandoori and
Mughlai-style dishes from the creators of the
award-winning San Francisco restaurant.
One of its main features is the Combination
Dinners, in which you can choose different
starters and entrées for an all-inclusive
price. Open daily 11.30am–2.30pm and
5–10.30pm. **$$**

Irish restaurants

Nine Fine Irishmen

**New York-New York, 702 740 6463,
www.ninefineirishmen.com**
In a town where everything is copied,
it was only a matter of time before an
'authentic' Irish pub with drink, food, music
and entertainment opened its doors. And
where better than the New York-New York
hotel, which is evocative of the city that is
home to so many Irish-Americans. Dishes
have been created by 9 of Ireland's top
chefs, though the name is based on the
lives of 9 Irishmen from the 19th century.
Open daily 11am–11pm. **$–$$**

Rí Rá Irish Pub

**Mandalay Bay, 702 632 7771,
www.mandalaybay.com/ things-to-do/the-
shoppes-at-mandalay-place/ri-ra.aspx**
The newest Irish pub on the Strip, Rí Rá –
which means 'celebration and good fun'
– at The Shoppes at Mandalay Place serves
traditional Irish fare such as Irish potato
cakes and beef and Guinness stew in an
olde worlde 19th-century pub atmosphere,
with live Irish music 7 nights a week.
Authentic artefacts restored in Wicklow
include a 8ft/2.4m, 500lb/227kg carved
plaster statue of St Patrick dating back to
1850. Open Mon–Thurs 11am–3am, Fri
11am–4am, Sat 9am–4am, Sun 9am–3am.
$$

Italian restaurants

B&B Ristorante

**Restaurant Row, Grand Canal Shoppes, The
Venetian, 702 266 9977,
www.venetian.com/Las-Vegas-Restaurants/
Fine-Dining/BandBRistorante/**
Celebrity chef Mario Batali, winner of the
2005 James Beard Foundation Chef of the
Year Award and the genius behind several
intensely popular New York restaurants
brings his genius to The Venetian along
with friend and expert wine maker Joseph
Bastianich. It is wine and Italian cooking
that 'captures the soul of an Italian
grandmother dancing the tango with pop
rock hipsters'. Open daily 5–11pm. **$$$**

Twist

© CityCenter

5

Bargain specials

Las Vegas abounds in great food deals, especially at downtown casinos and those off-Strip casinos that cater to local gamblers. Here are just a few:
Ellis Island Casino (in the Café): $7.99 Steak Dinner includes a 10-ounce sirloin steak, baked potato, bread, green beans and a beer. Look for 2-for-1 coupons you can use to buy 2 of these dinners for only $7.99. You have to ask for this special, as it is not on the menu (although there are notices at the blackjack tables). Its graveyard/breakfast special is New York steak and eggs for $3.45, available 11pm–11am.
Hard Rock Hotel: $7.77 Gamblers Special at Mr Lucky's offers steak, three grilled shrimp, a choice of potato or broccoli and a salad. It's not on the menu – you'll have to ask your server but is available 24/7.
California Casino: $4.75 for a Loco Moco (a bowl of rice topped with a hamburger patty, fried egg and drenched in brown gravy) is just one of the many specials at Aloha Specialties. Available Sun–Thurs 9am–9pm; Fri–Sat, 9am–10pm.
Tony Roma's in Fremont: $11.99 Steak and Lobster Special daily, 9pm–11pm.
Golden Gate: $1.99-cent Shrimp Cocktail at Du-Par's Deli gives you a mass of cold-water bay shrimp served in a large tulip glass with a side of homemade cocktail sauce. It also serves a $4.99 New York steak and eggs from midnight–2am.

Bartolotta Ristorante di Mare

Wynn Las Vegas, 702 248 3463,
www.wynnlasvegas.com
Paul Bartolotta, winner of the James Beard Foundation's Best American Chef Midwest award, has fresh seafood flown in daily from fish markets in Europe for his casual yet vibrant restaurant that offers outdoor seating near the lake and gardens. Alongside the signature seafood dishes are classic Italian specialities. Open nightly 5.30–10pm. **$$**

Battista's Hole in the Wall

4041 Audrie Lane, 702 732 1424,
www.battistaslasvegas.com
This old Vegas landmark serves Italian fare in a friendly atmosphere that makes it great for locals and tourists alike. Open for dinner only 5–10.30pm. **$$**

California Pizza Kitchen

Mirage Hotel 702 791 7111 and Town Square Las Vegas 702 896 5154
www.cpk.com
Part of a growing national chain that highlights 'California Fusion' food and serves mostly delicious pizzas with mouth-watering selections of fresh ingredients. Think chocolate pizza and Thai chicken pizza. Open Sun–Thurs 11am–midnight; Fri and Sat 11am–2am. **$**

Canaletto

Restaurant Row, Grand Canal Shoppes, the Venetian, 702 733 0070,
www.venetian.com/Las-Vegas-Restaurants/Fine-Dining/Canaletto/
Based on a concept by Il Fornaio's Larry Mindel, classics include homemade ravioli filled with fresh Maine lobster in a lobster cream sauce topped with shrimp, all overlooking the Grand Canal with gondolas passing by! Open Sun–Thurs 11.30am–11pm; Fri and Sat until midnight. **$$**

Casa Nicola

Las Vegas Hilton, 702 732 5755,
www.lvhilton.com/Hotel/dining
Specialises in fine northern Italian specialities in a beautiful setting. The exhibition kitchen gives customers the chance to watch chefs preparing the fresh pastas, pastries and sauces. Open 5.30–10.30pm. Note that the name of the hotel is likely to change by 2012. **$$**

Chicago Joe's

820 South 4th Street, 702 382 5637,
www.chicagojoesrestaurant.com
Chicago Joe's is an ageless Las Vegas standard and is famous for its Italian sauces. Try the cream garlic dressing with one of the many delicious salads, Mexican Gulf shrimp and Maine lobster. Open Tues–Fri 11am–10pm; Sat 5–10pm. **$**

Il Fornaio

New York-New York, 702 650 6403,
www.ilfornaio.com
A superb re-creation of an Italian restaurant from New York's Little Italy neighbourhood, here you'll find classic Italian cuisine and signature breads, rolls and pastries from the in-house bakery. By the way, most of the waiters migrated to Las Vegas from New York when the hotel opened, so the accents are real! Open Sun–Thurs 7.30am–midnight. **$$**

Wine and dine

If you like fine wines, Las Vegas with its 17 Master Sommeliers – more than any city in the country – is the place to come. Here are just a few highlights of where to find the best cellars in town.

Bellagio has established the record for the most Master Sommeliers at a single property anywhere in the world. The resort currently has a team of 17 Sommeliers, including 3 Master Sommeliers – Robert Bigelow, the property's director of wine, Robert Smith of Picasso, Jason Smith of Michael Mina. Additional on-property Master Sommeliers include William Sherer at Aureole (Mandalay Bay), Paolo Barbieri at Stratta (Wynn Las Vegas), Luis DeSantos at Spago (Forum Shops at Caesars), Kevin Vogt at Delmonico Steakhouse (The Venetian) and Thomas Burke at Red Rock Resort Spa Casino.

Master Sommelier Steven Geddes began his career at **Alizé** at The Palms under the tutelage of the restaurant's owner, André Rochat. Geddes began working for Rochat in 1977 as a busboy. After Geddes expressed his interest in wine, Rochat began mentoring him. He went on to earn the title of Master Sommelier at the age of 29, the youngest to earn the title at the time. Alizé now boasts a 65-page wine list with more than 1,000 varietals and 5,000 bottles.

In 1999, chef Charlie Palmer tapped Geddes to serve as wine director for his $11m restaurant, **Aureole** at Mandalay Bay. There, Geddes built an impressive list of fine wines backed by an inventory of more than 55,000 bottles. Today, many of those bottles are innovatively displayed in a 4-storey, $1.5m *Mission: Impossible*-inspired wine tower. Guests select their wines from a wine list contained in a tablet PC. Wine angels, who are trained acrobats and gymnasts, scale the tower with the aid of cables to retrieve each bottle from its carefully controlled 55-degree environment. The most expensive bottle in Aureole's collection is a $42,000 bottle of 1900 Petrus.

At **Wynn Las Vegas**, the property's wine director Danielle Price manages the wine lists for 9 fine dining and 6 casual restaurants, in-room dining, banquets, nightclub, and all lounges and bars. The property has an inventory of more than 100,000 bottles, including a $50,000, 6-litre 1990 Cristal Champagne. In addition, she supervises her team of 17 on-property sommeliers.

The Wine Cellar and Tasting Room at The Rio is home to an impressive public wine collection featuring 50,000 bottles valued at more than $10m. Amongst the bottles lies an 1800 Madeira from the cellar of Thomas Jefferson. The Cellar also has rare 'cult' wines and collectible labels from around the globe.

Napoleon's Champagne Bar at Paris Las Vegas ensures the French are known for more than just fine wine. Napoleon's boasts a selection of more than 100 Champagnes and sparkling wines by the bottle and by the glass. Guests can sip everything from Moët to Dom Perignon.

Onda Wine and Cheese Lounge at The Mirage is an Italian-inspired lounge where guests can enjoy a selection of wines by purchasing a tasting flute or individual glasses. A selection of artisan cheeses and meats complements each tasting and all wines are available for purchase.

Lupo

Mandalay Bay, 702 632 7410,
www.mandalaybay.com/dining/signature-restaurants/lupo-by-wolfgang-puck.aspx
Another of celebrity chef Wolfgang Puck's 6 eating outlets in Las Vegas, this one is pure Italian with traditional recipes cooked in pizza ovens and wood-burning rotisseries. The interior was designed by Adam Tihany, who has re-created a typical small, secluded piazza in Milan with views of pasta, meats and bakery production areas. Open Sun–Thurs 5–10pm; Fri and Sat 5–11pm. **$$**

Marinelli's

The M Resort, 702 797 1000,
www.themresort.com
Authentic regional Italian cuisine in an intimate setting. Menu selections include risottos, handmade pastas, seafood specialities, steaks, chops and veal dishes, as well as selections from the Marnell family (M Resort owners) recipe book and wines from their private label. Outdoor terraces overlook the adjacent steakhouse, Villaggio Del Sole events piazza and the Strip, Open daily 4–10pm. **$$**

Martorano's

Rio All-Suite Hotel, 3700 West Flamingo Road, 702 777 7740, www.riolasvegas.com
Martorano's makes an excellent choice for those in search of a delicious Italian meal and this place caters for the cast of *The Sopranos*! Don't miss the meatballs! Open Sun–Thurs 5.30–10pm; Fri–Sat 5.30–10.30pm. $$–$$$

Onda

Mirage, 866 339 4566, www.mirage.com/restaurants
Regional Italian and new American cuisine inspired by Todd English and served up in an elegant setting. All-you-can eat mussels Sun–Thurs 5–7pm for $20 per person. Open Thurs–Mon 5.30–10pm. $–$$$

Pizzeria Francesco's

Treasure Island, 702 894 7111, www.treasureisland.com
Filled with artwork by celebrities including crooner Tony Bennett, the menu here includes fresh pastas, antipasti, Mediterranean-style seafood and signature freshly baked breads. Open Sun–Thurs 11am–midnight; Fri and Sat 11am–1am (closed daily 11am–12pm). $

Scarpetta

Cosmopolitan, 877 893 2003, www.cosmopolitanlasvegas.com
Sophisticated Italian with a soulful menu of seasonally inspired Italian dishes. Open Sun–Sat 5.30–11pm. $$$$

Sergio's Italian Gardens

1955 East Tropicana Avenue, 702 739 1544, www.sergiosrestaurant.com
Consistently rated as one of the best Italian restaurants in town, Sergio's has a delightful garden with Roman columns. Dishes include calamari, Belgium endive salad, sautéed veal and filet mignon Rossini. Open Mon–Fri 11.30am–4pm, and nightly 5.30–11pm. $$

Sinatra

Encore Las Vegas, 702 248 3463, www.wynnlasvegas.com
Sinatra is a salute to Ol' Blue Eyes. Chef Theo Schoenegger's modern Italian cuisine riffs with Sinatra tunes as guests revisit the entertainer's legendary charisma. A must for Sinatra buffs.
Open nightly 5.30–10pm. $$

Sirio

Aria Resort & Casino, 877 239 2742, www.arialasvegas/dining/sirio-ristorante.aspx
Chef Sirio Maccioni serves a menu of Italian favorites such as veal Milanese, osso buco and authentic pasta dishes. Guests enjoy traditional Italian cocktails and one of Las Vegas's largest selections of Italian vintages at a wide array of price points. Designed by long-time Maccioni collaborator Adam Tihany, Sirio channels old-time Italy with its fantastical, Fellini-esque décor. Opening hours daily 5–10.30pm. $$

Valentino

The Venetian, 702 414 3000. www.venetian.com
A remarkable setting for award-winning celebrity restauranteur Piero Selvaggio to showcase the finest Italian cuisine. Seasonal menu with expert staff offering contemporary Italian cuisine that revisits and reinvigorates traditional recipes. Great wine list. Open 5.30–10pm. $$$$

Japanese restaurants

BARMASA

Aria Resort & Casino, 877 230 2742, www.arialasvegas/dining/barmasa.aspx
Making his Las Vegas debut, chef Masayoshi Takayama's concept comprises 2 distinct dining experiences. The restaurant's casual airy dining space features an à la carte menu of modern Japanese cuisine. Shaboo, an intimate and exclusive venue within BARMASA, offers the Japanese hot pot Shabu Shabu at weekends. Each table features its own induction cooking element to create the

Sirio

© CityCenter

ultimate dining experience. The restaurant, designed in collaboration with Richard Bloch, is refined and sleek, yet awe-inspiring with ceilings that soar to 35ft/11m. Open Wed–Sun 5–11pm. Closed Mon–Tues. Shaboo Fri–Sat 5–9pm. **$$**

Benihana

Las Vegas Hilton, 702 732 5755, www.lasvegashilton.com
Japanese fantasyland in an enchanting garden setting complete with thunder and lightning storms, lush flowers, flowing ponds and an authentic torii arch. There are 2 restaurants to choose from – the Hibachi where skilled chefs chop, slice and grill your food tableside and the Seafood Grille, where delicious delicacies are the order of the day. You can enjoy drinks and Oriental hors d'oeuvres in the Kabuki Lounge while your table is prepared. Open daily 5.30–10.30pm. **$$$**

BRITTIP
If you want an early evening appetiser, head for the Hamada's cocktail lounge, where you can get little plates of deep-fried tempura and sushi with your drinks.

Hyakumi

Caesars Palace, 877 346 4642, www.caesarspalace.com
Fresh sushi by masterchefs along with teppanyaki-style cooking and à la carte dishes including noodles – all served at traditional teppan tables. Open for lunch daily 11am–3.30pm; for dinner daily 5–11pm. **$$$**

MOzen Bistro

Mandarin Oriental, Las Vegas, 1-888 861 9367, www.mandarinoriental.com/lasvegas/dining
This all-day dining restaurant on the 3rd floor is a kitchen theatre of Pan-Asian and international cuisine with an exhibition noodle bar, rotisserie and grill. A clean, contemporary feel is complemented by deeply comfortable leather banquettes. Geometry and art introduce some striking creativity, with 3 spectacular circular steel and glass rod chandeliers suspended above round tables. Open daily breakfast 6.30–11.30am; lunch and light fare 12–5pm; dinner 6–10pm; brunch on Sundays. **$$**

Nobu

Hard Rock Hotel, 702 693 5090, www.hardrockhotel.com
Chef Nobu Matsuhisa's ground-breaking temple of Japanese cuisine with Peruvian influences has already set unmatched standards of excellence in Los Angeles, New York and London. Nobu Las Vegas has been hugely successful for the Hard Rock Hotel. Dishes include squid pasta, miso-infused cod and creamy, spicy, cracked crab. Open daily 6–11pm. **$$$**

Shibuya

MGM Grand, 702 891 3001, www.mgmgrand.com/dining
An expansive and spectacular environment forms the perfect backdrop to this stylish offering, which takes its name from the Tokyo district of Shibuya. Featuring freshly prepared ingredients and exquisite sushi, the restaurant also boasts one of the widest

5

Shibuya

© MGM

Lakeside dining

Lago Buffet: Caesars Palace
(see page 120)
Jasmine: Bellagio (see page 101)
Le Cirque: Bellagio (see page 103)
Olives: Bellagio (see below)
SW Steakhouse: Wynn Las Vegas
(see page 114)

sake selections available anywhere in
America. Open Sun–Thurs 5–10pm; Fri and
Sat 5–10.30pm. **$$–$$$**

Yellowtail Japanese Restaurant & Lounge

Bellagio, 702 693 8865, www.bellagio.com
Adventurous Japanese dining in a stylish
contemporary setting with an impressive
25-ft/8-m bronze wall-mounted installation
of the dorsal side of the yellowtail fish!
Award-winning chef Akira Back's menu
includes seasonal fish, sushi, sashimi,
tempura and hand rolls. Delicious! Open
Mon–Thurs 5–10pm; Fri and Sat 5–11pm.
$$

Mediterranean restaurants

Olives

Bellagio, 702 693 8865, www.bellagio.com
Todd and Olivia English bring their
famous Boston Olives to Las Vegas with
Mediterranean-style dishes in a lively café
setting. It serves pastas, steaks, rotisserie
dishes, brick oven pizzas and wines
recommended by Sommeliers. Open daily
11am–2.45pm and 5–10.30pm. **$$**

Picasso

Bellagio, 702 693 8865, www.bellagio.com
Julian Serrano, who dazzled diners at San
Francisco's Masa, brings his trademark
Spanish-tinged French cuisine to one
of the world's most opulent settings for
a restaurant – dine here and you'll be
surrounded by $52m worth of Picasso
originals and even some of the artist's
ceramics. The menu changes nightly
but usually includes Julian's foie gras in
Madeira sauce or warm lobster salad with
mangoes or potatoes. The views of the
Bellagio's dancing fountains finish off a
superb dining experience and you can be
confident of the food – it has received the
AAA Five Diamond Award eleven times.
Open Wed–Mon 6–9.30pm. **$$$**

Mexican restaurants

Blue Agave

The Palms, 702 951 7684,
www.thepalms.com
A fun, casual dining experience at the über-
trendy Palms hotel, named after the plant
that gives tequilas their flavour. The house
specialities are oysters, seafood cocktails
and pan roasts, plus a chilli bar with South
American favourites. Open 4pm–10pm;
Sunday brunch 10.30am–3pm. **$$$**

> **BRITTIP**
> For a real party atmosphere,
> head to the Blue Agave, where
> along with delicious Mexican-
> based cuisine, there is a range of 150
> tequilas and a whopping 350 different
> margaritas to choose from!

Border Grill

Mandalay Bay, 702 632 7403,
www.mandalaybay.com/dining/ signature-
restaurants/border-grill.aspx
Run by TV duo 'Too Hot Tamales', Mary
Sue Milliken and Susan Feniger, renowned
for their Border Grill in LA, their bold
and tasty Mexican dishes are served in a
vibrant beachside setting. Open Mon–Thurs
11.30am–10pm; Fri 11.30am–11pm; Sat
11am–11pm; Sun 11am–10pm. **$$**

Cabo Wabo Cantina

Miracle Mile Shops, Planet Hollywood
Resort & Casino, 702 866 0703,
www.miraclemileshopslv.com/dine.php
In autumn 2009, rock legend Sammy
Hagar opened his world-famous
Cabo Wabo Cantina. This 2-level,
15,000ft^2/1,394m^2 nightclub and
restaurant offers a blend of live music and
coastal Mexican food and a cocktail menu
with a heavy emphasis on tequila. Get the
slammers ready! Open daily 8am til late. **$**

Garduños

The Palms, 702 942 7777,
www.gardunosrestaurants.com and
www.palms.com
Authentic Mexican from this cantina chain.
Margaritas are also available. Go on
Sundays for its Margarita Brunch $16.99.
Open Mon 11am–9.30pm; Tues–Thurs
11am–10pm; Fri and Sat 11am–11pm;
Sun brunch 10.30am–3pm and 4–9pm. **$**

Gonzalez Y Gonzalez

**New York-New York, 702 740 6455,
www.nynyhotelcasino.com/restaurants**
A great spot to soak up the atmosphere
of the hotel's outdoor courtyard with
lanterns and Spanish piñatas, Gonzalez
Y Gonzalez serves authentic Mexican
cuisine at reasonable prices. Open daily
11am–1am. **$**

BRITTIP
The real secret of Gonzalez
Y Gonzalez is the long list of
margaritas, which can even be
served by the yard!

Isla Mexican Kitchen & Tequila Bar

**Treasure Island, 702 894 7111,
www.treasureisland.com**
Chef Richard Sandoval offers traditional
Mexican cuisine with a modern twist.
Innovations include the roving guacamole
cart armed and ready with freshly made
guacamoles. Dishes include grilled
Mexican spiced chicken breast with corn
dumplings, crispy red snapper with cactus
salad and Isla sirloin with mashed potatoes
and chimichurri sauce. Tacos, enchiladas,
tamales and burritos all get a modern twist,
with ingredients such as battered rock
shrimp and wild mushrooms. The Tequila
Bar features an impressive selection of
tequilas plus margaritas, sangrias and other
Mexican cocktail favourites. Open daily
4–11pm. The bar and lounge is open daily
11am–2am. **$$**

Pink Taco

**Hard Rock Hotel, 702 693 5000,
www.hardrockhotel.com**
A trendy restaurant offering celebrated
Californian chef Tacho Kneeland's fresh
and modern take on Mexican classics.
Choices include tamales nachos,
quesadillas, tacos and a whole range of
tequilas – served the traditional way, natch!
Open Mon–Thurs 7am–11pm; Fri–Sun
7am–3am. **$$**

Viva Mercado's

**3553 South Rainbow, 702 871 8826,
www.vivamercadoslv.com**
Regularly wins the local daily paper's poll
for best Mexican restaurant in town due to
its delicious food including chilli relleno,
carnitas and Mexican-style steak at great
prices. Open Sun–Thurs 11am–9.30pm; Fri
and Sat 11am–10pm. **$**

Private dining

If you want to impress, how about
booking a Krug Champagne Room at
Caesars Palace? The first of its kind in the
US, The Krug Room at Restaurant Guy
Savoy (702 731 7731, guysavoy.com)
offers private dining rooms for seasonal,
6-course pairing menus of decadent
cuisine served with a range of Krug
Champagnes including vintages. Cheque
books at the ready! **$$$**

BRITTIP
Be warned: although Las Vegas is
a 24-hour city, most of the top-
notch restaurants close as early as
10pm or 10.30pm.

Moroccan restaurants

Mamounia

**4632 South Maryland Parkway, 702 597
0092**
Delicious Moroccan dishes are served in a
simulated Middle Eastern desert tent setting
complete with low benches or pillows,
costumed waiters and belly dancers.
House specialities include all the Moroccan
classics such as hummus, kefta, tabbouleh,
briouats, cacic yoghurt dip, shish kebabs
and couscous. Great value. Open daily
5–11pm. **$$**

Marrakech Restaurant

**3900 Paradise Road, 702 737 5611,
www.marrakechvegas.com**
The oldest Moroccan restaurant in town
which takes the whole 'eating in the desert'
thing one stage further than Mamounia by
expecting diners to eat with their hands!
The house specialities include Moroccan-
style chicken in a light lemon sauce and
flambéed lamb brochette. Dinner features a
belly-dancing show. Open daily 5.30–
11pm. **$$**

Poolside dining

Caffe Nikki

**Tropicana Las Vegas, 702 739 3688,
www.nikkibeachlasvegas.com/cafe-nikki/**
Serving a blend of American cuisine
with unique global dishes from Nikki
Beach locations around the world, this
new restaurant is the ultimate in poolside

5

dining, especially in the evening, when entertainment includes mixes from the world's best DJs. Open for breakfast, lunch and dinner. **$$**

Seafood and steakhouses

American Fish

Aria Resort & Casino, 877 239 2742, www.arialasvegas/dining/american-fish.aspx
For his newest concept, James Beard award-winner chef Michael Mina draws inspiration from the bounty of American lakes, rivers and coasts to create a menu featuring refined American cuisine. Many products are purchased directly from fishermen, farmers and ranchers, allowing diners to enjoy unique regional dishes. The menu also will feature a wide array of well-sourced meats. Chris Sheffield of SLDesign, LLC, in collaboration with Mina, designed a room that resembles a traditional lodge, with masculine touches such as warm woods and leather accents. Open Tues–Sun 5–10.30pm. Closed Mon. **$$**

AquaKnox

Restaurant Row, Grand Canal Shoppes, the Venetian, 702 414 3772, www.Las-Vegas-Restaurants/Fine-Dining/Aquaknox/
Chef Tom Moloney, who honed his skills during 12 years with Wolfgang Puck, won Best New Restaurant in Vegas when his seafood extravaganza opened. Fresh seafood is flown in daily from around the world to provide a superb raw bar alongside wonderful dishes of filet mignon with truffle aioli and grilled lobster with herb butter. Favourites include the fresh stone crab claws from Florida Keys, sweet shrimp cocktail, Louisiana prawns, jumbo lump crab cocktail, dry-aged prime New

York steak, and oven-roasted guinea hen. Open daily 12am–3pm and Sun–Thurs 5.30–11pm; Fri and Sat 5.30–11.30pm. **$$–$$$**

Botero

Encore Las Vegas, 702 248 3463, www.wynnlasvegas.com
Diners can appreciate the art collection by Columbian artist Fernando Botero here while sampling Chef Mark LoRusso's modern cuisine, steaks and chops. It won an AAA Five Diamond Award in 2011. Open Sun–Thurs 6–10.30pm; Fri and Sat 6–11pm. **$$**

Búzio's Seafood Restaurant

Rio All-Suite Hotel, 702 777 7923, www.riolasvegas.com
Probably one of the best seafood restaurants in town with an extraordinary selection of seafood dishes. This is another fine restaurant based at the Rio All-Suite Hotel and well deserves its appearance in the annual Zagat survey of top restaurants in Las Vegas. Open Sun–Thurs 5–10.30pm, Fri–Sat 5–11pm. **$$**

Craftsteak

MGM Grand, 702 891 7318, www.mgmgrand.com/dining
Craftsteak was created by award-winning chef Tom Colicchio, founder of the critically acclaimed Craft restaurant in New York. The philosophy is simple: use the finest available produce and cook in such a way as to allow the flavours of the ingredients to shine through. Open Sun–Thurs 5.30–10pm; Fri and Sat 5.30–10.30pm. **$$$**

Delmonico Steakhouse

Restaurant Row, Grand Canal Shoppes at the Venetian, 702 414 3737, www.venetian.com/Las-Vegas-Restaurants/Fine-Dining/Delmonico-Steakhouse/
Emeril Lagasse's second outlet in Las Vegas features the food surprises that have made him famous. It seems to be on everybody's list of top steakhouses in the USA. Open Mon–Sat 11.30am–1.45pm, Sun–Thurs 5–10pm, Fri–Sat 5–10.30pm. **$$$**

Hugo's Cellar

Four Queen's, 202 Fremont Street, Downtown, 702 385 4011, www.hugoscellar.com
Very old school and a popular choice with locals and visitors alike, so book ahead to get a table. Famous for its excellent wine list. Open daily 5.30–11pm. **$$**

Craftsteak

© MGM

Michael Mina at the Bellagio

Jean-Georges Steakhouse

Aria Resort & Casino, 877 239 2742, www.arialasvegas/dining/jean-georges.aspx
At Aria, chef Jean-Georges Vongerichten eschews tradition by melding beloved steakhouse touches with a decidedly contemporary experience. The menu highlights the best ingredients and preparations, paying particular attention to an innovative array of side dishes and sauces. Designed by Dupoux Design, the restaurant's high-octane lounge and extensive bar program focuses on classic cocktails. Open daily 5–10.30pm. **$$**

Michael Mina

Bellagio, 702 693 8865, www.bellagio.com
Celebrity chef Michael Mina has replaced the top-notch Aqua with an even more amazing restaurant that has been drawing ecstatic plaudits for its innovative yet gourmet seafood dishes. Blending fresh ingredients from California, Britain and the Mediterranean, the incredible line-up of tastebud-tickling starters includes savoury black mussel soufflé with saffron Chardonnay cream, seared sea scallops and foie gras with a rhubarb-lime compote and Thai coconut soup with Dungeness crab. First courses include the tempura langoustine with young ginger, pickled fennel, saffron aioli, green papaya and mango. Entrées include Angus beef filet mignon, tapioca-crusted black bass with toasted almonds and Chile garlic vinaigrette, Maine lobster pot pie and roasted whole Hudson Valley foie gras.

Eat it and weep with sheer joy. Open daily 5.30–10pm. **$$–$$$**

N9ne Steakhouse

The Palms, 702 933 9900, http://n9negroup.com and www.palms.com
Another stylish offering from The Palms, the Chicago-style prime-aged steaks and chops are served in a sleek setting. Aside from the restaurant, a Champagne caviar bar sits amid comfy suede-covered booths from where you can gaze at the changing colours of the ceiling or try to spot the celebs arriving at the glass-enclosed private dining room. Open Sun–Thurs 6–10pm; Fri and Sat 6–11 pm. **$$**

Palm Restaurant

Forum Shops at Caesars Palace, 702 732 7256, www.thepalm.com/Las-Vegas
Following on from the success of the New York restaurant, the Las Vegas version also appears in the Zagat Top 40. Famous for crab cakes, lobster, prime rib and the house speciality, charcoal-burnt steak. Open daily 11.30am–11pm. **$$**

Prime Steakhouse

Bellagio, 702 693 7223, www.bellagio.com
Award-winning chef Jean-Georges Vongerichten uses only the highest-quality meats, seafood and chops to create a fine dining experience in a chocolate brown and delicate Tiffany blue interior. Open daily 5–10pm. **$$**

5

High Tea

Try an afternoon straight out of a Jane Austen novel at Strip hotels that offer English-style High Tea. Sit on brocade sofas or velvet high-back chairs in **The Petrossian Bar** at Bellagio, while you sip tea and nibble on open-faced English sandwiches, pastries and scones with Devonshire cream and Baxters preserves daily 2–4pm from $35 each.

At the south end of the Strip, delight in scones, sandwiches and pastries for English afternoon tea on the **Verandah** at the elegant Four Seasons Mon–Thurs 3–4pm from $30 ($38 with a glass of Premier Brut Champagne). For another elegant affair, with a stunning view, try Afternoon Tea 2.30–5pm at the **Tea Lounge** with delectable sandwiches and scones accompanied by a glass of Veuve Clicquot for $58 at The Mandarin Oriental.

Reserve in advance!

rm Seafood

Mandalay Bay, 702 632 9300, www.mandalaybay.com/dining/ signature-restaurants/rick-moonens-rm-seafood.aspx
With two restaurants in one, New York chef Rick Moonen offers the R Bar Café on the ground floor and the gourmet Restaurant rm upstairs. Delicious offerings include abalone in butter with Pacific sturgeon caviar, mussel soufflé with green curry sauce, halibut with foie gras and melted leeks in a red wine emulsion, and butter-poached lobster with corn chowder. There is also a 6-course tasting menu that will set you back just over $100. Open downstairs 11.30am–11pm; upstairs 5.30–10.30pm. $$–$$$

Ruth's Chris Steakhouse

3900 Paradise Road, 702 791 7011 and 4561 West Flamingo Road, 702 248 7011, www.ruthschris.com
A chain of franchised steakhouses that started in New Orleans, these places have a reputation for serving prime meat on a sizzling-hot platter with butter. Other offerings include lamb, chicken and fish with delicious vegetables from sautéed mushrooms to creamed spinach. Open daily 4.30–10.30pm. $$

Smith & Wollensky

3767 The Strip opposite Citycenter, 702 862 4100, www.smithandwollensky.com
Alan Stillman's New York steakhouse group's $10m free-standing, 3-storey restaurant seats up to 600 diners in a catacomb-like series of rooms, niches and chambers. Open Sun–Thurs 5–10pm; Fri and Sat 5–10.30pm. $$

The Steak House

Circus Circus, 702 794 3767, www.circuscircus.com/dining
An exception to every other rule at the family-friendly Circus Circus, this is definitely adult-friendly (the kids are running around the lobby outside). Zagat named it Top Steak House in Vegas in 2011 and it serves some of the best steaks and seafood in town, making it one of the finest in its price range. Happy hour daily 3–5pm. Open for dinner Sun–Fri 5–10pm, Sat 5–11pm. $$

The Steakhouse at Camelot

Excalibur, 702 597 7449, www.excalibur.com/restaurants
Gourmet cuisine served in the Excalibur castle overlooking make-believe English countryside creates a truly wonderful eating experience. Epicureans will find everything they are looking for from a fine wine cellar to a cigar room, lounge and private dining chamber, while the casual ambience makes it a friendly place for anyone to enjoy a meal. Dinner specials often available, such as 3 courses for $25. Open nightly 5–10pm. $–$$

STK Las Vegas

The Cosmopolitan, 702 6988 7575, www.cosmopolitanlasvegas.com/taste/restaurant-collection/stk.aspx
Glamorous take on a steak restaurant with plenty on the menu other than red meat. Executive chef Stephen Hopcraft offers sophisticated dishes such as tiger prawns served with shrimp rice crispys, sriracha chilli sauce, micro cilantro, shrimp bisque and fresh lime. Worth going for the sexy décor, classy cocktails and pleasing tunes from the talented in-house DJ. $$–$$$

SW Steakhouse

Wynn Las Vegas, 702 248 3463, www.wynnlasvegas.com
Star chef David Walzog redefines all the steakhouse classics here. Think charred,

prime-aged steaks and chops as well as poultry and seafood specialties. An elegant yet contemporary space, the restaurant offers the chance to dine outside overlooking the hotel's famous lake and mountain. Open nightly 5.30–10pm. **$$**

Terzetto Restaurant & Oyster Bar

The M Resort, 702 797 1000, www.themresort.com
Exhibition-style kitchen where charcoal-grilled steaks and seafood are expertly prepared such as hand-selected prime cuts of beef, including a reserve list from the Marnell family ranch and fresh-from-the-ocean seafood specialties. Terzetto Oyster Bar offers a casual dining option with made-to-order selections including soups, stews and pan favourites, oysters on the half shell, seafood salads, cocktails, ceviche and pastas. To top it off, guests can enjoy an extensive wine list or hand-crafted cocktails and the fabulous views both inside and outside. Open Sun–Thurs 5–10pm; Fri and Sat 5–11pm. **$$**

▪▶ BRITTIP

The Top of the World restaurant is one of the '10 Great Places to Pop the Question' according to America's wedding website, The Knot (theknot.com). Other locations include Paris and New York's Brooklyn Bridge.

The Top of the World

Stratosphere, 702 380 7711, www.topoftheworldlv.com
The name says it all! More than 800ft/240m up the tallest free-standing building in America, the Top of the World revolving restaurant makes a full 360-degree revolution every hour and 20 minutes. Awarded the Best Gourmet Room award by the *Las Vegas Review Journal*, the top-notch food includes sizzling steaks and fresh fish and seafood, tasty salads and flaming desserts. Even if the food wasn't great, the view would be worth it all by itself. Open Sun–Thurs 5–11pm; Fri and Sat until midnight. Happy hour in Level 107 Lounge (1 floor up) 4–7pm. **$$**

Outdoor and patio dining

Bartolotta Ristorante di Mare: Wynn Las Vegas (page 106)
Biscayne Steak, Sea & Wine: Tropicana (page 96)
BOA Prime Grill: Forum Shops
Brio Tuscan Grille: Tivoli Village
Bouchon: The Venetian (page 99)
Gonzalez Y Gonzalez: New York-New York (page 111)
Mix: THEHotel, Mandalay Bay (page 104)
Mon Ami Gabi: Paris Las Vegas (page 103)
Morels French Steakhouse & Bistro: The Palazzo
Nine Fine Irishmen: New York-New York (page 105)
Olives: Bellagio (page 110)
Pink Taco: Hard Rock Hotel (page 111)
Sinatra: Encore (page 108)

Yolie's

3900 Paradise Road, 702 794 0700, www.yoliesbraziliansteakhouse.com
A Brazilian steakhouse with large, wood-fired rotisseries that cook the meals in full view of the diners. The selection includes turkey, lamb, brisket, chicken, sausages and steak, plus side dishes of fried brown rice, potatoes and vegetables. Open 11am–3pm weekdays; dinner daily 5–11pm. **$$**

Southern restaurant

Crossroads at House of Blues

Mandalay Bay, 702 632 7607, www.mandalaybay.com/dining/casual-restaurants/house-of-blues.aspx
Las Vegas's version of Dan Aykroyd's famous House of Blues on Los Angeles' Strip at the majestic Mandalay Bay is living up to its 'hot' reputation. You'll find Cajun staples such as jambalaya and gumbo alongside new signature dishes from celebrity chef Aaron Sanchez such as shrimp and grits, meatball sliders, chilli braised short ribs and street tacos, incorporating flavours from around the world. Gospel fans will enjoy the Sunday Gospel Brunch, which features live music and an all-you-can-eat Southern-style buffet. At other times of the week expect blues-inspired and other live music. Open Sun–Thurs 8am–11pm; Fri and Sat 8am–midnight. **$**

South-western restaurants

Chili's Grill and Bar

2011 N Rainbow Blvd, 702 638 1482 and 3 other locations throughout the city, www.chilis.com
Mexican style with grills, sandwiches, steaks and fajitas at the restaurants in this chain. Open Mon–Thurs 11am–10.30pm; Fri–Sat 11am–11pm; Sun 11am–10pm. **$$**

Mesa Grill

Caesars Palace, 702 731 7731, www.caesarspalace.com
Celebrity chef Bobby Flay turns down the heat on a range of South-western classics that can usually set your throat on fire. A contemporary approach means smoked chicken and black bean quesadilla and lobster and cod griddle cakes with red cabbage slaw for starters. Main course signatures include the 16-spices rubbed rotisserie chicken, whole-fried striped bass with five-pepper ginger sauce and Flay's Cuban burger, sandwiched between slices of roast pork, cheese, ham and pickles. Open for lunch Mon–Fri 11am–2.30pm; for brunch Sat and Sun 10.30am–3pm; for dinner daily 5–11pm. **$$**

BRITTIP
Don't forget to check out your fun books (coupons usually found on line at sites like lasvegasfunbook.com) and local magazines for great 2-for-1 deals.

Spanish restaurants

Firefly

3900 Paradise Road, 702 369 3971, www.fireflylv.com
This small, sexy tapas kitchen and bar with Dali-esque green wooden chairs and live rock music serves the best small plates and finger food after midnight, with dishes originating from the Basque country of Northern Spain. Taste the house Sangria marinated for three days at happy hour 3–6pm. Open daily 11am–2am. **$-$$**

Julian Serrano

Aria Resort & Casino, 877 230 2742, www.arialasvegas
The internationally acclaimed chef's eponymous restaurant features a casual atmosphere with menus at different price points with French and Spanish influences. The expansive seafood bar highlights fresh shellfish and ceviches, while the dining room and lounge will serve tapas and other dishes from Serrano's native Spain. Open Sun–Thurs 11.30am–11pm, Fri–Sat 11.30am–11.30pm. **$$**

Tavern dining

Nobhill Tavern

MGM Grand, 702 891 7337, www.mgmgrand.com/restaurants/nobhill-tavern-restaurant.aspx
Nobhill Tavern by award-winning chef Michael Mina brings a new concept all of its own to Vegas – tavern cuisine. Just like the term 'B&B', tavern means something altogether more upmarket in the US. There's an innovative drink menu that pays homage to classic cocktails, an expansive lounge area and the menu is full of Mina's signature dishes including lobster rolls on buttery toasted brioche and tableside chicken and dumplings. Open Sun–Thurs 5.30–10pm; Fri–Sat 5.30–10.30pm. **$$**

BRITTIP
Men are advised to wear a jacket for dining at the sophisticated Nobhill restaurant – named after the famous Nob Hill in San Francisco.

Theme restaurants

Hard Rock Café

Showcase Mall, next to MGM Grand and adjacent to Monte Carlo, 702 733 7625, www.hardrock.com/lasvegas
Possibly the most rock 'n' roll of all the worldwide Hard Rock Cafes, this 42,000ft²/3,900m² of non-stop action is spread over 3 floors on an all new building that opened September 2009 right on the Strip. You can't miss it as there's a giant neon guitar on the side! There's an interactive 'Rock Wall', interactive Microsoft surface tables, a contemporary lounge and bar, a patio with Strip views, oh and quite a lot of good food! The café also features a built-in stage with an attached Green Room, so expect lots of celebs dropping by. Open Sun–Thurs 11am–midnight; Fri–Sat 11–1am. **$-$$**

Harley Davidson® Café

The Strip at Harmon Avenue, 702 740 4555, www.harley-davidsoncafe.com
This is the second outlet that pays homage to the 100-year-old motorbike and is hard to miss with its 28ft/8.5m high, 15,000lb/6,800kg $500,000 Harley Davidson Heritage Softail Classic bike outside! Inside the 20,000ft^2/1,860m^2, 2 storey café is a celebration of the free-spirit lifestyle of Harley Davidsons. And the food and drink lives up to it, too! You can sip on a range of cocktails with names such as Hill Climber, Rockin' Rita and Flat Tracker. Soak up the alcohol with fajitas, hamburgers, barbecue chicken, chillis, pasta or hot dogs. Open Sun–Thurs 11am–midnight; Fri and Sat 11am–2am. **$**

Hofbräuhaus Las Vegas

On Paradise and Harmon across from the Hard Rock Café, 702 853 2337, www.hofbrauhauslasvegas.com
Those who like their beer will enjoy this authentic replica of a Munich Hofbräuhaus complete with imported Bavarian beer, meat and sausage and even Bavarian pretzels. Lots of beer-swilling to the accompaniment of live German music! Daily lunch specials cost $9.95 Mon–Fri. Open Sun–Thurs 11am–11pm, Fri & Sat 11am–midnight. **$**

Jimmy Buffett's Margaritaville

The Flamingo, 702 733 3302, www.margaritavillelasvegas.com
For a themed night out with a difference, head to the great new Caribbean joint at the Flamingo where a 3-storey volcano erupts as it serves up delicious margaritas in the Volcano Bar. Spread over 3 levels, the restaurant has 5 bars and live music, and steaks, seafood, hamburgers (such as the 'Cheeseburger in Paradise') and Caribbean cuisine served up with toppings such as pineapple-rum sauce. At the top of the restaurant are 2 outdoor patios overlooking the Strip, one of which is home to the 12 Volt Bar, where live music is provided nightly on a theme of island and rock. Even if you don't plan to party the night away, do visit the bar if only to see the giant sails of the life-size Euphoria boat flying high! Open Sun–Thurs 8am–2am; Fri and Sat 8am–3am (dinner served until midnight). **$**

Lynyrd Skynyrd BBQ & Beer

Excalibur Hotel & Casino, 702 597 7777, www.excalibur.com
The band behind such classic American hits as *Sweet Home Alabama* and *Free Bird* is the inspiration for this new restaurant. Conceived by Michael Frey and Craig Gilbert of Drive This! Entertainment, the team behind classic Vegas venues as RHUMBAR and Tacos & Tequila this rock 'n' roll-inspired venue features classic hits, signature sips and down home, Texas-style BBQ on the strip. Open daily for breakfast, lunch and dinner (times not available as we went to press), it transforms into a high energy rock club in evening.

Planet Hollywood

Forum Shops at Caesars Palace, 702 791 7827, www.planethollywood.com
A chain famous more for their décor than the food, the place is overrun with photos and costumes and other Hollywood mementos. It seems every square inch has a Klingon costume or Freddie Kruger mask. The menu includes gourmet pizzas, pastas, fish, burgers and more. Open Sun–Thurs 9am–11pm; Fri and Sat 9am–midnight. **$**

The Rainforest Café

MGM Grand on the Strip, 702 891 8580, www.mgmgrand.com/restaurants/rainforest-cafe.aspx
A real-life simulation of a rainforest complete with tropical rainstorms featuring thunder and lightning that boom and spark across the entire restaurant. It's an untamed paradise brimming with exotic tropical birds, animated elephants, leopards and gorillas and tropical trees. You enter the dining area by walking under a massive double archway aquarium filled with marine fish from around the world in a 10,000gall/45,460l saltwater aquarium. The food, quite good by the way, consists of pastas, salads, sandwiches and delectable desserts. Signature dishes include tribal salmon, Mojo bones and sparkling volcano. Open Sun–Thurs 8am–11pm; Fri and Sat 8am–midnight. **$**

Olive's

© LVNB

Best gourmet-style dining in a hotel

Alizé: The Palms (see page 102)
Aureole: Mandalay Bay (see page 95)
Bartolotta Ristorante di Mare: Wynn Las Vegas (see page 106)
Búzio's Seafood Restaurant: Rio All-Suite Hotel (see page 112)
Central: Caesars Palace (see page 96)
Les Artistes Steakhouse: Rio All-Suite Hotel (see page 103)
Michael Mina: Bellagio (see page 113)
Mix: Mandalay Bay (see page 104)
Olives: Bellagio (see page 110)
Onda: Mirage (see page 108)
Picasso: Bellagio (see page 110)
Prime Steakhouse: Bellagio (see page 113)
Scarpetta: The Cosmopolitan (see page 108)
Sirio: Aria (see page 108)
Top of the World: Stratosphere (see page 115)

Trans ethnic restaurant

Restaurant Veloce Cibo & Bar Veloce

The M Resort, 702 797 1000, www.themresort.com
Gracing the summit of the M Resort, Veloce Cibo combines an extensive menu of appetisers, entrées, sushi, sashimi and nigiri with satisfying desserts and a range of hand-crafted cocktails and speciality drinks that take centre stage at Bar Veloce. The newest spot for dining and nightlife, Veloce Cibo offers amazing views of the Las Vegas skyline and one of the most spectacular terraces in the city. Open Sun–Thurs 5–11pm; Fri and Sat 5pm–midnight. **$$**

Lounge dining

Lounges are almost unique to Las Vegas. Relaxed yet stylish environments, they all provide live entertainment and in some cases delicious food. Here's a selection.

Firenze Lobby Lounge

Ravella at Lake Las Vegas, 702 567 4805, www.ravellavegas.com
For a light bite in a relaxing and romantic setting, this is the place to come. With views of the lake and beautiful art around the walls, you can enjoy hors d'oeuvres, desserts and soufflés before and after your meal. There's live music nightly plus an excellent selection of cocktails, Champagne, brandy and liqueurs. Open dinner 4pm–11pm. **$$**

BRITTIP
For a moment of refinement, try afternoon Florentine tea at the Firenze Lobby Lounge. Fresh flower arrangements and a live pianist create the perfect setting in which to enjoy scones, sandwiches and savouries while taking in the view of Lake Las Vegas and the mountains.

Peppermill Café & Lounge

2985 Las Vegas Boulevard South, 702 735 4177, www.peppermilllasvegas.com
For a taste of old-style Vegas hospitality, the Peppermill should be on your must-visit list. The food is excellent and portions are on the large side. Think burgers, sandwiches, steak, seafood and huge salads. While you're here, have a drink in the romantic lounge, which is famous for its fireplace, candlelit tables and comfy sofas. Open 24/7. **$**

Tea Lounge

Mandarin Oriental, Las Vegas, 1-888 881 9367, www.mandarinoriental.com/lasvegas/dining
A first for Vegas, the Mandarin Oriental's Tea Lounge brings authentic tea ceremonies to Sin City. Whether you fancy English tea and cupcakes or jasmine and some eastern delicacies, it's all here with gracious service and fab views. Open daily 10am–10pm; Afternoon tea 2.30–5pm. **$**

Cafés and diners

America

New York-New York, 702 740 6451, www.nynyhotelcasino.com/restaurants
A large, open restaurant with a few booths, serves classic casual American food such as roast turkey, meatloaf, pastas, salads and burgers. If all else fails to capture your imagination, try the all-day breakfast. Open 24/7. **$**

Binion's Original Coffee Shop

Binion's, 128 Fremont Street, 702 382 1600, www.binions.com
Binion's gets packed with downtown gamblers, so you have to pick your time to avoid long queues. Specialities include Benny Binion's Natural, considered to

24/7 gems

All the following serve excellent grub at around $10 throughout the day and night. These are perfect locations to get a great breakfast after a big night out or stock up on carbs before you hit the town.

Central: Caesar's Palace, 702 650 5921. Celebrity chef Michel Richard brings his 24/7 Washington DC eatery to Vegas for a bargain price, with beers on tap and cocktails. **$**

First Food Bar: The Shoppes at the Palazzo, 702 607 3478. From breakfast to late, and they mean really late, this is practically a 24-hour joint. Blending the casualness of a local eatery with the vibe of a late-night spot, chef Sam De Marco hits the mark. **$**

Liberty Café: 1700 Las Vegas Boulevard South, 702 383 0196. Just to prove good, old-fashioned grub works, here is an old-fashioned American drugstore with a counter. Famous for its monster breakfasts, it specialises in burgers and chicken-fried steak, while the retro drinks are a speciality. **$**

Monterey Room: Gold Coast Hotel, 4000 West Flamingo Road, 702 367 7111. Serving classic American grub throughout the day, plus great Chinese cuisine noon–5am, the Monterey is famous for its lunch and dinner specials. Lunch from $6.95 and dinners $5.95–15.95. **$**

Mr Lucky's 24/7: Hard Rock Hotel, 702 693 5000, hardrockhotel.com. You'll find excellent choices for breakfast, lunch and dinner, while afterwards you can check out the rock 'n' roll memorabilia and a large Jim Morrison mural. New York Steak & Eggs (an 8oz New York sirloin steak, two eggs, hash browns and toast) all for $4.99. **$**

Pelican Rock Café: Castaways Hotel & Casino, 702 385 9123. Traditional American breakfasts include omelettes, waffles and pancakes; lunch is soups, salads and sandwiches; while dinner offerings include steaks and burgers. This is one of the cheapest joints in town, still famous for its mega-cheap steak and egg deals. **$**

Hash House A Go Go: The M Resort, 702 797 1000, www.themresort.com. Guests can receive their morning jolt or evening 'pick-me-up' while surrounded by the restaurant's 1920s art-deco inspired atmosphere. The Red Cup Café menu offers a wide variety of American classics and Asian cuisine. Dining is available inside or on the outside terrace. 2-for-1 dining Fri and Sat 10pm–2am. **$**

Ristorante dei Fiore: Hotel San Remo, 115 East Tropicana Avenue, 702 739 9000. Sounds posh, but this is a cheap-as-chips joint serving excellent American and international food. Locals love its prime rib dinner and steak and egg breakfast, both $4.95, which are served 24 hours a day. **$**

Roxy's Diner: Stratosphere, 702 380 7777, www.stratospherehotel.com. A piece of 1950s America – everything from the decor to the singing staff in uniforms and music pay homage to the rock 'n' roll era. Food includes chicken, fried steak with homemade gravy and Mom's meat loaf with fresh vegetables and real mashed potatoes. Drinks include thick, cold milkshakes in tall, frosted glasses. Prime rib special from $10.99. **$**

Studio Café: MGM Grand, 1 800 929 1111, www.mgmgrand.com/restaurants. Upmarket hearty breakfasts or late-night snacks, this art deco-esque café is the place to head. Think eggs Benedict or filet and lobster. Average bill $18. **$**

5

be one of the best-priced, most delicious breakfasts in town, Binion's Delight, a hamburger platter with chips and the $9.95 Chicken & Rib special served from 4–11pm. Open Mon–Thurs 4pm–midnight; Fri–Sat 7am–1am; Sun 7am–midnight. **$**

Café Michelle

1350 East Flamingo Road, inside the local mall, 702 735 8686
The place to go for plenty of cheap grub far from the madding crowd. The red-and-white checked tablecloths and Cinzano umbrellas over tables in the plaza create a European ambience, while you tuck into omelettes, crêpes, salads and seafood. **$**

Enigma Garden Café

918 S Fourth Street, 702 386 0999
One of the best cafés downtown, it even has live music outside in the garden at weekends. During the summer it's open 24 hours a day (7am–10pm in winter). **$**

Jazzed Café & Vinoteca

8615 West Sahara Ave, 702 233 2859 and 2055 E Tropicana Ave, 702 798 5995

One of your best bets away from the Strip is this fun room on West Sahara Ave that's decorated as a bold piece of living pop art. It seats about 40 for dinner but stays open past the dinner hour as a cosy spot for live music. Open Mon–Thurs 5pm–1am; Fri and Sat 5pm–3am; Sun 10am–2pm and 5pm–1am. **$–$$**

Lago Buffet

Caesars Palace, 702 731 7778 (groups over 12), www.caesarspalace.com
Just to prove that the Bellagio isn't the only resort in town with water views, Caesars has opened this large café right by the Garden of the Gods Pool Oasis. This buffet offers international dishes and American and Asian favourites. The one drawback, of course, is that enjoying the beautiful setting doesn't come cheap. Open daily 7am–10pm. **$$**

Hotel and shopping mall restaurants

Many of the best restaurants that have been reviewed and listed are in the top resort-hotels. For quick reference, here is a run-down of the main restaurants and cafés in those resort-hotels and malls. The hotels also have their own buffets!

Aria Resort & Casino

877 239 2742, www.arialasvegas.com
The restaurants at Aria raise the bar in Las Vegas dining.
Fine dining:

American Fish	Seafood
BARMASA	Japanese
Blossom	Chinese
Jean-Georges Steakhouse	Steak
Julian Serrano	Spanish
Sage	Farm to table
Shaboo	Japanese
Sirio	Italian
Union Restaurant	American

Casual:

The Buffet	Buffet
Breeze Café	Café
Café Vettro	Café
JP Patisserie	Patisserie
Lemongrass	Thai
Skybox Sports Bar & Grille	Themed
Sweet Chill	Café
The Roasted Bean	Café

Bellagio

702 693 7111, www.bellagio.com

When the Bellagio opened at the end of 1998, it set a new standard both for hotels and for restaurants, and deliberately went out of its way to attract top celebrity chefs, including Elizabeth Blau, Julian Serrano and Todd English. All were a hit from the word go and have remained popular ever since.
Fine dining:

Jasmine	Chinese
Le Cirque	French
Michael Mina	Seafood
Picasso	Mediterranean
Prime Steakhouse	Steakhouse

Contemporary dining:

Circo	Tuscany
Sensi	Asian
Yellowtail Japanese Restaurant & Lounge	Japanese
Olives	Mediterranean
Fix	American
Noodles	Asian
The Petrossian Bar	Caviar

Casual:

The Buffet	Buffet
Café Bellagio	24-hour dining
Pool Café	Mediterranean

Quick eats:

Jean-Philippe	Pastry shop

Caesars Palace

702 731 7110, www.caesarspalace.com
The resort is posh and the restaurants reflect that, serving top-notch and largely pricey meals. If you're feeling flush, you can do no wrong by trying any of the following establishments.
Fine dining:

Hyakumi	Japanese sushi bar
Old Homestead Steakhouse	Contemporary American
Rao's	Italian
Restaurant Guy Savoy	French

Casual:

Beijing Noodle No.9	Chinese
Central	24 hour
Lago Buffet	Buffet
Cypress Street Marketplace	Self-service
Mesa Grill	Southwestern
Payard Patisserie & Bistro	Bistro
Serendipity 3	Café

Cosmopolitan

The unapologetic Cosmopolitan which opened in 2009 is naturally part of the new wave of gourmet offerings in Vegas, with 13 dizzying delectable and stylish temptations.

Fine dining:

Blue Ribbon Sushi Bar & Grill	Japanese
China Poblano	Mexican/Chinese
Comme Ca	French Brasserie
Estiatorio Milos	Greek
Jaleo	Spanish tapas
Scarpetta	Italian
STK	American

Casual dining:

D.O.C.G	Italian
Holstein's	Burgers
Overlook Grill	American
The Henry	American
Va Bene Caffe	Italian
Wicked Spoon	American

Circus Circus

702 734 0410, www.circuscircus.com

The Steak House is one of the finest of its kind in town and is regularly honoured by local newspaper polls as the Number One steakhouse of Las Vegas.

Fine dining:

Steak House	American

Casual:

Barista Bagels	Bagels and coffee
Blue Iguana	Mexican
Circus Buffet	Buffet
The Garden Grill	American
Rock & Ritas	American
The Pizzeria	Italian
Westside Deli	Deli

Crystals

www.citycenter.com

Opened 3 December 2009, Crystals at CityCenter features Eva Longoria Parker's BESO and Mastro's Ocean Club. There's Lemonsgrass, an exciting new Pub concept by Todd English, and Vegas old hand, Wolfgang Puck has opened 2 innovative new restaurant concepts, including a contemporary interpretation of a traditional French brasserie with tastes of the Mediterranean region. Many more luxury dining concepts will be announced at a later date.

Encore

888 320 7110, www.wynnlasvegas.com

In keeping with the culinary standards set by Wynn Las Vegas, Encore introduces a new all-star team of chefs, each of whom is in the kitchen cooking dinner every night.

Fine dining:

Botero Steak	Seafood and steak
Sinatra	Italian
Society Café Encore	American
Switch	French
WAZUZU	Pan Asian

Excalibur

702 597 7777, www.excalibur.com

Themes abound at the eating establishments of this resort that pays tribute to King Arthur's day. Lynyrd Skynyrd BBQ and Beer plays tribute to a musical legend and Excalibur Buffet calls to mind the famous sword.

Fine dining:

Lynyrd Skynyrd BBQ & Beer	American BBQ
The Steakhouse at Camelot	Gourmet dining overlooking the English countryside!

Casual:

Baja Fresh	Mexican
Dick's Last Resort	American
Excalibur Buffet	Buffet
Village Food Court	Fast food

Forum Shops at Caesars Palace

www.caesarspalace.com

The incredibly upscale Forum Shops have a tremendous number and range of dining options from celebrity chef to other upscale and more casual dining. In some cases you can even dine pavement style and watch the world go by.

Fine dining:

BOA Steakhouse	Steakhouse
Il Mulino	Italian
Joe's Stone Crab	Prime rib and stone crab
The Palm	Steakhouse
Spago	American fusion

Casual:

Cheesecake Factory	American
La Salsa	Mexican
Planet Hollywood	American
Sushi Roku	Sushi bar
PJ Clarke's	American saloon

5

© CityCenter

Lemongrass at the Aria

Cooking classes

If you've ever wanted to learn how to prepare food like a world-class chef, now you can as numerous restaurants offer cooking classes. **Mon Ami Gabi** at Paris Las Vegas is offering a new cooking class series on how to prepare French-inspired recipes and pair them with wine. Executive Chef Terry Lynch and a Mon Ami Gabi wine connoisseur will lead cooking demonstrations on select Saturdays during the year. Master Sushi Chef of Loews Hotels, Osamu 'Fuji' Fujita, conducts sushi classes in Marssa Restaurant at **Loews Las Vegas** Resort. **SUSHISAMBA Strip**, located on the retail level of The Shoppes at The Palazzo, has announced an interactive, 2-hour teaching and tasting event called SUSHI+SAKE 101. Participants learn what it takes to become a Master Sushi Chef while sipping sake alongside a 5-course meal. The class introduces students to the art and history of this unique cuisine. In addition to classes on the Strip, there are off-Strip cooking schools as well, such as **Le Cordon Bleu College of Culinary Arts Las Vegas**. Classes cover the culinary gamut, ranging from vegetarian cuisine to Thai to Southwest Thanksgiving. Classes are limited in size and available on a first-come, first-served basis. Las Vegas is now also home to a one-of-a-kind pastry school. At the School of Pastry Design, participants can work alongside world champion US Pastry Chef Chris Hamner, to create colourful edible life size pastry or chocolate art.

Four Seasons

702 632 5000,
www.fourseasons.com/lasvegas
Fine dining:

Charlie Palmer Steak	American
Casual:	
The Verandah	Eclectic

Grand Canal Shoppes at The Venetian

702 414 4500,
www.thegrandcanalshoppes.com
Along with everything else about this resort-hotel, the shops are beautiful and contain some wonderful restaurants.
Fine dining:

AquaKnox	Seafood
B&B Ristorante	Italian
Canaletto	Italian
Canyon Ranch Café	American
Pinot Brasserie	French/ Californian
Valentino	Italian
Wolfgang Puck's Postrio	American Italian/Seafood and steak
Zeffirino	Italian
Casual:	
Delmonico	Steakhouse
OTTO Pizzeria	Italian
Grand Lux Café	Café
Live music:	
Tao	Asian bistro

Hard Rock Hotel

702 693 5000, www.hardrockhotel.com
The rock 'n' roll memorabilia that adorns the first-ever hotel on this theme makes a visit to the casino a must – and while you're there you won't be disappointed by any of the dining establishments.
Fine dining:

Nobu	Japanese
35 Steaks + Martinis	Steaks
Casual:	
LTO Pizza & more	Italian
Espumoso	Coffee shop
Johnny Smalls	Tapas
Juice Bar	Juice bar
Mr Lucky's	Coffee shop
Pink Taco	Mexican
Starbucks	Coffee shop

Las Vegas Hilton

702 732 5111, www.lvhilton.com
The elegant resort-hotel has some fine restaurants. The prices are on the high side but then you are getting some of the best ingredients cooked to perfection and served in delightful settings. Note that the hotel name is likely to change by 2012.
Fine dining:

Benihana	Japanese
Casa Nicola	Mediterranean
Garden of the Dragon	Chinese
TJ's Steakhouse	Steaks
Casual:	
The Buffet	Buffet
Vince Neil's Tres Rois Cantina	Mexican
Paradise Cafe	Quick bites
Fortuna	Wine bar
Ice cream Shoppe	Ice Cream
Pizza Hut Express	Italian
Superbook Deli	Deli

Luxor

702 262 4444, www.luxor.com
The Luxor provides a good choice of dining
from healthy Asian fare at Rice & Company
to Mexican favourites at T&T. All offer a
lively environment and value for money.

Fine dining:

Rice & Company	Asian
Tender	Steakhouse

Casual:

Back Stage Deli	Deli
Blizz	Frozen yoghurt/
	dessert
Food Court	Self-service
MORE	Buffet
Pyramid Café	American
T&T	Mexican

M Resort

702 797 1000, www.themresort.com
All 9 restaurants are owned and run by
the Marnell family – long-time movers and
shakers in Vegas. The concepts are all their
own and everything is made fresh daily.

Fine dining:

Antony's	Seafood and
	steak
Marinelli's	Italian
Veloce Cibo	Trans ethnic
Terzetto	Seafood and
	steak

Casual:

Baby Cakes	Patisserie
Hostile Grape	Wine
Hash House A Go Go	American and
	Asian classics
Studio B	Buffet
The Vig Deli	Deli

Mandalay Bay

702 632 7777, www.mandalaybay.com
The hotel is in the top-end bracket and aims
directly at the more sophisticated traveller
in search of fun. It has a cracking live-music
venue – House of Blues – within a selection
of celebrity chef restaurants.

Fine dining:

Aureole	American
China Grill	Chinese
Fleur	French
Mix	Fusion
Red Square	Caviar
rm Seafood	Seafood
Shanghai Lilly	Cantonese
STRIPSTEAK	American
Lupo	Italian
Border Grill	Mexican

Casual:

Burger Bar	American

THEcafé	24-hour dining
Mizuya	Sushi
Noodle Shop	Chinese
Red, White and Blue	French
Verandah	International
Hussongs Cantina	Mexican

Live music:

Crossroads at House	
of Blues	Southern
Rí Rá Irish Pub	Irish

Mandarin Oriental, Las Vegas

1-888 881 9367,
www.mandarinoriental.com/lasvegas/dining
Drama is definitely on the menu at the
Mandarin Oriental. Guests arrive at the
23rd floor Sky Lobby with expansive views
of Vegas, while dark marble floors lead to
all restaurants.

Fine dining:

MOzen Bistro	Japanese
Twist	Fusion

Casual:

Pool Café	Tapas
Tea Lounge	Teas

MGM Grand

702 891 7777, www.mgmgrand.com
Celebrity chefs Wolfgang Puck, Joël
Robuchon and Emeril Lagassé all have
restaurants here.

Fine dining:

Craftsteak	Steakhouse

Witchcraft

Joël Robuchon	French
L'Atelier du Joel Robinson	French
Specialty dining:	
Nobhill Tavern	Californian
Shibuya	Japanese
Fiamma Trattoria	Italian
Emeril's	New Orleans/ Creole
Pearl	Chinese
SeaBlue	Seafood
Wolfgang Puck Bar & Grill	American
Casual:	
Cabaña Grill	American
Grand Wok	Asian
MGM Grand Buffet	Buffet
Rainforest Café	Bistro
Stage Deli	New York deli
Starbucks	Coffee shop
Studio Café	24 hours
Studio Wok	Chinese
Wichcraft	Deli

Mirage

702 791 7111, www.mirage.com
You won't go wrong dining at any of the eateries here, and many offer fine food at mostly reasonable prices.
Fine dining:

Fin	Contemporary Chinese
Japonais	Japanese
Kokomo's	Seafood
Onda	Italian
Samba Brazilian	Steakhouse
Stack	American bistro
Casual:	
BLT Burger	American
B.B. Kings Blues Club	Southern American
Blizz	Frozen yoghurt/ desserts

California Pizza Kitchen	Californian
Carnegie Deli	NY deli
Cravings	Buffet
Dolphin Snack Bar	Café
Paradise Café	Café
Roasted Bean	Coffee shop

Monte Carlo

702 730 7777 or 877 2-DINE-LV, www.montecarlo.com
Here you will find one of the best restaurants in town – André's – and 3 run by top Californian restaurateurs, Salvator Casola, his son Sal, and Chipper Pastron. Their Market City Caffé is an Italian eatery featuring fresh homemade bread and pasta dishes and the Dragon Noodle Company features the Tea Bar with a range of exotic teas.
Fine dining:

André's	Gourmet French
Brand Steakhouse	American
Casual:	
Café	Fusion
d.Vino	Italian
Diablo's Cantina	Mexican
Dragon Noodle Co	Asian
Golden Bagel	Deli
Food Court	International
Market City Café	Italian
The Buffet	Buffet
The Pub	American

New York-New York

866 815 4365, www.newyorknewyork.com
Each of the hotel's restaurants provides a themed dining experience based on the New York areas including Little Italy, Chinatown and Manhattan. The quality is good and the prices are reasonable.

Fine dining:

Chin Chin	Chinese
Gallagher's Steakhouse	Steakhouse
Il Fornaio	Italian

Casual:

America	24-hour bistro
Broadway Burger Bar	American
Gonzalez Y Gonzalez	Mexican
Nathan's Hot Dogs	New York street
New York Pizzeria	Italian
Nine Fine Irishmen	Irish
The Sporting House	American

◀️ ▶️ BRITTIP

Delis originated in New York and are basically the American version of our sandwich bars, with a heavy Italian feel.

The Palms

702 942 7777, www.palms.com
The newest casino hotel on the block is also one of the hippest and has an excellent line-up of restaurants.

Fine dining:

Alizé	French
Garduños	Mexican
Little Buddha Café	French
N9ne Steakhouse	American
Nove Italiano	Italian
Simon Resturant	International

Casual:

24 Seven Café	American
Bistro Buffet	Buffet
Blue Agave	Oyster bar
Cathay House	Chinese

Paris Las Vegas

702 739 4111, www.parislasvegas.com
The Paris-inspired resort keeps the French theme in all of its dining outlets ranging from true gourmet to casual. The restaurants have gone from strength to strength and new ones have even opened in this successful resort-hotel.

Fine dining:

Eiffel Tower Restaurant	Gourmet French
Le Provençal	Regional French
Les Artistes Steakhouse	Gourmet French
Mon Ami Gabi	Brasserie

Casual:

Café du Parc	Poolside bistro
Café Ile St Louis	French
JJ's Boulangerie	Pastries, salads
La Crêperie	Crêpes
Le Village Buffet	Buffet
Le Burger Brasserie	American
Sugar Factory American Brasserie	American

Planet Hollywood

702 736 7114,
www.planethollywoodresort.com
PH has an exceptional range of innovative restaurants and retains the Spice Market Buffet from its days as the Aladdin, still one of Vegas's best-value places to eat.

Fine dining:

Koi	Japanese
PF Chang's China Bistro	Chinese
Strip House	Steakhouse
Yolo's	Mexican

Casual:

Earl of Sandwich	Deli
Pink's Hot Dogs	American
Planet Dailies	American brasserie
Spice Market	Buffet
Starbucks	Coffee bar

Miracle Mile Shops

702 866 0703,
www.miraclemileshopslv.com
Great places for dining and people-watching.

Fine dining:

Pampas Churrascaria	Brazilian grill

Casual:

Aromi D'Italia	Italian bistro
Blondies Sports Bar & Grill	Sports bar
Cabo Wabo Cantina	Mexican
Cheeseburger Las Vegas	American
FRESH Grill & Bar	American
Hawaiian Tropic Zone	Hawaiian
La Salsa Cantina	Mexican
Lobster ME	American seafood
Lombardi's Romagna Mia	Italian
Merchant's Harbor	Coffee house
Panda Express	Chinese
Ocean One Bar & Grill	American
PBR Rock Bar & Grill	American
Stripper Bar	Light bites
Todai	Japanese seafood buffet

5

Diablo's Cantina at the Monte Carlo

© MGM

Rio All-Suite Hotel

866 746 7671, www.riolasvegas.com
One of the most successful off-Strip resort-hotels with a tremendous range of *Zagat*-rated restaurants.
Fine dining:

Búzios	Seafood
Gaylord India Restaurant	Indian

Casual:

All-American Bar & Grille	American
Carnival World Buffet	Buffet
Mah Jong	Asian noodle bar
Martorano's	Italian/American
McFaddon's	Bar and grill
Sao Paulo Café	24-hour diner
Sports Deli	American
Village Seafood Buffet	Buffet
VooDoo Steak & Lounge	Cajun/Creole
Whopper Bar	American

Town Square Las Vegas

702 269 5000,
www.mytownsquarelasvegas.com

Blue Martini	Tapas and Martinis
Brio Tuscan Grille	Italian
California Pizza Kitchen	American
Claim Jumper	American
english's	English
Johnny McGuire's	Deli
Kabuki Japanese Restaurant	Japanese
Nu Sanctuary Lodge	Fusion
Texas de Brazil	Brazilian-American Steakhouse
Tommy Bahama's Restaurant & Bar	Caribbean
Whole Food Market	Organic
Yard House	American fusion

Treasure Island

702 894 7111, www.treasureisland.com
The resort tribute to the world of the Caribbean has some great restaurants.
Fine dining:

Isla	Mexican
Phil's Steakhouse	Steakhouse

Casual:

Buffet at TI	Buffet
Canter's Deli	Deli
Delicatessen	Deli
Pizzeria Francesco's	Italian
Kahunaville	Hawaiian
Pho	Vietnamese
Starbucks Coffee	Coffee bar

Tropicana

702 739 2222, www.troplv.com/dining
There is a distinctly tropical theme to many of the restaurants at this resort-hotel.
Fine dining:

Bacio	Italian
Biscayne	Steakhouse/ seafood
Café Nikki	American

Casual:

South Beach Marketplace	International

The Venetian

702 414 4100, www.venetian.com
This hotel has a host of celebrity-chef restaurants.
Fine dining:

AquaKnox	Seafood
B&B Ristorante	Italian
Bouchon	French bistro
Canaletto	Italian
Carnevino	Steakhouse
CUT	Steakhouse
Delmonico Steakhouse	Steakhouse
LAVO	Italian
Morels	French Steakhouse/ Bistro
Pinot Brasserie	Gourmet French
Postrio Bar & Grill	American
SUSHISAMBA	Brazilian/ Peruvian/ Japanese
Table 10	New Orleans
Tao Asian Bistro	Asian
Valentino	Italian
Zeffirino	Italian seafood

Casual:

Canyon Ranch Cafe	Healthy
Grand Lux Café	Global
Grill at Valentino	Italian
i love burgers	American
Noodle Asia	Noodles
OTTO Pizzeria	Italian
Taqueria Cañonita	Mexican
Tintoretto bakery	Italian bakery
Trattoria Reggiano	Italian

Wynn Las Vegas

877 321 9966, www.wynnlasvegas.com
Perfect for the more sophisticated diner.

Bartolotta	Italian
Bolero	Steakhouse
Country Club	Steakhouse
La Cave	French
Lakeside	American seafood
Okada	Japanese
Sinatra	Italian

Society Café Encore	American
Stratta	French
Switch Steak	Steakhouse
SW Steakhouse	Steakhouse
Wazuzu	Asian
Wing Lei	French/Asian

Buffets

These all-you-can-eat-for-little-bucks feasts are what Las Vegas used to be most famous for in the culinary stakes and they are still going strong. The mega-feasts date back to the 1940s when the owner of the El Rancho devised a plan to offer a Midnight Chuck Wagon Buffet – 'all you can eat for a dollar' – and found the crowds rolling in. Other hotels quickly followed suit, introducing breakfast, lunch and dinner spreads, and the buffet boom was born. Open for breakfast, lunch and dinner, the average buffet features around 45 food selections including salads, fruits, roast beef, baked ham, roast turkey, vegetables and a variety of desserts. They are known as the gambler's revenge – a way to fill up on food for as little as $3 for breakfast to $15 for dinner – though some of the more upmarket, speciality buffets run to $30 a head. In fact, there's a whole new wave of gourmet buffets, and knowing Vegas, it could become the in-thing, especially in times of recession.

You'll find buffets at just about every hotel on the Strip and downtown but both the choice and the turnover vary considerably. The Rio All-Suites has the biggest buffet, serving upwards of 12,000 hungry gamblers a day, but the queues are incredibly long!

For a Sunday brunch with a difference, try the Southern cuisine at Crossroads at House of Blues. Sittings at 10am and 1pm.

Getting the most out of buffets

- Generally, avoid breakfast buffets as you won't be able to walk for the rest of the day and the choice is not as good as at other times.
- A lot of buffets change from breakfast to lunch at around 11am. Arrive at 10.45am to pay the breakfast rate and get the lunch spread!
- Never, ever attempt more than one buffet a day or you will explode!
- Try to avoid peak lunch and dinner times or you'll find yourself standing in a queue for an hour and a half. At weekends, even at off-peak times, the queues can

take 45 minutes.
- If the queues are long, take a good book or magazine to read – and opt for comfortable shoes!
- Always check out the local magazines for 2-for-1 coupons.

 BRITTIP
At some buffets you have to queue up to get a table after you've queued to get your food!

Buffets on (or near) the Strip

Buffet of Champions: Champagne brunch at the Las Vegas Hilton, $19.99, Sat and Sun 8am–2.30pm.

Carnival World Buffet at the Rio All-Suite Hotel: On West Flamingo, this is both the biggest and best. The food is laid out in separate kiosks that have different cuisines from around the globe such as American, Chinese, Japanese and Mexican. It's so impressive you'll want to go back again and again, but the long queues may put you off as this is a real favourite with locals.

Excalibur Buffet: New Take 2 Buffet Pass for $32 allows you to eat all day at the Excalibur and/or the Luxor.

Harrah's resorts: Flavors at Harrah's Las Vegas which has live cooking stations, freshly prepared seafood, prime rib, Churrasco (Brazilian BBQ), hand-rolled sushi and Italian casseroles prepared in a wood-burning oven.

Imperial Buffet: Champagne brunch in the Imperial Palace, Sat and Sun 8am–3pm, $12.99.

Luxor Steakhouse: Champagne brunch, Sun 10am–3.30pm, $17.99.

MGM: Grand Buffet invites guests to take advantage of a $29.99 dinner. Available daily 4.30–9.30pm. Breakfast $17.95 Mon–Fri 7–11am, lunch $19.99 Mon–Fri 11am–2.30pm. Sat–Sun brunch 7am–2.30pm.

Mirage: Champagne brunch, 8am–9.30pm, $20.50.

Monte Carlo: Champagne brunch, 7am–3pm, adults $18.95.

Palatium Buffet: Caesars Palace offers a Champagne brunch, Sun 10.30am–3.30pm, adults $23.50.

Paris Las Vegas, Le Village Buffet: Showcases 5 provinces of France. Breakfast Mon–Sun 7–10am; lunch Mon–Fri 10am–3.30pm; Champagne brunch Sat and Sun 10am–3.30pm; dinner Mon–Sun 3.30–10pm.

Seasons Buffet at Silverton Casino Hotel Lodge: Brunch Sat and Sun 9am–3pm;

5

lunch Mon 11am–9pm; Tues–Fri 11am–3pm, dinner daily 4–9pm; Fri–Sat until 10pm. Don't miss the Surf & Turf buffet Fri 4–9pm $21.99.

Sterling Brunch: At Bally's Hotel on the Strip, this is truly expensive ($65) but also truly worth it if you want to splash out on a great dining experience, 9.30am–2pm.

Stratosphere: At the northern end of the Strip, this has a wide selection of good quality food at very good prices.

Studio B: New-age gourmet buffet at M Resort. The 500-seat Studio B revolutionises the buffet concept, integrating a state-of-the-art restaurant with a live-action cooking studio. Within the show kitchen, chefs prepare delicious appetisers, entrées and out-of-this-world patisserie desserts. Beer and wine can also be enjoyed as part of lunch and dinner meals at no additional cost. Fast-paced, entertaining and ever-changing live cooking and technique demonstrations by culinary experts have guests routinely coming back for more, choosing from over 200 items daily. Studio B is open for breakfast Mon–Fri 7–10.30am; lunch Mon–Fri 10.30am–2.30pm; dinner 4–11pm; dinner Mon–Thurs 4–9pm; seafood dinner Fri 4–10pm and brunch Sat and Sun 9am–2.30pm and seafood dinner Sat and Sun 2.30–10pm.

Treasure Island: Champagne brunch, 7.30am–3.30pm, $18.

Tropicana: Champagne brunch in the El Gaucho restaurant, 10.30am–2pm, adults $32. The hotel's Island Buffet also has a cheaper Champagne brunch, Sat and Sun 10.30am–2.30pm, $16.25.

Village Seafood Buffet: Also at the Rio in the new Masquerade Village, this is more expensive than the norm (around $18) but offers an incredible selection of all the different types of seafood in the world.

> **BRITTIP**
> A $44.99 Buffet of Buffets day pass gives unlimited access to 7 Sin City buffet restaurants: Caesars Palace, Paris Las Vegas, Planet Hollywood, Ballys, Harrahs, Rio All-Suites, Flamingo Las Vegas and Imperial Palace.

Greater Las Vegas

If you really want to get the best out of a Las Vegas buffet then you need to travel downtown to the Garden Court Buffet at Main Street Station. While a bit on the smaller side, compared to the massive resorts, the Champagne brunch is a mere $10.99 and the food is rated excellent.

In the opposite direction, the Feast at Boulder Station on the Boulder Highway provides an excellent stop on your way to or from the Hoover Dam. Here you'll find a good choice of quality foods ranging from tacos to pizzas and rotisserie chicken from $7.99.

> **BRITTIP**
> For a Sunday brunch with a difference, try the Southern cuisine at Crossroads at House of Blues. Gospel Brunch sittings are at 9am, 11.30am and 2pm, $34.60.

Round Table Buffet at the Excalibur

© MGM

BARS, LOUNGES AND NIGHTLIFE

Bars, lounges, nightclubs, live music venues and strip clubs

With its 24-hour party mentality, there's no doubt that Las Vegas has nightlife to rival anywhere in the world. Over the last few years an erotic force of ultra-lounges and lavish nightclubs has taken over Sin City with pounding EDM (electro dance music), intimate corners with oversized couches, sexy dancers, interactive tables and long queues vying to pass the entrance across a velvet rope. Internationally renowned DJ Markus Schulz with his new residency at The Marquee, one of the hottest clubs in town, has gone so far as to say that Vegas is on track to be the new Ibiza (see page 139). Places like XS, iBar, Gold Diggers, LAX, eyecandy sound lounge & bar, The Bank, The Gallery, Club Nikki, Tryst, Pure and Tao are magnets for the movers, shakers, beautiful people and celebrities with their 'crews' who flock to where skin is flaunted, liquor flows and we little people fight for a glance at the rich and famous. A whole raft of VIP rooms, private booths and sky bars at many of the nightclubs command hundreds of dollars for access. Many of these places actually pay famous party animals fees to come and be seen, and notorious naughty girls Lindsay Lohan and Jessica Simpson reportedly get up to $10,000 for partying at some top clubs.

There is also a druggie side to many of these power party joints. Ecstasy, the popular club drug of choice, is downed like candy in many of these places, along with cocaine. Another open secret, which is pointedly not talked about lest it cut down on the numbers of visiting and near-naked young women, is that these are hunting grounds for those creatures who use 'date rape' drugs like GHB. So make sure that if you go to one of these ultra-lounges, you go with people you trust implicitly.

Even though hotspots abound, you don't have to reveal all or spend a fortune to have a great night out in Sin City. Vegas now has many more nightclubs, lounges and bars where times are good, entertainment is great and prices are reasonable. Even better, most of them are conveniently located along the main drag of the famous Strip.

For those who really need a raunchy fantasy, there are many establishments both

In this chapter

on and off Strip where beautiful bodies gyrate in nothing but the briefest of g-strings before panting customers clutching $5 bills. Not just males, either, as a swath of gin joints cater to the erotic fantasies of single girls on holiday.

Many top nightspots start off as restaurants or bars early in the evening and transform into something altogether hotter around 10 or 11pm. Other venues are dedicated nightclubs, while live music can be found in the plethora of lounge bars – mostly at hotels and usually free, though the drinks are expensive! – and dedicated live music venues, where drinks are cheaper.

Bar Vdara

© CityCenter

Here's a selection of all types of venues that are available to keep you well amused during your time in Vegas. As with the restaurants, it is usually quicker to go to the hotel-resort website, where appropriate, then follow the entertainment or nightlife link, rather than keying in a long URL.

◀◀▶ **BRITTIP**
For help in planning your big night out, skipping the queues at nightclubs or arriving to a reserved lounge table get in touch with Red Carpet VIP at www.vipnight.com.

Bars

Bar at Times Square

New York-New York, 866 815 4365, www.nynyhotelcasino.com/entertainment
The duo of pianists here are famous for trying to outdo each other and have become the best piano show in town. Give them a song and enjoy singing along in a cosy bar based on an old New York City pub. Open nightly. You must arrive by 7.30pm for table reservations. $10 cover.

Bar Vdara

Vdara, 702 590 2111, www.vdara.com
Described as a glowing jewel box in the centre of Vdara, one of the first hotels to open in the new CityCenter development, Bar Vdara connects to an intimate outdoor space where guests can lounge on spacious swings. Open for a morning espresso or a late-night cocktail. We like! Open Sun–Thurs 11am–1am, Fri–Sat 11am–2am.

Bar Veloce

M Resort, 702 797 1000, www.themresort.com
High atop the M Tower, Bar Veloce's social and contemporary atmosphere is coupled with spectacular views of the Strip. An open-front bar allows mixologists to interact with guests and prepare cocktails to order. Open Sun–Thurs 5pm–11pm; Fri and Sat 5pm–midnight.

C Bar

Stratosphere Hotel, www.stratospherehotel.com/hotel/nightlife
The 360 degrees of pulsating beats from a live DJ, banks of plasma screens showing music videos and a bottomless Happy Hour, make for a good time. Try the C Bar Martini.

Center Bar

Hard Rock Hotel, 4455 Paradise at Harmon, 702 693 5000, www.hardrockhotel.com
A flashy circle bar at the heart of the hippest hotel in Vegas, this is filled with the hottest babes in town flashing their cleavage and g-strings. Drinks are pricey but the people-watching is priceless. Celebs spotted here include Gwyneth Paltrow, Ben Affleck and the Backstreet Boys. The only downside, say insiders, are the desperados trying to hit on 'hot chicks' – you know you've been had when you hear the line, 'Are you a model?'. Follow the party link on the website. Open 24/7.

Centrifuge

MGM Grand, 702 891 7777, www.mgmgrand.com/nightlife
The newest bar at the MGM Grand near the Lion Habitat and Poker Room. Remixed top-40 hits pump out of the speakers and hand-crafted cocktails are served along the circular black bar. Twice an hour the music pumps up and the bartenders, male and female, ascend the bar for a hip-grinding dance to the delight of the crowd. Open Mon–Thurs 2pm–Close; Fri–Sun from noon.

◀◀▶ **BRITTIP**
Nevada's legal drinking age is 21. Most places will 'card' you if you appear under 30 so always make sure you've got ID with you – preferably a passport. You can buy alcohol 24 hours a day at both on-premises (bars, etc, assuming they're open) and off-premises (off-licences, etc). It is one of the more relaxed states, with state law rendering public intoxication legal.

Coyote Ugly

New York-New York, 702 740 6969, www.nynyhotelcasino.com/entertainment
This is by far the wildest bar in town. It is like the wild fraternity parties from *Animal House* you've seen on the movies, only like a Southern bar. Based on the New York namesake, this saloon with a dance floor is designed to look like a bar that has seen years of partying. The hot and sassy female bartenders are part of the entertainment – they have not only elevated pouring drinks to an art form, but also get on the bar for an act of sexy dance numbers and amazing stunts from fire-blowing to body shots. Once bartenders have done their thing, female punters are

invited to dance on the bar as well and even nail some of their undies on the Bra Wall of Fame. No fancy concoctions served here, only straight shots of liquor and beer. Open Sun–Thurs 6pm–2am; Fri and Sat 6pm–3am. $10 cover after 9pm.

Double Helix Wine & Whiskey Lounge

Town Square Las Vegas, 702 735 9463, www.doublehelixwine.com
Located between Yard House and nu Sanctuary lounge and below Johnny McGuire's, this bar offers 30 unique wines by the glass and 50 whiskies and a unique twist in the form of Double Helix's signature winetails. Sink into a lounger with a drink on the patio around a fire pit, cooled by a mister and pick at tasty small-plates created by chef Doug Vega, from Daniel Boulud's DB Brasserie. Other locations are at The Palazzo and Tivoli Village. Open Mon–Wed 3pm–midnight, Thurs–Sun noon–midnight.

Drai's After Hours

Bill's Gamblin' Hall & Saloon, 3595 South Las Vegas Blvd, 702 737 0555, www.drais.net
A decadent after-hours joint which resembles some kinky salon decked out in lacquered wood, red sofas and plenty of leopard skin, with fine wines, Champagnes and cigars. Don't be put off by its location in the basement of Bill's Gamblin' Hall (previously Barbary Coast Hotel). Open Thurs–Mon 1am–close.

Gilley's Saloon

Treasure Island, www.treasureisland.com/nightlife
Billing itself as the only real honky tonk saloon on the Strip, bikini bull riding and the Gilley Girls dressed in bikinis, chaps and cowboy hats and boots show off their casino dealing skills in the Party Pit. Budweiser and barbecues are on menu. Open Sun–Thurs 11am–2, Fri–Sat 11am–4am.

Gordon Biersch

Restaurant Row, 3987 Paradise Road at Flamingo, 702 312 5247, www.gordonbiersch.com
Filled with beautiful people, this is one of the city's hottest pick-up parlours. Great brews, good food and live swing music make it a fun place to go. Open Sun–Thurs 11am–midnight; Fri and Sat 11am–1am.

Bar and club awards

Best for beautiful people: Surrender, XS, Marquee, V-Bar, Venus, Tabu and Risqué
Best for celeb spotting: The Bank, LAX, Tao, Moon and Pure
Best for cowboys: Gilley's Saloon
Best party time: Coyote Ugly
Best for salsa/Latin: Club Rio, Thursday nights, Dulce Latin Night at Gonzalez Y Gonzalez and Vida!
Best Strip views: Curve, Mix Lounge, VooDoo Rooftop Nightclub, Hush, Pure, Moon, Tao and Bar Veloce
Hippest: Surrender, XS, Marquee, Shadow, Ghost Bar
Hottest club in town: eyecandy sound lounge, Tao, Moon, XS, Club Nikki
Swankiest: Tabu, Ghost Bar and The Bank, Marquee, Surrender, XS, Club Nikki
Wildest: Coyote Ugly

BRITTIP
For a romantic cocktail with a view, head to Romance At The Top of the World at the Stratosphere. www.stratospherehotel.com/Hotel/Nightlife.

Harrah's Carnival Court

Harrah's, 702 731 7778, www.harrahslasvegas.com
Join the carnival of fun at one of the liveliest of Vegas's outdoor venues. If you're not enamoured with the new sophistication of Vegas and just want a really good knees up, this is the place for you. Bar staff are well trained to entertain with singing and dancing to juggling bottles on the bar. Open Sun–Thurs noon–2am; Fri and Sat noon–3am.

Kahunaville Party Bar

Treasure Island, www.treasureisland.com/nightlife
This Hawaiian-inspired bar has a little bit of the frat bars about it, but just manages to keep a lid on it despite the flamboyant bartenders and dancing servers. Live sports on TV, live DJ, oxygen bar and lei girls. Open Sun–Thurs 11am–2am; Fri and Sat 11am–3am.

Petrossian Bar

Bellagio, 702 693 7111, www.bellagio.com/nightlife
Those who enjoy the finer things in life

6

The Bank

should head to the chichi Petrossian. Champagne, smoked salmon, Petrossian caviar, vodka tastings and a choice of cigars are the order of the day here. Open 24/7. Afternoon tea 2–5pm, caviar Sun–Thurs noon–midnight; Fri and Sat noon–1am.

BRITTIP
In this city that never sleeps, Pour 24 at New York, New York does what it says on the label, and is open 24/7. It also celebrates 24 of the best American Craft Beers, which amusingly includes Newcastle Brown Ale! www.nynyhotelcasino.com/entertainment

The Pub

Monte Carlo,
www.montecarlo.com/restaurants
This contemporary 'Pub' has more than 200 beers on tap, stacked in lit up large kegs behind the bar. If not in beer mode, choose from milkshakes such as The Luck of the Irish and Peppermint Snowflake or an international food menu. It also has big screen sports, duelling piano players and dancing to live DJs. Open Sun–Thurs 11am–11pm, Fri–Sat 11am–3am.

Rouge

MGM Grand, 702 891 7433,
www.mgmgrand.com/nightlife
Designed by the famed Adam Tihany and

featuring sleek chrome and red Ferrari leather decor around a towering wall of liquors, this is a cool cocktail hangout (formerly Teatro). Signature flavoured ice cubes and model servers add to the mix! Open Mon–Thurs 3pm–close; Fri–Sun noon–close.

Zuri

MGM Grand, 702 891 7433,
www.mgmgrand.com/nightlife
With live nightly entertainment, this 100-seat bar just off the hotel's main lobby specialises in fruit-infused spirits such as frozen Woodford Reserve bourbon infused with peaches, cinnamon-infused vodka and speciality beers from around the globe. Open 24/7.

BRITTIP
If you've had a heavy night, try Zuri's For the Morning After the Night Before menu, which includes a variety of liquid brunch drinks and Bloody Marys!

Hotel lounges

One of the most wonderful things about Las Vegas is the lounge scene, a phenomenon that's unique to the city. Best of all, there is no entrance fee, although there may be a minimum drink order. The lounges all provide live music and just about every hotel has a good one.

The Beatles REVOLUTION Lounge

Mirage, 702 693 8300,
www.thebeatlesrevolutionlounge.com
Along with Cirque du Soleil®'s Beatle's tribute show *LOVE*, the Mirage opened up this '60s retro lounge inspired by all things Beatles. It has a modern twist on '60s psychedelic décor, including viewing holes behind the bar inspired by a yellow submarine. Open Wed–Mon 10pm–4am, Thurs–Mon 6pm–4am.

Le Cabaret

Paris Las Vegas, 702 739 4111,
www.parislasvegas.com
Designed to create the feeling of sitting outside in a garden area, this lounge allows you to sit under trees laced with twinkling lights while sipping your drinks and enjoying the live entertainment.

Caramel Lounge

Bellagio, 702 693 7111,
www.bellagio.com/nightlife
This is an excellent spot to enjoy a pre-show or late-night drink. Opaque marble tables, hand-blown glass sculptures, oversized round ottomans and leather sofas create an elegant and sophisticated setting for a trendy, yet relaxed lounge. It's all done on a theme of caramel – hence the name. Music ranges from the Rolling Stones to Frank Sinatra and the Beatles. The food menu includes the classic Las Vegas shrimp cocktail, pâté, smoked salmon and an assorted cheese plate, but the thing to go for here is the signature Martini served in chocolate and caramel-coated chilled glasses. Open daily 5pm–4am; DJs on at 10pm.

BRITTIP
Drinks take centre stage at many bars and lounges. At **Caramel** in Bellagio, speciality drinks are served in chocolate and caramel-coated Martini glasses. **Red Square** at Mandalay Bay not only offers more than 100 types of vodka but also keeps drinks cold on their bar made out of ice.

Fleur Lounge

Mandalay Bay, 702 632 9400,
www.mandalaybay.com/dining/signature-restaurants/fleur.aspx
A cosy and intimate lounge with live music, it opens pre-dinner for drinks, although the globally-inspired small plates by celebrity chef Hubert Keller, which may tempt you to stay. Open daily 5pm–10.30pm.

Galleria Bar

Caesars Palace, 702 731 7778,
www.caesarspalace.com
An elegantly laid-back lounge in which to relax and enjoy a happy hour cocktail. Open 24 hours a day.

BRITTIP
Fancy a pit stop on your way up and down the Strip, but don't want to sit in a freezing cold, air-conditioned bar? Then head for the poolside Dolphin Bar at the Mirage, where it's cool, not cold.

Ghost Bar

The Palms, 702 942 6832,
www.n9negroup.com/#/ghostbar/main/
A sultry indoor-outdoor lounge and sky deck on the 55th floor of The Palms, with a 360-degree view of the glittering Las Vegas skyline, that has quickly become one of the hottest places in town. Decked out in silver, white, greens and greys, it has floor-to-ceiling windows, a 30ft/9m ghost-shaped ceiling that changes colour and custom-made ultra-contemporary lounge furniture including plastic egg-shaped chairs that would be perfect in a 1960s sci-fi show. Celebs such as David Schwimmer, Cuba Gooding Jr, Samuel Jackson and Mark Wahlberg have all enjoyed the private VIP lounge and the eclectic music and the bar has featured in MTV's *Real World: Las Vegas*. Miss it and miss out. Open nightly 8pm–late.

The Beatles REVOLUTION Lounge

© MGM

Best alfresco hangouts

The Boulevard Pool, The Cosmopolitan (page 140)
Ghost Bar, The Palms (page 133)
Harrah's Carnival Court, Harrah's (page 131)
Hyde Lounge, Bellagio (page 137)
Nikki Beach, Tropicana (page 140)
Pure Nightclub, Caesars Palace (page 139)
Tryst, Wynn Las Vegas (page 140)
VooDoo Rooftop Nightclub, Rio All Suite Hotel & Casino (page 135)

Ignite Lounge

Monte Carlo, 702 730 7423,
www.montecarlo.com/restaurants/lounges/
aspx
The newest lounge to open at the Monte Carlo, meet and mingle over cocktails in a sexy red ambience.

Japonais Lounge

The Mirage, 866 339 4566,
www.mirage.com/nightlife
Overlooking the Mirage casino floor, this lounge is pure Vegas with chandeliers and sushi. Open Sun–Wed 3pm–midnight; Thurs–Sat 3pm–1am.

La Scena Lounge

The Venetian, 702 414 1000,
www.venetian.com
You won't escape the video games here, but you will enjoy the nightly entertainment of high-energy bands performing anything from rock 'n' roll to Motown, disco and top 40 hits. Open Sun–Mon 7.30pm–1am.

◀️🇬🇧▶️ **BRIT**TIP
Lounges may provide free music, but drinks can start at a pricey $5 and rise to an even more hefty $12 a hit – so sip, don't glug!

Mix Lounge

Mandalay Bay, 702 632 9500,
www.mandalaybay.com/nightlife
Atop THEhotel on the 64th floor, the 300-capacity lounge features wall-to-wall black leather décor with red accents and a balcony with a dizzying view. The lounge is located adjacent to Alain Ducasse's restaurant of the same name that features one of the largest chandeliers in Las Vegas

as well as music spun by savvy DJs. Opens 5pm. Cover Thurs–Sat $15. THEhotel guests $10 and local ladies free!

Rhumbar

The Mirage, 702 792 7615,
www.mirage.com/nightlife
A relaxing lounge bar serving minty mojitos, Latin Manhattans and other great rum-inspired cocktails. With Strip views and a cigar humidor on the patio, this is laid-back lounging, Caribbean style.
Open Sun–Thurs noon–1am; Fri–Sat noon–2am.

Risqué

Paris Las Vegas, www.parislasvegas.com
This nightclub-style lounge has hot sounds, VIP bottle service and Strip views from the second-storey balcony. Watch out for celebs slipping past the velvet ropes.

Seahorse Lounge

Caesars Palace, 702 731 7778,
www.caesarspalace.com
Inspired by the most captivating elements of the sea world, a towering 1,700-gall/7,730-l aquarium filled with seahorses announces your arrival at one of the most chilled lounges in town. Tuck into seafood appetisers and sip on Champagne or any one of the speciality Martinis as you get a 360-degree view of Australian pot-belly seahorses.

Shadow Bar

Caesars Palace, 702 731 7778,
www.caesarspalace.com
This 'destination' lounge sets itself apart with its provocative shadow dancers, whose silhouetted performances dance to house and hip-hop while punters knock back high-energy cocktails.

◀️🇬🇧▶️ **BRIT**TIP
Shadow is the perfect place for a drink after a show and before hitting your chosen nightclub.

THELounge

Mandalay Bay, 702 632 7777,
www.mandalaybay.com/entertainment
Slink into plush, club chairs, enjoy a match from the TV at the bar or get in a round at the billiards table in THEHotel.

V Bar

**The Venetian, 702 414 3200,
www.venetian.com**
Known to celebrities and Martini
aficionados, V Bar was created by the
owners of New York's superclub Lotus. This
upscale lounge wrapped in translucent
glass is both relaxing and upbeat. The
focal point is a custom-designed oversized
bed made of pearlised silver leather and
hollowed in the centre to allow space for a
table holding a selection of exotic cocktails.
Open Sun–Wed 5pm–2am; Thurs–Sat
5pm–3am.

VooDoo Rooftop Nightclub

**Rio All-Suite Hotel, 3700 West Flamingo,
702 777 6875, www.harrahs.com**
The view of the Strip is fantastic from the
51st floor and so are the bottle-juggling
bartenders. Sit inside or outside on the
terrace while sipping one of the many
speciality drinks, such as the Witch Doctor,
a mix of 4 rums and tropical fruit juices and
dance the night away to live DJs 7 nights a
week. Open nightly from 9pm.

BRITTIP
The lifts to the VooDoo Rooftop
Nightclub are on the second floor
of the Masquerade Tower.

Non-hotel lounges

Armadillo Lounge

**Texas Station, 2101 Texas Star Lane, 702
631 1000**
A real hit with the locals, thanks to the fair
prices, this lounge is a happening place
most nights of the week. Almost every
musical style plays here from rock to blues,
jazz, country and reggae. Phone the
entertainment hotline for more information
on 702 631 1001.

Fireside Lounge

**The Peppermill Coffee Shop, 2985 Las
Vegas Boulevard South, 702 735 4177,
www.peppermilllasvegas.com/lounge**
One of the swankiest and oldest surviving
lounges with cosy booths, an intimate
atmosphere and the famous fire pit – a
circular fireplace surrounded by a pool of
bubbling water. Recently named one of
America's 10 Best Make-out Bars by *Nerve*
magazine, this kitschy spot has attracted

Best nightspots for views

Bar Veloce, M Resort (page 130)
The Boulevard Pool, The Cosmopolitan
(page 140)
Chateau Nightclub & Gardens, Paris Las
Vegas (page 137)
Ghost Bar, The Palms (page 133)
Moon, The Palms (page 138)
Pure, Caesar's Palace (page 139)
Top of the World, The Stratosphere
(page 115)
VooDoo Rooftop Nightclub, The Rio
(see left)

the likes of Sharon Stone and Joe Pesci.
One of the quirks of the joint is that the
waitresses – clothed in long black dresses
split to the thigh – sit down at your table
to take your order. Try the Scorpion, the
giant-sized house special cocktail for 2, a
64oz/1.8l glass with 6 shots of various
spirits, ice cream and two 2ft/60cm long
straws! Open 24/7.

Ultra-lounges

Is it a bar? Is it a music venue? Is it a
nightclub? Is it a decadent den of iniquity?
The new breed of nightlife in Las Vegas is
called the ultra-lounge and it combines all
of the above. Think luxurious decor, ultra
comfy seating, sensuous music and a sense
that anything goes and you'll start to build
up a picture of the newest kind of scene
on the block. Another element that marks
an ultra-lounge out from a lounge or a
nightclub is the relatively small dance floor
– it's all about getting intimate, baby!

eyecandy sound lounge & bar

**Mandalay Bay, 702 632 7777,
www.mandalaybay.com/nightlife**
Located at the centre of Mandalay Bay's
casino floor, this ultra, ultra-lounge features
interactive touch tables, revolutionary
iPod® sound stations which, on promotional
nights, allow guests the chance to hear their
personal music mixes integrated into the
lounge's repertoire. The best of Deftal DJs
and VJs spin seven nights a week. Instead
of traditional bottle service, eyecandy
features tables that can be purchased by
the hour, where guests can drink their
choice of libations – including cocktails
from Master Mixologist Tony Abou-Ganim
– throughout the evening. eyecandy bar is
open daily 11am–late and eyecandy sound
lounge is open 6pm–late.

6

Flirt Lounge

Rio Las Vegas, 866 746 7671,
www.riolasvegas.com
One of the breed of ultra lounges, this bar
is pitched at women gathering after seeing
the Chippendales show, and as the blurb
goes, in the mood to flirt! Whether that's
true or not, it's a cool bar. Open to ticket
holders Thurs–Tues 6.30pm and to general
public Sun–Thurs 8.30pm–late.

I-Bar

Rio All-Suites Hotel, , www.riolasvegas.com
The 'I' stands for Ipanema and this is a
cool, quiet but erotic place. There are
ten I-Girls – part model, part provocative
dancer and part gifted mixologist – who
serve up fruity drinks like Tropicana
Hypnosis and Peachy Keen. Open from
2pm–2am or later.

Risqué

Paris Las Vegas, 702 946 4589,
www.parislasvegas.com
On the second floor of the chic Paris
hotel with dramatic views of the Strip,
this ultra-lounge combines classic Parisian
architecture with contemporary Asian style
and discreet lighting elements in which to
lounge or dance until dawn. What makes
this place so special, though, are the
balconies, plush couches, ottomans, beds,
piles of pillows and intimate, lighted dance
floor. Open Wed–Sun 10pm–4am.

BRITTIP
Drink-drive penalties are severe
and strictly enforced in the
city so don't even think about it.
Besides, most of the best bars, lounges
and nightclubs are around the Strip so
you can either walk or take a taxi (see
page 14).

Eyecandy

© MGM

Tabu

MGM Grand, 702 891 7183,
www.mgmgrand.com/nightlife
The MGM Grand's cutting edge nightclub
for the ultra sophisticated beautiful people
combines luxury with state-of-the-art
technology and excellent service from
models. The funky furniture, marble tops,
wooden floors and gorgeous textiles are
highlighted by saucy images of body parts
that bounce off every surface with reactive
imagery. The main room leads to 2 private
rooms, one with a bar made of ice and
metallic fabrics. Music goes from classic
lounge tunes earlier in the night to more
progressive vocals later in the evening.
Champagne and vodka are the house
specials. Open Fri–Mon from 10pm.

BRITTIP
Ensure yourself a reserved table
at the trendy Tabu by ordering
a bottle in advance of your visit,
through the VIP services manager on
702 891 7129.

Tao

Venetian, 702 388 8588,
www.venetian.com
Tao is not only a top restaurant but it also
hosts what has become the hottest and
sexiest ultra-lounge in Vegas. It is an odd
mix of Oriental spirituality – with sensitive
rock gardens, candles and waterfalls – and
New York modernism in the clean lines
and colours. Just see the modernistic bar
surrounded by hundreds of tiny Buddha
statues and you will understand. It is also a
hands-down favourite with celebrities and
home to some of the most raucous parties
in Sin City. Think gorgeous go-go dancers
and a 40-ft/12-m long outside terrace
with stunning views of the Strip. Everyone
from Mariah Carey to Janet Jackson have
sampled. Lounge open Sun–Weds 5pm–
midnight, Thurs–Sat 5pm–1am; Nightclub
open Thurs and Fri 10pm–5am; Sat
9.30pm–5am.

Hotel nightclubs

10AK

The Mirage, 702 693 8300,
www.mirage.com/nightlife
The Jet nightclub has held this space for 6
years and frequented by celebrities such as
Sean 'Diddy' Coombes, Rhianna and Lady
Gaga is reincarnated as 10AK on New

Year's Eve 2012 as the latest evolution of nightlife artistry developed by the Light Group in partnership with New York City's Butter Group. With 1OAK NYC already celebrity haunt, the Vegas opening looks set to be one of the city's hottest new clubs.

The Bank

Bellagio, 702 693 8300,
www.bellagio.com/nightlife
Previously hot celebrity hangout Light, The Bank is Bellagio's signature nightclub by The Light Group and has helped revolutionise the Vegas club concept with a high energy atmosphere in 6,600 ft^2/613m^2 that includes VIP booths and a glass-encased dance floor. Open Thurs–Sun 10.30pm–4am.

Chateau Nightclub & Gardens

Paris Las Vegas, 702 776 777,
www.parislasvegas.com
The newest nightlife venue at Paris Las Vegas, Chateau Nightclub & Gardens spanning more than 45,000ft^2/4181m^2 and 2-storeys combining classic French opulence with modern eclectic style and with 6 bars, a DJ booth and VIP seating, it has three separate experiences – a high-energy nightclub; Strip-side Chateau Terrace – a 10,000ft^2/9300m^2 balcony – and Parisian gardens. The Chateau Terrace is a beer garden by day, opening 10am, with luxury cabañas for a good view of the Bellagio Fountains. Perhaps most magical though is taking the glass elevator to dance under the stars on the rooftop dance floor in the lavish gardens with cabañas below the Eiffel Tower encircled by an 8ft/2.4m glass wall with a spectacular view over the Vegas skyline. Open 10pm–late.

Cleopatra's Barge

Caesars Palace, 702 731 7778,
www.caesarspalace.com
A theme offering from the Greco-Roman resort, this always popular club is housed in an ornate replica of the kind of craft that once transported royalty down the River Nile. Statues and centurions abound in the beautiful setting where live contemporary dance music is on the menu and drinks are served by luscious hand maidens in diaphanous Cleopatra costumes. Open Tues–Sun 8.30pm–4am.

Gallery Nightclub

Planet Hollywood, 702 818 5700,
www.planethollywoodresort.com

© CityCenter

Marquee at The Cosmopolitan

The provocative Gallery Nightclub has opened as the newest nightlife venue in Planet Hollywood resort. Designed by burgeoning talent Amy Kim of AK DesignNETWORK, the 20,000ft^2/1858m^2 space fuses vintage gothic design with contemporary touches, dancers styled in voyeuristic fashions perform nightly in a playfully sexy backdrop which includes candlelit glass fireplaces creating a mysterious sexy glow, and erotic photography. The Main Room has a sprawling dance floor, 2 bars and an elevated DJ booth, where renowned DJs spin a mix of house, mash-ups, hip-hop and top 40. Open Weds–Sat 10pm–late.

Gold Diggers

The Golden Nugget, 129 East Fremont Street, 702 385 7111,
www.goldennugget.com
Gold Diggers, the newest nightlife experience at The Golden Nugget, is a state-of-the-art entertainment venue boasting a large dance floor bordered by bartenders serving up enticing libations in a fun-filled atmosphere. Just steps away from the party, the nightspot opens to a 180-degree, oversized balcony providing stunning views of Fremont Street Experience. Open Wed–Sun 9pm–late.

Hyde Lounge

Bellagio, www.bellagio.com/nightlife
The Fontana Bar reopens as well-known LA nightclub brand The Hyde Lounge, on New Years Eve 2011. Designed by Philippe Starck, it will operate as a lounge until 10pm and then transform into an indoor–outdoor nightclub. It is the place to take in the stunning dancing waters of Bellagio's 8acre/3ha lake.

6

LAX

The Luxor, 702 262 4529,
www.luxor.com/nightlife
One of LA's hottest nightclubs lights up
Luxor with star power courtesy of celebrity
investors DJ AM and Christina Aguilera.
From the creators of Pure Nightclub, LAX
Las Vegas combines the best of its Los
Angeles namesake with the energy and
excitement that only Pure Management
Group can create. Catering to a
sophisticated Hollywood crowd, LAX is
a 'see and be seen' place for club-goers,
A-list celebrities and the social jet set. Open
Wed–Sat 10pm–late.

Marquee Nightclub and Dayclub

The Cosmopolitan, 702 333 9000,
www.marqueelasvegas.com
From the same people that created the
popular Tao and LAVO nightclubs, pumped
$60m into the 60,000ft^2/5574m^2 Marquee
Nightclub in Las Vegas's hottest new
hotel, has three lavish rooms with varied
musical experiences. Resident and visiting
DJs including Markus Schultz – including
Kaskade spin house music in the main room
with a 40ft/12m LED screen, dance floor
surrounded by spacious leather booths and
go-go dancers on the catwalks. There's
usually hip hop in the Boom Box Room
which has dark tones, silhouetted paintings
and faux crocodile skin flooring. Then
there's a library with billiards and a bar.

The Day Club completes the experience
in spring and summer, with 2 large pools
and cabañas with private plunge pools,
outdoor gaming and 3-storey bungalows
with rooftop pools. Open Mon, Thurs, Fri
and Sat 10pm–4am. Marquee Dayclub
seasonally 10am–6pm. Men pay $30 and
women $20.

Moon

The Palms, 702 942 6832,
www.n9negroup.com/#/moon/main/
With the opening of the Palms' Fantasy
Tower, the hotel added yet another
nightclub, Moon. Located at the top of the
tower and featuring a retractable roof, it
boasts panoramic views of the city below
as well as an outdoor patio, private VIP
room and exclusive table service. Open
Tues, Thurs–Sun 11pm–late.

Pure

Caesars Palace, 702 731 7873,
www.caesarspalace.com or

www.purethenightclub.com
This insanely popular ultra-club was
actually launched by a group of Hollywood
personalities and local tennis hero, Andre
Agassi. It offers 4 distinct areas over 2
storeys each featuring its own DJ and sexy
style. The cream, white and silver decor of
the main room contrasts sharply with the
VIP-only Red Room with its plush fabrics,
chandeliers and upholstered walls. A glass
lift will then take you up to the terrace with
its dance floor, private cabañas and tables
that offer spectacular views of the Strip.
Open Thurs–Sun, Tues 10pm–4am.

✈ BRITTIP

Want to experience the VIP
treatment? Well, money talks
in Vegas. You don't need to be a
celeb – you just need to hand over the
dosh. You may have to part with at least
$150–200 for a booth – could be worth
it for the special treatment if you're with
a crowd. Call in advance to check out
the prices.

Rain

The Palms, 702 942 6832, www.palms.com
The massive multi-level Rain doubles as
a nightclub and concert venue and is
famous for its special effects, which include
water, fire and fog. The back of the stage
is flanked by a 16ft/5m, colour-changing
water wall and the front by a rain curtain.
You enter through a gold-mirrored mosaic
tunnel and can either head straight for the
elevated bamboo dance floor surrounded
by a computer-programmed river of water
or find a private booth with water sofas
(there are only 8, so it's best to book one!).
VIPs and the very wealthy can opt for one
of the cabañas with mini-bars or a sky box
with a private balcony on the third floor.

Food is available and appetisers include
shrimp cocktail, smoked salmon canapés,
crab cakes, tenderloin skewers with
dipping sauce and full oyster and caviar
menus. Drink specialities include a sake
selection, premium tequilas, Champagnes
and Martinis. Serious clubbers should note
that Paul Oakenfold, one of the world's
leading DJs chose Rain as his first resident
DJ position, while DJ Pauly D has taken up
the hot seat. Open Fri and Sat 10pm–5am.

Rok Vegas

New York New York, 866 815 4365,
www.nynyhotelcasino.com/entertainment
Expect rock-inspired imagery, outdoor VIP
lounge and high energy music from Rok's

Why Vegas is the new Ibiza

Following in the footsteps of Paul Oakenfold and Pete Tong, DJ Markus Schultz, resident DJ at The Marquee club at The Cosmopolitan explains why he thinks Las Vegas is poised to rival Ibiza in the clubbing stakes

'Ibiza has 3 decades of serious clubbing history. Las Vegas has around 2 years, so give it another 10 years and the club scene will be as big as Ibiza. Nevada has a history of rave culture, at its height in the late nineties with raves out in the desert and community-led events like the Burning Man Festival. Now a lot of those young rave promoters who created that scene have grown up and are behind the big Vegas clubs. There's a lot of influence coming from California, and in particular Los Angeles, which is the epicentre for EDM (electronic dance music or techno). It's a bit like the relationship between London and Ibiza and clubs are evolving with boutique clubbing coming to the fore. The new style of DJing is the residency where the whole room is built for the DJ. When you look back at Vegas, it's going to be Paul Oakenfold who paved the way with Planet Perfecto at The Palms in 2008 and now I feel proud to be resident DJ at The Marquee.

'Whereas in a city like New York, clubs have to shut their doors at 7am, Vegas truly is a 24-hour city, and whereas in Ibiza people chill on the beach then go clubbing, here there's no beach, so the clubbing can go on 48 straight hours. There really should be a mandatory siesta in Vegas! In Ibiza you come for a week of partying, in Vegas the maximum is 2 or 3 nights. There are many niche clubs that open up during weekdays and if you want to hear local DJs, head down to Fremont East to venues like The Vanguard Lounge, Insert Coins and The Griffin. There's been a coming together of hip hop music and dance music in Vegas. Dance music was never able to get on MTV and hip hop artists were never able to tour the clubs, so it makes the perfect marriage as seen by the success of 50 Cent in Ibiza. I've been coming to Las Vegas for over 15 years, and I've never felt the electricity like it has right now. Everything is coming together like a perfect storm of clubbing. All of a sudden there's a new generation of creativity and energy.'

6

resident DJ followed by resident VJ (video jockey) who mixes lighting effects with vivid images displayed through the club. Open Wed–Sun 10pm–5am. Cover charge $10 ladies, $20 men.

BRITTIP

Vegas is fast becoming a hotspot for electronic music, with the Electric Daisy Carnival (www. electricdaisycarnival.com) in 2011 and DJ guest residencies by some of the world's most famous DJ's - Tiesto, Lil' John DJ Vice, Pete Tong, Markus Schultz and David Guetta.

Studio 54

MGM Grand, 702 891 7254, www.mgmgrand.com/nightlife
The namesake of the '70s and '80s New York nightclub that defined an era, Studio 54 was recently named 'Best Place to Dance' by the *Las Vegas Weekly's* Readers Poll. A high-energy nightclub, it has state-of-the-art sound, video and lighting along with a troupe of live dancers. There are 4 separate dance floors and bars, an exclusive area for invited guests, plus the

Rainforest Café, a giant show bar with 50 video screens and music. Tuesday evening is Eden – Erotically Delicious Entertainer's Night – and Thursday is Dollhouse night when guests can dress up beautiful life-size 'dolls' in outfits from the club's reach-in closets. The dolls then serve as hosts in place of cocktail waitresses. Tues–Sat 10pm–5am.

Surrender

Wynn Las Vegas, 702 770 7300, www.surrendernightclub.com
The most recent collaboration between Steve Wynn and nightlife impressario Sean Christie, a 120ft/37m long sleek silver snake lies seductively behind the main bar of this indoor/outdoor nightclub. Plush banquettes and VIP seating overlooks the dance floor surrounded by go-go dancers and Cirque de Soleil® artists on 8 dance platforms. Outside, a 45,000ft²/4181m² oasis has 3 tiered pools, 26 VIP cabañas with flat screen TVs and private balconies and 8 decadent bungalows and a glass DJ booth with electronic music every Friday. Open Weds, Thurs, Fri, Sat 10.30pm–closing.

Tryst

Wynn Las Vegas, 702 770 3375,
www.wynnlasvegas.com

This could be the cause of the ultimate romantic moment and something like this could only be found at the lavish Wynn Las Vegas. This fiendishly luxurious nightspot has intimate seating under an open-air main room and a sizeable dance floor that ends at a 90ft/27m waterfall that falls under cunning mood lighting. Service and drinks are decadently wonderful – and costly. Cover charge sometimes applies. Open Thurs–Sat 10pm–4am.

⚡ BRITTIP

Smart dress is essential to get into most nightclubs. Generally no trainers, denim or shorts are allowed, while baggy jeans are also banned and tank tops for men are a real no-no almost everywhere!

Vanity

Hard Rock Hotel, 702 693 5555,
www.hardrockhotel.com

The Hard Rock's sensualist's playground is firmly aimed at the kind of Hollywood celeb who loves to enjoy the adult environment of Las Vegas at the weekend. With mirrored walls and rich velvet and satin tapestries rubbed brass and black chrome, it screams high class. 50 VIP booths, and outdoor terrace with five cabañas and a women's lounge are luxurious surrounds to the centrepiece – a sunken dance floor with world-class DJs and a cyclone chandelier dripping with 20,000 lit cut crystals. Two marble bars provide space for mere mortals to stand and watch the action. Open Fri–Sun 10pm–4am.

⚡ BRITTIP

Las Vegas has no shortage of bias. Men pay more to get into nightclubs than women and many clubs charge out-of-towners double. Think $10–30 for men and up to $20 for women. In fact, in Vegas, there simply isn't a party if there aren't enough women in a club, so if girls turn up before 11pm on a regular night, it's possible that they might get their hands stamped for free and even given a complimentary glass of Champagne. You could even go round a few clubs before this time and get all the stamps so that you can pick and choose as the night goes on.

XS

Encore, 702 770 0097,
www.encorelasvegas.com

At XS, the new nightclub at Encore, after-dark impressario Victor Drai combines an outdoor pool environment with a sizzling club atmosphere and DJs The Manufactured Superstars and Afrojack have taken up residency. Destined to be the gold standard in Vegas nightlife, the club's design is inspired by the sexy curves of the human body and embraces the European pool and island bar it envelopes. The dance floor at XS is highlighted by a 10-ft/3-m rotating chandelier. If you're a high roller, or just plain stupid, order the Ono Signature cocktail priced at $10,000. Open Fri–Mon 10pm–4am.

⚡ BRITTIP

Avoid queuing to get into the hippest nightclubs in town. Buy front-of-line tickets in advance from www.vegas.com.

Hotel beach and pool clubs

These are the hottest new thing in town. See page 134 for the best al-fresco hangouts.

The Boulevard Pool

The Cosmopolitan, 702 698 7000,
www.cosmopolitanlasvegas.com

With its stunning location both looking down on the Strip and up at the mighty skyscrapers with a cracking view of the Eiffel Tower, The Boulevard Pool is a sophisticated open air place to chill out, drink or party. It's often used as an intimate live music venue where the likes of the Arctic Monkeys and TV on the Radio have played. Lounge chairs and day beds create a communal atmosphere round the pool. Open daily 9am–6pm and evenings. Subject to change based on events.

Nikki Beach

Tropicana Las Vegas Hotel Resort & Casino,
www.troplv.com/club-nikki or
www.nickkibeachlasvegas.com

In the same spirit of European sophistication and tropical élan as its venues in such locations as Miami, St. Tropez, Marbella and Cabo San Lucas, the ultimate beach club, Nikki Beach, has arrived in Vegas. Set in over 2acres/0.8ha of lush natural pool landscape, this is the newest, sexiest place to sun yourself on sleek loungers and opium beds, or enjoy premium bottle service and hors d'oeuvres as part of the VIP experience in one of the secluded cabañas.

A restaurant in view of a waterfall, outdoor café and bar, swim-up blackjack and a private island in the center of the tropical pool complete the picture, as well as the signature entertainment – high-energy dancers, professional musicians, interactive performance artists and an outdoor concert space for world-class musicians. At night, steps away from the Beach Club is 16,500ft²/1533m² Club Nikki, with glamorous ultra-lounge and dance floor with globe-travelling DJs within its all-white decor.

Palms Pool

Palms Pool & Bungalows, The Palms, 702 942 7777, www.palms.com
By day, a luxurious outdoor lounge with 2 pools, a lavender-shaded swimming pool and the Mermaid Cove – an elevated pool with portholes where mermaids swim after dark – plus 27 private cabañas and fibre-optically lit water salons, billiard tables, outdoor swings, poolside blackjack, trampolines, massages and other spa services. Three bars include The Waterfall Bar, behind a cascading 12ft/3.6m waterfall and The Glass Bar under an elevated glass bottomed deck pool, gives a clear view to those at the bar below.

Come night-time in the summer, the lounge is transformed into one of the most spectacular outdoor nightclubs and concert venues in Vegas for Ditch Fridays. It has a concert stage, 2 dance floors, including Plexiglass dance platforms where aqua go-go girls emerge from the lavender pool. An elevated pool-top dance floor allows you literally to dance on water. Atmosphere is added with lighting and fog effects.

Along with the rest of The Palms' venues, this has become a fast hit with locals and visitors alike – a true haven of voyeurism for adults. Poolside dining is provided by N9ne Steakhouse and includes specialities such as sashimi and ceviche.

During the day, Palms Pool is only open to hotel residents, but in the evening it is open to the public. Cover charges vary depending on the entertainment, while the beach party element is only on in summer.

Pool & Lounge Vdara

Vdara, 702 590 2030, www.vdara.com
Merging the boundaries between pool club and lounge, the Pool & Lounge Vdara has world class DJs, private spa cabañas with

plunge pools. Above Harmon Circle, on the rooftop, cocktails and tapas are served. Hours vary seasonally.

Rehab

Hard Rock Hotel, 702 693 5555, www.hardrockhotel.com
Home to some of the naughtiest night scenes in town (and that's saying something), the Hard Rock's poolside paradise comes complete with swim-up blackjack, waterfalls and private cabañas in an Indonesian-style setting. There are Sunday Pool Parties with Rockstar lemonade and world famous DJs that only just stop short of being called orgies (and sometimes cross the line).

Live Music Venues

Back Alley Bar

Stratosphere Hotel, www.stratospherehotel.com/Hotel/Nightlife
One of the newest bars on the Vegas scene, there's live music Thurs–Monday 10pm–3am. There are daily drink specials, plus 12 different beers on tap.

B.B. King's Blues Club

Mirage, 702 242 5464, www.mirage.com
Live music from blues greats, with the occasional appearance from the man himself Tues–Sat 8pm–1am. Seats have a good view of the stage and southern comfort food helps you get in the spirit.

House of Blues

Mandalay Bay, 702 632 7600, www.mandalaybay.com/nightlife
The legendary chain of restaurants-cum-live music venues and nightclubs provides an eclectic mix of music to serve all tastes. The venue, which can hold 1,900 people, plays host to every kind of band from rock to R&B, reggae, hip-hop, country, jazz and, of course, blues. You can catch anyone from B.B. King to Stevie Nicks here. A Sunday Gospel Brunch at the Crossroads at House of Blues features the best of gospel music and a Southern-style buffet with seating at 10am and 1pm. Live blues Thurs–Sat. The 500-seater restaurant under new TV celebrity Chef Aaron Sanchez serves old favourites like jambalaya and updated versions of staples like cornbread, pulled pork sandwiches and signature burgers. He has also created new dishes such as shrimp and grits, meatball sliders, chilli braised short ribs and street tacos.

Downtown on the up

Downtown Las Vegas's 3rd Street is quickly gaining popularity as one of the newest hotspots in Las Vegas as a dining and entertainment district featuring some of the best known nightlife hotspots. New York's famous **Hogs & Heifers** (www.hogsandheifers.com) opened with its unique brand of entertainment where bartenders wear halter tops and leather pants and are armed with megaphones to keep the mood as raucous as possible. Next door, **Triple George Grill** (www.triplegeorgegrill.com) features not only great food, but also a classic lounge where patrons can relax in oversized leather armchairs, smoke cigars and banter with the pianist. Near to the Triple George is **Sidebar** (www.sidebarlv. com), an intimate bar specialising in classic cocktails – its Martini voted Best of Las Vegas. Nearby, on Fremont Street East, **Beauty Bar** (www.thebeautybar.com/las_vegas) offers patrons a nail polish with their cocktail amidst décor taken straight out of an old New Jersey beauty parlour. Next door is **The Griffin** (702 382 0577), a new tavern with a movie-set feel, vaulted ceilings and 2 fire pits. Opposite, and adjacent to the Fremont Street Experience, is the new videolounge and games bar, **INSERT COIN(S)** (702 477 2525, insertcoinslv.com). Just around the corner, locals discover a cosy, sophisticated lounge called the **Downtown Cocktail Room** (www.thedowntownlv.net), serving signature Martinis in a classy atmosphere. And finally, downtown's Main Street Station houses the popular **Triple 7 Restaurant & Brewery** (www.mainstreetcasino.com/dining), recently named by the *Las Vegas Review Journal* as 'one of Vegas's hidden gems'.

BRITTIP

Don't hang around the bar at the House of Blues if you want to catch a good view of the band, the low-lying ceiling will obscure your view.

The Joint

Hard Rock Hotel, Harmon Avenue, 702 469 6295, www.hardrockhotel.com
Famous for its cracking live music in a great rock 'n' roll environment. Phone for live music updates. As Brandon Flowers, front man of The Killers and Las Vegas local said in *HRH* magazine, 'Before that, it was dismal – there were a couple places that nobody wanted to play at. Then I saw Oasis play at The Joint when I was about 17 and my life was changed.' Tiësto, known as the world's number one electronic DJ, had a residency here in 2011.

BRITTIP

Generally gig tickets go for $20–80, but can rise to a staggering $1,000 a hit if you want to see the Rolling Stones, for instance, at The Joint!

Jazz

Jazz Festival at the Fremont Street Experience

Downtown Las Vegas, 702 678 5600, www.vegasexperience.com
Go to the city during the last weekend in May and you'll enjoy the now annual free jazz festival that takes place throughout the 5 city blocks that make up the Fremont Street Experience.

Napoleon's

Paris Las Vegas, 702 946 7000, www.parislasvegas.com
One of the best Champagne bars in the city, with more than 100 varieties to choose from, it also has a full-service bar. So enjoy a glass of bubbly and sit back to soak up the smooth live jazz. The bar also has a fully stocked cigar humidor and a carving station for fresh rolls piled high with steak, mustard-rubbed roast turkey and wine-braised pork loin. Open Sun–Thurs 4pm–2am; Fri and Sat 4pm–3am. Live music nightly 9pm–1am.

BRITTIP

Phone Napoleon's in advance to check Happy Hour times, when you get a complimentary carving station roll if you buy a drink.

Onda Lounge

Mirage, 702 791 7111, www.mirage.com/nightlife
Just outside the Onda restaurant (see page 108), this is where you can sip wines by the glass and nibble on artisan cheeses or indulge in a cocktail while enjoying the live jazz. Rush Hour complimentary wine tastings on Fridays 5–7pm. Open nightly 5pm–10pm.

BRITTIP

Weird but true: women can 'entertain' men, but are not allowed entry to 'gentlemen's' clubs unless they arrive with a man!

Burlesque

Ranging from sexy through steamy and ribald to flat-out raunchy, sex sells, and the Las Vegas tradition of beautiful bodies reaches new levels as dancers and strippers from both sexes peel down to the very briefest of g-strings to the delight of panting crowds. The main admission prices may be reasonable, but guaranteed entry and the best seats in the house come with a hefty price tag.

Pussycat Dolls Burlesque Saloon

Planet Hollywood Resort, 702 818 3700, www.planethollywoodresort.com
The famous Pussycat Dolls of Hollywood lore have re-created their sexy show in a new saloon-style venue in Planet Hollywood Resort, complete with sultry bartenders pouring shots and non-stop performances. Clad in fishnet tights and leather bustiers, the Dolls sing, dance and generally tantalise their audience from the stage and swings that hang from the ceiling. Open Tues–Sat 9pm–4am.

Strip clubs

The sex industry is big business in Las Vegas and to prove it a raft of swanky new clubs has recently opened. Indeed the latest – Sapphire – cost $25m and is so upmarket you may even feel you've wandered into the lobby of a 5-star hotel. Kid yourself not though, the club is purely about titillation with a spot of elegance thrown in! The following are the major topless clubs.

Club Paradise

4416 Paradis Road, 702 734 7990, www.clubparadise.net
One of the older-style clubs, but extremely popular thanks to its lack of seediness (which in Las Vegas equals classy!). It consists of a large room with a nightclub atmosphere, 1 main stage and 2 other dance floors, plus go-go type dance stages near the ceiling. The club also has a restaurant and VIP room. Open Mon–Fri 5pm–8am, Sat and Sun 6pm–8am. Cover price: varies; lap dance $20.

Strip club etiquette

- First of all, in Las Vegas anyway, there is a distinction between a strip club and a gentlemen's club – the former offers full nudity and the latter topless only. Both have strict rules governing behaviour.
- While many strip clubs don't necessarily have a dress code, you won't get in if you look really scruffy or if you're drunk.
- If you try to touch one of the girls, you'll find yourself out on your ear pronto.
- Have plenty of cash. The girls are not paid and work for tips only. It's a big no-no to take in the sights and not tip.
- Don't even think about sitting stage side without a wad for both drinks and tipping.
- While the dancers are working girls, they're not THAT kind of working girl. Prostitution is illegal in Las Vegas – ironic or what! – so don't even think about it. It's also not on to ask for a date or even suggest dinner.

BRITTIP

If you really want to get up close – but not personal – the going rate for a lap dance is generally $20. VIP rates, usually for 4 dances in a private room, start at around $100.

Sapphire Gentlemen's Club

3025 South Industrial Road, 702 796 6000, www.sapphirelasvegas.com
The newest, swankiest, largest club in town, at 71,000ft^2/6,600m^2, it is massive, and at peak times there can be up to 800 topless dancers entertaining the crowds. The huge, multi-layered central stage can be seen from any part of the club, while music includes a variety of dance and top 40 hits. The 3 main bars are the Martini Bar, which has an enormous Martini glass as its centrepiece, Pete's Bar and the Off Broadway bar, generally used for private parties. Other facilities include the Stake restaurant, serving steaks, which has its own separate entrance, and VIP sky boxes, which allow clients to overlook the main dance floor from a private room. Typical cover price is $30. Lap dances $20; VIP lap dances $100 for 3; an hour in the VIP area $400; sky box $250 an hour including drinks, plus $500 an hour for lap dances. Open 24/7.

6

Other topless-only clubs

Cheetah's Topless Lounge

2112 Western Avenue between West Oakey Boulevard and Sahara Avenue, 702 384 0074, www.cheetahslv.net
One of the friendliest clubs, it puts a big emphasis on providing coverage of major sporting events. It has 5 intimate little stages and is a favourite with locals. Open 24/7. Cover price: $10, free with shuttle.

Crazy Horse III

3535 West Russell Road
At one time the premier strip club in Las Vegas, Crazy Horse Two was closed down and has been renamed to appear in a swanky new venue with a red glow, and good exotic dancers. Open 24/7. No cover price but $30 if arriving by public transport.

Girls of Glitter Gulch

20 East Fremont Street between Casino Center and Main Street, 702 385 4774, www.vegas.com/nightlife/stripclubs/glittergulch.html
Thanks to its location close to the Fremont Street Experience, this attracts a fairly touristy crowd. Open daily 1pm–4am. No cover price but drink minimum may apply.

Olympic Garden Cabaret

1531 Las Vegas Boulevard South at Wyoming Avenue, 702 386 9200, www.ogvegas.com
Once one of the largest topless clubs in Vegas – prior to the opening of Sapphire's – the main room has several stages, while the second has 2 stages and a catwalk. An exotic male dance revue takes place in the VIP lounge upstairs. Open 24/7. Cover price: free before 6pm, $30 after 6pm.

Play It Again, Sam

4120 Spring Mountain Road, 702 876 1550, www.playitagainsams.com
A gentlemen's-style club with an almost restaurant-like atmosphere, booths and video poker machines, the intimate club features an all-you-can-eat lunch buffet. Open 24/7. Cover price: $10 after 7pm.

The Spearmint Rhino

3340 South Highland Drive, 702 796 3600, www.spearmintrhinolv.com

Considered one of the best strip clubs in town, it offers excellent dancers, seating options and a choice of stages. Open 24/7. Cover price: $30 non-residents; free with complimentary limo service.

Total nudity

For classic dark and steamy, make for any of these old-time strip clubs, which all feature total nudity.

Can-Can Room

3155 Industrial Road, one block west of the Stardust Hotel, 702 737 6846, www.cancanroom.com
There are 5 stages and 7 fantasy theme rooms. The club offers private dances in VIP bedrooms – at a cost of $150 for 30 minutes. Open daily 9pm–dawn. No cover price.

✚ **BRITTIP** ————
Some strip clubs do a big, hard-sell number on private dances. Do not feel you have to commit yourself to something that could easily cost $150 unless you are happy with the quality of the dancer.

Little Darlings

1514 Western Avenue, half a mile south of Charleston Avenue/Interstate 15 intersection, 702 366 1141, www.littledarlingsnv.com
Open Mon–Sat 11am–6am daily; Sun 11am–4am. Cover prices: $10 for locals, $30 for non-residents with bottomless soft drinks.

Palomino Club

1848 North Las Vegas Boulevard, 500m south of the intersection with East Lake Mead Road, 877 399 2023, www.palominolv.com
Open daily 4pm–5am. Cover prices: $15 for locals and women, $30 non-residents.

Talk of the Town

1238 South Las Vegas Boulevard, one block south of the intersection with East Charleston Road, 702 385 1800
Open daily 4pm–4am; dancers start at 8pm. Cover price $20.

GAMBLING

Everything you need to know about having a flutter without blowing all your cash

You've seen the erupting volcano, watched the fountains of Bellagio and witnessed amazing circus acts – all in the most opulent, best-that-money-can-buy settings. Now let's get down to the nitty gritty, the *raison d'être* of the city – the casinos.

Most of the Strip resorts have their casinos laid out in such a way that you can't fail to notice them even before you've got to your room. That is so you don't need to spend 5 straight hours taking a chance, but just hit a few dollars here and there to and from the show or dinner. It's no surprise really: you have to accept that there is only one reason for all the glamour and razzmatazz: the making of money – absolutely billions of it. Vegas's gaming revenue in 2010 was a whopping $5.8bn with the average visitor spending $466.

BRITTIP
Remember the golden rules of gambling: stick to your own limits and always, always quit while you're ahead!

The casinos want people to have fun and to know when to walk away because they want them to return again and again and again. That way, they know, the odds are that they'll always get their money back – and more besides! High-roller baccarat players, the very latest slot machines, state-of-the-art video gambling machines and sports betting are the big money-spinners, and you'll also find everything else from roulette to craps and poker to blackjack.

To this end, the industry has been working hard to make casinos more user-friendly by providing free lessons in easy-to-find locations. A move to put 'comps' (see page 156) on a more straightforward footing has led to the creation of loyalty cards by many establishments where the amount of money you spend along with the time you spend gambling generates points to put towards free meals, free rooms and free shows.

Whether you intend to spend $20 or $2,000 gambling, or just sit in one of the many bars and watch the action, all these factors mean you can have a fantastic time in Las Vegas without parting with

huge amounts of money – as long as you follow the rules: stick to your own limits and always, always quit while you're ahead!

BRITTIP
Money raised from gambling was used to buy uniforms, provisions and bullets for troops fighting us Brits during America's fight for independence from 1775 to 1783.

Casino trends

As if the resorts and casinos weren't seductive enough, Las Vegas is putting a new spin on gaming, making it sexier and more exciting than ever before. The latest trend is the emergence of intimate, themed casinos within a casino.

The Pussycat Dolls Casino at Caesars Palace is located just across from The Pussycat Dolls Lounge inside Pure Nightclub. The casino features a mixture of sexy slot machines, blackjack, craps and roulette tables, a big 6 wheel and merchandise area, featuring the brand's sexy burlesque look. Playboy Enterprises, Inc., the Palms Casino Resort and N9NE

History of gambling in Vegas

It all began on 19 March 1931 when Governor Fred Balzar signed a bill that legalised gaming in Nevada. Since that day, Nevada, and especially Las Vegas, has become recognised worldwide as a premier gaming destination. From traditional card and dice games, to slot machines and race and sports book betting, the casino industry has flourished and evolved into an international phenomenon. Now, more than 75 years later, Nevada celebrates the very industry that has supported economic growth in the state.

Las Vegas has come a long way from its first legalised gaming establishment, Northern Club on Fremont Street, in 1931. Owned by Mayme Stocker and her family, the Northern Club and others like it on the infamous Block 16 in downtown Las Vegas pumped $69,000 into the state coffers during their first 2 years of operation. Today, gaming revenue in Clark County alone totals more than $10.9bn per year.

In the early 1940s, Thomas Hull selected a plot along the 2-lane highway that led to Los Angeles as the site for the El Rancho. His themed resort – the first in Las Vegas – would become the first hotel along what is now known as the Strip. Five years later, Benjamin 'Bugsy' Siegel would open his lavish Flamingo Hotel, ushering in the era of celebrity glitz in Las Vegas. Some of the world-famous entertainers who became synonymous with Las Vegas included The Rat Pack, Elvis and Liberace.

Further development occurred in the late 1960s when business, aviation and movie mogul Howard Hughes introduced corporate financing to the Las Vegas resort landscape. In 1989, Steve Wynn opened the Mirage, the first of many mega-resorts now lining the Las Vegas Strip. Today, gaming is still the centrepiece of Las Vegas, one of the world's most desirable destinations.

Group opened Las Vegas's first **Playboy Club** atop the new Fantasy Tower at The Palms. The club and casino showcase the iconic Playboy bunnies dealing high-limit table games, as well as a Diamond Bar built out of 10,000 diamond-shaped crystals.

While slot machines are the runaway favourite among gamblers in Las Vegas, table games have seen new additions and a tremendous resurgence in the popularity of poker. Some of the newer games, such as 3-card poker, and timeless favourites like pai gow continue to draw people to the tables. The increased exposure and popularity of poker, specifically Texas hold 'em, has prompted many casinos to re-open poker rooms that had been shuttered for a number of years. Las Vegas is featured regularly as the site of televised celebrity poker showdowns as well as professional poker tournaments.

High-rollers

The casinos like to keep all their customers happy, but they go to extraordinary lengths to accommodate high-rollers (big betters) – and I mean HIGH! Baccarat, the game they tend to play, accounts for a massive 13% of casino takings. With its high-bet limits and liberal odds, baccarat is worth a cool $1bn in gambling income worldwide and Las Vegas casinos have been working hard to cash in. Bally's casino on the Strip has

hired a high-roller expert to weed out the big fish – gamblers willing to bet $300,000 to $1m each hand – from the 'whales', who only bet around $250,000 a hand!

High-stakes poker is big business, too, and Las Vegas has been home to the World Series of Poker (WSOP) title for the last 4 decades. For 35 years, Binions Casino in the Fremont Street area hosted this gathering of card sharks. However, in 2005 Harrah's bought the rights to the WSOP and eventually moved it to the Rio All-Suite and Casino. This came as internet poker sites began to explode in popularity, and the WSOP exploded in size, besides being moved from May to a June–July setting.

The move included an increase in the number of events, and what was once a single poker tournament has reached a stunning series of 51 poker tournaments held over 6 weeks. The main event, a no-limit Texas hold 'em tournament that costs a cool $10,000 just to enter, attracted over 8,200 contestants in 2007. The winner in 2006, Jamie Gold, took home a breathless $12,000,000 from a single tournament played over 7 days. A set of laws enacted by the US Government which cut into the ability to transfer gambling money from US-based credit cards and bank accounts cut down on the 2007 WSOP event. The 2007 winner, Jerry Yang, overcame only 6,358 players and won a 'mere' $8,250,000.

The law

You must be over 21 to gamble in Las Vegas and under 18s are not allowed in arcades 10pm–5am during the week and midnight–5am at weekends. In a further move to appease the anti-gambling lobby, the city has passed a new law that bans under 18s from walking down or cruising the Strip after 9pm without a parent or guardian.

How to get in on the action

I remember the first time I visited Las Vegas, the bright lights were so overwhelming and the sheer scale of everything so overpowering that it seemed far too daunting to go into the casinos and play a game or more. Removing some of the mystique surrounding these games of chance is not to remove the magic of the setting, but it will give you the right kind of edge.

BRITTIP

When in a casino always remember that Big Brother is watching you! Mirrors or dark glass in the ceilings house cameras to record almost every square inch of the casino. In the old days, similar mirrors hid people who stood on catwalks to watch casino action to stop cheating by players or dealers.

When it comes to a weekend gambling spree, the average American will allow a budget of $200–500. When a touring Brit arrives in town, their budget of $100–200 is usually simply there to fritter away while downing complimentary drinks. If you do want to have a go, though, here is a guide to the different games, the rules and the best ways to place your bets, so that even if you don't win, you won't blow your entire budget straight away.

The aim of the game is to make your spending money last as long as possible while having fun – and, who knows, you may even come out a winner! Bear in mind that these tips are aimed at those people who are new to gambling as opposed to those looking for more detailed and advanced information. But I have included details of where you can go for further information and more in-depth advice.

Gambling milestones

1931	Nevada Governor Fred Balzar signs a bill legalising gaming in Nevada
1955	Nevada Gaming Control Board is established
Mid-1950s	Gaming revenue tops $100m
1964	Nevada Electronic introduces first electronic slot machine
2003	Non-gaming revenue surpasses gaming revenue in Clark County
2005	Nevada gaming revenue tops $11.6bn
2011	Nevada celebrates 80 years of gaming

The odds

There are 2 aspects to every game you play – the chance of you winning inherent in each game (the odds) and the rules designed to favour the house, including payoffs at less than the actual odds or predetermined payoffs, as in slot machines (the edge). It is because of this edge that, no matter how well you are playing or how much luck you seem to be having, the odds almost always favour the casinos, who will win everything back in the long run. That's why when you've come to the end of a winning streak you should always walk away.

Table games with the best odds on winning or on reducing your losses are baccarat and blackjack (in fact, you can expect to win money if you are an accomplished 'card counter' in blackjack). Craps is not good, roulette is terrible and in keno you have about as much chance of winning as you do with our National Lottery. Of course, a keno bet is usually $1 or less, so you may not care.

The 2 games on which you can actually expect to win money are blackjack (if you are a skilled card counter) and poker (if you are better than the other players). The other side of the coin, though, is that if you are not skilled, you will likely lose your coin quite fast.

As a general rule, the smaller casinos away from the Strip are what are known as the 'loosest' – they will offer the best returns on slot machines. For some time, the downtown casinos have been rated as the 'loosest slots in America' by the *Casino Player* magazine (www. casinoplayer.com). For instance, slot machines will give 95–99% return on your play. That means if you bet $1, you'll get

7

95–99 cents back over the long term if you win. Downtown, you have more chance of finding machines with a 98–99% return. Sometimes, as part of promotions, a casino will offer a few slot machines that offer a 100–101% return! But then it is only a few machines and they'll be available for only a short time.

BRITTIP
Be careful of places that have gaudy signs that say 'Loosest Slots'. Often they will have only one or two 99% machines in some hard-to-find corner, while the rest of the machines are 95% money-eaters.

The exception on the Strip is the Stratosphere, which has made a corporate decision to lure in punters with the promise of the best returns in town. Their deals include 100 times odds on craps, single-zero roulette, hand-dealt double-deck blackjack, double-exposure blackjack (where you see both the dealer's cards), 98% return on 100 $1 slots and more than 100% return on 100 video poker machines. But do bear in mind that there are only a certain number of the high-paying machines, so always check the returns on a machine before you play.

Limits

The table limits are an important consideration because the higher the minimum bet, the quicker you'll get through your money. Unless you're a serious gambler, you'll steer clear of baccarat. The minimum at most Strip resorts is $100! Cheapest, though, is New York-New York, which has games with minimum bets of $10. You can also play mini-baccarat at the Stratosphere with minimum bets of $5 per hand.

High rollers' area at Caesars Palace

Most Strip resorts have a minimum of $10 on blackjack. The cheapest are Circus Circus ($5), Excalibur ($5), Luxor ($5), Monte Carlo ($5), Stratosphere ($3) and Treasure Island ($3). In comparison, you'll find $2 blackjack tables aplenty and $1 roulette at casinos away from the Strip.

BRITTIP
Limits fluctuate. Minimum bets tend to be higher in the evening, at weekends and during special events. The Strip hotels all have higher minimums than downtown casinos.

Table games

Baccarat

There is normally an aura of glamour surrounding this game as it tends to attract high-rollers and is usually played in a separate, often more refined, area, cordoned off and staffed by croupiers in posh tuxedos. But don't be put off by the glamour of it all. The mega-bucks, high-roller games will be played in special VIP rooms, so the areas you see really are for mere mortals! What's more, it is an easy game to play and offers the best chance of you beating the casino.

Generally, up to 15 players sit around a table where 2 cards from an 8-deck shoe are dealt to each of the players and to the bank (see Gambling lingo, page 000). You can bet either on you winning, the bank winning or there being a tie, but you are only playing against the bank, not the other players. Each time you win, the casino takes a commission, though not if you lose.

The idea is simple: you're aiming to get to a total of either 8 or 9 and the value of the cards are: ace to 9 – face value; 10 and face cards – zero. If the cards add up to more than 10, only the second digit is counted. For instance, if your hand contains a 9 and a 4, it adds up to 13 but is worth 3 as you drop the first digit from the total. In this case you'd ask the dealer for another card.

The house edge in baccarat is very low, which is why it is such an attractive proposition. The edge when betting on a bank hand is 1.17% (though that is increased by the fact that a commission is always paid to the house on with-bank bets) and the edge on a player is 1.36%.

A version that is becoming very popular is mini-baccarat. Basically it is the same game, but it is played around a table about the size of a blackjack table, with spaces for 6 or 7 players.

 BRITTIP

In blackjack, avoid high minimum/low maximum tables like the plague – they'll eat up your bankroll in a very short space of time.

Blackjack or 21

After baccarat, blackjack (or 21) is one of the easiest games to play and the rows of blackjack tables in casinos reflect the huge number of gamblers who play the game. The object is to get as close to 21 as possible without 'busting'. There can be up to 6 people around a table, all playing against the dealer.

Bets are placed first, then the dealer gives 2 cards to each player and himself, the first face down (known as the hole card), the second showing (upcard). Numbered cards count as their face value, face cards count as 10 and aces are worth either 1 or 11. You can either decide to stand with the 2 cards you received or take a hit (another card from the dealer) until you're happy with your hand or you go bust.

When all the players have finished, the dealer turns over his hole card and takes hits until his total exceeds 17. If the dealer busts, everyone around the table wins, otherwise only those whose hands are higher than the dealer's win. If the

first 2 cards you are dealt total 21, then you've got what is known as a natural, i.e. a blackjack, and you automatically win. If both you and the dealer are dealt a blackjack, then it is a stand-off and no one wins.

As a general rule, if you have a hand without an ace against the dealer's 7 or higher, you should take hits until you reach at least 17. Against the dealer's 4, 5 or 6, you can stand on a 12 or higher; if against the dealer's 2 or 3, hit a 12.

With a soft hand (one which includes an ace), hit all totals of 17 or lower. Against the dealer's 9 or 10, hit 18.

What gives the house the edge is that you have to play your hand first, so even if the dealer busts after you have, you're still a loser. But there are 2 ways to help you even the odds – you can double down or split pairs. If you feel you may have a good hand and will only need one more card, you double down – i.e. you double your initial bet and accept one extra card to complete your hand.

If you are dealt a pair, you can opt to split them, thereby increasing your chances of winning. You separate the cards to create 2 hands, thereby doubling your bet, and draw extra cards for each hand. When splitting aces you are only allowed to take one extra card for each ace. If the next card is an ace, though, you can split again. The rule is always to split aces and 8s.

A word about 'insurance'. When the dealer's 'show' card is an ace, you will

7

Playing craps

Fun books and other freebies

Whether or not you intend to do any gambling, always check the casino cages for their free fun books. These will give free goes on slot machines, may entitle you to double a bet at the blackjack table or increase the value of a keno ticket. They will also be full of bargains on food and drink or offer discounts on souvenirs such as T-shirts. These books are also available from car rental agencies, hotels, motels and other locations in the city. Some tour operators – most notably Funway – have put together their own fun books, which include some fantastic deals on excursions and attractions.

The monthly *Las Vegas Advisor* gives subscribers lots of information on deals and freebies available in Las Vegas and sometimes includes valuable coupons or arranges special deals for subscribers. Sign up online at www.lasvegasadvisor.com. Subscriptions are $37 a year, but you'll generally get back that cost in money-saving coupons the first day in Las Vegas, let alone all the other tips! Also, check out their website for up-to-the minute top bargains and information.

be offered the chance to insure yourself against the dealer getting a blackjack to win 2–1 if the dealer holds a blackjack, so you break even. But it is not a good bet to make because even if you end up with a blackjack, you'll only get 2–1 on a bet that should pay 9–4.

Another way the casino gets an edge is by using a shoe containing 6 packs of playing cards. This makes busts less likely, which helps the dealer, who is forced by the rules to take more hits than the player. And blackjacks are also less frequent, another drawback as you get paid 3–2 for those.

If you want to learn more, call into the Gambler's Book Club (5473 S Eastern Ave (between Tropicana & Russell), 702 382 7555, www.gamblersbook.com, open Mon–Fri 9am–7pm, Sat 10am–6pm) where you'll find copies of just about every book ever written about blackjack, and experts on the game – including card counters – who are happy to answer questions. Also, most gift shops have blackjack strategy cards, playing-card sized helpers that give the 'book' answer to when to hit and when to stand.

Craps

We've all seen this game played down New York alleyways in gangster movies, now here's your chance to give it a go! Sadly it is one of the most complicated table games on offer, but it is also the one that produces the most excitement.

You join a game by standing anywhere around the table, start betting any time and wait for your turn to shoot. When rolling the dice you have to do it hard enough for them to bounce off the far wall of the table to ensure a random bounce. Basically, the shooter rolls a pair of dice that determine

the outcome of everyone's bets. The first roll is called the 'come-out roll'. If it is a 7 or an 11, the shooter and all those who bet with him or her win. If the shooter rolls a 2, 3 or 12, that is craps and the shooter and all those betting with him or her lose. If the shooter rolls a 4, 5, 6, 7, 8, 9 or 10, he or she must roll the same number again to win. If the shooter rolls a 7 before that number, he or she '7s out' and loses.

 BRITTIP

Carry a sweater – the air con is deliberately chilly to put you off facing the desert heat outside. Some casinos pump scented oxygen in to keep tired players pepped up so they carry on gambling.

There is a whole series of bets that can be made – with the most bizarre titles you could imagine – from 'pass lines' to 'don't pass', 'come' and 'don't come', 'field', 'big 6' or '8', 'any craps', 'hard ways', 'bet the horn', 'any 7' and 'under or over 7'.

The odds on winning and payouts vary wildly.

Best bets: The **pass line**, where you are betting with the shooter, and the **don't pass line**, where you are betting against, pay even money. **Come** and **don't come** bets are the same as the **pass** and **don't pass** bets, with the same odds, but can only be placed after the first roll of the dice. The best bet of all is the **free odds**, which is only available to the above betters, but is not even indicated on the table. Once the point has been established by the first roll of the dice, you can make a bet equal to your original and get true odds (2–1 on the 4 and 10, 3–2 on the 5 and 9 and 6–5 on the 6 and 8) rather than even money.

Poor bets: The **field**, where you bet that any number in the field, i.e. not 5, 6, 7 or

8, will be rolled. If the numbers mentioned come up, you lose. **Place bets**, where you bet the 4, 5, 6, 7, 8, 9 or 10 will be thrown before a 7, sound like a good idea but the casino edge is so great that you should not consider any bets other than placing the 6 and 8.

BRITTIP
Many casinos have moving walkways that take you in but rarely take you out again!

The downright daft bets!: Big 6 and **big 8** bets on either the 6 or 8 or both can be made at any time and either must appear before a 7 is thrown to win. But the bet only pays even money so the casino's advantage is high. Worst bets of all are the **proposition** bets, which include the **hard ways** and **one-roll** bets. The casino's advantage is so great that you shouldn't even consider these.

Roulette

This game has been growing in popularity in America since Europeans started visiting the city in greater numbers, but generally it does not carry very good odds even in the European version. The American roulette table has 36 numbers, plus a green zero and a green double zero – as opposed to the European wheel, which does not have the extra double zero (the only Strip exception is at the Stratosphere). This turns the roulette wheel into a game heavily tilted to the casino's favour.

You place chips on the game board, gambling that either a single number, any of a dozen numbers, a column of numbers, corner of 4 numbers, red or black, or odd or even numbers comes up on the wheel. After all the chips have been put down, the dealer sends a small metal ball spinning around the roulette wheel, which spins in the opposite direction. When the ball drops into one of the slots, the owner(s) of the chips in that slot collect(s).

BRITTIP
Exits from casinos are hard to find and even if you do see a signpost it won't be plain sailing getting there, as your way will be blocked by a maze-like arrangement of slot machines!

The lure is that if your number comes up you're paid at the rate of 35–1, but what makes roulette a poor game for strategists

Card counters

You will probably have heard of card counters. These are people who basically keep a track of the low and high cards that are being played in blackjack to try to determine the likelihood of drawing a high or low card at a crucial moment – e.g. when you've got a 15, which is unlikely to be enough to win but you can't guarantee you'll get a 6 or under. There are many different forms of card counting, but the most simple is the one used with single-deck blackjack. Basically, 10, J, Q, K and aces are worth minus one, while 2, 3, 4, 5 and 6 are worth one, and the other cards (7, 8, 9) have no value. Starting from zero, you count upwards and downwards according to the cards dealt. Generally you should bet the minimum when the score is negative (you're more likely to bust) and higher when the count is positive 2 or more.

It is not illegal to count cards but the casinos in Las Vegas frown on this misguided attempt by players to play the game well. They consider it an attempt to cheat them out of money and tend to refuse to let card counters into their casinos. This is why it's best to practise your technique in advance so you won't be noticed!

is that it basically involves blind luck. The best way to reduce the chance of losing is to stick to betting that the ball will drop on either a red or black number; and odd or even number of numbers 1–18 or 19–36. Worst bet is any one number. Other bets include groups of 12 numbers (2–1), groups of 6 numbers (5–1), groups of 4 numbers (8–1), groups of 3 numbers (11–1), groups of 2 numbers (17–1) and a group of 0, 00, 1, 2 and 3 (6–1).

Card games

Poker

For the real Wild West experience, this is a must! There are many variations, but most follow the same principles: all players play for themselves, paying a commission, or 'rake', from each pot (or a certain sum of money per half hour of play at high limits) to the casino, and a regular deck of cards is used. Before joining a game, always check with the dealer to find out the specific game being played.

In the past there were many different styles of poker games available. At the

© MGM

Casino at the Venetian

World Series of Poker tournaments, held at the Rio All-Suites, you can still play old-time poker games like 7 card stud, Omaha which is favoured in most European casinos, deuce to 7 and 5 card draw. With the enormous increase in interest caused by the televised events of the World Poker Tour and the European Poker Tour, Texas hold 'em has become the game of choice in Las Vegas.

Poker is a game that requires nerves of steel and the skill to know when to cut your losses and drop out. Professional poker players reckon that you'll have a pretty good idea of your chances by the time the first 2 cards have been dealt, and there are basic combinations that you need to have if you are going to continue.

Texas hold 'em: This is the game of the high-stakes World Series of Poker and is now the most popular poker game in the world. There are 2 types of game offered: limit hold 'em, where there are only set amounts that can be bet at each betting round, and no-limit hold 'em, where you can bet any amount during any betting round, up to and including your entire stack of chips.

In both limit and no-limit there is a 'dealer button' which advances round the table at the start of each hand. It indicates which 2 players, called the 'big blind' and 'small blind', are required to make forced bets before any cards are dealt, so that there is some money on the table to fight for. Everybody is then dealt 2 cards face down and a round of betting starts. Obviously, the first 2 cards you're dealt are the most important and should be either a

pair of aces, kings, queens or jacks or 2 high-value cards.

After the first round of betting, the dealer places 3 cards in the middle of the table, called 'the flop'. These are community cards that all players use, with the 2 cards in their hand, to make their best 5-card poker hand. There is another round of betting. Then a fourth card is placed on the table by the dealer, 'the turn'. Another round of betting is made, then the last card is placed in the middle, 'the river'. There are now 7 cards, 2 in your hand and 5 on the table. You use the best 5 cards of the 7 to make your best 5-card poker hand. The last round of betting ensues and when the last bet is covered or called, the dealer calls for the showing of hands and the highest one wins.

Most casinos now have poker rooms, where Texas hold 'em is offered. Most also hold a series of daily tournaments, where you play poker against other players. You keep playing until you have no more chips. Usually 10% of the top-placing players get cash prizes, and the top prizes typically run into the thousands of dollars.

There are other poker games that are offered with the other table games, where blackjack and baccarat are offered.

Pai gow poker: Played with a deck of 52 playing cards plus 1 joker, which can be used only as an ace to complete a straight, a flush or a straight flush. Players are dealt 7 cards which they arrange to make 2 hands – a low hand of 2 cards and a high hand of 5. The cards are arranged according to high-draw poker rankings, i.e. the highest 2-card hand is 2 aces and the highest 5-card hand is a royal flush. The object is for both hands to beat the banker's hands.

Caribbean stud poker™: Played with a standard 52-card deck and no joker, it is the first casino table game to offer a progressive jackpot. You start by placing your bet in the box marked 'ante' and then have the option to bet $1 to enter the progressive jackpot, after which all the players and the dealer are dealt 5 cards. None of your cards is exposed, though one of the dealer's is, but you cannot draw any more cards.

Now you have to decide whether to play or fold; in the latter case your ante is lost. To carry on playing, you have to wager double your ante in the box marked 'bet' to see the dealer's hand. If the dealer's hand is less than ace-king high, then he folds and automatically pays the ante bets at even money. The bet wagers are considered 'no action' and returned to the player regardless of their hand. If the dealer's hand is ace-king high or higher, then he calls all bet wagers. If the dealer's hand is higher than yours, he takes both the ante and the bet. If it's lower than yours, he pays the ante at even money and the bet according to the signposted rates, based on your hand. Regardless of the dealer's hand, if your hand qualifies for the progressive jackpot, you will win the appropriate amount for your hand (shared if there is more than one winner).

Let it ride poker™: In this game, you are not playing against the dealer or the other players but simply trying to get a good poker hand. To play, you place 3 equal bets as indicated on the table layout and then get 3 cards. After looking at your cards, you can ask for your first bet back or 'let it ride'. The dealer then exposes 1 of his cards, which becomes all of the players' fourth card. At this point you can either ask for your second bet back or again let it ride, after which the dealer exposes another card to complete the 5-card hand. Winning hands are then paid according to the payout schedule.

BRITTIP
The average electricity bill for a large Las Vegas casino is around $3m a year!

Keno

This game originated in China more than 2,000 years ago but is basically a form of our lotto. You mark anywhere between one and 15 of the 80 numbers on the keno ticket, then place your bet with the keno writer. You then keep a duplicate ticket to match against the 20 numbers drawn by the casino at a set time. All the casinos have their own rules about winning combinations, so check before playing. The alternative to this game is throwing your money in a bin, but the lure is the massive payouts.

Slots

Las Vegas is home to the most sophisticated, state-of-the-art machinery in the world and gamblers get so mesmerised by the idea of their winning line coming up that they spend hours feeding money into these machines. But slot machines are such big business now that they account for around 60% of total casino earnings – and so fill a staggering amount of floor space in the casinos.

BRITTIP
Most of the newer slot machines have coloured lights on top to signify the machine's denomination. A red light means it's a 5-cent machine, green 10 cents, yellow 25 cents, orange 50 cents, blue $1 and purple $5.

Mechanical penny and nickel slot machines that took one coin at a time have been replaced by computerised dollar slot machines that can accept multiple coins simultaneously and now feature poker, keno, blackjack, bingo and craps. Some even accept credit card-style gambling and the linking up of machines has led to massive $10m-and-more jackpots. You can still play for as little as a nickel a go, but some slots now allow you to use $500 tokens – usually in special VIP slot areas!

BRITTIP
Only play on machines that tell you the return and look for a 98–99% return on $1 slots.

Playing the slots

© MGM

7

Gambling lingo

Acorn	Player who is generous with tips
Ante	Money you bet in card games
Bank	Inventory of coins and chips on all table games
Big digger	Ace of spades
Book	Place where bets are made on sporting events
Boxcars	When a gambler rolls 2 sixes for a point of 12
Boxman	Craps table dealer who sits over the drop box and supervises bets and payoffs
Bumble puppy	Careless or inexperienced card player
Bust	Exceed the maximum score allowed, for instance 21 in blackjack
Buster	Term used for illegally altered dice
Casino cage	Secure area within the casino for banking services and casino operations
Casino boss	Person who oversees the entire casino
Comp	Free meal, gift, etc. (short for complimentary)
Coupons	Redeemable for nearly everything from a free meal to a free pull on a slot machine
Crossroaders	Card cheats who travel across America in search of games
Dealer	Person who conducts table games
Drop box	Locked box on 'live' gaming tables where dealers deposit your cash
Eye in the sky	One-way mirror used for surveillance of the casino area
Flat top	Slot machine with a fixed jackpot, as opposed to a progressive slot machine where the jackpot increases according to the amount of play
Frog skin	Old-time gamblers' name for paper money
Gaming	Las Vegas euphemism for gambling
Green	Gambling chip worth $25, also known as a quarter
High-roller	Someone who bets large sums of money
Hit me	What you say when you want another card from the dealer in a blackjack game
In red	If you get a free meal, your name will appear in red on the maître d's reservation list
Ladderman	The person who supervises baccarat games and has the final say over any disputes
Limit	Minimum and maximum bet, as decided by the casino
Loose	Term used to describe slot machines that pay out at the best percentages
Marker	IOU
Nevada lettuce	$1,000 bill
Pit	Area of the casino containing gambling tables
Pit boss	Person who oversees a number of table dealers
Red	Gambling chip worth $5, also known as a nickel
RFB comp	If the casino is impressed with someone's credit rating, they will arrange free room, food or beverages (RFB) during a hotel stay
Shoe	Contains the packs of playing cards used in blackjack and baccarat
Shooter	Person rolling the dice in craps
Snake eyes	Craps term used when the dice holder rolls a point of 2
Soft hand	When you have at least one ace in your blackjack hand; it is counted as either 1 or 11 so you have 2 possible totals
Spoon	A device used by slot machine cheats
Stand	To refuse any more cards in blackjack
Stickman	Dealer who moves the dice around on a craps table with a hook-shaped stick
Table games	Everything from blackjack and baccarat to roulette
Toke or gratuity	Tip
Whale	Gambler who is willing to bet $250,000 a hand
Whip shot	In craps, the way of rolling the dice to hit the table in a flat spin so the desired numbers are on top when the dice stop rolling

Progressive slots are machines that are computer-linked to other machines throughout the States and pay out incredible jackpots. One of the progressive slots is known as Megabucks, which is computer-linked to other machines in the state of Nevada. The CircusBucks progressives start the jackpot climbing at $500,000, but the most recent Super Megabucks starts climbing at $10m! What's more, gamblers can now check online at www.megajackpots.com to find out the current jackpot total on Megabucks and 7 other progressive slot networks run by International Game Technology.

◀▶ **BRITTIP**
The coin trays of slot machines are not anchored to the machine so that the money falls with a 'play-me' ting-ting-ting-ting!

Video games

These are basically interactive slot machines aimed directly at the new generation who grew up with computers and computer games. Multiple-use videos can offer up to 10 games with anything from poker to keno and blackjack, plus regular slot machines and are activated simply by touching the screen. Some machines even allow you to play for a $1m poker payout with a 25-cent bet! Another reason for the increase in popularity of video games is that you can play at your own pace, without pressure from dealers, croupiers or other players. The returns that you should be looking for on all the different games are as follows:

All-American poker: Also known as gator bonus poker. Go for machines that pay 8–1 on full houses, a flush and a straight.

Bonus deuces: Best machines are those paying 20–1 for a wild royal flush, 10–1 on 5 of a kind and straight flush and 4–1 on 4 of a kind and a full house.

Deuces wild: Look for a 5–1 payout on 4 of a kind, which is considerably better than 4–1 for 4 of a kind that you'll find on many of these video machines.

Double bonus poker: Find a 10/7 machine – one that pays 10–1 on a full house and 7–1 on a flush.

Flush attack: Do not play on a machine that needs more than 3 flushes to go into attack mode, and look for one that pays 8–1 for a full house and 5–1 on flushes (known as an 8/5 machine).

Jacks or better: Look for 9/6 machines, which pay 9–1 for a full house and 6–1 on flushes.

Joker wild: Kings or better. Look for a machine that pays 20–1 for 4 of a kind, 7–1 for a full house and 5–1 on a flush.

Sports betting

The race and sports book, as it is known, gives you the chance to bet on horse races and major sporting events. For horse races you can bet on a win (first place only), a place (first or second) and a show (first, second or third). Further bets include naming the first 2 horses in any order, naming the first 2 horses in the correct order or the horses that will win any 2 specified races.

Details of races, the horses and odds are displayed or you can read local newspapers, racing sheets and other publications before making up your mind. Then watch the action on closed-circuit broadcasts live from race tracks across America. The latest innovation in sports betting is proposals for a progressive prize MegaSports jackpot, where the final payout is determined by the amount of betting over a certain period. The prize pools will start at $1m.

The surge in televised coverage of sporting events in America has also created a surge in sports gambling. During one Super Bowl weekend (held every February), nearly 200,000 visitors flocked to Las Vegas to bet more than $50m on their favourite team and spent a further $50m in the city in the process! At Caesars Palace Race and Sports Book – the first to open in Las Vegas – they have a total of 50 different ways to part with your cash, including betting on the number of quarterback sacks or the total field goals. The Las Vegas Hilton [to change its name] is home to The 'Best of Las Vegas' Race and Sports Superbook – the largest in the world. Over 30,000ft2/2788m2, it has more than 300 seats, 28 giant screens and a massive 15x20in/38x50cm screen for over 60 viewing monitors. This is the place to wager on sporting and racing events, and follow live action from around the world.

Internet betting

Online casinos have exploded in popularity, especially those sites offering poker. Many different sites often have more than 10,000 punters playing at the same time, all in the comfort of their own homes. The casinos also offer home access to gambling on blackjack, craps, video poker, roulette, bingo and 3-dimensional,

7

interactive slot machines. In fact, many industry experts credit much of Las Vegas recent explosive growth to the internet. It is estimated that over 100,000,000 people gamble on internet sites worldwide (62,000,000 in the US alone!) and soon get the urge to give the lights of Vegas a try!

Gambling lessons

For first-timers or for those who just want to brush up on their skills, many casinos in Las Vegas still offer complimentary gaming lessons. Rediscover classic Las Vegas at any of the famous casinos Downtown. The Golden Nugget offers free, daily gaming lessons for a variety of table games including craps, 3-card poker, Pai gow, Texas hold 'em, roulette and blackjack.

On the Strip, The Venetian and The Palazzo offer complimentary gaming lessons for blackjack, roulette and craps. The Venetian also offers 1-on-1 and group poker lessons for no-limit and limit Texas hold 'em. All gaming lessons are available 24 hours based on availability. Off-Strip, the Gold Coast offers craps lessons every Fri, Sat and Sun in the casino pit. Its sister property, Suncoast, offers instructional handouts on table games. Dealers provide personal instruction and assistance on the floor even during live games.

BRITTIP

Floral fragrances are pumped around selected slot machines, which increases play by up to 50%.

Many hotels are linked to the Players Network (www.playersnetwork.com), which you can access through the TV for tips on how to play different games, table etiquette and sports betting.

For tips on how to play all the different video poker machines, it is worth taking the trip to north-west Las Vegas for Bob Dancer's weekly lessons at the Fiesta Rancho Hotel & Casino (2400 North Rancho Drive, 702 631 7000, www.fiestacasino.com).

Comps

Many Vegas veterans are misty over the good old 'mobbed-up days' when the mob-owned casinos offered free drinks, cheap food and cheap or even free hotel rooms to draw in the punters. The new age of corporate casinos brought a waft of business managers who demanded all areas, including the hotel and restaurant sides, show a profit along with the gambling hall.

Most casinos still liberally hand out free drinks for gamblers. And you can still get comps on everything from free rooms to

You can take lessons to help understand the games

© MGM

Fremont Casino

food, show tickets, front-row seats and limos, without being a high-roller. You just have to earn them.

To qualify for a comp, you'll need a player's card, which you can request from the casino as soon as you arrive. Blackjack used to be the fastest way to get comps. Over the last 2 decades casinos began to recognise that slot machines were more profitable so they now offer their best comps for slot players. In fact, the old players cards are now as often referred to as 'slot club cards'.

BRITTIP

Savvy locals know that if they play at a slot machine that offers a 99% return on $1 slots, plus play with their slot club card to get comps from the casino (generally a 1–3% value), they can actually expect to beat the casino!

But while slots get the best comp values, some savvy blackjack players have learned some tricks to maximise their comps. As soon as you sit down at a table, ask to be 'rated', presenting your player's card to the pit boss. This effectively starts the clock on your play and the idea from this point is to make it look as if you're placing good bets for as long a period of time as possible, while reducing your risk of losing money by playing as little as possible.

BRITTIP

Part of the fun of a visit to Las Vegas is to check out all the different resorts and attractions. However, try to do most of your gambling at one casino to maximise your freebies.

Once the floor person has walked away, bet as little as you can, depending on the table's minimum. Also, don't play every hand. If the dealer is on a winning streak, tell him or her you're going to sit things out until they've busted a couple of times. A natural break in a game is provided when the dealer starts to shuffle and at this point you can whiz off (not forgetting your chips!) to another table out of your pit boss's jurisdiction, though you must always tell them where you're going. Then lay your chips on the table and chat to the dealer, making it look as if you're playing without actually making one bet. After an hour of 'play', take a break, asking the dealer to mark your seat.

About every half hour, the floor person normally comes around with a clipboard to check on play. Bump your bets back up to $25 while he's there.

It's a pleasant enough way of spending a few hours, but always remember the golden rule of never going beyond the amount

Swimup blackjack at the Tropicana

of money you have given yourself to play with. Obviously, you'll need to walk around the casino for a while before you start playing so you know which pit bosses cover which tables. Thereafter, it will be down to your ability to act in a natural way!

Deception and subterfuge are not always necessary when it comes to earning freebies, though. Many of the casinos are so determined to foster good relationships with their customers that they have introduced loyalty cards, where the amount of play gives you points that can be put towards meals, rooms, shows or even getting cash back. Ask at your hotel, but the following are a few of the best.

BRITTIP

If you're a regular gambler or plan to gamble a lot when in Las Vegas, join a slot club and see what deals you're offered. Apart from free drinks, you may get a comp room or even free show tickets.

a-List Players Club: Available at Planet Hollywood Resort, the a-List Players Club gives you great rewards such as room nights, restaurant meals and show tickets. It also gives you access to PH Perks. This includes PH Award Play that lets you redeem your slot points for free slot play right at your favourite slot machines. PH Bonus Play allows you to earn extra rewards by participating in a-List Players Club promotions and special gaming offers sent to you based on your play.

Circus Circus Players Club: Players can earn dollars redeemable at Slots-of-Fun and Circus Circus for hotel stays, airport limousine transportation, meals and tickets to shows at other MGM Mirage properties in Las Vegas.

Club Palms: Earn 1 point for every $1 of coin-in on slot and video poker machines. Points can be redeemed at the rate of 400 points = $1 for comps or for Free Slot Play. Comps for your points can be redeemed at over 35 outlets including The Pearl Concert Theater, Simon at Palms Place, N9NE Steakhouse, ghostbar, Drift Spa, Brenden Theatres, Playboy Club and Moon Nightclub. You can even get a tattoo at Huntington Ink or a palm reading at Cosmic Corner.

Island Winners' Club: At the Tropicana, this rewards slot, video poker and table-game players. Slot and video poker players can earn both comps and cash by inserting their club card into the slot machine. On average, about 2 hours of play on a dollar

slot with maximum coins played on each 'pull' will earn about $10 cash back. Table-game players present their card to a floor person to earn comp credits at blackjack, craps or roulette tables. Credits are based on the average bets and length of time you play.

MGM Mirage Players Club: With just 1 card you can earn valuable rewards based on slot and table games play, such as cash, complimentary rooms, show tickets and invitations to promotions and special events. The card is valid across the MGM Grand, Bellagio, Mirage, Treasure Island, New York-New York, Mandalay Bay, Luxor, Excalibur and Monte Carlo.

Play Rio Card: This card, at the Rio All-Suite Hotel and Casino in Valley View Boulevard at Flamingo Road, will allow you to earn points during both slot and table play towards reduced-price or comp suites, comp dining or tickets to a show. Sign up at the Play Rio Center.

Total Rewards: The new Harrah's card lets you build up points at all Harrah's properties; especially valuable at Caesars Palace.

Trop Plus Players Club: The newly transformed Tropicana casino has one of the most liberal in Vegas with up to $200 losses reimbursed on your first day's membership.

BRITTIP

GOLD to goTM anyone? High rollers can cash in at America's second Gold-dispensing ATM at the Golden Nugget Hotel & Casino. For mere mortals, traditional gold coins and signature gold bars with the Golden Nugget logo are dispensed along with the 1-250 gram 24-karat gold bars.

The casinos

As much imagination has gone into the decor of the casinos as in every other part of the resort-hotels.

Aria: www.arialasvegas.com. The new resort at CityCenter brings gambling out of the dark ages, literally, with its use of natural light which streams through the gaming floor in pools of illumination. Unthinkable only a year or so ago!

Caesars Palace: www.caesarspalace.com. At Caesars Palace Forum Casino you can take a break from gambling and have your photo taken with Caesar and Cleopatra as they stroll around with their royal entourage, while the west corridor is home to animatronic Atlantis statues!

Gambling fast facts

- In 2010, Clark County's casinos (Clark County includes Las Vegas, Laughlin, Mesquite, Primm and Jean) took in $8.9bn in gross gaming revenue. Las Vegas strip casinos alone accounted for $5.8bn.
- In 2010, the average gambling budget per trip was approximately $466 per visitor.
- The average visitor gambled 2.9 hours per day.
- 80% of visitors said they gambled during their stay.
- Slot machines reign in the casinos – 70% of visitors hit the slots during their stay.
- Blackjack came in a distant second at 11% with video poker rounding out the top 3 with 7%.
- The statewide Megabucks games experienced a first in September 2005 when a player hit the progressive jackpot for the second time. The 92-year-old winner took home $4.6m in 1989 and then hit the jackpot again last year for $21m.
- Nevada's casino and gaming areas are off-limits to people younger than 21. When Bellagio opened on the Las Vegas Strip in October 1998, the hotel barred patrons from the premises who were under 18 years of age unless they were registered guests of the hotel; this policy was a first, although it is not strictly enforced today.
- Race and sports betting tops $2bn per year. Some Las Vegas casinos treat gamblers to plush seating, free drinks and buffets in the race and sports book complexes where live racing and athletic events are viewed on giant, satellite-fed screens.

Cosmopolitan: www.cosmopolitan lasvegas.com. The Cosmopolitan Race & Sports by Cantor on the second floor adjacent to Marquee Nightclub. Wagering is by fixed bets or trading stations. There are 43 plush trading stations with viewing screens and Cantor's In-Running sports trading technology.

Excalibur: www.excalibur.com/casino. The Excalibur casino continues its theme with staff dressed in medieval costume and trumpet players blowing on horns straight out of Robin Hood.

Flamingo: www.flamingolasvegas.com. Margaritaville Casino at the Flamingo has launched a new gaming experience. This 15,000ft^2/1394m^2 casino adjoining Jimmy Buffet's Margaritaville restaurant it has 22 gaming tables, 220 slot machines and the 5 O'Clock Somewhere bar as its centrepiece.

Imperial Palace: www.imperialpalace. com. If you're having trouble parking, then you can always place your bets at the drive-up sports book at the Imperial Palace! In fact, more casinos would offer the same service but just don't have the space. The manager at the Imperial drive-up says business is always brisk – especially in summer when gamblers prefer to remain in their air-conditioned cars.

Las Vegas Hilton: Note that this hotel is changing its name by 2012. The Las Vegas Casino is one of the most beautifully decorated, with marble, rich woods and tier after tier of crystal chandeliers. The largest race and sports book is also to be found here.

Luxor: www.luxor.com/casino. At the Luxor you'll find a sumptuous setting surrounded by the Nile.

MGM Grand: www.mgmgrand.com/ gaming. If you want to see how the other half lives, take a sneak look into the VIP high-limit area at the MGM Grand. Here high-rollers rub cheeks with celebrities in a setting based on the elegance and style of the grand old casinos of Monte Carlo. Tall, classic columns, rose-coloured curtains and cherry wood and suede tables embroidered with the gold MGM Grand monograms are a real sight!

The Palms: www.palms.com. Gambling with the beautiful people and the high-rollers in the Mint Hi-Limit Lounge.

Planet Hollywood Resort & Casino: www.planethollywoodresort.com. Nearly 3acres/1.2ha of action in typical slick PH style. The Pleasure Pit, for example, features blackjack and roulette dealt by women in lingerie as go-go dancers keep the guys playing with their moves.

Tropicana: www.troplv.com/casino. You can beat the heat of the summer at the Tropicana by swimming up to the blackjack table, open daily 9.30am–5pm. In the indoor area of the resort's indoor-outdoor swimming pool, up to 14 players sit on marble stools up to their hips in water. They play with plastic cards and use either chips

Slots at Circus Circus

or cash. The paper money is kept in mint condition by specially heated rotating drop boxes that dry the cash in less than 60 seconds! It also has race and sports book.

BRITTIP
Many of the casinos have information on how to play the games on their websites.

Downtown casinos

Now home to the last neon signs of what used to be Glitter Gulch city, the downtown casinos are generally more friendly and relaxed, have cheaper-play slot machines, better returns and more comps. Regular visitors to Las Vegas may like staying at the ritzy, glamorous Strip hotels, but often enjoy a trip downtown to play on the nickel slot machines.

BRITTIP
So many people are so rude, the waitresses always remember the nice punters who tip in advance, and make sure they get their free drinks.

Binion's Gambling Hall: 128 East Fremont Street, 702 382 1600, www.binions. com. Once home to the world poker championships, this casino which opened as the Horseshoe Club in 1951, celebrated its 60th anniversary in 2011. It's famous for its single-deck blackjack and liberal rules, single-zero roulette, great odds-on crap, loose nickel and quarter machines and loads of comps. Binion's is also known for its friendly atmosphere.

Four Queens Hotel: 202 Fremont Street, 702 385 4011, www.fourqueens. com. You'll find the world's largest regular slot machine at the Four Queens Hotel downtown. It is the size of a small motorhome and allows 6 people to play at the same time!

Gold Coast: 4000 West Flamingo Road, 702 367 7111, www.goldcoastcasino. com. The karaoke bar at the Gold Coast is excellent for entertainment (locals dressed as stars such as Roy Orbison, Dean Martin and Elvis) and cheap drinks.

Gold Spike: 217 Las Vegas Blvd North, 702 384 8444, www.goldspike.com. This down to earth casino offers sportsbooks, keno, video poker and slot machines as well as a $250 cash draw at its Seigels Club 10pm Saturday nights, after a slap up prime rib and Saturday pool party.

Golden Gate: 1 Fremont Street, 702 385 1906, www.goldengatecasino.net Another friendly establishment, this still serves up its famous $1.99-cent shrimp (huge prawn) cocktail.

Sam's Town: 5111 Boulder Highway, 702 456 7777, www.samstownlv.com. The favoured haunt of locals is Sam's Town on Boulder Highway (going out towards the Hoover Dam). The free light and laser show is excellent and you'll find great odds on slots and video machines, and good comps.

Casino Promenade at the Beau Rivage

GOING TO THE CHAPEL

Getting married on any budget in the wedding capital of the world

Las Vegas has more chapels per square mile and more options on how you tie the knot than any other city in the world – and it's all so easy. Liberal state laws mean that Nevada is one of the few states that does not require a blood test, and to get you quickly on your way to the altar, the Marriage License Bureau is open 8am–midnight daily, including holidays.

If you do decide to go ahead, you'll be in star-studded company – this is where Elvis wed Priscilla, Frank Sinatra wed Mia Farrow, Jane Fonda wed Roger Vadim and Paul Newman wed Joanne Woodward. Others include Bruce Willis and Demi Moore, while Brigitte Bardot, Britney Spears, Bob Geldof, his daughter Peaches Geldof, David Cassidy, Richard Gere, Michael Jordan and Joan Collins all said 'I do' at a chapel in Las Vegas.

Getting married here is so simple that an amazing 120,000 get marriage licences here every year. The most popular day is Valentine's Day, closely followed by New Year's Eve, while the date 7 July 2007 (7/7/07) was considered lucky and it also happened to be a Saturday – 4,450 weddings were performed that day. On 8 August 2008 (8/8/08) 2,196 wedding took place in Vegas.

And you can do it all in such style. Dress up as a medieval prince and princess at the Canterbury Chapel in the Excalibur, allow an Elvis impersonator to wed you at Graceland Wedding Chapel, or try any of the other themes available from *Star Trek* to gangsters and rock 'n' roll. Then again, you could decide to make your vows before diving off a bungee-jump platform, soaring high above Las Vegas in a hot-air balloon or flying over the Grand Canyon. You can even stay in your car at the world's first ever drive-up wedding chapel or try the Tunnel of Love chapel at A Little White Chapel on the Strip.

It costs $60 for a marriage licence, which must be paid in cash, and $35 for the ceremony. A very basic package starts at $100, but the sky's the limit depending on where you wed, what you do and the accessories you choose.

The good news is that while many of the high-profile marriages may have ended in

the divorce courts, a Las Vegas wedding is not synonymous with one that ends in tears. People tend to opt for the wedding capital of the world because here they are free of family pressures and can make all their own choices. Furthermore, thanks to the raft of amazing accommodation, romantic restaurants, shows and nightlife, the city is also becoming a honeymoon mecca where the wedding can also be combined with a visit to the Grand Canyon and its surrounding attractions.

BRITTIP

Avoid Valentine's Day unless you want to queue for 4 hours to get your licence!

Wedding chapel at the Mandalay Bay

© MGM

What you need to wed

- A marriage licence from one of 3 bureaux (see below) – you can speed things up by pre-applying online. Once the licence has been issued it is valid for 1 year.
- Proof of age (driving licence, passport or birth certificate).
- Minimum age for adults is 18. Those aged 16–17 must have either a parent present at the time the licence is issued or a notarised affidavit.
- If you have been divorced, you will need to specify the date, city and state/country when it became final.

Licence bureaux

Clark County Marriage Bureau: 201 Clark Avenue, 702 671 0600. For recorded information: 702 455 4415, co.clark. nv.gov/Depts/recorder/Pages/Marriage. aspx Open 8am–midnight daily.
Laughlin, Nev. Marriage License Bureau: 101 Laughlin Civic Drive, 702 298 1097. Open Thurs–Sat 8am–5pm. Closed holidays.
Mesquite, Nev. Marriage License Bureau: 500 Hillside Drive, 702 346 1867. Open Wed 8am–11.30am and 12.30pm–3:30pm; Fri 3pm–9pm; Sat 9am–3pm. Closed Mon, Tues, Thurs, Sun and holidays.

Fascinating facts

Ancestry.com, the world's largest online family history resource, has launched a collection of Nevada's marriage and divorce records of the more than 9 million people who said their 'I do's' and 'I don'ts' in Nevada between 1956 and 2005. A cross-section of the collection reveals some fascinating and fun facts on getting together, splitting up, celebrity sightings, most popular days of the week to get married, percentage of marriages that take place in Nevada versus nationwide, shortest marriages in Nevada history, repeat offenders and much more. And, in true betting fashion, the site also launched www.VegasWeddingOdds.com, an online marriage-predicting site which, based on your first name, will give you the first names of the people you're most likely to marry in Nevada.

Ceremonies

Like every other aspect of Las Vegas, the business of helping people to tie the knot is booming. Hotel ceremonies tend to be more ostentatious than those at ordinary chapels, but they have prices to match, too! One couple were taken to their wedding site at the Venetian's St Mark's Square in an oversized white gondola, with a host of actors cavorting about as if it were a renaissance fair. After the gilt ceremony, the reception was held in the gardens area, where champagne and caviar celebrated the blessed union. All for a mere $12,000.

Not quite as expensive, but definitely unusual, is a wedding on the roller-coaster at New York-New York Hotel & Casino (702 740 6607, www.nynyhotelcasino. com/entertainment/entertainment_ therollercoaster). Ceremonies take place at 67 mph/108kph and cost $600 in the morning and $700 in the evening. Or how about saying 'I do' at Chopper Chapel at the Harley-Davison Café (702 740 4555 #26, www.harley-davidsoncafe.com/ chapel.php) on the Strip from $199?

Wedding queen of the West

Possibly the most famous wedding chapel in the world is the Little White Wedding Chapel (alittlewhitechapel.com) owned by Charolette Richards, dubbed the 'wedding queen of the West'. In her time, she has married celebs including Joan Collins, Patty Duke and Bruce Willis. She is also a savvy business woman as well as a wedding planner and has an empire of wedding chapels and more exotic options. Contact details are in the A–Z of major wedding chapels on page 166.
- Little White Wedding Chapel
- Chapel l'Amour
- Chapel of Promises
- Crystal Chapel
- Gazebo Chapel
- Tunnel of Love Drive Thru: In 1991, Charolette noticed a disabled couple having difficulty getting out of their car to go into her chapel so she hit upon the idea of a drive-up window and opened it at the Little White Wedding Chapel on the Strip. It became such a novelty that couples began queuing up for the drive-through wedding. They come on motorcycles, roller-skates, in cars, limos, trucks, taxis and even boats! Now it includes a Tunnel of Love in which couples are surrounded by floating cherubs, twinkling stars, birds on ribbons and signs everywhere saying 'I love you, I want you, I need you and I can't live without you'.

- A Little White Chapel in the Sky for balloon weddings

BRITTIP
If you do get married in Las Vegas you need copies of your marriage certificate, which you can now order via the internet. Go to www.co.clark.nv.gov.

At the Little White Wedding Chapel you pay anything from $229 for the Lover's Package, which includes a decorated chapel, traditional music, a witness (if required), a religious or civil ceremony, 12 digital photographs, a rose bouquet for the bride and a boutonniere for the groom plus a 'beautiful love recipe, keepsake rules for a happy marriage and a keepsake' to $829 for the Honeymooner Package, which includes all of the above plus 82 digital photographs and a photo album, a large bridal bouquet and bridesmaid bouquet, best man's boutonniere, a DVD of the ceremony, padded marriage licence holder and bride and groom champagne glasses. All the packages include a courtesy limousine service from your hotel to the Marriage License Bureau, on to the Little White Wedding Chapel and back to your hotel.

The chapel fee is $55, drive-through weddings cost from $40, hot-air balloon weddings start at $1,500 and helicopter deluxe weddings cost $1,179.

BRITTIP
A useful website for chapel hunting is las-vegas-weddings.co.uk.

Co-ordinators

In addition to the chapels there are several very good wedding specialists. Co-ordinators have no chapel themselves, but co-ordinate with a variety of vendors to make a memorable wedding for you, from themed to decadent.

Viva Las Vegas Weddings

702 384 0771,
www.vivalasvegasweddings.com
This company arranges an extraordinary number of differently themed weddings from Star Trek to Elvis and rock 'n' roll. Here are some examples.
Bond: You can choose a Bond wedding ceremony for $1,100, which includes a limousine pick-up by Bond baddie Oddjob, 2 dancing Bond girls and a ceremony performed by a 007 impersonator who arrives by sports car.
Camelot: The Camelot theme includes Merlin or King Arthur as the minister, while you'll be treated like a king and queen. The basic package costs $700 and includes period music, knights, trumpeters and fair ladies. For an extra $100 you can have a soloist perform a medieval tune.
Elvis in Blue Hawaii: Here you have an Elvis impersonator and dancers from the Tropicana's *Folies Bergères* at your ceremony, which takes place in the Elvis Chapel. In addition to all the Elvis memorabilia, Hawaiian sets, showgirls and hula dancers, there will be theatrical lighting and fog, while 'Elvis' will sing 'Love Me Tender', 'Viva Las Vegas' and 'I Can't Help Falling In Love With You' ($700).
Gangster: Here you'll step back in time to a 1940s mafioso shotgun wedding where the Godfather/minister opens the door to wedded bliss accompanied by 2 bodyguards and a waiter/soloist singing in Italian ($650).
Intergalactic: Your special day is presided over by Captain James T Quirk or Captain Schpock in the Starship Chapel, surrounded by life-size cut-outs of your favourite characters. The package comes with a Minister Transporter, an illusion entrance, theatrical lighting and lots of fog for $700.
Las Vegas: This package includes showgirls, keno runners, cocktail waitresses, card dealers and a Las Vegas-style singer/minister, plus theatrical lights and fog. It costs $700 and for another $250 you can even have Elvis or Marilyn Monroe at your wedding. Other packages include the Pirate ($700), the Disco ($650) and the Beach Party ($700).
Rock 'n' Roll: This is all about rock 'n' roll, complete with memorabilia and an electric guitar version of the Wedding March, while a rock star impersonator will sing during the ceremony for $650.

LV Wedding Connection

702 236 8728,
www.lvweddingconnection.com
Joni Moss can arrange anything from a wedding in a luxury 14-passenger cadillac while driving down the Strip, to vows on a Harley Davidson (in a private room, not on the road!) and of course, impersonators for themed weddings. She also works with 3 contrasting chapels (but can also assist with weddings anywhere throughout town) and reception locations range from ranch to a lakeside marina.

8

Las Vegas Weddings

2550 East Desert Inn Road, Suite 562, 702 737 6800, www.lasvegasweddings.com
This company can book your rooms and organise every aspect of your wedding. Open 24/7, they arrange flowers, transport, clothes, reception and entertainments. They have 17 chapels and themes include Elvis and nature weddings. Or you can choose to take one of the packages arranged by tour operators from Britain (see page 214).

⚡ BRITTIP
If you're coming to Las Vegas to propose, yourhandinmarriage. com is ready to assist. Services include a proposal written in the sky to finding the perfect engagement ring.

Wedding chapels at major resort-hotels on the Strip

Nearly every major casino resort in Las Vegas has its own unique wedding chapel, offering simple celebrations to elaborate affairs and range from the romantic Terrace of Dreams at Bellagio to the storybook charm of The Venetian. With all the resort-hotel websites, it's usually quickest to key in the main website address, then navigate via the menus. If you can't immediately see a weddings option, look under 'amenities' or sometimes 'meetings'.

Bellagio

702 693 7444, www.bellagio.com
East Chapel: The more intimate chapel holds a maximum of 30 guests, and is decorated in hues of cream, rose and peach, with antique green and bride's blue. The classy design allows you to say your vows at the altar with a beautiful full-length stained glass window as the backdrop.

The Luxor wedding chapel

South Chapel: Holds up to a maximum of 130 guests in an elegant and refined classic European-designed environment. Beautifully decorated in gold and muted colours with stained glass windows, it is also light and airy.

Terrazza di Sogno: Marry Italian-style on a balcony overlooking Lake Como, which can hold up to 34 guests and where the Fountains soar into the air at your first kiss!

⚡ BRITTIP
Most resort hotels are very willing to put together hen parties for the bride and her maids.

Caesars Palace

702 731 7110, www.caesarspalace.com
Caesars specialises in customising weddings to suit the most romantic tastes and a recent flurry of developments have led to the opening of some of the most attractive and varied chapel settings in any resort-hotel. For something even more special, you can also hire ancient characters – Caesar, Cleopatra, Roman guards, handmaidens and sirens are the favourites – to attend your ceremony at any of the chapels. There's even an aromatherapy package – the smell of rose representing the journey of lovers. Packages cost $850–4,300 but the sky's the limit with extras.

Classico: Having opened in August 2005, this now offers the chance for 196 guests to enjoy a wedding ceremony in a classical environment. On a theme of beige, light blue and cream, it has chandeliers, stained glass windows and magnificent floral arrangements.

Romano: A more intimate affair for 35 guests, its décor is based on Rome of course!

Venus Garden: Small, beautiful and secluded, the Romanesque temple is surrounded by tropical palm trees, a blooming floral landscape, koi fish pond and fountains. Seats 114.

Tuscana: Based on the romance and charm of old world Tuscany, the colour scheme is creams and browns. Seats 80.

Circus Circus

702 794 3777, www.circuscircus.com
Chapel of the Fountain: One of the first and longest-running hotel-casino wedding chapels in town. Packages cost $325–$1,100.

Excalibur

702 597 7777, www.excalibur.com
Canterbury Wedding Chapel: In keeping with the theme of the hotel, the chapel in a lovely gazebo has a medieval-gothic flavour with domed ceilings, stained glass windows and lots of dark wood which houses up to 87 guests. A large chandelier over the altar forms the perfect backdrop for photos and you can even look the part, too, by hiring period costumes and rounding off the day with a medieval tournament. Now, where is that knight in shining armour ...? Wedding packages from $199.

Four Seasons

702 632 5000,
www.fourseasons.com/lasvegas
Fountain Terrace and suites: The Four Seasons offers the serenity and prestige of the city's most acclaimed hotel in an exclusive, non-gambling environment. In addition to an outdoor venue, the Fountain Terrace, the Four Seasons also offers the chance to get married in some of the most amazing suites available in Las Vegas for wedding parties of up to 30 guests. Normally reserved for those who like to pay up to $10,000 a night for their hotel accommodation, this is a wonderful way to experience how the other half lives, for $1,800–5,500 a night! The Presidential and Panoramic suites, on the 35th to 39th floors of the hotel, come with stunning views of the mountains and desert. They are decorated in rich woods with floral and warm-hued upholstery and drapes. The Las Vegas Strip View suites feature floor-to-ceiling windows and – you guessed it – amazing views of the Strip. Prices for wedding ceremonies on application.

Imperial Palace

866 228 0918, www.imperialpalace.com
Skyline Chapel: The focal point of this elegantly appointed chapel decorated in white, cream and black which opened on 11.11.11, is the Las Vegas Skyline. Seating up to 70, there's a 50ft/15m aisle to create maximum impact.

Southwestern Chapel: A quaint and intimate chapel with a desert landscape theme, it seats up to 20. The most popular of its range of packages is 'Glitter and Lights', but co-ordinators can arrange Elvis impersonators and more for your dream wedding.

Luxor

702 262 4444, www.luxor.com
Luxor wedding chapel: Surprisingly, given the strong theming throughout this hotel, the chapel is in keeping with the hotel, but not overtly Egyptian in feel. Elegantly decked out in creams and peaches, it seats 100 guests. Packages such as Ameythst from $525. Themes including *Titanic*, cowboy, rock 'n' roll and Vegas, of course.

Mandalay Bay

702 632 7490, www.mandalaybay.com
Mandalay Bay chapels: There are 3 chapels within this resort, set within an exotic island built on the shores of an 11acre/4.5ha tropical lagoon. The interiors are decorated in peaches and cream, while outside, the chapel fountain provides a superb photo backdrop. Many themed weddings are also available in different venues around the resort ranging from a shark reef wedding to a cabana ceremony. Packages such as Crystal Waters from $1,100.

Mandarin Oriental Las Vegas

702 590 8888, www.mandarinoriental.com
Intimate to ballroom: In true Mandarin Oriental style, weddings are tailormade and can be as intimate or grand as you wish. Events ideas include an exotic ball against the backdrop of The Strip, a private party in its VIP bar 23 floors up, tying the knot in a luxury poolside cabana or a private dinner in the black and white Emperor Suite. Prices on request.

MGM Grand

1 800 646 5530,
www.mgmgrandweddings.com
Forever Grand Wedding Chapel: A magnificent, cathedral-like archway announces your arrival at the lobby of this dual chapel. Lining the walls of the marble-floored area is a series of black and white photographs of movie stars in their wedding finery. Both chapels come in creams and blue with pretty domed ceilings. Other venues around the hotel include the ballroom, poolside, spa wall or the Terraza. Themes include Hollywood glamour. Packages from $800.
Cherish Chapel: Seats 45 guests.
Legacy Chapel: Seats 70 guests.
Terraza: Seats 100 guests.

8

A–Z of major wedding chapels

Allure Wedding Chapel: 823 South 3rd Street, 702 291 2667, www.allurewedding chapel.com

Bally's Celebration Wedding Chapel: 3645 Las Vegas Blvd S, 702 892 2222

Chapel L'Amour: 1301 Las Vegas Blvd S, 702 382 5943, www.alittlewhitechapel.com

Chapel of Dreams: 3377 Las Vegas Blvd S, Suite 2001, 866 841 3739, www.madametussauds.com

Chapel of Love: 1430 Las Vegas Blvd S, 702 387 0155

Chapel of Promises: 1301 Las Vegas Blvd South, 702 382 5943, www.alittlewhitechapel.com

Chapel of the Bells: 2233 Las Vegas Blvd S, 702 735 6803, www.chapelofthebells lasvegas.com

Chapel of the Flowers: 1717 Las Vegas Blvd, 702 735 4331, www.littlechapel.com

Chaplain at Large: 3162 Cadbury Dr., 702 898 2694

China Town Wedding Temple: 4215 Spring Mountain Rd, 702 252 0400

Crystal Chapel: 1301 Las Vegas Blvd South, 702 382 5943, www.alittlewhitechapel.com

Cupid's Wedding Chapel: 827 Las Vegas Blvd S, 702 598 4444, www.cupidswedding.com

Divine Madness Fantasy Wedding Chapel: 111 Las Vegas Blvd S, Suite H, 702 384 5660

Elvis Chapel: 1205 Las Vegas Blvd South, 702 384 0771, www.theelvisweddingchapel.com

Emerald at Queensridge: 891 S Rampart, 702 242 5700, www.emeraldgarden.com

Flamingo Garden Chapel: 3555 Las Vegas Blvd S, 702 733 3232, www.flamingolasvegas.com

Gazebo Chapel: 1301 Las Vegas Blvd S, 702 382 5943, www.alittlewhitechapel.com

Gothic Weddings: 1205 Las Vegas Blvd S, 702 384 0771, www.gothicweddings.com

Graceland Wedding Chapel: 619 Las Vegas Blvd S, 702 382 0091, www.gracelandchapel.com

Hartland Mansion: 1044 South 6th Street, 702 387 6700, www.lasvegashartlandmansion.com

Heavenly Bliss Wedding Chapel: 710 S. Third Street, 702 444 5444, www.heavenly blisschapel.com

Hollywood Wedding Chapel: 2207 Las Vegas Blvd S, 702 731-0678, www.ahollywood weddingchapel.com

Las Vegas Wedding Chapel: 727 South 9th St, 702 383 5909, www.lvchapel.com

Little Church of the West: 4617 Las Vegas Blvd South, 702 739 7971, www.little churchlv.com

Little White Chapel in the Sky: 1301 Las Vegas Blvd S, 702 382 5943, www.alittlewhitechapel.com

Little White Wedding Chapel: 1301 Las Vegas Blvd, 702 382 5943, www.alittlewhite chapel.com

Long Fung Wedding Temple: 4215 Spring Mountain Rd, 702 252 0400

Maverick Helicopter: 6075 Las Vegas Blvd. S, 702 948 1325, www.maverickhelicopter.com

Rainbow Gardens: 4125 West Charleston Blvd, 702 878 4646, www.ilv.com/rainbowgardens

Resort on Mount Charleston: 2275 Kyle Canyon Road, 702 872 5500, www.mtcharlestonresort.com

San Francisco Sally's Victorian Chapel: 1304 Las Vegas Blvd South, 702 385 7777

Shalimar Wedding Chapel: 1401 Las Vegas Blvd S., Phone: 702 382 7372, www.shalimarweddingchapel.com

Silver Bell Wedding Chapel: 607 Las Vegas Blvd S, 702 382 3726

Special Memory Wedding Chapel: 800 South 4th Street, 702 384 2211, www.aspecial memory.com

Speedway to Love Wedding Chapel: 7000 North Las Vegas Blvd, 702 644 3000

Sunset Gardens: 3931 East Sunset Road, 702 456 8004, www.sunsetgardens.com

Sweethearts Wedding Chapel: 1155 Las Vegas Blvd South, 702 385 7785, www.sweetheartschapel.com

Tunnel of Love Drive Thru: 1301 Las Vegas Blvd South, 702 382 5943, www.alittlewhitechapel.com
Valley Outreach Synagogue: 1692 Long Horizon Lane, 702 436 4900, www.valleyoutreach.com
Victoria's Wedding Chapel: 2800 West Sahara, 702 252 4565, www.avictorias.com
Wedding Bells Chapel: 375 E Harmon, 702 731 2355, www.weddingbellschapel.com
Wedding on Wheels: 1301 Las Vegas Blvd S, 702 385 5943, www.alittlewhitechapel.com
The Wedding Room at the Cellar: 3601 West Sahara Ave, 702 362 6712, www.theweddingroom.com
Wee Kirk o' the Heather: 231 Las Vegas Blvd S, 702 382 9830, www.weekirk.com

Mirage

702 791 7155, www.mirage.com
Customised ceremonies: The Mirage does not have a chapel, but can customise ceremonies so you can exchange vows beside the volcano and celebrate your reception poolside. You meet with their design team to discuss your requirements and tailor-make your own fairytale wedding.

Monte Carlo

1 800 822 8651, www.montecarlo.com
French-Victorian-styled chapel: The upmarket resort offers a refined chapel, which is decorated in soft, neutral colours with hand-painted murals. It seats 100 guests. Packages from $385.

Palazzo Las Vegas

702 607 7777, www.palazzolasvegas.com
Upmarket weddings around the hotel including private use of the Palazzo Waterfall for 1 hour.

Paris Resort

1 877 650 5021, www.parislasvegas.com
In addition to 2 of the most romantic chapels in any resort hotel, you can also choose to get wed in a cabana by the rooftop pool or on the observation deck at the top of the Eiffel Tower. Packages cost $1,000–10,000!
Chapelle du Jardin: An intimate chapel seating 30, it is decorated in pastel tones accented by charming garden murals.
Chapelle du Paradis: The cathedral-style setting of this beautiful chapel is enhanced by elegant columns, detailed gold-leaf designs, crystal chandeliers and angelic cherubs painted onto the blue-sky ceiling. Seats 90.

Planet Hollywood

702 702 785 5933, www.planet hollywoodresort.com
The chapel: The new Planet Hollywood is about cool lines and chic, designer flair and so is the chapel which seats up to 60 guests. Wedding packages cost from $550 for *What Happens in Vegas* right up to $11,000 for a maximum 50 people at *Twilight*.

Stratosphere Casino, Hotel & Tower

1 800 789 9436, www.stratospherehotel.com
or www.chapelintheclouds.com
Bella Luna Salon – Chapel in the Clouds: The Stratosphere Tower holds the unique position of offering the highest chapels in all of America, sitting 800ft/240m above the ground and offering truly awesome views, especially at night. Couples can also get wed on the indoor observation deck and then use the outdoor patio overlooking the Strip for up to 240 guests for their reception. Prices from $299. Elvis impersonator (of course!) is also available at an extra cost.
Bella Luna Salon: The smaller chapel seats 20.
Bella Vista Chapel: This seats 90 and is decorated in orange and grey.

Treasure Island

702 894 7700, www.treasureisland.com
Elegant Wedding Chapels: White benches contrast with the terracotta hues of the décor to provide a romantic setting for your wedding or for a less conventional flavour take your vows aboard the pirate ship. Packages from $350.

8

Tropicana

702 739 2451, www.tropicanalv.com
Island Arbor: The outdoor island gazebo,
an unusual and romantic chapel with a
Polynesian theme, seats 30.
  Island Wedding Chapel: This has been
voted Best Wedding Chapel and Most
Romantic Setting by the *Las Vegas Bride*
magazine. Tucked away in the lush tropical
foliage and tumbling waterfalls for which
the hotel is famous, it seats 76.
  Island Courtyard: Seats up to 70 guests.
Packages start at $399.

The Venetian

866 548 1807, www.venetian.com
Chapels: This resort-hotel is themed around
the ageless beauty and romance of Venice
and the storybook charm of old-world Italy.
There are 3 chapels, each holding 40–50
guests and overlooking the pool deck and
lush gardens. Cleverly, all 3 chapels can be
opened out to provide space for a larger
event. The chapel terrace overlooking the
Venezia Courtyard Gardens, is another
romantic option.
  Ponte al di Piazza: Alternatively, couples
can choose to say their vows on the bridge
over the square, which is said to serve as
the stairway to longevity and prosperity as
man and wife. Afterwards, you can start
married life by floating down the Grand
Canal in a beautiful gondola while being
serenaded. Packages from $2,000.

Wynn Las Vegas

702 770 7400, www.wynnlasvegas.com
In keeping with the standards for privacy
that pervade all aspects of Wynn's mega-
resort, each of the wedding salons has its
own private foyer where guests can gather
before the ceremony, and a private bridal
room for last-minute touch-ups! Delicate
tones, deluxe upholstery and beautiful
lighting are the other hallmarks of each
chapel and expert consultants are on hand
to create the perfect day. Packages for
these glamorous venues cost $1,190.
  Lavender Salon: Designed to be intimate,
yet can accommodate 120 guests. Despite
its name, back-lit rose murals and rose
petals strewn along the aisle are the main
features of this chapel.
  Lilac Salon: This chapel is perfect
for smaller wedding parties and seats
65. White, creams and terracottas run
throughout the salon and are reflected in
the choice of flowers that line the aisle and
altar.

Primrose Court: Think luxurious fabrics
in genteel Caribbean colours draped over
an exterior altar and you get a good idea
of what this chapel is about. A private
courtyard under a canopy of trees that is
surrounded by 2 fountains, it can seat up
to 100 guests. It also available for pre-
event cocktails or post-wedding cake and
Champagne for up to 70 guests.

Resort-hotels off the Strip

Hard Rock Hotel & Casino

702 693 5000, www.hardrockhotel.com
Tailormade weddings can be anything from
a ceremony under billowy drapery to one
surrounded by black roses at the hotel's
rock 'n' roll wedding. Receptions can be a
brunch buffet to a poolside party.

Las Vegas Hilton

702 732 5755, www.lvhilton.com
At the time of going to press, the Hilton was
about to change its name.
  La Bella Wedding Chapel: Traditional
cream chapel and a variety of packages
available.

M Resort

702 797 1919, www.themresort.com
A variety of venues with stunning views
over Vegas.

Rio All-Suite Hotel

702 252 7777, www.riolasvegas.com
Tie the knot in the Palazzo Gardens, on
the 51st floor in the VooDoo Lounge or
poolside.

Resort-hotel at Lake Las Vegas

Ravella at Lake Las Vegas

702 567 4700, www.ravellavegas.com
or www.ravellaweddings.com
Capella di Amore: sits directly over the
shimmering waters of 320acre/130ha
Lake Las Vegas on the resort's landmark
Ponte Vecchio-inspired bridge. Offering
spectacular lake views and charming
Tuscan design, the chapel lies within steps
of the hotel. Other options include the
Presidential Suite, on a white sand beach
by the lake, in the Tuscan Courtyard (20–
50 guests), sculpted Florentine Garden or in
a unique Ponte Vecchio Pavilion suspended
over the lake. Packages from $5,500.

A full guide to restaurants, bars and clubs

Surprisingly, for a city that claims to be so adult, there is relatively little available for the gay community. Nevadan anti-sodomy laws were only repealed in 1995 and a decade later, the city now has its first openly gay nightclub on the Strip – Krave. Despite this, Las Vegas was ranked as one of the top 10 gay-friendly destinations in the US according to a survey conducted by the Travel Industry Association.

There may not be the gay areas you'll find in many other cities, but there is an active scene and the annual Gay Pride Parade in April or May (866 930 3336, www.lasvegaspride.org for details) is testimony to the presence of a gay community. For the most part, though, a lot of gay activity is immersed in the mainstream. Here is a guide to the specific amenities available to gay men and women.

Information

Gay and Lesbian Center

953 East Sahara Avenue between 6th Street and Maryland Parkway, 702 733 9800, www.thecenterlv.com
A good place to start is the Gay and Lesbian Center. It is open Mon–Fri 11am–7pm – call ahead for schedules. It is a relatively new building and a new meeting point for gay people. The Center's website is very helpful.

BRITTIP
A leading gay newspaper, QVegas, maintains a great website, www.qvegas.com full of information for the gay community. www.gayvegas.com and www.outinlasvegas.com are other useful websites.

The Gay Triangle

The Gay Triangle area around Paradise Road has several hangouts, such as Get Booked and the Mariposa Restaurant. Pick up copies of the free *QVegas* at either of those locations. This area is also lovingly

referred to as the Fruit Loop by local gay and straight residents, for the business signs that show the rainbow colours of gay pride. Hotspots include **Suede**, a piano bar and restaurant, and **Gipsy**, the city's original gay dance club. Popular among celebrities, **Piranha Nightclub** and **8½ Ultra Lounge** feature a second floor with a beautiful view of the Strip, VIP cabañas and sky boxes and a private bar. You'll also discover **Freezone** and, as the name implies, there is never a cover at this popular bar and nightclub. A favourite among lesbian visitors, Freezone offers daily drink specials, good times and an ever-friendly welcoming staff.

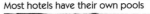

Most hotels have their own pools

Get Booked: At Paradise Plaza, 4640 South Paradise Road, 702 737 7780, www.getbooked.com this is a bookstore at the heart of the Gay Triangle at the corner of Naples Drive and Paradise Road, just south of Hard Rock Café, and a great source of information. It is open Sun–Thurs 10am–midnight; Fri–Sat 10am–2am.

Another great gay area can be found in the Commercial Center between East Sahara and Karen Avenue, just to the west of Maryland Parkway. Here you will find **Entourage, Crew'N, Spotlight Lounge, Badlands Saloon** and **Rainbow Lounge.**

BRITTIP
Nevada Gay Rodeo Association, www.ngra.com, is an all-volunteer, non-profit organisation dedicated to preserving the Western lifestyle and producing gay rodeos with a commitment to raise funds for charitable organisations.

Accommodation

Alexis Park

375 East Harmon, 702 796 3300, www.alexispark.com
The closest hotel to the Fruit Loop area and host to a number of gay events.

Blue Moon Resort

2651 Westwood Drive, just off the Strip, 702 784 4500, www.bluemoonlv.com
The $3.1m Blue Moon Resort opened in December 2002 providing a full-service gay resort for men only with 45 rooms and suites. Amenities include a Jacuzzi Grotto with 10ft/3m waterfalls to relax and enjoy the sun, a lagoon-style pool and sundeck with a clothing-optional area, plus a steam room.

Parlour suites provide 800ft^2/74m^2 of space that are ideal for small meetings, entertaining guests or simply watching the TV and have large beds and armoires, large TVs, cable TV and electronic door locks.

Lucky Club Casino & Hotel

3227 Civic Center Drive, 702 399 3297, www.luckyclublv.com
An exclusively gay B&B just 2 blocks from the Strip within walking distance of gay bars. Well priced – from $29 per night – but no credit cards accepted.

Riviera

2901 The Strip at Riviera Boulevard, 702 794 9433, www.rivierahotel.com
The most openly gay hotel on the Strip, it is the home of *La Cage*, a top drag show starring Frank Marino as Joan Rivers, now reincarnated at the Imperial Palace.

Rumor Boutique Hotel

455 East Harmon Ave, 877 997 8667, www.rumorvegas.com
Right across the street from the Hard Rock Hotel, this girly all-suites stylish hotel with DJs, poolside chilling and Addiction Restaurant (see page 95), also has a wedding service.

BRITTIP
Visit www.gaybars.com for up-to-date information and location maps for all the local gay bars.

After dark

After dark, myriad options await, beginning with one of the hottest shows on the Strip, Cirque du Soleil's **Zumanity** at New York New York. **Celine Dion** is performing for a 3-year engagement at The Colosseum at Caesars Palace. Frank Marino's **Divas Las Vegas** stars Frank Marino as comedy icon Joan Rivers and an all-star cast of female impersonators.

Clubs and bars

Backdoor Lounge

1415 East Charleston Blvd, 702 385 2018
There's fun to be had here 24/7. It has a happy hour every night 5–7pm. Monday night a free poker party starts at 7pm and there is a free barbecue on Saturday nights at 6pm, weekend dancing and drag shows. Very popular with gay Latinos at the weekends.

Badlands Saloon

Commercial Center, 953 East Sahara Avenue, 702 792 9262
New home of the Gay Rodeo Association, this country and western style neighbourhood bar is probably the friendliest bar in town. The best times to visit are Sun around 4pm and Tues and Thurs around 7pm when the line-dancing classes get going.

Charlie's Las Vegas

5012 Arville Street (Tropicana), 702 876 1844, www.charlieslasvegas.com
Part of a well-known chain of gay bars popular in Chicago, Phoenix and Denver. It sports a Country and Western theme with live DJs Wed–Sun, line dancing Thursdays 7–9pm and Sun afternoon Beer Blasts Sundays from 4pm – $2 drinks for guys in underwear.

Crews'N

Commercial Center, 1000 E Sahara Ave, Suite 105, 702 731 0951, http://crewsnlv.com
Downtown piano lounge, this neighbourhood gay bar serving stiff drinks is open 24/7.

Escape Lounge

4213 West Sahara Avenue, 702 364 1167, www.escapeloungelasvegas.com
This is a new place with great specials and a friendly atmosphere.

Flex

4371 West Charleston Blvd, 702 878 3355, www.flexlasvegas.com
A great mixed club off the Strip with drink specials, dancing and go-go boys or amateur strip contests.

Freezone Night Club

Paradise Fruit Loop, 610 East Naples, 702 794 2300, www.freezonelv.com
A down-to-earth bar with cheap drinks and bar menu and something on nightly. Tuesday is the Ladies 4 Ladies revue night, Thursday the all-male revue for Boys Night, and What a Drag! is held on Friday and Saturday. As its name implies: never a cover charge to enter.

BRITTIP
Some of the gay night spots are in quite out-of-the-way locations. For help finding them, look up addresses on mapquest.com.

Gipsy

4605 Paradise Road, 702 731 1919, www.gipsyvegas.com
The city's original gay dance club with live music some nights. Expect a young crowd, go-go boys and drag queens. Open 9pm–dawn.

Goodtimes

1775 East Tropicana, 702 736 9494, www.goodtimeslv.com
A night of drag entertainment and an open bar mean 'good times'. Happy hours 5–7am and 5–7pm. Monday is the most popular. No credit cards.

Krave

Miracle Mile Shops at Planet Hollywood, 702 836 0830, www.kravelasvegas.com
The only gay nightclub on the Strip has been voted the best venue in town by many of the leading gay papers. There are events for men throughout the week – all starting at 11pm – with CandyBar for the girls on Sat 9pm–3am. For dining, check out Lucky Cheng's inside Krave. This popular drag queen Chinese restaurant originally debuted in Manhattan's East Village to rave revues. True to its New York counterpart, Lucky Cheng's serves Pan Asian cuisine as well as a nightly cabaret.

Las Vegas Eagle

3430 E Tropicana Ave, 702 458 8662
The true adventure-seeker will earn free drinks and beer every Wed and Fri at Las Vegas Eagle, but only under one condition: that bar patrons strip down to their boxers or briefs!

BRITTIP
Take a look at www.gaylasvegasfun.com for gay things to see and places to visit.

Piranha Boutique Nightclub & 8½ Ultra Lounge

4633 Paradise Road, 702 791 0100, www.piranhavegas.com
Popular amongst celebrities, this venue offers a beautiful view of the Strip from the second floor, VIP cabañas and sky boxes and a private bar. Thursdays is Comedy Drag Night. Open nightly 10pm–dawn.

BRITTIP
Head for the Mirage's gorgeous ultra-lounge Revolution (www.lightgroup.com) for gay night on Sundays.

Pool party

Snick's Place

1402 South 3rd Street, 702 385 9298,
www.snicksplace.com
One of Vegas's oldest gay bars, and still
going strong with happy hours Mon–Fri
2–4pm and 2–4am.

Spotlight Lounge

Commercial Center, 957 E Sahara Avenue,
702 696 0202
Over the last few years, this low-key lounge
with a welcoming atmosphere and strong
drinks has grown into a leader of the gay
community, hosting a number of meetings
and charity events to raise money for gay
causes. It is also a great working class bar
in which to relax.

Suede Restaurant & Lounge

4640 Paradise Road, 702 791 3463
Slick ultra-lounge and restaurant.
Wednesdays is Sheila's Karaoke at 9pm,
Thursday is Sheila's Pajama Karaoke,
Fridays is Queer as Food, a Queer-as-Folk
themed evening, and Saturday is singles
night. Open Wed–Sat 5pm–2am.

Gay bath house

Entourage Spa & Health Club

Commercial Center, 953E Sahara Avenue,
Suite A-19, 702 650 9191,
www.entouragevegas.com
Located in the north-west corner of
Commercial Center, this is a bath house
that caters for men, with gym, steam room,
dry sauna, two Jacuzzis, pool, video room
and 60 private rooms all with video feed.
The first Monday of each month is Manhunt
Monday. For out-of-towners this is a great
place to get clued up about the Vegas gay
scene.

BRITTIP
There are no exclusively female
bars in Las Vegas, but 2 of the
most popular with gay women are
Freezone and Charlie's.

Pool parties

The Luxor's **Temptation Sundays** are the
biggest LGBT pool party in town where
DJ's spin themed parties weekly – such as
'Christmas in July' and 'I love the 80s' – at
the South Pool. **Heaven Saturdays** are held
at **Bare** at the Mirage once a month on hot
summer nights.

Goodtimes

Thrill rides, children's attractions, museums and animal habitats

Yes, there really is more to Las Vegas than bright lights and gambling dens. There are a whole host of attractions that appeal to people of all ages, some amazing thrill rides and even a little – some overpriced – culture in the form of art museums.

The high-tech wizardry that can be seen in so many nightclubs and production shows is also put to use in heart-thumping simulator rides and 3-D movies. And there is a raft of museums that celebrate aspects of the city's history and people – including Elvis – and the Las Vegas Natural History Museum, while animals can be seen at several resort-hotels and the local zoo.

As in other chapters, to save keying in a long website address, you can go to the home page for the resort-hotel, then follow the entertainment or attractions links.

Thrill rides

Many resorts around the Las Vegas area have added a number of thrill rides to get the blood pumping before you hit the gambling tables. Circus Circus draws top hand for the most rides at its Adventuredome, while the Stratosphere's sky-reaching thrillers are some of the most gut-wrenching. There are more too,

including the great roller-coaster at New York-New York. The Las Vegas High Roller – the world's tallest ferris wheel – 107ft/32.6m taller than the London Eye – will make for heart-stopping moments when it opens in 2013.

Adventuredome Theme Park

Circus Circus, 702 794 3939, www.adventuredome.com
The desert may be scorching hot outside, but here in this 5acre/2ha, fully enclosed elevated theme park – the largest space-frame dome in America – the temperature stays a comfortable 22ºC/72ºF all year round. Grand Slam Canyon is designed to

Chaos at the Adventuredome

© MGM

look like a desert with a large rock canyon that gives way to caverns, pinnacles and steep cliffs, while a stream flows gently through the lush landscape. But this canyon is home to prehistoric creatures – well, life-sized replicas of them at least! – that make themselves known between two 140ft/43m peaks, a fossil wall, archaeological dig and a replica of an Indian cliff dwelling.

The 25 rides and attractions in the Adventuredome divide into Premium Rides, Large Rides, Junior Rides, Family Rides and Featured Attractions. Below are some of the most popular.

The **Canyon Blaster** is the only indoor, double-loop, double-corkscrew roller-coaster in America, and sends you careering between canyon walls at 55mph/86kph.

The 2-minute long **Inverter** involves a 360-degree rotation in which you are held upside-down with only a harness and a T-bar separating you from the concrete floor 50ft/15m below.

Chaos twirls and whirls you anti-clockwise, backwards and upside-down on a circular platform amid the tracks of the Canyon Blaster. Lasting 2 minutes, it creates a 3-D effect as you rise, tilt and spin all at the same time, and due to the variation in speed and motion, no 2 rides are the same.

In the **Slingshot** you are shot up a tower at 4Gs of acceleration and then shot straight back down again.

The **Rim Runner** is a more relaxing ride, taking you on a scenic journey through botanical landscaping before plunging over a heart-stopping 60ft/18m waterfall.

◀✦▶ **BRITTIP**
Save the Rim Runner thrill ride until the end of your Adventuredome visit as you will get soaked through!

Lazer Blast is where sharpshooters take part in a high-tech war. There are also bumper cars and a swinging ship, plus an IMAX simulator thrill ride (see page 175). Younger children are well catered for from plane and train rides to clown shows, bumper-mobiles, plus strolling entertainers who juggle, mime and do magic tricks. There's also the new **FX Theater** with Dora & Diego and Happy Feet 4-D rides.

One of the newer rides to try is **Disk'O** which once you're strapped in, rocks and spins you at the same time.

Open: Daily from 10am. It closes at 6pm Mon–Thurs, midnight Fri and Sat and 8pm Sun, though exact hours may vary according to the seasons – in September it

opens some days at 11am for example, so do check.

Tickets: Entrance to the park is free; you just pay for the rides of your life! The main thrill rides cost $5–8 each or you can buy an All Day Ride Pass at $26.95 for people 4ft/1.2m tall or taller and $16.95 for those under 4ft/1.2m. Children under 2' 9"/84cm ride free with an adult.

Fremont Street Experience Flightlinez

425 Fremont Street, Suite 160, 702 410 7999, www.fremontstreetflightline.com
Fly like an aerialist under the glittering lights of Fremont Street Experience canopy and light show on 800ft/244m of ziplines, up to 30mph, 60ft/18.3m in the air. Before 6pm $15, after 6pm $20. Open Sun–Thurs noon–midnight, Fri–Sat noon–2am.

The Roller Coaster

New York-New York, 702 740 6969 or 866 815 4365, www.newyorknewyork.com/ attractions/the-roller-coaster.aspx
Based on the kind of roller-coaster that made Coney Island in the real New York so famous, the **Roller Coaster** twists, loops and dives around the perimeter and even through the New York-New York hotel, which can be a worry when you are sitting in 'Central Park' and hear a roar and rattling through the rafters. It has the world's first heart-line twist and dive that simulates the sensation felt by a pilot during a barrel roll in an aeroplane when the centre of rotation actually becomes the same as your centre of gravity! The roller-coaster lifts you up 203ft/62m, drops you down 144ft/44m and leaves you coasting at 67mph/108kmh. Incidentally, the roller-coaster has been voted Best Thrill Ride in Nevada by *Nevada Magazine*'s reader survey.

Open: Sun–Thurs 11am–11pm, Fri–Sat 10.30am–midnight

Tickets: $14 per person; all-day Scream Pass $25 or Family Fun Flight for 4 $60

Stratosphere Tower Rides

Stratosphere Casino Hotel and Tower, 702 380 7777 or 800 998 6937, www.stratospherehotel.com/ Tower/Rides
Four extreme thrill rides are found here. The **Big Shot** thrusts 16 passengers 160ft/50m into the air along the 228ft/70m spire at speeds of around 45mph/72kph, producing up to 4Gs with negative Gs on the way back down. What is so scary

about the ride is not just the speed and force of it all, but the fact that you are so high up in the air in the first place as The Stratosphere Tower is 100 floors up and over 900ft/274m high.

Insanity, the Ride thrusts passengers 64ft/20m over the north edge of the tower at speeds that create forces of up to 3Gs, while at a 70-degree angle, providing a perfect view of nothingness beneath you – except a 900ft/274m drop to the Strip below (though no time for photos, folks!).

In **X-Scream** (i.e screaming to the extreme) passengers are propelled 27ft/8m over the edge of the tower at 30mph/48kph – again providing excellent views of the 900ft/274m drop.

The newest is **SkyJump** a plummet 855ft/261m through the sky from the 108th floor – the highest controlled free fall in the world. Yikes.

Open: Sun–Thurs 10am–1am; Fri–Sat 10am–2pm. However, the rides are often not open on windy days

Tickets: $16 for adult admission to Stratosphere Tower. Tickets to ride X-Scream and Insanity are $12 each and the Big Shot is $13. Tower admission and 3 rides is $31, and an unlimited day pass $34. SkyJump is $109.99 and up (with free admission to the tower).

✚▶ **BRITTIP**
For the best selection of thrill rides in town, the Stratosphere is the place to go. Thrill seekers with a car should head out of town to Buffalo Bill's Adventure Canyon in Primm.

Thrill Rides at Buffalo Bill's

Buffalo Bill's Resort & Casino, 31900 South Las Vegas Boulevard, Primm, 702 386 7867 or 1-800 FUN STOP, www.primmvalleyresorts.com
For amazing thrill rides on a Wild West theme, head to Buffalo Bill's in Primm, which is just 35mls/56km south of Las Vegas on Interstate 15.

One of America's tallest and fastest roller-coasters, **Desperado**, has a top speed of around 90mph/145kph and creates a G-force of nearly 4. A high-speed dive down a 55-degree hill into a tunnel starts the ride and is then followed by a 155ft/47m second hill, which leads to a zero-gravity sensation – 2.43 minutes of heart-pounding fun.

Turbo Drop creates a similar sensation to flying straight towards the ground in a

jet fighter. Riders are nestled in padded saddles and shoulder harnesses, lifted 200ft/60m up in the air and plunged to earth at 45mph/72kph, creating positive G-forces close to 4.5.

The **Vault** is the first 3-D, digital projection motor ride in America. Each of the 6 motion pads drops, twists and turns as the screen takes you on one of 10 different rides ranging from a dizzying magic carpet ride in Arabia to the seriously rickety mine car on the Haunted Mine Ride.

Adventure Canyon Log Flume starts as a classic flume ride with a 35ft/11m drop, but once you splash down, you continue through an electronic shooting gallery that follows the park's Wild West theme. You take out a pistol as targets are lit up along the way, then if you shoot a bad guy you get points and if you shoot a good guy you lose points!

Other rides to make your visit worthwhile include the **Maxflight Cyber Coaster** and the **Froghopper** and there's also the **Attraction Zone Arcade** and the **Carolee Theatre**, showing big name movies.

Open: Fri–Sun 12.15pm–9.45pm. Although only open at weekends at the moment, times can change, so best to call ahead for hours of operation

Tickets: The main rides cost $3–10 each or $30 for a full-day wristband, $22 for a half-day wristband. Little Wrangler passes for those under 4ft/1.2m are $12

Simulator rides and 3-D movies

SimEx and FX Theaters

Adventuredome Theme Park, Circus Circus, 702 794 3939, www.adventuredome.com
Fans of the Nickelodeon cartoon will love **SpongeBob SquarePants 4-D Ride** in the new FX Theater, where they get the chance to dive into Bikini Bottom and join SpongeBob and co on a 4-D adventure – wind, bubbles and scent are just a few of the 4-D effects. For children over 3' 6"/106cm only.

There's a new **Dora & Diego's 4-D Adventure: Catch that Robot Butterfly** and **Happy Feet: Mumble's Wild Ride 4-D** – excitement on ice – in the SimEx Extreme Ride Theater.

Open: Daily from 10am. It closes at 6pm Mon–Thurs, midnight Fri and Sat and 8pm Sun, though exact hours may vary according to the seasons, so do check

Tickets: $8 per ride. All-day passes for

10

Circus Circus

the Adventuredome are also available (see page 174)

BRITTIP
The website www.vegas.com/
attractions lists free attractions,
thrill rides, kids activities and more
and sells tickets to top attractions
online.

Insanity

Excalibur rides

**Excalibur, 877 750 5464 or 702 597 7777,
www.excalibur.com/attractions**
Here you'll find a series of hilarious rides.
SpongeBob SquarePants 4-D Ride, also
shown at The Adventuredome above,
Happy Feet 4-D and **Extreme Log Ride**
are the newest rides. You must be 3'
6"/106cm tall to ride. Arcade games and
childhood favourites can be found at the
Fun Dungeon.
   Open: FX Rides: Mon–Thurs 11am–9pm;
Friday 11am–10pm; Sat–Sun 10am–10pm
   Tickets: $9.99 per ride

BRITTIP
Get 3 must-see attractions for
$54. Choose out of 7 from Shark
Reef at Mandalay Bay to the Roller
Coaster at New York New York.

Fremont Street

Fun rides

Eiffel Tower – The Ride

**Paris, 877 796 2096 or 702 946 7000,
www.parislasvegas.com**
You take a lift to about two-thirds of the
way up the replica Eiffel Tower and then
look out at the desert through an iron mesh
460ft/140m above ground. The hotel's
tower is, in fact, only two-thirds of the
height of the real Eiffel Tower, so your view
is blocked by many of the tall buildings
about. Although voted 'Best Place to View
the City', it is hard to get a decent view of
the entire Strip and impossible to take any
worthwhile pictures through the grille.
Open: Daily 9.30am–12.30am, weather
permitting
Tickets: Adult $10.50 daytime, $15.50
at night

BRITTIP
The Eiffel Tower Experience is
probably the most expensive
elevator (lift) ride in the world. Save
your money and enjoy Strip views from
any one of the fab restaurants with
views (see page 98).

Gondola rides

**Venetian, 702 414 4300,
www.venetian.com/gondola.aspx**
Supplying the full Venetian experience, the
hotel puts on indoor gondola rides around
the Grand Canal Shoppes. They're pricey,
but still cheaper than gondola rides in

© LVNB

The Strip

Venice! Tours start from St Mark's Square.
Better yet are the newest outdoor gondola
rides by the main entrance of the Doge's
Palace. These gondoliers are required to be
Italian, or at least have travelled enough in
Italy to be able to talk about it first hand.
Plus, they must have great singing voices
as they croon romantic melodies to their
passengers. Many a wedding proposal has
been made here. They even have a special
wedding gondola, oversized and all in
white, if you'd like to take your vows here.
Open: Indoor Sun–Thurs 10am–11pm;
Fri–Sat 10am–midnight; outdoor daily
11am–10pm
Tickets: Adults $16, private 2-passenger
gondola $64. Reservations must be made
in person, same day

10

Gondola ride at the Venetian

BRITTIP
The gondola rides are so popular that tickets sell out every day and the average wait for a ride is 1 hour.

Observation Deck Stratosphere Tower

Stratosphere, 800 99 TOWER or 702 380 7711, www.stratospherehotel.com/Tower/Observation-deck
Take a ride up the Stratosphere's lifts to the top of the tallest free-standing observation tower in America, which has an indoor and outdoor observation deck where all the landmarks seen from different points of the circular deck are explained. The best time of day to see the Strip is just before sunset when you can make out all the landmarks before the town goes dark and everything lights up. Better still, start at the observation deck, then move up to the AirBar – the highest in Vegas – or Top of the World Restaurant for a romantic dinner.
Open: Sun–Thurs 10am–1am; Fri–Sat 10am–2am
Tickets: Adults $16, children 4–12 $10, senior and Stratosphere guests $12 (see pages 174–5 for the details of the tower's thrill rides)

BRITTIP
The **Las Vegas Power Pass** is the passport to top attractions from the Stratosphere Tower to Hoover Dam for a fixed fee starting from a day pass for $79.99 adults and $49.99 children (www.visiticket.com/LasVegas).

Free shows

CBS Television City

MGM Grand, 800 646 7787 or 702 891 5752, www.mgmgrand.com
A research centre in the MGM Grand Casino that allows audiences to view TV shows in production and comment on them. A new addition is The Sony 3-D Experience, a research centre focusing on perceptions of 3-D – from previews of programmes to Playstation's upcoming 3-D titles.
Show times: Free screenings are conducted every half an hour daily 10am–8.30pm

Circus acts at Circus Circus

Circus Circus, 2880 Las Vegas Boulevard South, 702 734 0410, www.circuscircus.com/las_vegas_entertainment/circus_acts.aspx
World-renowned circus acts include African acrobats, a 15-year-old contortionist, a stilt-walking juggler and a blindfolded triple somersault, all in the world's largest permanent circus.
Show times: Daily from 11am–midnight every 30 minutes

Fountain at Miracle Mile Shops

Planet Hollywood Resort & Casino, 3667 Las Vegas Boulevard South, 702 866 0710, www.miraclemileshopslv.com
This multi-million dollar popular water feature sees the fountain leaping 5 storeys high with effects such as colour-changing fog, bursts of light and surround sound.
Show times: Daily on the hour noon–11pm

Fountains of Bellagio

In the lake outside the Bellagio, 702 693 7111, www.bellagio.com/amenities/fountains-of-bellagio.aspx
An incredibly stunning visual and audio experience as more than a thousand now world-famous fountains set in an 8-acre/3-ha lake perform carefully choreographed movements in time to operatic, classical and whimsical music.
Show times: Mon–Fri 3pm–midnight; Sat–Sun noon–midnight. Shows every half hour until 8pm, then every 15 minutes until midnight

Fremont Street Experience

425 Fremont Street, 702 678 5600, www.vegasexperience.com
Towering 90ft/27.4m above 4 of the blocks of the Fremont Experience pedestrian mall in Downtown is a massive space-frame lit up by 12.5 million lights and 540,000 watts of sound.
Show times: Nightly on the hour, 6pm–midnight

Lake of Dreams

Wynn Las Vegas, 3131 Las Vegas Boulevard, 702 770 7000, www.wynnlasvegas.com
This secluded 3-acre/1.2-ha lake surrounded by a lush forest is a tranquil idyll in the midst of the city and provides free vantage points to view the water and

light show, if you don't want to wander into one of the bars and restaurants.

Show times: Nightly every half hour from 8.30pm–1am

Live Runway Shows

Fashion Show Mall, 3200 Las Vegas Boulevard (near Saks Fifth Ave/Nordstrom), 702 369 8382, www.thefashionshow.com
The fullest line-up of fashion on the Strip is on this 80ft/24m runway which rises out of the ground for 1,000 shows a year. Think Saks, Bloomingdale's and Macy's.

Show times: Weekends hourly midday–6pm

> **BRITTIP**
> For just $12.95 guests can ride in the float with the dancers at Masquerade Show in the Sky. Buy tickets at the Rio Hotel's box office.

Masquerade Show in the Sky

Rio All-Suite Hotel, 3700 West Flamingo, 702 252 7777 or 866 746 7671, www.riolasvegas.com
A $25m Disney-esque spectacle in which dozens of Mardi Gras floats containing exotically costumed dancers literally 'float' about 20ft/6m above your head, accompanied to music. Different shows on different nights, on Mon–Wed, they're accompanied by hot live Latin rhythms.
Show times: Thurs–Sat hourly 6–11pm

> **BRITTIP**
> If you are travelling with children, be warned that the Masquerade Show in the Sky includes topless showgirls during the evening performances.

Mirage Volcano

The Mirage, 3400 Las Vegas Boulevard, 702 791 7111, www.mirage.com/attractions/volcano.aspx
The newest free show on the Strip, this man-made wonder blasts fireballs 100ft/30.48m into the air with fiery lava flames flowing down its sides into the lagoon, close enough for spectators to feel the heat. The accompanying soundtrack was composed by Grateful Dead drummer Mickey Hart and Indian tabla virtuoso Zakir Hussain.

Show times: Erupts nightly, every hour 8pm–midnight, weather permitting

Sirens of TI

Treasure Island, 3300 Las Vegas Boulevard, 702 894 7111, www.treasureisland.com/shows/sirens_of_ti.aspx
A rowdy bunch of buccaneers do battle against alluring but treacherous Sirens in a spectacle full of singing, sword play, canon shots and, of course, at least one walking of the plank.

Show times: Daily at 5.30pm (autumn/winter only); 7pm, 8.30pm, 10pm and 11.30pm (spring/summer only)

Streetmosphere at the Grand Canal Shoppes

Venetian Hotel and Casino, 3555 South Las Vegas Boulevard, 702 414 4500, www.venetian.com or www.thegrandcanalshoppes.com/dining-entertainment/streetmosphere
Street performers, Artiste del Arte – singers, actors and entertainers who put on shows throughout the day – Living Statues and The Venetian Trio – who offer elegant music in the evening – all adds fun to the shopping experience. Most of the action is around St Mark's Square.

Show times: Daily, about 30 performances a day at various times. *Artiste del Arte* 1pm, 2pm, 4pm, 5pm and 6pm; *Living Statues* 10am–6pm; *The Venetian Trio* 6–10pm; *The Gondolier March* 9.45am and 4.15pm

Sunset Stampede at Sam's Town

Sam's Town Hotel & Gambling Hall, 5111 Boulder Highway (less than 10mls/16km from the Strip), 702 456 7777, www.samstownlv/com/entertain/mystic-falls
This 8-minute show in Mystic Falls Park starts with the plaintive howl of a wolf and goes on to create a symphonic journey through the Wild West with water, laser, light and animation.

Show times: Daily 2pm, 6pm, 8pm and 10pm

Animal magic

Lion Habitat

MGM Grand, 702 891 7777, www.mgmgrand.com/entertainment/lion-habitat.aspx
In this $9m multi-level lion habitat at the MGM Grand, visitors are encircled by lions and cubs via a see-through glass tunnel running through it. Out of 31 lions cared

Mirage Volcano

Shark Reef

Mandalay Bay Hotel, 3950 Las Vegas Boulevard S, 702 632 7777, www.sharkreef.com

An aquarium you walk underneath so you are completely surrounded by water giving you a 360 degree view of some of the world's most dangerous aquatic animals and fish from the world's tropical waters. More than 2,000 animals can be seen here in 14 exhibits from a 100ft/30m nurse shark to a tiny clown fish. Divers in the aquarium talk about the animals and answer questions via a high-tech underwater communications system.

The largest display of golden saltwater crocodiles outside Thailand can be seen here too. This is a seriously endangered species as there are only 12 left in the world. Other animals include moray eels, southern stingrays, angelfish, puffer fish, jellyfish and serpents and dragons featuring green tree pythons, known for their vivid green colour and razor-sharp teeth. A touch pool includes sharks, rays and horseshoe crabs. Certified divers staying at the Mandalay can dive with the sharks in the largest 'Shipwreck' exhibit.

Open: Sun–Thurs 10am–8pm; last admission at 9pm, Fri–Sat 10am–10pm

Admission: Adults $18, under-13s $12, under-4s free

for on a ranch by a veteran animal trainer, up to 7 can be viewed here at any time. Three of the lions – Goldie, Metro and Baby Lion – are direct descendants of the MGM Studios lion, Leo.

Open: Daily 11am–7pm. Feeding at 11.15am and 4.30pm daily

Admission: Free, though an 'official' picture costs around $10. There's a gift shop on the way out

Shark Reef

Siegfried and Roy's Secret Garden and Dolphin Habitat

Mirage Hotel, 3400 Las Vegas Boulevard S, 702 791 7111, www.mirage.com/attractions/secret-garden.aspx or www.miragehabitat.com
Here is your chance to get a closer look at the rare breeds of animal that Siegfried and Roy used in their magical illusion show. The $15m, 2.5acre/1ha natural Secret Garden habitat was specially built to house their white tigers, lions, panthers, snow leopards and Asian elephants.

BRITTIP
Make the most of the Mirage's free attractions by taking a look at the enormous tropical fish tank behind the resort's lobby during your visit to see the beautiful white tigers.

Next door is the massive **Dolphin Habitat**, which is home to a family of Atlantic bottlenose dolphins. Four connected pools, an artificial coral reef system and a sandy bottom replicate the dolphin's natural environment, which aims to provide a healthy and nurturing home for the marine mammals and educate the public about their role in the ecosystem – you can even see bottlenose calves.

Open: Mon–Fri 11am–6.30pm; Sat–Sun 10am–6.30pm

Admission: Adults $17, children (4–12 years) $12, under-3s free, includes entrance to both habitats. Tickets can be booked online. VIP 1-hour group tours run at 11am, 1pm, 2.30pm and 4pm daily. Call 702 792 7889 for prices

Be a dolphin trainer

One of the most exciting – although expensive – attractions to hit Las Vegas is the chance to become a dolphin trainer for the day at Siegfried and Roy's Secret Garden and Dolphin Habitat at the Mirage. For a hefty fee of around $595 per person (with 2 people per family as a maximum, participants must be at least 13 years old) – observers pay $150, it is possible to learn how to feed and play with dolphins as you accompany real trainers 9.45am–3.15pm. Throughout the day, your activities and contact with the dolphins will be captured on camera and the photos put on a CD to take home. For further details or to make a reservation, phone 702 792 7889.

Southern Nevada Zoo

1755 North Rancho Drive, 702 647 4685, www.lasvegaszoo.com
A small zoo committed to conservation, education and recreation, it houses more than 50 species of reptiles and small animals of the great south-western desert. It is also home to other animals including an African lion, Bengal tiger, Barbary apes, monkeys, wallabies, flamingos, king vultures and North America's only tigrina, an endangered tropical cat, as well as many species of plants.

Open: Daily 9am–5pm

Admission: Over-12s $9, 2–12s and seniors $7, under-2s free

10

Siegfried and Roy's Secret Garden and Dolphin Habitat

© LVNB

The Tank

Golden Nugget, 702 385 7111 or 866 946 5336 for seat reservations, www.goldennugget.com/LasVegas/pool_thetank.asp

While primarily for guests staying at the Golden Nugget in downtown Las Vegas, sometimes staff will let you slide in. The Tank is the new $30m swimming pool complex, including a 3-storey waterslide. But the coolest part is the shark tank – yes, sharks! The Tank is designed in such a way that while going down the water slide you go through a tube through the middle of the sharks. It is the closest you can come to these cold-blooded killers without donning a mask and fins.

Open: Daily 10am–8pm. Jacuzzi and H20 bar open until 2am

Admission: Non-hotel guests 12s and over $20, 11 and under $15, under 2s free; Rent 1 of the 7 private cabañas for the day for $175 Mon–Thurs or $250 Fri–Sun

Wildlife Habitat at the Flamingo

Flamingo Hotel, 3555 Las Vegas Boulevard S, 702 733 3111, www.flamingolasvegas.com

Surrounded by lush pines, palms, magnolia and waterfalls, this is the only place in town where you can see flamingos up close who have come all the way from Chile. Over 300 birds can be seen here, including Impeyn and silver pheasants along with Gambel's quails, a crown crane and ducks, ibis and swans as well as koi and turtles.

Open: 24/7
Admission: Free

Art galleries and exhibitions

Being but 100 years old, Las Vegas has a limited run of culture to draw on and what there is happens to be imported at a tidy cost. So it's perhaps no surprise then that the exhibitions have been dropping like flies since the onset of the credit crunch, due to poor ticket sales. Museums and galleries may be a bit pricey here, but they are a good way to avoid the searing heat!.

One lovely counterpoint, though, is that several of the high-end shopping areas, including places like Grand Canal Shoppes and Forum Shops, have some dazzling art galleries. And away from the resorts, there are some fascinating places to check out.

The Arts Factory

105 East Charleston Boulevard, 702 676 1111, www.theartsfactory.com

The Arts Factory is a collection of artists, architects, photographers, graphic designers and galleries are gathered under one roof in Downtown, just around the corner from the 18b Arts District. Opening within it is Sin City Gallery 'to stimulate the naughtier side of art' with edgy art exhibitions. First Fridays monthly event from 6–10pm is free.

Bellagio Gallery of Fine Art

Bellagio, 877 957 9777 or 702 693 7871, www.bellagiolasvegas.com/amenities/gallery-of-fine-art.aspx

This originally opened to show off the previous owner Steve Wynn's masterpieces, which included Rembrandts, Monets and Picassos, but he took the paintings with him when he sold the hotel to the MGM Grand. Now it showcases travelling art exhibitions and is theoretically non-profit-making. The exhibitions are on a small scale, rarely more than 12–20 pieces or so, but the cost is steep, so you should only come by if the current exhibition is particularly of interest to you. In 2009, the gallery was showing 'Classic Contemporary: Lichtenstein, Warhol and Friends' and in 2011, 'A Sense of Place' landscapes from Monet to Hockney.

Open: Sun, Mon, Tues, Thurs 10am–6pm; Weds, Fri and Sat 10am–7pm

Admission: Adults $15, seniors $12, students $10. Children 12 and under go free

Luxor exhibitions

Luxor Hotel 800 557 7428 or 702 262 4400, www.luxor.com/entertainment

Bodies – the Exhibition showcases 21 real bodies and 260 organs dissected – not for the squeamish but a fascinating look into our system and a wake-up call for a healthy lifestyle!

Titanic: The Artifact Exhibition tells the story behind the ill-fated journey of the 'Ship of Dreams' with more than 300 artifacts recovered from below the icy Atlantic – whose temperatures can be felt on the Promenade deck— and a full-scale recreation of the Grand Staircase as well as passengers' memories.

Open: Daily 10am–10pm. Last admission 9pm

Admission: Bodies: $32 adults, $30 seniors, $24 children (4–12 years). Titanic:

$28 adults, $26 seniors, $21 children (4–12 years). Audio tours available for $6

The Wynn Collection

Wynn Las Vegas, 877 321 9966 or 702 770 3590, www.wynnlasvegas.com
Casino mogul Steve Wynn's private collection scattered around this resort includes Picasso's *Le Rêve*, (the painting that originally inspired him for Wynn Las Vegas), Matisse's *The Persian Robe* and *Pineapples and Anemones* and Manet's *Portrait of Mademoiselle Suzette Lemaire in Profile*. Oh, and there's also a portrait of Steve Wynn himself by Andy Warhol! Named one of the top 10 private collectors by US magazine *ARTnews*, Wynn has been collecting art for years and now has a collection that spans 400 years of art history. The one drawback? There are only 13–15 pictures on display at any one time.
Open: 24/7
Admission: free

Attractions

Bellagio Conservatory and Botanical Gardens

Bellagio, 3600 Las Vegas Boulevard S, 702 693 7111, www.bellagio.com/amenities/botanical-garden.aspx
This glorious display of exotic plants and flowers provides row upon row of blooms that create a unique tapestry to reflect each season and holiday. The combination of the fragrances, textures and colours are heavenly, while the inspirational conservatory with its glass-topped atrium and sweeping staircase is simply divine. This is a wonderful place to come and release the tension of otherwise intense Las Vegas.
Open: 24/7
Admission: Free

BRITTIP
Feel a photo opportunity coming on? Then the perfect spot to capture yourself in Vegas is at the gorgeous Botanical Gardens in the Bellagio.

The Cloud

Fashion Show Mall, 3200 Las Vegas Boulevard, 702 369 8382, www.thefashionshow.com
One of the most eye-catching attractions on the Strip hovers 128ft/39m above a pedestrian plaza right outside the Fashion Show Mall. Nearly 500ft/152m long, the steel canopy is called The Cloud and is a wonderful source of shade during the day. At night, giant images are projected on to its surface to highlight promotions and events happening at the mall, while a further 4 massive LED screens are used to broadcast videos and other live broadcasts from the city.
Open: Mall hours are Mon–Sat 10am–9pm; Sun 11am–7pm
Admission: Free

CSI: The Experience

MGM Grand Hotel and Casino, 877 660 0660 or 702 891 7006, www.mgmgrand.com/entertainment/csi-the-experience.aspx
This latest blockbuster show to hit the Strip opened in September 2009 and is based on the hit US show. Participants join forces with the team of investigators to crack crime cases in this interactive exhibit using forensic evidence.
Open: Daily 9am–10pm. Last admission 8.30pm
Admission: Adults $30 (12 years and up), children 4–11 $23. Book tickets in advance

Ethel M Chocolate Factory and Cactus Gardens

2 Cactus Garden Drive, Henderson, 800 471 0352 or 702 435 2655, www.ethelm.com
This large American sweet-making factory, just 5mls/8km from the Strip, gives an insight into the entire process. The tour ends with a free sample, but as you'll also find yourself in the factory shop, you won't be alone in deciding to buy a box of chocolates. Afterwards, step outside to see the 2.5acres/1ha of cactus gardens with over 350 species of desert plants and the Living Machine, a revolutionary new waste water recycling plant – the first of its kind designed for treating industrial waste water.
Open: Daily 8.30am–6pm; Chocolate Factory Tours Mon–Thurs 8.30am–4.30pm.
Admission: Free

Imperial Palace Auto Collection

Fifth floor, Imperial Palace Hotel, 3535 Las Vegas Boulevard S, 702 794 3174, www.autocollections.com
More than 600 cars make up this collection but only 300 are ever on show at one time.

10

Las Vegas Mini Gran Prix

However, that still makes this the 'World's Largest Classic Car Showroom'. Some of the vintage, classic and special-interest cars include the Chaser, the world's fastest petrol-powered police car; a 1986 Ford Mustang, which was specially built for the Nevada Highway Patrol; President Woodrow Wilson's 1917 Pierce Arrow car and a 1961 Lincoln Continental that was once owned by Jacqueline Kennedy Onassis.

Open: Daily 10am–6pm
Admission: Adults $8.95, seniors and under-13s $5, children under-3s free

Las Vegas Mini Gran Prix

1401 North Rainbow Boulevard, 702 259 7000, www.lvmgp.com
In the unlikely event that you do turn up in Sin City with children in tow, then this is the place to come to stop them feeling they have to spend their entire sojourn being kept out of all the adult activities. There are a few fun coasters, including the Dive Bomber, Tornado Twister and Dragon Coaster, but the real draw here is the fun mini-car races, which take place in Grand Prix-style cars of various shapes and sizes. To ride a Kiddie car you must be 4 years old or at least 4'6"/1.37m tall. To ride a Gran Prix car you must be 16.

Open: Sun–Thurs 10am–10pm; Fri and Sat 10am–11pm
Admission: $7 per ticket or $6.50 each if buying 5; 1 hour Megaride wristbands $20

✛ **BRITTIP**
Another fun outing is a trip to Laser Quest (see page 210).

Madame Tussauds

Venetian Resort Hotel Casino, 3355 Las Vegas Boulevard S, 702 862 7800, www.madametussauds.com/lasvegas
This is the Las Vegas version of the popular wax museum franchise with over 100

Conservatory at the Bellagio

© MGM

Old Las Vegas Mormon Fort

10

celebrities. Five theme areas include the Big Night, a special VIP party with Whoopi Goldberg and Brad Pitt among others; the Sports Arena with Mohammed Ali, Babe Ruth and Evander Holyfield (who is missing part of his right ear!); Rock and Pop with Elton John and Tina Turner; Las Vegas Legends with Frank Sinatra and Marilyn Monroe; and the Finale, a state-of-the-art tribute to modern Las Vegas legends including Wayne Newton and Siegfried and Roy. The entrance is just off the Doge's Palace at the south end of the square.

Take the moving walkway until you see 2 wax figures standing guard at the entrance. These figures change regularly, rotating between basketball's Michael Jordan, Johnny Depp as *Pirates of the Caribbean's* Jack Sparrow, Muhammad Ali and Don King (the wild-haired boxing promoter). It is a great photo opportunity! Inside are loads of other photo opportunities from staging a wedding with George Clooney to auditioning in front of Simon Cowell.

Open: Times vary but generally Sun–Mon 10am–9.30pm, Fri–Sat 10am–10.30pm

Admission: Adults $25, seniors and students $18, children $15 (children 6 and under go free). Book online to get 10% discount

Marine Gallery at LVNHM

© LVNB

Old Las Vegas Mormon Fort

State Historic Park, 500 E Washington Ave, 702 486 3511, www.parks.nv.gov/olvmf.htm
This is the oldest surviving non-native-American structure in Las Vegas and dates back to 14 June 1855 when the Mormon missionaries arrived in New Mexico Territory. Their aim was to convert the indigenous inhabitants and provide a safe way-station between Mormon communities in Salt Lake City to the north and San Bernardino to the east. The 150ft^2/14m^2 adobe-walled fort was still being built when the fort was abandoned in 1858 and subsequently was used by lead miners before becoming a ranch. To think, Sin City could have been a conservative Mormon haunt like Salt Lake City!
Open: Tues–Sun 8am–4.30pm
Admission: $1 13 and up, under-13s free

Planetarium and Observatory

College of Southern Nevada, 3200 East Cheyenne Avenue, North Las Vegas, 702 651 4759/4SKY, www.csn.edu/planetarium
This is star-gazing with a difference. Escape from the glitz and glamour into Southern Nevada's only public planetarium and observatory which has multimedia shows on astronomy plus hemispheric motion pictures. Public observing sessions are held after the last showings.
Open: Shows are on Fri 6pm and 7.30pm, Sat 3.30pm and 7.30pm. Public observing sessions are held at about 8.30pm, weather permitting. The shop is open Fri 5–8pm and Sat 3–8pm
Admission: Adults $6, under-12s and over-55s $4. It fills up fast

Museums

Atomic Testing Museum

Desert Research Institute, 755 East Flamingo Road, 702 794 5161, www.atomictestingmuseum.org
Once classified as top secret, the most chilling episodes in Nevada's history have been re-created at this museum. Tracing the history of the Nevada test site, which from 1951 until 1992 saw more than 900 nuclear weapons being tested for the US government, you enter an interactive bunker to witness bomb blasts. As the seats vibrate and gusts of air blow through the theatre, it is easy to get a feel for the power of the bombs. Exhibits include replicas of bomb

shelters, offices and guards station from the Nevada test site and nearly 400,000 declassified documents. They include letters from Albert Einstein and the captain of a Japanese fishing boat caught in the fall-out tests carried out in the Pacific.
Open: Mon–Sat 10am–5pm; Sun noon–5pm
Admission: Adults $14, students, children (7–17) and seniors $11, children 6 and under free

Las Vegas Natural History Museum

900 North Las Vegas Boulevard, 702 384 3466, www.lvnhm.org
Wildlife existed in the Las Vegas valley long before humans arrived and created casinos! Here you can take a walk on the wild side and discover the scenic and wild natural beauty of southern Nevada. It includes exhibits representing the many different habitats in the Las Vegas area with a diverse variety of plants and wildlife. The historical side is represented by animated dinosaurs, while there is an international wildlife room, small live sharks in the aquarium, and a hands-on exploration room for children. There is also an extensive wildlife art gallery with award-winning wood sculptures. There are travelling exhibits as well as changing exhibitions. The Egyptian Pavilion, its centrepiece a replica of King Tut's tomb, arrived in 2010.
Open: Daily 9am–4pm
Admission: Adults $10, seniors and students $8, 3–11s $5, children 2 and under free

Lied Discovery Children's Museum

833 North Las Vegas Boulevard, 702 382 5437, www.ldcm.org
Here children can touch, see, explore and experience more than 100 hands-on exhibits in one of America's largest – and most exciting – children's museums. Children crawl and slide through the Toddler Towers, become a star on the Performing Arts stage, pilot the Space Shuttle or Gyrochair, create colour computer prints and toe-tap a tune on the Musical Pathway. They can also stand in a giant bubble, play at being a disc jockey at the KKID radio station or use their bodies to generate electricity.
Open: Tues–Fri 9am–4pm; Sat 10am–5pm; Sun noon–5pm. Closed Mon. 1 Jun–5

Sept: Mon–Sat 10am–5pm; Sun noon–5pm
Admission: Adults $9.50, children 1–17 and seniors $8.50, under-1s free. Children under the age of 11 must be accompanied by an adult

Marjorie Barrick Museum of Natural History

4505 South Maryland Parkway, 702 895 3381, http://barrickmuseum.unlv.edu
Another genuinely fascinating offering at the University of Las Vegas campus, the real interest in this museum is its emphasis on the lives and traditions of the Paiute and Hopi Indians. A museum dedicated to the natural history of the region, one of the other main exhibits shows the reptiles that live in Nevada's deserts, including the venomous Gila Monster lizard, plus an open-air habitat for desert tortoises.
Open: Tues, Wed, Fri 10am–6pm; Thurs 10am–8pm, Sat–Sun 10am–2pm. Closed Mondays.
Admission: Free. Suggested donation: adults $5, seniors $2

The Mob Museum

300 Stewart Avenue, 702 229 2734, www.themobmuseum.org
The Las Vegas Museum of organised crime and law enforcement dedicated to the history of the mob who created and shaped Las Vegas opened its doors in downtown in February 2012 at a cost of $42 million. Constructed inside a federal court house which in 1950 tried notorious gangsters of the past, like Al Capone and Bugsy Siegel, history is explored its collection of over 1,000 artefacts from famous gangsters, film and interactive. Immersive exhibits include first person accounts by apparitions of famous gangsters where visitors hear about everything from human trafficking to money laundering activities. Call for opening and admission times.

Neon Museum

East end of the Fremont Street Experience, 702 387 6366/NEON, www.neonmuseum.org
Once the City of Neon, now all that remains of many of Vegas's most famous older hotels are their neon signs. Here you'll find the Hacienda Hotel sign before the building was imploded to make way for the Mandalay Bay, plus the original Aladdin's genie lamp and many other historical neon signs with their spectacular colours, intricate animation and sheer size.

Shoot 'em up at The Gun Store

The Gun Store (2900 East Tropicana Ave, 702 454 1110, www.thegunstorelasvegas.com) Just off the Strip is a chance to star in your very own shoot 'em up, calm and cool as James Bond, crazy as *The A Team* or intense as John Wayne in *The Good, the Bad and the Ugly*. Choose from 50 varieties of gun, with classes in how to use them, from authentic fully automatic machine guns, handguns, rifles and shotguns, fired at an indoor shooting range. Try your hand at famous guns seen in the movies like the Glock, Smith & Wesson, Dirty Harry.44, AR-15, Springfield M1A, Beretta Cx4 Storm, Colt M16 or Uzi or Shoot in the Dark – the latest idea.
Open: Daily 9.30am–6.30pm.
Admission: Handguns $25 for 20 rounds; 25–50 rounds with a machine gun start at $50; M249 Saw is $60 for 40 rounds. Under 18s need to be accompanied.

A small museum with big appeal!
While there are lots of exhibits inside, the best part is out the back at 'The Boneyard' where the massive signs are kept. This area is constantly being used by movies and TV shows for location shoots. Many of the best signs have been refurbished and mounted in the areas of the Fremont Street Experience and the East Fremont Street Entertainment District. You can download a free walking tour from the website.
Open: By appointment. Tours Tues–Sat 10am, 12pm and 2pm, advanced booking necessary
Admission: Free. Guided tour $15 per person

Nevada State Museum

Springs Preserve, 309 South Valley View Boulevard, 702 486 5205, www.museums.nevadaculture.org
The history of southern Nevada from mammoths to gambling is presented in 3 galleries – Biology, Earth Science and History/Anthropology. There is also a display explaining how neon has been used in the city. A new 2-storey, 70,000ft^2/6503m^2 building at The Springs Preserve is the new home for Nevada State Museum as of October 2011 (see below),

10

with new exhibits showing how dinosaurs lived in Southern Nevada millions of years ago. Call for opening hours and admission prices.

BRITTIP
Don't forget to get your picture taken below the 'Welcome to Fabulous Las Vegas' sign at 5200 Las Vegas Boulevard South – a must!

Springs Preserve

333 South Valley View Boulevard, 702 822 7700, www.springspreserve.org
A recently opened 180acre/73ha cultural and historical attraction situated on the site of the natural springs which encouraged the early settlers. Over 300 interactive exhibits include activities for kids – such as digging for fossils in the Mojave Desert Gallery, video games to learn about Las Vegas in the New Frontier Gallery and a playground resembling a desert canyon with wildlife replicas and a 'nature exchange' popular with little ones. There are Native American dwellings and a myriad of live animals here as well as trails through desert vegetation. Four hiking trails lead off through the picturesque Springs Preserve with interesting interpretative displays. The Springs Preserve has hosted the Nevada

State Museum from October 2011 (see above).
   Open: Daily 10am–6pm
   Admission: Adults $18.95, seniors $17.05, children (5–17 years) $10.95. Children 4 and under go free

BRITTIP
If you've a couple of thousand dollars to burn, opt for one of 2 new private sunset helicopter tours at sunset with Papillon Airways (www. papillon.com) which, with limousine pick up from most Strip hotels, takes in the Grand Canyon and the Strip.

Coming soon

The World's First Indoor Ballooning Attraction is coming to a Strip-side location. **Parabounce® Vegas**, due to open at the end of 2011, will be an air-inflated, 100,000ft²/930 m² bubble-style dome where up to 20 flyers can simultaneously float, soar and bounce in individual, 22ft/6.7m, Parabounce helium balloons. Anyone from children to seniors, can safely soar up to 100ft/30.4m in the air and bounce up to 600ft/183m in one jump. The attraction will also have aerial bumper cars and a flying bicycle – the Parabike.

Springs Preserve

OUTDOOR ADVENTURE

Every kind of fun from cowboy cook-outs to horseback riding

Las Vegas is a wonderful city, and practically everything you'd like to do in the great outdoors in America can be found in the stunning desertscape that surrounds it. Nearby are Red Rock Canyon, where ponderosa pines and Joshua trees grow out of towering cliffs of Aztec sandstone; the Valley of Fire, a Martian landscape of vivid red, pastel and white sandstone, and Mount Charleston, which looms 12,000ft/3,658m above sea level.

BRITTIP

If you want to time your visit to tour Hoover Dam at the least crowded times, go between 9am and 10.30am and 3pm and 4.45pm.

The biggest jewel in Las Vegas's crown of outdoor splendours, though, is the Grand Canyon. A whole raft of companies organise plane and helicopter flights to – and even down to the bottom of – the 10ml/16km wide and 1ml/1.6km deep natural wonder. Many of those companies also offer trips a little further north to the

In this chapter

stunning Bryce Canyon and Zion National Park, famous for cascading waterfalls.

On top of that, there are a whole host of brilliant ways to experience this great region, from white-water rafting and rock climbing, to horse riding and quad biking and following the cowboy trail. At certain times of the year, it is possible to go skiing in the morning at Lee Canyon on Mount Charleston, then head off to Lake Mead for a spot of water-skiing in the afternoon. Where else could you find such a dramatic mix of marvels? In Las Vegas you are just moments away from a world of beauty and adventure.

Hoover Dam

© LVNB

Places to see

Hoover Dam

South on Highway 93 just past Boulder City, 30mls/50km south-east of Las Vegas at the Nevada-Arizona border. 702 494 2517, www.hooverdam.com and www.usbr.gov/lc/hooverdam/service
Visitor Center: Open daily, except Thanksgiving and Christmas Day, 9am–5pm. Tickets sold until 4.15pm
Admission: Visitor Center: adults, seniors, juniors $8, under-3s free; Powerplant Tour: adults $11, 4–16s $9, under-3s free; Hoover Dam Tour $30, not accessible to those on wheelchairs/crutches.

This amazing construction – it's 726ft/221m high and 1,244ft/379m long – is filled with enough concrete to build a 2-lane highway from San Francisco to New York, and it literally changed the face of America's West. Blocking the Colorado River at the Black Canyon, which spans Nevada and Arizona, the dam put an end to centuries of droughts and floods caused by the mighty Colorado. Work began on the dam in 1931 and the $165m project was completed by 1935. Its offspring, Lake Mead, now produces drinking and irrigation water for the entire Las Vegas Valley, while the electric power plant creates enough energy to sell to Nevada, Arizona and California.

BRITTIP

If you're touring in an RV (recreational vehicle, or camper van) you will have to park on the Arizona side of the dam as they have been banned from the parking garage at Hoover Dam for security reasons.

Discovery Tour: This gives you access to the 165m Visitor Center, a 3-level, 110ft/34m diameter circular building, which stands 700ft/213m above the base of the dam. From the indoor and outdoor observation decks are stunning views of the dam, Lake Mead and the waters of the Colorado River re-entering the Black Canyon after passing through the dam's giant turbines.

A gallery houses an environmental exhibit, technology exhibit and the story of the settlement of the lower Colorado River area. The rotating theatre is divided into 3 segments and you move between the 3 areas to see different films about the making and history of the dam.

Powerplant Tour: This tour includes presentations by reclamation guides, audio and film presentations, exhibits and other media to give a comprehensive view of the massive dam and its operations. Tours last around 2 hours and tickets can be bought 9am–5.15pm.

Hoover Dam Tour: The longest tour, this is a guided exploration of lesser known parts of the dam. It is offered from 9.30am every half an hour until 4pm, on a first come first served basis.

Boulder City/Hoover Dam Museum: At Boulder Dam Hotel, Boulder City, museum 702 294 1988, bcmha.org, Mon–Sat 10am–5pm, Sun closed, admission adults $2, seniors/children $1. Here you'll see a free movie about the building of the dam plus historical memorabilia from the workers. While you're there, take a peek at the renovated home in the museum, which in its time has accommodated movie star James Cagney and reclusive billionaire Howard Hughes.

BRITTIP

As you leave Boulder City and head for Hoover Dam, watch out for stupendous views of Lake Mead at the junction with Highway 93.

Other activities: While you're in the area you can also take a river raft trip (see page 199) or try a tandem jump (see page 212). An excellent stop-off point during your day trip is Harry's Café (512 Nevada Hwy, 702 293 1950, open 7am–8pm). Boulder's oldest diner, its 1950s-style environment makes for a fun pit stop.

Lake Mead

Visitor Center is 4mls/6km north-east of Boulder City, 702 293 8990, www.nps.gov/lake or www.lakemead.areaparks.com
Open: Year round, 24 hours a day. Visitor Center open daily 8.30am–4.30pm
Admission: $5 per vehicle; $3 others
Other useful numbers: Lake Mead Marina 702 293 3484; Park Information Desk 702 293 8906 (Mon–Fri)

The dazzling-blue Lake Mead, created by the construction of the Hoover Dam, is about 25mls/40km south of Las Vegas. It is 110mls/177km long and has 550mls/885km of freshwater shoreline. It is the Las Vegas outdoor retreat of choice and many permanent residents have boats here. Here you can try out anything from boating to swimming, scuba-diving, kayaking, water-skiing, camping, biking and fishing, while 6 marinas provide docking space for boats, plus restaurants and other services. Every December, a Parade of Lights is held at Lake Mead marina, with a flotilla of powerboats, houseboats and sailing boats covered in lights. A newer, annual event is the hydroplane race held in September.

The Visitors Center contains a botanical garden and exhibits on natural history. Here you will find details of a self-guided tour, with tape recording, of the lake's Northshore and Lakeshore roads, plus information about facilities and services. It was closed for year-long renovations at the time of writing, and a temporary one in its place. It will have a new park film to show when it opens.

Marinas: Two not-so-scenic roads – Lakeside Scenic Drive (Highway 146) and Northshore Scenic Drive (Highway 167) provide access to the marinas around the Nevada shoreline of Lake Mead, which include **Las Vegas Boat Harbor** (702 293 1191), **Calville Bay Resort** (702 565 8958) and **Echo Bay Resort** (702 394 4000). These are all full-service marinas offering houseboat and daily deck cruiser rentals, restaurants and gift shops. At night, Callville Bay provides a barbecue on the patio overlooking the lake. Lake Mead Cruises (702 293 6180, www. LakeMeadCruises.com) has sunset, dinner dance and breakfast cruises.

If you'd like to explore a little further afield, head off south to Lake Mohave and Cottonwood Cove Resort and Marina (1000 Cottonwood Cove Road, Cottonwood, 702 297 1464). It's a full-service marina offering luxury houseboats, small boats and personal watercraft rentals about one and a half hours south of Las Vegas. For a thrill, Forever Resorts (702 294 1414) offer The Black Canyon River Adventure – a smooth water-rafting trip in the Black Canyon.

Hiking: During the cooler months, from November to March, you can take a hike in the Lake Mead National Recreation Area on Saturday mornings to learn about the history of the people of the area, from the mining era onwards. Each hike is limited to 25 people and you can make reservations by phoning 702 293 8990.

Valley of Fire State Park

6mls/10km from Lake Mead and 55mls/88km north-east of Las Vegas using Interstate 15 and Highway 169, 702 397 2088, www.desertusa.com/nvval/index.html
Open: Year round, dawn to dusk; Visitor Center: Open daily 8.30am–4.30pm
Admission: $10 per vehicle

The park – the oldest in Nevada – gets its name from the red sandstone formations that were formed from great, shifting desert sand dunes during the age of the dinosaurs 150 million years ago. Complex geological movements and extensive erosion have created the spectacular wind carvings in the colourful rock formations. There are shaded areas with restrooms at Atlatl Rock, Seven Sisters, the Cabins, near Mouse's Tank trail head and White Domes. At the Visitor Center, there are exhibits on the geology, ecology and history of the park, plus the nearby region.

This whole area was extensively used by basket-making peoples and later by the Anasazi Pueblo farmers from the nearby Moapa Valley from 300bce to 1150ce. It was probably visited for hunting, food gathering and religious ceremonies, though the lack of water limited their stays. Wonderful reminders of the time these ancient tribes spent here can be seen in the extraordinarily detailed Indian petroglyphs that tell the stories of their lives. The fantastic scenery and fascinating history make it well worth a day's visit.

Nature's way: The whole area is dominated by creosote, burro and brittle bushes, plus several different types of cactus. Spring is a wonderful time to visit as this is the time to see desert marigold, indigo bushes and desert mallow in bloom. The park is visited by many species of bird, but those in residence include raven, house finch, sage sparrow and, of course, the famous road runner – beep beep!

The animals tend to be nocturnal, coming out to forage for food when the desert heat has begun to fade, and include many different types of lizard, as well as snakes, coyote, kit fox, spotted skunk, black-tailed jack rabbit and ground squirrel. The desert tortoise is now so rare it is protected by Nevada State law. Early mornings or late afternoons are the best time to see the wildlife, but keep your distance.

One of the best ways to explore the park is by hiking through it and maps of trails are provided at the Visitor Center.

Arch Rock: A 2ml/3km scenic loop road provides views of some of the valley's most interesting rock formations, for example Arch Rock and Piano Rock. You'll get a true wilderness experience at the secluded Arch Rock Campground with its primitive facilities!

Atlatl Rock: Here you will find outstanding examples of ancient Indian

11

rock art or petroglyphs, including a depiction of the atlatl (at'-lat-l), a notched stick used to throw primitive spears and the forerunner of the bow and arrow.

◢◣✠ BRITTIP

Atlatl Rock is a great location for campers and the campsite is well-equipped with modern WC and shower facilities.

Beehives: Unusual sandstone formations weathered by the eroding forces of wind and water, there are 3 group camping areas nearby, available by reservation only.

Cabins: Now a picnic area, these historic stone cabins were built with native sandstone by the Civilian Conservation Corps in the 1930s as a shelter for passing travellers.

Mouse's Tank: Named after a renegade Indian who used the area as a hideout in the 1890s, this is a natural basin in the rock where water collects after rainfall, sometimes remaining for months. A half-mile/800m round trip trail leads to Mouse's Tank from the trail head parking area, passing numerous examples of prehistoric Indian petroglyphs.

Petrified logs: Logs and stumps washed into the area from an ancient forest about 225 million years ago are exposed in 2 locations.

Rainbow vista: A favourite photo point with a panoramic view of multicoloured sandstone.

Seven Sisters: Fascinating red rock formations, which are easily accessible from the road. Picnic areas provide a relaxing stop.

White Domes: Sandstone formations with brilliant contrasting colours, picnic area and trail head. White Domes is an 11ml/17.7km round trip drive from the Visitor Center. Duck Rock is a short hike.

Other sights: Clark Memorial, Elephant Rock, the deep red sandstone of Fire Canyon and the amazing Silica Dome.

Red Rock Canyon

17mls/27km west of the Las Vegas Strip on Charleston Boulevard (Highway 159), 702 515 5350 or 702 363 1921 (Visitor Center), www.redrockcanyonlv.org or www.sunsetcities.com/redrock.html

Red Rock Canyon is part of the Red Rock Canyon Conservancy Area and encompasses a large part of the Mojave Desert, the unearthly landscape where Steven Spielberg's sci-fi classic was filmed. Red Rock Canyon also includes the Spring Mountain Range, home of the Spring Mountain Ranch, Mount Charleston and Bonnie Springs Old Nevada.

Once the home of ancient Native American tribes, this magnificent canyon was formed by a thrust fault – a fracture in the earth's crust where one plate is pushed horizontally over another – 65 million years ago. It is home to feral horses and burros (donkeys), as well as native wildlife such as desert bighorn sheep and coyotes, which you can see on the 13ml/21km Scenic Loop Drive (see opposite).

The Calico Vista points are good stopping points, offering great views of the crossed-bedded Aztec sandstone. For easy access to the sandstone, stop at the Sandstone Quarry car park where you can see large blocks of stone and other historic

Watersports on Lake Mead

© IVNB

Red Rock Canyon

evidence of quarry activity that took place during the turn of the last century. You can have a picnic at Red Spring and Willow Spring, where there's also a Petroglyph Wall Trail, while there are also great views of wooded canyons and desert washes at Icebox Canyon, Pine Creek Canyon and Red Rock Wash.

With 30mls/48km of trails, hiking, mountain-biking, horse-riding and rock-climbing tours are all available at Red Rock Canyon and cost from $69 per person.

Stop at the Visitor Center at the entrance to the Scenic Loop Drive for touring and adventure activities information, trail maps and tours. Open 6am–5pm November to February, 6am–7pm March and October and 6am–8pm April to September. Costs $7 which includes scenic drive.

◀🇬🇧▶ BRITTIP
You need to stop at the Visitor Center before going into the park's Scenic Drive Loop to acquaint yourself with the park regulations, including where you can drive and park.

Scenic Loop Drive: Open daily, changing by season, but generally from sunrise to sunset; Nov–Feb 6am–5pm, Apr–Sep 6am–8pm and Mar–Oct 6am–7pm. Entrance to the loop costs $5 for motorists and $2 for motorcyclists; free for hikers and cyclists.

The 13ml/21km scenic drive is a one-way road. Cyclists are permitted to ride on the scenic drive, but must obey traffic laws. Sightseeing, photography and hiking trails are accessible from the designated pullouts and parking areas. If you would like to go hiking or rock climbing in Red Rock or Mount Charleston, see page 000.

Pahrump Valley Winery: 3810 Winery Road, Pahrump, 775 751 7800, www.pahrumpwinery.com. Just north of Red Rock is Nevada's only vineyard and it regularly produces award-winning Chardonnay, Cabernet and Burgundy. In 2009, it released Nevada's first ever commercial red – a 2005 Zinfandel called Nevada Ridge. Free tours offered most days at 11.30am, 1.30pm, and 3.30pm; call to check schedule.

Death Valley

11

Bonnie Springs Old Nevada

16mls/26km west of Las Vegas, 702 875 4191, www.bonniesprings.com
Open: Wed–Sun 10.30am–6pm (summer), Weds–Fri 11am–5pm, Sat–Sun 10.30am–5pm (winter)
Admission: $20 per car (up to 6 people and includes a $10 restaurant coupon); petting zoo $5 per person Mon–Fri; $7 per person Sat–Sun.

Originally built in 1843 as a stopover for the wagon trains going to California down the Old Spanish Trail, Bonnie Springs has been used as a tourist attraction since 1952. Now this replicated old American West mining town includes gunfights in the street, hangings, an 1880 melodrama, miniature train, US Post Office, blacksmith display, wax museum and Boot Hill Cemetery.

A 1-hour guided horseback ride through Red Rock Canyon costs $55 (no children under 6) is offered 9am–4.45pm in summer and 9am–3.15pm in winter– and there is a petting zoo, duck pond and aviary for families as well as daily shows such as gun fighting in the street and even a hanging. Breakfast, lunch, dinner – ranch food including Cowboy Toast and Bronco Burgers – and cocktails are also available. A shuttle service from Las Vegas gets you here in half an hour and is provided through Star Land Tours (702 296 4381) or for $90 by Bonnie Springs for groups of 6 or more.

Spring Mountain Ranch State Park

15mls/24km west of Las Vegas, via Charleston Boulevard (Highway 159), in the Red Rock Canyon National Conservation Area, 702 875 4141, http://parks.nv.gov/smr.htm
Open: Daily 8am–6pm. The main ranch house is open daily 10am–4pm
Admission: $9 per vehicle; walk-ins, bicycles and bus $1

The many springs in these mountains once provided water for Paiute Indians and later brought mountain men and early settlers to the area. This 520acre/210ha oasis was developed into a combination working ranch and luxurious retreat by a string of owners who have given the area a long and colourful history. Chester Lauck of the comedy team Lum & Abner, and millionaire Howard Hughes are past owners of the ranch.

In the mid-1830s a campsite was established along the wash that runs through the ranch. The spring-fed creek and grassy meadows formed a welcome oasis for travellers using this as an alternative route to the Spanish Trail through Cottonwood Valley. The use of the site by pack and wagon trains continued until their replacement by the railroad in 1905.

At the ranch house, you can find information about the ranch and surrounding areas and take a self-guided tour. Guided tours throughout the historic area are available weekdays at noon, 1 and 2pm; weekends at noon, 1, 2 and 3pm.

◄█► BRITTIP ————
There are often fire restrictions in this area, so check the website for the latest information.

The remote trail was also perfect for outlaws and was used extensively by those involved in slave trading, horse stealing and raids on passing caravans. One of the most famous was mountain man Bill Williams, after whom the ranch was first named.

In 1876 it was taken over by 2 men and named Sand Stone Ranch. The name stuck until it was leased in 1944 to Chet Lauck, the Lum part of comedy duo Lum & Abner, and renamed Bar Nothing Ranch. A ranch house was built as a family retreat and Lum created a boys' camp. In 1955, German actress Vera Krupp bought the property, expanded the ranching business side and renamed it Spring Mountain Ranch.

At 3,800ft/1,158m, it is usually up to 10ºC/15ºF cooler than Las Vegas with cold winters and thunderstorms and flash floods in summer. Visitors can see wonderful plants including the Joshua tree, Mohave yucca, indigo bush, desert marigold and globe mallow. Animals are harder to spot as many are nocturnal, but include lizards, snakes, antelope ground squirrels, kit fox, jackrabbits, coyote, rock squirrel, badger, mule deer and bighorn sheep.

What's on: The programme includes hikes by moonlight into Sandstone Canyon. A Living History programme re-creates the ranch's past in the spring and autumn, including demonstrations of pioneer skills. The Super Summer Theater puts on outdoor performances every June, July, August and September while the Theatre under the Stars features musicals and plays for the whole family. Gates open at 6pm, shows start at 8pm (7pm in September). Tickets cost $12 in advance (children 5 and under go free). There is also a picnic area as well

Further afield

Full details of the Grand Canyon, Zion, Bryce and Death Valley are given in Chapter 15 on pages 233–48 and details of air and bus tours are in this chapter on page 197.

Grand Canyon: www.nps.gov/grca. If you're planning to go on a bit of a tour, then you're bound to want to see the Grand Canyon close up and for real. But it is also possible to take plane and helicopter rides to this, the most spectacular canyon on earth – even landing on the canyon floor and having a spot of lunch on the banks of the Colorado. With Papillon Grand Canyon Helicopters you can land and have lunch inside the canyon and with Heli USA combine a flight to the Grand Canyon with a river rafting trip.

Zion National Park: 435 772 3256, www.zion.national-park.com. North of Las Vegas and the Grand Canyon in southern Utah is the majestic Zion National Park with its beautiful waterfalls cascading down red rocks, and its hanging gardens. Once a home to the ancient Anasazi, its history and majesty are presented in an adventure film at the Zion Canyon Giant Screen Theatre (435 772 2400, www.zioncanyontheatre.com) along with Hollywood movies, some in 3D.

Bryce Canyon: 435 834 5322, www.nps.gov/brca. Nearby in Utah is the equally beautiful Bryce Canyon, once home to both Native Americans and cowboys of the Old West. Both Zion and Bryce offer hiking, biking, horse riding, rock climbing and bird watching and in winter, snow shoeing.

Death Valley: 760 786 3200, www.nps.gov.deva. West of Las Vegas in eastern California, this is the hottest place on earth, with average summer temperatures of 45°C/113°F. Here you will see miles of sand that has been hardened into a sea-like landscape by the heat of the sun, extinct volcanoes and wind-carved rock formations.

Many companies offer day trips to Death Valley and to break up the monotonous terrain on the way, you'll be taken through the beautiful Titus Canyon and some ghost towns and be shown Native American Indian petroglyphs. Once there, you'll be shown all the Death Valley highlights including Furnace Creek, Zabriskie Point, Bad Water and Scotty's Castle.

---

as summer activities with crafts rangers for children.

Mount Charleston

35mls/56km north-west of Las Vegas on Highways 95 and 157, 702 515 5400, www.sunsetcities.com/mt-charleston.html or www.fs.usda.gov
Camping: 1-877 444 6777. Seven campgrounds are open from May to September. Cost is from $10 per night depending on campsite, picnic area and trail, for a maximum 5 days

Set in the lush Humboldt-Toiyabe National Forest, The Spring Mountains National Recreation Area known as Mount Charleston to locals looms nearly 12,000ft/3,658m above sea level. One of the most beautiful areas in the Las Vegas Valley, Lee Canyon Road, the Kyle Canyon section of Charleston Park Road and Deer Creek Road have all been designated Scenic Byways because of their extraordinary scenery and panoramic views. The area is about 17°C/30°F cooler than Las Vegas, making it a perfect escape from the city heat for a day.

Charleston Peak was the birthplace of the Paiute people, so for the Native

Americans it is sacred land. To respect this, the scale and extent of the road system remains fairly limited.

Camping is popular here, along with horse riding, mountain biking, hiking and rock climbing and in the winter you can ski at Lee Canyon (see Activities, page 000).

◀▓▶ BRITTIP

Day trips to the Grand Canyon, Bryce Canyon and Zion Canyon from Las Vegas are available via helicopter, small plane or coach (see page 197).

Spooky sights

ET Highway

About 140mls/225km north of Las Vegas, 1 800 NEVADA 8, www.byways.org/explore/byways/2029

A 98ml/158km stretch of road on Route 375, a few miles north of the notorious Area 51 and the super-secret Groom Lake Air Force Base, this is where the American Air Force is believed to have tested the Stealth and U-2 aircraft and

11

where numerous American TV shows have claimed aliens from outer space have undergone examinations at the top-secret Department of Defense site. UFO buffs often gather on ridges above Area 51 and use high-powered telescopes and binoculars to spy on the secret location. Their favourite meeting points are at the bars in nearby Rachel (www.rachel-nevada.com/ethighway.html), where they exchange tales about extra-terrestrials.

Now the road has been officially dubbed the ET Highway by the Nevada Commission on Tourism, which has even created a new programme called the ET Experience.

Pioneer Saloon

Goodsprings, south of Las Vegas, 702 874 9362, www.pioneersaloon.info

Founded in the old mining town, this has much historical memorabilia and is worth dropping into to soak up some old-Americana atmosphere. Sitting on top of the US Army Cannon Stove, once used to warm people up on cold winter nights, is a piece of melted aluminium from the aeroplane in which film star Carole Lombard died. The plane crashed into Double Deal Mountain in January 1942 and her husband Clark Gable sat in the bar for days after, hoping for a miracle. Open daily from 10am.

Bonnie and Clyde's 'Death Car'

Primm Valley Hotel, 702 386 7867, www.primmvalleyresorts.com

The original car driven by Bonnie Parker and Clyde Barrow in their final shoot-out with the FBI on 23 May 1934 is on display at Whiskey Pete's Hotel. The infamous duo who held up gas stations, restaurants and small banks in Texas, New Mexico, Oklahoma and Missouri were shopped by a friend. At a cost of $75,000, Clyde's bullet-ridden and bloodstained shirt is now on display too! Worth visiting if you're going to Buffalo Bill's Turbo Drop and Desperado (see page 175).

Ghost towns

The old gold and silver mining towns are the stuff of many a Western movie and it is possible to visit some of these abandoned sites.

Goldfield Ghost Town (4650 N Mammoth Mine Road, Arizona – on Interstate 95 north of Scotty's Castle, 480 983 0333, www.goldfieldghosttown. com) was once Nevada's largest city after gold was discovered in 1902. Known for its opulence, it was called the Queen of Camps and had 20,000 residents at its peak, with mines producing $10,000 a day in 1907. A flood in 1913 and a fire in 1923 destroyed much of the town, but still standing are the Courthouse and Santa Fe Saloon among others. Open 10am–5pm daily.

In 1904 gold was discovered in the Amargosa Valley and the town of Rhyolite (just outside Beatty on Interstate 95, then 374) was born. At its peak, it housed 10,000 people and had more than 50 saloons, 18 grocery stores and half a dozen barbers. But it became a ghost town in 1911 after losing its financial backing. You can still see the Cook Bank Building,

Pioneer Saloon

Helicopter over the Grand Canyon

school and jail, plus a house built in 1905 entirely of bottles. Visit www.ghosttowns. com to find other ghost towns in the area or see Creative Adventures in the A–Z of tour operators on page 201.

BRITTIP

Take the 3-hour Haunted Vegas Tour in town, leaving at 9.30pm and costing $66.25 (www. hauntedvegastours.com; tickets at www.vegasexplorers.com or by calling toll free 866 218 4935).

Tours

Air tours

You can fly to all the major sights mentioned in this chapter either in a small plane or by helicopter. Flight packages or helicopter flights are offered by many of the tour companies listed. Scenic Airlines is the largest. These tours may be pricey – anything up to $650 – but they offer a marvellous opportunity to see amazing scenery in a very short space of time.

Generally, a short flight will include the Las Vegas Strip, Western Grand Canyon, Hoover Dam and Lake Mead and will cost around $60. The next step up will be the above plus a complete aerial tour of the Grand Canyon for around $200. The more expensive prices will include extras such as a Champagne lunch on the Grand Canyon

rim or, in the case of a helicopter flight, on the Canyon floor next to the Colorado. Combination tours may include lunch with Native Americans, river rafting, hiking and canyon sunset/sunrise. Some companies offer an overnight stay at the Grand Canyon, Bryce Canyon or Monument Valley. Tour companies are listed on pages 200–04.

Bus tours

The prices are cheaper, but the days are longer as you get to see all the sights covered by the air tours – only on the ground, of course! Tour companies are listed on pages 200–04.

Activities

All the contact details for the various companies are in the A–Z on pages 200–04.

Bike tours

Bootleg Canyon Trails: With names like The Reaper, Dominatrix and Armageddon, the world-class downhill and cross country trails at Bootleg Canyon Mountain Bike Park near Boulder City are for real mountain bikers. The most extreme is Elavator Shaft – flying down a 22% degree hillside.

Escape Adventures: Runs mountain bike trips in Red Rock Canyon from a half day to a weekend for $525.

Las Vegas Cyclery: This professional outfit offers half, full and multi-day mountain,

Flying to the Grand Canyon

The Maverick Helicopters' pilot looked the spitting image of Tom Cruise and the theme from *Mission: Impossible* was blasting down our earphones as we took off from McCarran Airport. Suddenly the helicopter banked steeply and we 5 passengers had an altogether too-close-for-comfort view of the ground. Then, just as suddenly as we'd banked to the right, the helicopter straightened up and we found ourselves inching over the 'matchbox' houses at what seemed to be a snail's pace. In reality, we were speeding out of the Las Vegas Valley at 130mph/210kph, heading east to the West Rim of the Grand Canyon.

Within minutes, we were flying over the $1m homes in the exclusive community of Lake Las Vegas and its 2 golf courses. Next came the 110ml/177km long Lake Mead, the largest man-made lake in America providing a beautiful blue contrast to the pale brown rocks, and then the Hoover Dam. My thoughts that the scenery had a volcanic look to it were confirmed when our pilot pointed out an extinct volcano.

It took half an hour to reach the Grand Canyon and after a brief flyover, we landed on its rocky floor. Our pilot immediately jumped out and started preparing our Champagne drinks with light snacks. It seemed a perfect way to spend 40 minutes – quaffing Champagne and looking around at this millions-of-years-old natural wonder.

All too soon, it seemed, we were taking off again, but before we started our return journey we were flown through the canyon. The half-hour ride back to Las Vegas sped by and we headed for our final treat – a flight down the entire length of the famous Strip for a bird's-eye view of all those amazing buildings. (For information on helicopter flights to the Grand Canyon see page 238.)

road and multi-sport cycling adventures for casual to experienced cyclists. The Red Rock Scenic Loop costs from $99 self-guided and $109.99 guided.
Single Track Tours Las Vegas: Professionally guided mountain bike tours and road trips in Las Vegas, Red Rock and Lake Mead for both the beginner and professional at $115 per person.

Hiking

Escape Adventures: 6-day hiking adventures include Color Country Hiker – a moderate hike through Bryce, Zion and Grand Canyon National Parks ($1390 camping) and Death Valley to Red Rock Canyon ($1,290 camping and Inns).

Grand Canyon Tour Company: They do half-day trips to Red Rock Canyon ($119.99), a hike to the Hot Springs ($139) and full-day hikes of the Grand Canyon with guides who tell you all about the geology and human and natural history. You will be given drinking water, high-energy drink mixers and snacks.

HikeThis!: Moderate or moderately strenuous guided hikes start at $119 per person for 2–5 people and cover 4–6mls/6.5–9.5km (4 hours' round trip). The more popular, moderately strenuous to strenuous rock scrambling adventure deep in the canyons, over creek bed stones and massive sandstone boulders is 3–4mls/5–6.5km and takes up to 5 hours. Free pick-up and drop-off and lunch included.

Horse riding

Available at Red Rock Canyon, Bonnie Springs Old Nevada, Mount Charleston and Valley of Fire.

Cowboy Trail Rides Inc: You can go on horseback rides, custom and group trail rides and pack trips in southern Nevada, Utah and Northern Arizona. Trips are tailor-made and can last an hour or 7 days. They offer day rides for kids through to a sunset ride with a Western-style barbecue under the stars through Red Rock Canyon and a 5-hour Wow Ride through untouched Wild West wilderness. Rides cost $69–329 per person.

Wild Wild West Horseback Trail Rides: Both novice and experienced riders can choose from a Red Rock Canyon Breakfast Ride or an Old Spanish Trail Ride with lunch ($119 and 6 hours each) or the Wild West Sunset Dinner Ride ($149), bookable through LookTours (see A–Z below).

Off-road adventures

ATV Action Tours: ATV has the sole licensing permits for many desert regions, mountains and other points of interest in south-west Nevada. They combine the off-road experience in Land Rovers, Jeep Cherokees, Wranglers and ATVs with short hiking excursions, climbing large rock formations and searching for petroglyphs. Definitely the most fun way to get back to nature without breaking into a sweat! Tours cost from $89, with free hotel pick-up and daily departures. Book online for the cheapest prices.

Awesome Adventures: has off-road ATV tours that explore the lives and trails travelled by pioneers and explorers of the past such as The Anasazi, a lost civilisation; Outlaws and Gunfighters of the Wild West and Gold Chasing Miners. The Eldorado Canyon tour takes around 5 hours (lunch included) and costs $169.

LookTours: This company offers ATV tours alongside the 6-hour Hoover Dam and Lake Mead, 4x4 Off-road Hummer Adventure. This includes around 2.5 hours of 4-wheel, off-road adventure through the Mojave Desert, including Lava Butte, Rainbow Gardens and Lizard Eye Ridge, plus Hoover Dam and Lake Mead and costs $188.99 including lunch. It's $148.99 for a 6-hour Desert ATV Adventure, which includes 2.5 hours on an ATV through the Valley of Fire. Other off-roading experiences on offer include a Hidden Valley Primm Extreme Dirt Bike Adventure through the Mojave Desert ($278.99).

Pink Jeep Tours: The first independent company to set up in Death Valley, Pink Jeep's off-road adventures are in custom-designed Tour Trekkers that seat 10 people or 6-passenger SUVs, with 12 nature-based guided tours to choose from including a 6-hour Valley of Fire tour for $135 and a 4-hour Red Rock Canyon tour, for $94.

Other companies: Since ATV set the ball rolling, many other tour companies are now offering Hummer Tours – the term used to describe off-road adventures in 4x4 Hummers. Those companies include Grand Canyon Tour Company and Rebel Adventure Tours. The Hummer tours can be combined with other activities such as jet-skiing and rafting.

◀✚▶ **BRITTIP**

For excitement seekers the Bootleg Canyon Zipline Tour from LookTours ($148.99 online) may be just the ticket.

Rafting

Rafting the Grand Canyon's Colorado River is rated as America's top adventure. Two basic types of rafting are easily available from Las Vegas.

Black Canyon River Raft Tours: You can take a gentle ride in a motorised raft down an 11ml/18km stretch of the Colorado, starting at the base of the mighty Hoover Dam and stopping for lunch (and a cooling swim). Along the way you will see hot water springs bubbling out of cliffs, flora and fauna and the amazing desert bighorn sheep, who think nothing of living on the perilous slopes of the Grand Canyon. These rides usually last around 7 hours and cost $87.95 (plus $44 round trip transport) from February to November. Plenty of other tour companies offer similar tours.

Grand Canyon Tour Company: The other kind of rafting is a lot more expensive, but more authentic and involves rapids. One- or 2-day trips on rapids with strengths of 4–7 (on a scale of 1–10) are available with Native Americans from the Grand Canyon area. The Grand Canyon Tour Company offers trips from Lees Ferry in Arizona (about 2.5 hours' drive from the South Rim of the Grand Canyon) that can also be combined with a hike down the Grand Canyon between April and October. A long day trip (children must be over 8) aboard a motorised raft with Hualapai Indian guide takes you across class 3–6 rapids with an optional hike before being lifted by helicopter to Grand Canyon West ($459 per person). Otherwise most of their trips start at 2 days and go up to 10, in an oar craft or motorised, on class 3–6 water, between April and September, costing $225 per day. If you're coming in the off-season, you can take a day trip on the Colorado River from Diamond Creek to Pierce Ferry (about 3 hours from Vegas). Trips need to be booked well in advance as permits need to be arranged.

Skiing and snowboarding

Just 35 minutes away from Las Vegas in Mount Charleston's Lee Canyon, you can ski or snowboard from Thanksgiving to Easter. Beginner packages for skiing or snowboarding cost $70 for ski rental equipment, lift ticket and a 2-hour group lesson or the whole morning for kids (age 6–12). Lift prices for those with experience are $50 a day for adults and $30 for under-12s. In summer (mid-June to October) ski-lift chair rides to the top of the ski runs are only $5 for adults and $3 for under-12s.

Water activities

Cruising, boating, fishing and jet-skiing are all available on Lake Mead.

Great Venture Tours: White-water rafting on the Colorado river. Prices and options vary.

Lake Mead Cruises: The largest provider of cruises and jet-skiing runs brunch, midday and dinner (Sun–Thurs) cruises

11

on the glassy waters of Lake Mead on board the Desert Princess, an authentic 300-passenger paddle-wheeler, which is climate-controlled inside. Sunday brunch cruises cost $39 (under-12s $18), April to October; midday sightseeing cruises $24 (under-12s $12) daily 12pm and 2pm; dinner cruises $49 (under-12s $25) April to October. Under-2s go free and all prices include tax. You can either board at Hoover Dam or at Lake Mead Marina.

Lake Mead Jetski Tours: Rents powercraft from $200 per day. Package (from $200) includes a 2-day orientation class and 90 minutes on the water. Each tour is accompanied by a guide who will narrate the trip via a hands-free, waterproof, 2-way radio on each jet-ski. Lunch is provided.

 **BRITTIP**

Tight on time? Discover the diversity of the desert in style on the Fantastic 4 Mojave Desert Tour which takes in Hoover Dam, Lake Mead, Red Rock Canyon, Mount Charleston and The Valley of Fire (costs $199 per person from www.anniebananie.com).

At Overton Beach Marina you can hire everything from personal watercraft to patio and fishing boats. Overnight packages are even available. Personal watercraft can seat 2–3 people and have storage compartments with a built-in cooler for your packed lunch. Patio boats for up to 10 people are perfect for fishing or cruising and come with a motor, radio/cassette, cooler, cushioned bench seating and an awning. Costs are $125 for 4 hours, $195 for 8 hours. Fishing boats hold 4 people and come with a Fish Finder and Pole Holder to increase your odds! Costs are $65 for 4 hours, $100 for 8.

A–Z of tour companies

As you can see, the outdoor options are numerous, so to make life a little simpler I have tried to list most of the major tour companies in this simple A–Z format. In many cases the companies have their own websites through which it is possible to book excursions and trips in advance. This is probably most useful for those planning to do something quite specialist, such as rock climbing or trying to go off the beaten track, as times and dates may be specific.

Adventure Photo Tours: Toll free 1-888 363 8687 or 702 889 8687, www. adventurephototours.com. Private or semi-private photo safaris with professional and well-informed guides to Red Rock, Valley of Fire, Lake Mead, Zion, Death Valley, Bryce Canyon and ghost towns in 7-seater Ford Expeditions, with pick-up from your hotel.

All Las Vegas Tours: 1 800 566 5868 or 702 233 1627, www.alllasvegastours. com. A whole range of adventure tours available online from day tours of the Grand Canyon include the Skywalk, Hummer tours and an optional helicopter ride to the floor of the canyon and a raft ride on the Colorado River, and with testimonials from those who have done them.

Annie Bananie's Wild West Tours: 702 804 9755, www.anniebananie.com. Experienced 'cowboy' guides take you on a trip through ancient and western history and show the diversity of the desert landscape.

ATV Action Tours: 702 566 7400 or toll free 888 288 5200, www.actiontours. com. Get to the other side of Las Vegas Valley in a Jeep Cherokee or Wrangler off-roader and then take a short hike, or take an adventure by ATV, or go horse-riding

Rafting on the Truckee River

Lake Mead

or white-water rafting. Also offers custom tours – including overnight stays at a dude ranch (see page 000), in a mountain cabin or even camping under the stars.

Awesome Adventures: Toll free 1-866 999 961 or 702 257 7338, www. awesomeadventureguide.com. This company is a one-stop shop for outdoor adventure tours, offering ATV tours, ziplining at Bootleg Canyon, hiking, biking and horse-riding, white-water rafting and kayaking. It also offers combo-tours such as the Eldorado kayak, ATV and horse ride.

BRITTIP

Watch out! Some tour companies offer 2-for-1 or other big discounts, making their prices appear very competitive, but they don't include taxes and other extras, which can bump up the cost considerably.

Black Canyon River Raft Tours: 702 294 1414 or toll free 800 455 3490, www. blackcanyonadventures.com.

Bootleg Canyon Mountain Bike Park: 702 293 9356, www.bootlegcanyon.net. World-class downhill and cross-country trails at Bootleg Canyon Mountain Bike Park near Boulder City. 'Flightlines' or ziplines are a recent addition.

Coach America/Gray Line Tours: Toll free 1-800 472 9546 or 702 384 1234, www. grayline.com. The big bus trip specialist, covering everywhere from Hoover Dam to Bryce Canyon and Death Valley. If you pay

for your tour in advance, you'll get a free round trip transfer from the airport to your hotel or a free Laughlin Day Tour.

Cowboy Trail Rides: 702 387 2457, www.cowboytrailrides.com. Fun horse rides from day rides for kids and sunset rides through Red Rock Canyon to multi-day rides.

Creative Adventures: 702 893 2051, www.creativeadventuresltd.net. Specialists in the Ghost Town Tour, which takes you to the wild country along the Colorado to Native American country before touring Searchlight, once a bustling mining town at the turn of the last century. They also offer a Historic Spanish Trail through Red Rock Canyon, The Valley of Fire State Park and Mount Charleston Tour with horse riding as an added attraction and the Grand Canyon Adventure Tour.

11

Death Valley

Cowboys ...

You can't get away from them in Nevada – even the casinos are packed with Stetsons bobbing around among the slot machines. One of the most exciting festivals the city has to offer is the annual National Finals Rodeo held in the second week of December. Great contests include saddle bronco riding, bareback riding, bull riding, calf roping, steer wrestling, team roping, steer roping and barrel racing.

Annie Bananie's Wild West Tour: Here you can get the best of the Wild West in comfort and style at $60–199 per person. Experienced 'cowboy' guides take you to Lake Mead for lunch at the historical Calville Bay Marina, before your air-conditioned coach whisks you off to the Black Mountains, Rogers' Springs, the Valley of Fire and the Moapa Indian Reservation.

Bonnie Springs Old Nevada: A visit here (see page 194) will give you a real taste of the Wild West.

Cowboy Trail Rides: Offer a 1.5-hour sunset ride with Western-style barbecue under the stars through Red Rock Canyon ($169) and a 5-hour WOW ride that takes you through untouched wilderness, making you think you are in 1800s Old West.

Grand Canyon West Ranch: You can get a taste for real-life ranch action at any of the many ranches dotted throughout Nevada, Arizona and California that allow non-cowboys on board for a bit of fun (see page 234 for a full description of the different types and how to get in). One of the nearest – just 45 minutes by helicopter from the Las Vegas Strip – is the Grand Canyon West Ranch (1 800 359 8727 or 702 736 8787, www. grandcanyonranch.com), which nestles in the mountainous area between the west end of the Grand Canyon and the 6,000ft/1,829m Music Mountains of Arizona. Heli USA (see below) offers VIP overnight packages, including helicopter flight, at this working cattle and guest ranch for $749 adults, $649 children, plus $50 fee each, other packages available.

Accommodation consists of rustic 2- or 4-person cabins with authentic roll-top bathtubs and log fires. A herd of long-horn Corriente cattle roam the ranch along with the wild animals such as deer, mountain lion, bob cats, rattlesnakes and lizards. Self-drive packages with cabin stay and Western-style entertainment start at $99 per person mid week.

Oatman: About 20mls/32km east of Laughlin is Oatman, a ghost town in Arizona. Once a thriving mining town during the gold rush, wild burros now wander the streets of this popular TV and Western movie backdrop. At weekends you can take a trip back to the Old West with free cowboy gunfights and showdowns on Main Street. For details phone the Chamber of Commerce (928 768 6222 or 928 768 3839).

Wild West Horseback Adventures: 702 792 5050 or 1-877 945 3978, www. wildwesthorsebackadventures.com. If time doesn't permit a stay, try these trail rides available through LookTours, including a free pick-up from your hotel to the Sage Brush Range on the Moapa Indian Reservation. Choose from a Maverick Breakfast Ride ($109 for 5 hours), Old Spanish Trail Ride with lunch ($129 for 5 hours) or the Wild Wild West Sunset Dinner Ride ($129.99). Including a hearty feast prepared by cowboys and cowgirls, the trails are designed to be user-friendly for both novice and experienced riders.

Escape Adventures: 702 596 2953, www.escapeadventures.com runs mountain bike, road and multisport as well as hiking trips in Red Rock Canyon and beyond.

Grand Canyon Tour Company: 1 800 2 CANYON/1 800 917 5156 (UK) or 702 655 6060 (Las Vegas), www. grandcanyontourcompany.com. All kinds of tours by most methods of transport including self-drive.

Heli USA Airways: 01462 488227 (UK) or 702 736 8787 (Las Vegas), www. heliusa.com. Offers a comprehensive selection of flights to the Grand Canyon with overnight stays, plus exclusive stays at the Grand Canyon West Ranch (see Cowboys panel, above).

Helicop-Tours: Toll free 1-800 653 1881 or 702 736 0606, www. sundancehelicopters.com. Mostly helicopter trips to the Grand Canyon – landing on the canyon floor – but also do combinations with rafting and pontoon boat rides.

... and Indians

Three tribes have dominated Nevada's Native American history – the Northern Paiute, Southern Paiute and the Shoshone. Between them they have etched their stories in the rock petroglyphs of the Valley of Fire and other sacred places including Mount Charleston. The modern-day Native Americans still remain an important force in Nevada, with major Indian reservations at Moapa plus Fort Mojave Reservation in the southern-most tip of the state. They still live by their ancient codes and, even though they now run their own casinos and restaurants, maintain their heritage through traditional pow wows.

Originally, the pow wow was designed to bring various tribes together in a friendly way. It was a festive gathering where they exchanged gifts, heard the latest news and sold foods and crafts. Rodeos were an attraction, but the highlight was always the tribal dance competition for which they would dress in tribal regalia.

Bruno's Indian and Turquoise Museum: 1306 Nevada Highway, Boulder City, 702 293 4865. This promotes and gives information about the Native American artists of the south-west, of which 2,000 are represented by the museum. Open 9.30am– 5pm.

Great Venture Tours: (1 800 578 2643, www.greatventures.com) Another way to get the 'Indian' experience is to go on a rafting trip with a Native American river guide on the Colorado River. This company (see page 199) offers a 1-day rafting trip on class 2–4 rapids with Hualapai River Guides from Sedona for $599 (minimum age 8), Tues, Thurs and Sat.

Grand Canyon West Ranch: (1 800 359 8727, www.grandcanyonranch.com). This company offers accommodation in Indian Tipis or pine cabins.

Heli USA: See below. Offers overnight packages, including sunrise helicopter flight for $649 adults, $549 children, plus $50 fee each, or self-drive package for $399 adults, $299 children, plus $15 fee.

Hualapai Indians: Most of the major tour companies offer Grand Canyon flights or helicopter tours to the West Rim combined with a barbecue lunch with the Hualapai Indians, who will tell you about their legends and culture. The trips have been so successful that the Hualapai have even built a tiny village overlooking the Grand Canyon where you can shop for souvenirs or check out the small museum.

Lost City Museum of Archaeology: 721 South Moapa Valley Boulevard, Overton, 702 397 2193, www.sunsetcities.com/lost-city-museum.html. Another great place to go, this is just north of Red Rock Canyon. For $5 admission you will be able to see artefacts from the Anasazis who lived in the Moapa Valley from the 1st to the 12th centuries AD. Displays include a reconstruction of the basket-maker pithouse and pueblo dwellings. The museum is located 66mls/106km north-east of Las Vegas on Highway 15 and Highway 169 near Overton. Open Thurs–Sun 8.30am–4.30pm.

Moapa River Indian Reservation: Pow wows still take place today and are a wonderful way to experience the Indian culture. Of course, it cannot be guaranteed that a pow wow will be organised for your trip, but you can still get a taste of the Native American way of life by going here, just east of the Valley of Fire off Interstate 15. The store at the entrance is famous for its duty-free tobacco, alcohol and fireworks. But be warned: fireworks are not allowed outside the reservation and police do stop and search cars periodically.

11

Hike This!: 702 393 4453, www.hikethislasvegas.com. Offers guided hiking and rock scrambling tours around some of the most spectacular scenery in southern Nevada. Costs from $159 for a single person; $119 each for 2 people.

Keith Prowse: 0203 1377420, www.keithprowse.com. For helicopter, aircraft and land tours. The West Rim Indian Country Bus Tour includes lunch with the Hualapai Indians.

Lake Mead Cruises: 702 293 6180, www.lakemeadcruises.com. Cruises and jet-skiing on Lake Mead.

Lake Mead Jetski Tours: 702 558 7547, www.worldwidejetskis.com. Jet-ski tours and rental on Lake Mead.

Las Vegas Cyclery: 702 596 2953, www.lasvegascyclery.com This professional outfit offers half, full and multi-day mountain, road and multi-sport cycling adventures for casual to experienced cyclists as well as hiking tours in Red Rock Canyon.

Las Vegas Tour Desk: 1 866 GC Tours or 702 310 1320, www.lasvegastourdesk. com. Specialises in air tours to the Grand Canyon.

LookTours: 1 800 566 5868 or 702 233 1627, www.looktours.com. Winner of the 2005 Best Sightseeing Tour Company by the Nevada Commission on Tourism, the company offers every conceivable tour option and combination you could wish for – by aeroplane, bus, helicopter, raft and ATV or Hummer. It's worth checking out the website and booking directly to take advantage of the internet deals.

Maverick Helicopters Inc: 888-261 4414, www.maverickhelicopter.com. Custom charters and tours to Grand Canyon, Bryce, Zion, Monument Valley and Death Valley. Also offers personalised videos to take home.

Overton Beach Watercraft: 702 394 4400. Hire of anything from personal watercraft to patio and fishing boats.

Papillon Grand Canyon Helicopters: 0800 404 9767 (UK toll free) or 702 736 7243 (Las Vegas), www.papillon. com. Offers helicopter trips ranging from the Vegas strip at night to packages which plunge into the Grand Canyon. New are a blow-the-budget private sunset helicopter rides.

Pink Jeep Tours: 888 900 4480 or 702 895 6777, www.pinkjeep.com. Pink Jeep Tours have been operating here for 50 years and offer a choice of 12 nature and culture-based tours including Death Valley, Hoover Dam, Grand Canyon, Red Rock Canyon, Valley of Fire, Mt Charleston, Zion National Park and Eldorado Canyon.

Rebel Adventure Tours: 800 817 6789 or 702 380 6969, www. rebeladventuretours.com. Off-road Hummer tours to Lake Mead and Hoover Dam and Grand Canyon, also combined with jet-skiing, lunch with Native Americans and white water rafting. Rebel also offer ATV, helicopter and horse-riding adventures.

Scenic Airlines: 866 235 9422 or 702 638 3300, www.scenic.com. Since Eagle Airlines bought out Scenic, this is now the largest air tour company in Las Vegas. It offers every single destination you could think of – and every combination. In addition to the Grand Canyon, Zion Canyon, Bryce Canyon, Monument Valley and Lake Powell, you can also do overnight stops and get the Native American experience. Plus, of course, the night flight over the Strip.

Showtime Tours: 1-888 827 3858 or 702 895 9976, www.showtimetourslv.com. Tours include a Night on the Town, Grand Canyon Bus Tour, Colorado River Rafting and a Lake Mead Dinner Cruise.

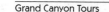 **BRITTIP**

Some tour companies offer free day-long trips to Laughlin, but these are just a classic way to get you to spend money at the casinos there.

Single Track Tours: 702 813 5730, www.singletracktours.com. Professionally guided mountain bike and road tours of the Las Vegas area.

Ski & Snowboard Resort: 702 593 9500, www.skilasvegas.com. Las Vegas Ski & Snowboard resort is a fully-serviced resort offering ski packages for adults and kids, in Mount Charleston's Lee Canyon, just 30 minutes from the strip.

Sky's the Limit: 702 363 4533, www. skysthelimit.com This company provided hiking and rock climbing tours but, at time of going to press, they were unavailable to update their entry.

Grand Canyon Tours

12 GOLF AND OTHER SPORTS

Getting some golf action, plus spectator and extreme sports

Las Vegas is most famous for staging big-name fights between boxers, but its climate – especially in the spring, autumn and winter months – makes it perfect for golf. With a massive increase in courses built over the last decade, there are now over 60 top-flight golf courses to choose from. Many of the world's most famous golfers have played here, including Tiger Woods, former US President Bill Clinton and NBA Legend, Michael Jordan. Designers include Billy Casper, Greg Nash, Arnold Palmer, Tom Fazio, Jack Nicklaus and Pete Dye and Las Vegas has hosted stops on some of the world's major tours including the LPGA, Seniors Tour, PGA Tour and NCAA Championships.

The irony is that the time when most Brits visit Las Vegas – the summer – is actually low season, so you should get some pretty good deals at golf courses then. The peak season is October to May, as the Americans consider the summer months far too hot to be playing golf! Fortunately, in the summer golf courses are open early in the morning and later in the afternoon.

BRITTIP

If you want to arrange a round of golf, go for an afternoon slot as the early mornings tend to get very busy. It's also a lot cheaper at many places – ask about 'twilight' rates, which means any time after 1pm.

Many hotels are affiliated to different golf courses, which offer resort guests reduced-price tee fees. All the same, fees for those courses and others in central Las Vegas will be 2 to 3 times more expensive than those out of the city, although with more courses competing for business, fees came down in 2009, so I have given details of golf courses in Boulder City, North Las Vegas, Laughlin and Pahrump. A few Henderson courses are still well priced, but most of those in the sought-after Lake Las Vegas area are now very expensive. Generally, the prices given include a cart.

A full listing of golf courses open to visitors follows below, but several very useful numbers are:

Stand-by Golf: 1 866 224 BOOK or 760 321 2665 (daily 7am–9pm), www. standbygolf.com. For same-day and next-day play at reduced prices (10–50% off) at many golf courses in the Las Vegas area

Las Vegas Golf: 1 866 456 9912, www. lasvegasgolf.com is a newer site offering a similar service.

Golf Reservations of Nevada: 702 732 3119, www.worldgolf.com/courses/usa/nevada. For advance tee-time reservations for individuals and groups at major courses in the area.

Golf courses in Las Vegas

Angel Park Golf Club

100 South Rampart Boulevard, 888 446 5358 or 702 254 4653, www.angelpark.com
Designed by Arnold Palmer, two 18-hole resort courses offer 36 holes of Championship golf with spectacular views of Red Rock Canyon. Rounds cost $55–135 depending on the season with

Angel Park Golf Club

very reasonable stay and play packages available. Twilight and reduced summer rates available. Reservations up to 4 months in advance, bookable online.

Badlands Golf Club

9119 Alta Drive, 1 800 675 1458 or 702 363 0754, www.badlandsgc.com
This 27-hole resort course designed by Johnny Miller is a true desert course experience. Rounds cost from $45 depending on season, if booked online. Twilight rates available. Reservations up to 60 days in advance.

 BRITTIP

The Badlands is considered the golfing equivalent of an ultimate thrill ride. Carved through canyons, each of the 27 holes – the 3 nines called Desperado, Diablo and Outlaw – is known for dramatic shot values.

Bali Hai Golf Club

5160 Las Vegas Boulevard, 888 427 6678, www.balihaigolfclub.com
With 4,000 trees and 7acres/2.8ha of water hazards, this stunning tropical-themed course just south of the Mandalay Bay with a fabulous clubhouse was named by GolfWeek as one of the 'Top 40 Resort Courses in America'. Rounds cost $89–325 depending on the season. Reservations up to 6 months in advance.

 BRITTIP

The Bali Hai Golf Club is not only fantastically located just by the Four Seasons and Mandalay Bay hotels, but also has a divine restaurant, Cili, run by celebrity chef Wolfgang Puck.

Bear's Best Golf Club

11111 West Flamingo Avenue, 1 866 385 8500 or 702 804 8500, www.clubcorp.com
A collection of Jack Nicklaus's favourite 18 holes in a dramatic setting with a desert-style clubhouse. Rounds cost $59–179 booked online. Booking is up to 90 days in advance.

Callaway Golf Center/ Divine Nine

6730 Las Vegas Boulevard South at the corner with Sunset Road, 1 866 897 9500 or 702 896 4100, www.callawaygolfcenter.com

Nine par-3 holes. Rounds cost $25–30. Driving range hits on to 12 greens with various hazards among grass and synthetic trees. Open 7.30am–9.30pm.

 BRITTIP

The Callaway Golf Center is also home to the Eric Meeks School of Golf that offers free golf instruction to children aged 11–16. Lessons cost $50 an hour with cheaper packages available.

Desert Pines Golf Club

3415 East Bonanza Road, 1 888 427 6678, www.desertpinesgolfclub.com
Named after the thousands of mature pines that line the 18-hole public course, it also has covered hitting areas and an automatic ball delivery system. Just 15 minutes from the Strip, rounds cost $35–160 booked online. Reservations up to 6 months in advance.

Desert Rose Golf Club

5483 Club House Drive, 702 431 4653, www.desertrosegc.com
Palm trees, water and bunkers highlight the 18-hole county course, which has a wash between the holes. Rounds cost $49–59. Twilight rates available. Tee times 7 days in advance.

Las Vegas Golf Club

4300 West Washington Avenue, 702 646 3003, www.americangolf.com
The oldest golf course in Vegas, this 18-hole city course is also one of the busiest and a local favourite. Recently renovated, rounds cost $59–79. Reservations 60 days in advance.

 BRITTIP

Don't forget your sun protection factor 30 and a hat when playing in summer. In autumn, take a sweater with you for late-afternoon games as it can get quite chilly when the sun goes down.

Las Vegas National Golf Club

1911 East Desert Inn Road, 1 866 695 1961 or 702 734 1796, www.lasvegasnational.com
18-hole public course less than 2mls/3km from the Strip. Rounds from $79-119. Twilight rates available. Floodlit driving range. Reservations 60 days in advance.

BRITTIP

Las Vegas National Golf Club is home to the Las Vegas Golf Hall of Fame, featuring photos and memorabilia from Las Vegas golf champions Jim Colbert, Arnold Palmer, Jack Nicklaus, Annika Sorenstam and others as well as trophies used for the PGA's Tours Las Vegas and memorabilia from other tours and events.

Las Vegas Paiute Golf Resort

10325 Nu-Wav Kaiv Boulevard, 20mls/32km north of city on the Snow Mountain exit near Mount Charleston, 1 800 711 2833 or 702 658 1400, www.lvpaiutegolf.com
Three 18-hole public courses designed by Pete Dye on the Las Vegas Paiute Tribe Indian Reservation. Green fees start at $59–119 depending on the season. Twilight rates are available. Reservations up to 120 days in advance.

BRITTIP

The Snow Mountain course at Las Vegas Paiute Golf Resort is considered the best public access course in Las Vegas by **Golf Digest** magazine.

Painted Desert Golf Club

5555 Painted Mirage Drive, 1 800 468 7918 or 702 645 2570, www.painteddesertgc.com
This 18-hole public course was the first desert course in the area – expect holes shaped by desert landscape and cacti. Rounds cost $69–99 according to the season. Twilight rates are available. Reservations up to 60 days in advance.

Rhodes Ranch Golf Club

20 Rhodes Ranch Parkway, 1 888 311 8337 or 702 740 4114, www.rhodesranchgolf.com
This is a Ted Robinson-designed course tucked in the shadows of the Spring Mountain range, with tough, intriguing par-3s and numerous water features. Rounds cost from $45, varying according to the season. Reservations up to 60 days in advance.

Shadow Creek

3 Shadow Creek Drive, 1 888 778 3387 or 702 791 7161, www.shadowcreek.com

This 18-hole extraordinarily beautiful resort course is specifically for the MGM Mirage group, which includes the MGM Grand, the New York-New York, Bellagio, Treasure Island and the Mirage. One of the highest ranking courses in the world – accessible to MGM Mirage guests from a mere $500!

BRITTIP

When reserving your tee time, also check the cancellation policy and how much notice you need to give before forfeiting any money!

Tournament Players Club (TPC) Las Vegas

9851 Canyon Run Drive, 1 866 447 4653 or 702 256 2500, www.tpc.com
This 18-hole resort course is the only public PGA course in Vegas and includes a meandering canyon. Rounds cost from $149 booked online depending on the season. Reservations up to a year in advance.

BRITTIP

Did you know that Tiger Woods earned his first PGA Tour victory at the Tournament Players Club in Summerlin.

Wynn Golf Club

Wynn Las Vegas, 888 320 7122, www.wynnlasvegas.com
You can find 18 holes of world-class golf right on the Strip. Designed by Tom Fazio and Steve Wynn, 800,000 yds^3/611,644m^3 of earth were moved to create the dramatic elevation changes for this par 70 golf course of which 11 holes include a water element – think waterfalls and streams among the trees. Golf packages from $609 per night.

Golf courses north of Las Vegas

Aliante Golf Club

3100 East Elkhorn, North Las Vegas, 1 877 399 4888 or 702 399 4888, www.aliantegolf.com
Voted the Best New Course in Las Vegas by *Vegas Golfer Magazine*, this is a challenging tournament-quality course of 18 holes, with green fees running at $30–130 depending on the season.

12

Craig Ranch Golf Course

628 West Craig Road, 702 642 9700, http://thegolfcourses.net/golfcourses/NV/4123.htm
An 18-hole public course, with rates from $30, according to season. Reservations 7 days in advance.

North Las Vegas Golf Course

324 East Brooks Avenue, 702 633 1900, www.cityofnorthlasvegas.com
Nine-hole lighted city course (the ninth hole is on a hill and has a great view of Las Vegas) which is a bargain option for beginners. Rates under $50 for adults, according to season. Reservations 7 days in advance.

Golf course in Boulder City

Boulder City Golf Course

1 Clubhouse Drive, Boulder City, 702 293 9236, www.bouldercitygolf.com
This 18-hole city course near the Hoover Dam is shadowed by hundreds of large trees and has large greens, wide open fairways and 2 lakes. Rates from $40-50, depending on season, with twilight rates available. Reservations 1 week in advance.

Golf courses in Henderson and Green Valley

Black Mountain Golf and Country Club

500 Greenway Road, Henderson, 702 565 7933 x 113, www.golfblackmountain.com
This 27-hole semi-private mature course catering to all levels in the Vegas Valley underwent a $2m renovation in 2008. Rates from $65 depending on season, with twilight rates available. Tee times up to 4 days in advance.

Dragon Ridge

DragonRidge Country Club

552 South Stephanie Street, Henderson, 702 614 4444, www.dragonridge.com
With great views of the Las Vegas Valley and bent-grass greens, this private 18-hole course will test even the best golfers and offers lessons from the Jack Nicklaus Academy. Cost $175–275. Reservations up to 30 days in advance.

The Legacy Golf Club

130 Par Excellence Drive, Henderson, 1 888 629 3930 or 702 897 2187, www.thelegacygc.com
This 18-hole resort Champion course is ranked by *Golf Digest* as one of the top 10 courses in Nevada. Designed by Arthur Hills, it features tee boxes on the 10th hole in the shape of each suit in a deck of cards: spades, clubs, diamonds and hearts. Cost $135–155 depending on the season with twilight rates available. Tee times up to 90 days in advance.

Reflection Bay Golf Club

75 MonteLago Boulevard, Lake Las Vegas, 702 740 4653, reservations 1 877 698 4653, www.nicklaus.com/design/lakelasvegas
Jack Nicklaus's second prestigious course created on Lake Las Vegas includes 5 holes played alongside 1.5mls/2.4km of shoreline, while other holes are decorated with water features. Green fees start from $120 but vary daily. Tee times up to 30 days in advance.

Rio Secco Golf Club

2851 Grand Hills Drive, Henderson, 1 888 867 3226 or 702 777 2400, www.riosecco.net
This 18-hole resort course, which includes desert and canyon holes, is owned by the Rio All-Suite Hotel. Mostly for Rio's and Harrah's hotel guests. At the Butch Harmon School of Golf here, golfers can analyse their swing using state-of-the-art computer equipment. Rates from $110. Reservations 90 days in advance.

BRITTIP
Jack Nicklaus's nationally ranked Reflection Bay Golf Club is part of the exclusive MonteLago Lake Las Vegas Resort, which includes shops, restaurants, a casino and 2 waterfront hotels. For more details of the whole area, visit www.lakelasvegas.com.

Wildhorse Golf Club

2100 Warm Springs Road, Henderson 702 434 9000, www.golfwildhorse.com
An 18-hole public course with rates from $87 if booked online, that vary seasonally. Reservations up to 60 days in advance.

BRITTIP
The Wildhorse Golf Club's 18th hole is one of the most difficult in the Las Vegas Valley, thanks to the surrounding bunkers and 4 lakes!

Golf course in Laughlin

Mojave Resort Golf Club

9905 Aha Macav Parkway, Laughlin, 702 535 4653, www.mojaveresortgolfclub.com
An 18-hole course that hosts the Southern Nevada Golf Association Championships, this desert experience includes sand dunes and marshes and a GPS system on golf carts so you can't get lost! Rates are $54–109, depending on the season. Reservations 1 week in advance or 30 days with a credit card.

Golf course in Summerlin and Pahrump

Sun City Summerlin Golf Club

0800 803 0758, www.golfsummerlin.com
Palm Valley: 9201 Del Webb Boulevard, 702 363 4373. 18-hole semi-private (preference is given to residents).
Highland Falls: 10201 Sun City Boulevard, 702 254 7010. 18-hole course.
Eagle Crest: 2203 Thomas Ryan Boulevard, 702 240 1320. 18-hole course. Rates vary – check for web specials. Call for reservations.

Spectator sports

Las Vegas has it all still to do in the sporting arena. It doesn't have a professional football or basketball team – both are university (or college, as they are called in America) teams, but sometimes NBA (basketball) friendlies are held during October, which are worth going to see.

The city is most famous for hosting major championship boxing events 2 or 3 times a year – and has done so since 1960, largely as a result of the fact that this was the only city in America where you could legally gamble on a winner. Most of the middle and heavyweight fights take place at Caesars Palace, the MGM Grand or the Mandalay Bay. Tickets start at $100 and rise to a steep $3,500 or more for ringside seats. The best place to do your homework is on www.ticketmaster.com.

American Football

Sam Boyd Stadium, 7000 East Russell Road, Boulder Highway, 702 895 3761, www.unlvtickets.com
The UNLV team's season runs Sep–Dec. Tickets cost $15–25.

Baseball

Cashman Field, 850 Las Vegas Boulevard North at Washington Avenue, 702 386 7200, www.minorleaguebaseball.com
Home of the Las Vegas 51s, who play April–Sep as part of the Pacific Coast League.

Basketball

Hoop Hall Experience, Planet Hollywood Resort & Casino, 3667 Las Vegas Boulevard South, 702 785 5555, www.planethollywoodresort.com
Basketball fans can immerse themselves in interactive fun displays and exhibits in a celebration of the game and even give it their best shot at the 'dunk zone' to get in the mood.

Thomas & Mack Center, 4505 Maryland Parkway on the UNLV campus, 702 895 3900 or 1 866 388 3267 (box office), www.thomasandmack.com and www.unlvtickets.com
The city's team is the UNLV Runnin' Rebels, who play all their games here Nov–May. During October, NBA teams sometimes play exhibition games here, and in 2007 the NBA's All-star Game was hosted here. There is also a strong movement to move an NBA franchise to Sin City.

Mojave Resort

Ice hockey

Las Vegas Wranglers, 702 471 7825, www.lasvegaswranglers.com
Ice hockey is a big deal in America and desert-bound Las Vegas doesn't disappoint. For some fierce action try the local Wranglers' matches. Visit the website or phone for a schedule.

For general sports events try UNLV Sports on 702 895 3761, www.unlvtickets.com.

BRITTIP
Try Nevada Ticket Services on 702 597 1588 or www.lasvegasticket. com to book anything from basketball to football, hockey, baseball, National Finals Rodeo, pro bull rides, Superbowl and Final Four.

Motor Sports

Las Vegas Motor Speedway, 7000 Las Vegas Boulevard North, 1 800 644 4444, www.lvms.com
Lying 17mls/27km north of the Strip, the 1,500acre/607ha speedway opened in 1996 at a cost of $200m and seats 107,000. Facilities include a 1.5ml/2.4km superspeedway, a 2.5ml/4km road course, a 0.5ml/0.8km dirt oval, drag strip, go-kart tracks and racing school. Check out Midnight Madness on Fridays and Saturdays for drag racing that starts at 10pm as part of the test-and-tune sessions that begin at 5pm. Phone ahead for schedules of upcoming events and tickets.

Wrestling

www.wwe.com
The city doesn't hold its own events, but does play host to several World Wrestling Federation and World Championship Wrestling events. Either check out the local paper when in town or look at the website in advance.

Extreme sports

There are many different ways to have fun in Las Vegas and if extreme thrills are your thing, then you can do anything from taking part in a race at the Speedway to skydiving.

Laser Quest

7361 West Lake Mead Boulevard, Suite 100, 702 243 8881, www.laserquest.com
You wear a laser-sensing vest and shoot it out with other laser-wielding players in a maze of corners, turns, walkways and mirrored walls. Lasers are, of course, lightbeams, so you can even hit someone from around a corner if you get it to ricochet off the right point. Great for children up to the age of 80!

Open: Mon–Thurs 2–9pm; Fri 4–11pm; Sat noon–11pm; Sun noon–6pm.

Cost: Flat rate of $8.50 per person for 20 minutes of play. Book in advance to avoid the queue.

BRITTIP
Going to fight it out at Laser Quest? Remember that lasers are just like light beams and can ricochet off reflective spots throughout the Quest – a pretty neat way to do away with your opponents (or be done away with)!

Race Car Tours

This can mean anything from family fun in the Mini Gran Prix to the experience of riding or driving a racing car at high speed at on the Las Vegas Motor Speedway, home to the city's NASCAR events and drag races.

Las Vegas Mini Gran Prix

1401 North Rainbow Boulevard, 702 259 7000, www.lvmgp.com
Take Exit 82a off US 95 for the family ride of a lifetime on sprint cars, go-karts and kiddie karts and adults' Gran Prix cars. This place also offers fairground style rides guaranteed to get little ones' hearts pumping. Try the new dip and glide Dive Bomber, fly and spin on the Tornado Twister and take a trip on the Dragon Roller Coaster. There is also a games arcade and snack bar.

Open: Sun–Thurs 10am–10pm; Fri–Sat 10am–11pm except Christmas Day and depending on the weather.

Cost: $7 per ticket or $32.50 for 5. Cars available for from 4- to over 16-year-olds.

Mario Andretti Racing School

1 877 722 3527 or 702 651 6317, www.andrettiracing.com
Billed as the World's Fastest Racing Experience, hold onto your seat as for $114.39 you race 3 laps as a passenger in a Champ Ride as a professional racing driver reaches speeds of up to 180mph/290kph. The Qualifier allows you to get behind the wheel of a full-sized,

Major annual sporting events

March: NASCAR Winston Cup at the Las Vegas Motor Speedway, 1 800 644 4444
April: Big League Weekends (baseball) – Cashman Field Center, 702 386 7100; Spring
Pro-Am Golf Tournament, 516 292 4055

September: NCCA College Football – UNLV Rebels – 1 866 459 9233; Pro-Am Golf
Tournament – Sahara Country Club, 1 800 332 8776

October: Ice hockey season – a schedule is available in August for the Thomas and
Mack Center, 702 895 3761, thomasandmack.com; Las Vegas Invitational PGA Golf
Tournament – buy tickets from the Thomas and Mack Center; US Open of Supercross
sees top supercross riders racing in and around the hotels on the strip, 1 866 459 9233;
Professional Bull Riders meet for a 4-day competition at the Thomas and Mack Center,
702 895 3761.

December: The first week kicks off with the Las Vegas Marathon which starts in front of
Mandalay Bay, 702 731 1052; National Finals Rodeo at the Thomas and Mack Center,
702 895 3761; Las Vegas Bowl Collegiate Football Game at Sam Boyd Silver Bowl, 702
895 3761

For other events visit http://las.vegas.eventguide.com. The Event Channel has tickets
for many of the above sporting events, 1 866 459 9233, http://tickets.eventchannel.net

600HP racing car yourself, where after minimal instruction you'll reach speeds of up to 150mph/241kph at a cost of $290.39–378.39. These costs reflect a 25% online discount.

Richard Petty Driving Experience

7000 North Las Vegas Boulevard, 1-800 237 3889, www.drivepetty.com
This offers a similar experience of driving a racing car at high speed (140mph/225kph) for $109–3,000. Try to go on a weekday or early at the weekend to avoid the crowds. If you're too nervous to drive, 'Ride Along' at 165mph/266kph!

Rocks & Ropes

Nevada Climbing Centers, 3065 East Patrick Lane, Suite 4, 702 898 8192, www.rocksandropes.com
This indoor climbing facility has more than 7,000ft2/650m2 of sculpted and textured walls for climbing, 30ft/9m ceilings, top rope and lead climbing and a mega-cave with a leadable 40ft/12m roof so people can learn everything they need to know to go rock climbing for real!
Open: Mon–Fri 3–10pm; Sat–Sun 11–8pm; first time users must arrive 2.5 hours before closing.
Cost: $13 adults per day, $9 for children under 12, $12 first-time instruction (ages 12 and up), $6 equipment rental.

Xtreme Zone

Adventuredome Theme Park, Circus Circus, 702 691 5861, www.adventuredome.com
A combination of rock climbing and aerial bungee jumping creates an interactive experience with multiple difficulty levels. The Zone's rock-climbing attraction combines traditional harnesses and handholds with cutting-edge belay technology to make it as safe as possible. The aerial trampoline combines a standard trampoline with a hydraulic system and bungee cords so you can climb up to 20ft/6m and then flip and spin yourself back and forth. You must weigh 40–265lb/18–120kg to climb the wall and 30–220lb/13.5–100kg to experience the bungee.

Skydiving

Skydiving has become big in Las Vegas and can be done indoors or outdoors, in tandem or solo, for those who dare.

BRITTIP

Dress the part for your indoor skydive – make sure you're in comfy clothes with socks and trainers.

Flyaway Indoor Skydiving

200 Convention Center Drive, toll free 877 545 8093 or 702 731 4768, www.vegasindoorskydiving.com
Learn how to fly in Vegas's only indoor

12

skydiving simulator, where the vertical wind tunnel allows you to beat gravity and fly! First-time flyers are given a 20-minute class in safety and body-control techniques. Experienced skydivers can also get valuable 'air' time to improve their skills without having to pack a rig and wait for the right weather. Video coaching programmes are also available in which your air tunnel flight is recorded to help you improve your style.

Open: Daily 9.45am–8pm. Classes every half hour from 11am to an hour before closing

Cost: Peak rates $85 for single flight, $50 for same day repeat flight, $250 for 5 flights, $400 for a 15-minute family block and $25 for a video of you in action! Off-peak rates available.

Las Vegas Skydiving Center

Just behind the Goldstrike Hotel at Jean airport, 702 303 3914 (south-west of Las Vegas), www.lasvegasskydivingcenter.com
Take a tandem skydive after a 30-minute lesson from $199 (including complimentary shuttle from the Strip). Daily 7.30, 10am and 12 noon; jumps that can be captured on camera or video for an extra fee, are by appointment only (minimum age 18, weight less than 240lb).

Skydive Las Vegas

Boulder City Airport, 1401 Airport Road, Boulder City (near Hoover Dam), toll free 1-800 875 9348 or 702 759 3483, www.skydivelasvegas.com
You freefall for 45 seconds before enjoying a 7-minute parachute ride in a tandem jump. By appointment only.

Skydive Las Vegas

Vegas Extreme Skydiving

23600 S Las Vegas Blvd, 702 303 3914, www.vegasextremeskydiving.com
View the Las Vegas strip from 2mls/3km up with the thrill of descending at 120mph/193kph before putting on the air brakes to savour views over the Hoover Dam, Lake Mead and the Colorado River. Vegas Extreme Skydiving offers tandem dives for first-time jumpers and solo dives for the experienced.

Open: By reservation only.

Cost: From $199 for a tandem sky dive with instruction. Video and photographic services available.

Boulder City

GETTING THERE

The tour operators, doing it your own way and specialist holiday planners

Of course, with Las Vegas your dream destination, you still have to get there. You have a lot of choices. After all, if you are going to fly across an entire ocean and most of a continent to get there, you might as well make it worth the trip! Do you use the city as a fantastically cheap base for visiting all the natural wonders on its doorstep? Maybe you head off on a fly-drive tour; or even start in Los Angeles and San Francisco and take in all the wonderful places that you can reasonably visit in the amount of time available to you?

Then there are the other factors, like how many of you are travelling, or whether you will be visiting friends in, say, San Diego or Phoenix. In that case you could take advantage of the incredibly cheap offers to Las Vegas that are advertised in the local papers and travel from there. If you have children and teenagers in your party, you'll probably be best with an airline/tour operator that caters well for the family market. You may even want to do a part fly-drive and add on a ranch or golfing holiday or an adventure trek.

The visitor figures show that Brits tend either to go on a long-weekend package to Las Vegas or do a combination of any of the above. It is for this reason that if you have ever picked up a brochure on visiting Las Vegas and California there seems to be so much information and so many options to wade through: multi-centre packages,

Palazzo Hotel

fly-drives, coach tours, open-jaw flights (see page 217) and so on. It'll take some time to make sense of one brochure, let alone compare a few to see what suits you best. Then there is the other option – to organise your trip totally independently.

To try to make life easier, I've tried to outline the options available, what to look for and what to ask for.

> ◀🇬🇧▶ **BRITTIP** ————————
> When shopping around for flight prices, make sure the figure you are given includes all taxes and airport fees to make a proper comparison.

Specialist tour operators

These are not your local travel agents, but those who specialise in organising holidays to Nevada and California and produce a brochure to display their products. This is important because Las Vegas in particular has quirks all of its own and someone with little local knowledge is unlikely to provide you with the best deals or choice of options.

What's good about the specialist North American tour operators is that the big outfits have massive buying power and so can offer some of the best prices available for both hotels and car-hire services. In many cases you can go for a 'land-only' deal for a nominal charge, which gives you the option to arrange your own flights through some of the cheap flight brokers who advertise in the weekend national newspapers (more about that in the independent travel section, page 225). Most do not advertise this, though, so you will have to ask.

All the main specialist North American operators provide tailor-made packages, which mean that you can take advantage of any special deals and arrangements they may have with, for instance, hotels, theme parks and local airline companies offering scenic flights around the Grand Canyon area and San Francisco.

The bigger guys – such as Virgin Holidays, Kuoni, Premier Holidays, Thomas Cook and Gold Medal – can pack in a lot of added-value extras, especially in these competitive, 'credit crunch' times. You can get room upgrades for honeymoon and anniversary holiday-makers, free transfers to the hotel (rarely part of a North American package), free accommodation and/or free meals for children, extra nights free, free flights to London from regional airports and so on. You may also like to know that out of the large tour companies operating in North America, Virgin Holidays, Kuoni, Travelsphere, Jetsave and Page & Moy did particularly well in the 'would you recommend this tour operator to a friend?' stakes as part of a *Which?* tour operator survey.

Local knowledge

Big is not always best in this market, as good knowledge of the location is very important, along with the operator's determination to provide you with what is best for you (which may involve making alternative suggestions to your own best-laid plans) and offer a generally good level of service. Smaller outfits such as Just America (www.justamerica.co.uk) do not claim to be the cheapest, but with a high level of return custom and recommendation-to-friends business, they know their emphasis on getting things right for a slightly higher cost means all the difference between an okay holiday and a fantastic one. Their policy is based on not packing too much into one trip so that you travel to see destinations, not see destinations as you travel. Overall, it makes them very good value for money.

Another smaller UK operator, Funway Holidays, (www.funwayholidays.co.uk) works alongside United Vacations, which sends more than one million people a year to Las Vegas, so they have tremendously good buying power and very good access to hotels in Las Vegas. More than 50 hotels are featured in the brochure (the average tends to be about 10 to 15), including all the recently opened resorts such as The Encore.

In addition, Funway's parent company is one of the largest in America meaning they are likely to be able to get you into top resort-hotels when other tour operators may not – with the best choice and competitive rates and a whole raft of extras including discount vouchers. Overall, it makes them one of the best operators to Las Vegas. They also have some great arrangements for self-drive tours.

What to look for

Using a tour operator is great if you want to get everything sewn up before you go, but remember they're in business to make money and, while their brochures may be in one sense accurate, not all of them will point out any negatives. Also, it is useful to bear in mind that even if something is not

Frequent-flyer points

Did you know that every time you fly you could be clocking up frequent-flyer mileage points that will eventually give you free air travel or other perks such as last-minute availability, lounge access and free upgrades or discounts off attractions and excursions in the USA? Very often your holiday booking does give you free air miles, but you may not know about it. Even if you do not claim the benefits, your travel agent still has the right to do so and some like to keep this nice little perk under their hats! So, before you go on holiday, register with the airline for their loyalty scheme and keep your booking passes to prove that the flights were taken. Discounted flights may not qualify, but it's always worth checking. A useful site to browse is www.frequentflier.com which has links to many airlines.

Many of the North American specialists will automatically offer frequent-flyer points on American Airlines flights, though you may have to pay an additional fee for the privilege of collecting them. Having said that, AA give you one Advantage mile for every mile you fly, which is over 10,000 if you're flying from London to Los Angeles – enough to earn you one free ticket to certain European destinations (www.aa.com).

If you have a family, it is a good idea to register the whole family in the scheme so each person can build up their points. Some schemes, such as Virgin's Flying Club Frequent Flyer (0844 412 2414, www.virgin-atlantic.com), expect their economy-class passengers to complete 3 return economy flights before qualifying, though upper class or premium economy passengers qualify immediately. British Airways offer both air miles – 1 mile per every mile flown – and travel points, the latter granting lounge facilities and even free travel insurance with enough credits. As most major airlines are members of alliances, you can collect air miles on different airlines, making it all the quicker to gain miles.

When arranging to join a frequent-flyer programme, ask if there is a bonus for joining at that particular time as different airlines offer bonuses. For instance, not so long ago Virgin was offering a bonus of 2,000 points on joining and Continental a special activation bonus of a whopping 5,000 miles when you take your first Continental Airlines holiday. The scheme offers free upgrades and free tickets.

Also, for those who have an American Express card, they have an excellent travel site (www.membershiprewards.com) where you can book everything you need, get frequent travel points for Amex and double up frequent flyer points for the airlines and hotels you use. These transcontinental trips can add up quickly when you are dipping twice.

Finally, following the lead of a partnership between MGM Mirage and American, most major resorts have teamed up with one airline's frequent-flyer programme or other to get points bonuses. So any time you spend money at the hotel you can earn even more points, or use your points for free shows, tours, or what have you.

included in the brochure, such as open-jaw tickets (see page 217) or air passes (see page 219), you should always ask your preferred operator if they can arrange those for you.

The following sections will show you how to take the good, watch out for the bad and reject the downright ugly that tour operators have to offer.

Scheduled flights

Charter services to Las Vegas come and go – and are seasonal at best, so it really is down to scheduled flights. In the case of America generally, and Las Vegas in particular, this is a good thing as most of the airlines fly every day to a whole range of locations in North America – many at easy-to-catch times of the day – and from a range of regional airports in the UK.

Given the way most Brits tend to move around Nevada, Arizona and California during a holiday to the region, this provides the essential flexibility required when organising a trip. What tends to follow on from scheduled services is the ability to make a stop on the way to your final destination (stopover); fly into one city and out from another (open-jaw) and even fly between cities (using multi-centre packages or air-pass vouchers). And if you tend to do a lot of long-haul travelling, you can even arrange it so that you get frequent-flyer points. Most of the operators offer a minimum of 3 airline prices, some up to 6, except for airline-run operators, such as American Holiday (American Airlines); NorthWest Airlines; United Vacations (United Airlines) and Virgin.

Paris Las Vegas

Assessing flight choices

Flights to Las Vegas from Britain have multiplied at a happy rate. Direct service is with Virgin via London or Manchester, and in October 2009, a daily British Airways (BA) flight was added, from London Heathrow and first class introduced in 2011 so you can now go in style. Competition for passengers, though, has made going indirect through hubs much

cheaper and you can save hundreds of pounds by waiting for changeovers in airports.

Indirect service is available through a host of airlines, including a partnership of British Airways/USAir, plus Continental, BMI, Virgin, American and United, although recently KLM Royal Dutch/NorthWest has consistently been having the lowest fares, with their London-Amsterdam-Minneapolis-Las Vegas route generally much cheaper than others, although you will spend at least 7 extra hours travelling.

BRITTIP
Always check around for best flight prices before booking, as there may be good deals on offer. Check prices online at comparison sites such as www.cheapflights.co.uk and www.travelsupermarket.com.

So when comparing prices for flights, the first thing you need to look for is whether you are getting a direct flight with Virgin or BA or whether you are going via a hub city – which you will do with any of the other carriers – and how much longer that will add on to your travel time. When weighing up cost differences, bear in mind that flying into a hub city tends to involve changing planes to a less comfortable domestic plane, where you will also be charged for your drinks.

The Luxor

The Rialto Bridge at the Venetian

If you do opt to use a non-direct service, also remember that some tickets may provide better stopovers than others, which will make arranging a decent multi-centre deal easier.

The next thing is to take into consideration any differences between flying at the weekend or midweek – there is normally a surcharge for Friday and Saturday flights.

Finally, always ensure the price you are quoted includes all airport taxes and non-negotiable fees – they can amount to a fair bit and you don't want those kinds of surprises!

Open-jaw flights

This means flying into one city and out from another. It's usually very simple to work out the cost – in most cases, you add the cost of flying to one destination to the cost of flying to the other, divide by 2 and add £1. Open-jaw flights means you don't have to backtrack and can save you quite a lot of money on a touring trip. Very few operators advertise open-jaw so you will have to ask whether it can be arranged or shop around.

Caesars Palace

13

Multi-centre packages

Fly into one city, look around, fly on to another, look around, fly on to another, look around and then fly home. This kind of package tends to be one of the most popular in the Las Vegas/California holiday market with the trio of Las Vegas, Los Angeles and San Francisco as the leading lights. It's a good idea if you don't want to drive, or don't have enough time to drive between all the main places you want to see, but it is a more expensive option, generally, than using your full quota of stopovers, or the open-jaw system.

Stopovers

The alternative to the above is to use the stopover system whereby you break your journey at various points. Most of the airlines offer this service, with the first stopover usually free and subsequent stopovers (up to a maximum of 3) being charged at around £70 a stop. Some airlines now offer 2 free stopovers.

BRITTIP
Do bear in mind that if you opt for the direct Virgin or British Airways flight there will be no stopovers to take advantage of.

If you want to use this system, you have to ensure that the route you are booking is the correct one for you as the first, free, stopover is usually limited to the 'gateway' city – the first place where the plane lands in the United States and where you'll go through American immigration. Watch this, as many of the American airlines use 'hub' cities as their gateway cities, such as Detroit or Minneapolis in the case of NorthWest Airlines, and you may not consider Delta's hub cities of Atlanta or Cincinatti to be as exciting a stopover point as New York or Los Angeles, for instance. As NorthWest is now allied with KLM, it may pay to route your trip via Amsterdam so that you get a more interesting 'gateway' city.

BRITTIP
To make best use of your free stopover, check your 'gateway' city is a reasonable destination, such as New York or Chicago, rather than Cincinatti or Atlanta!

Extra stops

These are similar to stopovers, except you'll pay an extra fee, usually £70. If you want to fly to more than one place not covered by your free stopover allowance, or if the place you want to go to isn't on the route, go for an air pass (see below).

BRITTIP
When booking flights, be sure to claim your free air miles or find out about the airline's loyalty scheme before you go, to be on track for free air travel or other benefits such as priority booking, lounge facilities and upgrades.

Child and youth discounts

Most airlines give child discounts (ages 2–11), usually at 50% off the published price during mid and low seasons and at 40% during peak season. The peak season does vary a little but a rough guide is July–August and the Christmas period around 15–27 December. Very few airlines offer youth discounts for 12- to 16-year-olds (a paltry 10%, which could be matched by shopping around the flight shops) but your best bets are tour operators who use United Airlines and Virgin.

Infant fares

The old days of tour operators publishing very cheap infant fares, but then adding on up to £70 of taxes are, thankfully, mostly gone, though some still continue this practice. Even BA charge £30 for infants with £70 tax – though £100 is a good fully inclusive price these days. Do check that the price you have been quoted includes all taxes.

Travelling with children

One point to stress is that many airline crews are being quite strict with child passengers. There have been numerous instances in recent years of children not being allowed to travel because of bad behaviour. It is quite a long trip, so make sure you bring enough things to keep your children merrily occupied.

Regional departures

More and more airlines are running routes directly from regional airports in the UK to Las Vegas and California, but in most cases you will have to pay a supplement to fly to London (from Newcastle or Glasgow, for example, this is around £60). However, United Vacations and US Airtours offer free connections from many regional UK airports and Kuoni offers free flights in connection with transatlantic BA and United Airlines flights.

Air passes

If you plan to visit more than the one city covered by your free stopover or, for whatever reason, are likely to make quite a few flights between certain destinations, an air pass is the way to go. But you must buy before you go as North American residents are not permitted to buy air passes, so they won't be available once you get to the US.

Smoking

Virgin and most of the American airlines have a total non-smoking policy on their transatlantic flights; in fact, smoking is banned by law on all flights in US airspace, as it is on transatlantic flights, so you won't be smoking on your journey.

Code share

Many airlines enter into alliances with each other to share routes, which can offer you more choice of routes and fares. It means that your flight is marketed by one airline, with the airline's flight number, but when you board you find the service is operated by a different airline. Some tour operators will inform you in advance, but they may not always know as these alliances are constantly changing. Be careful of this if you have a particular dislike for one airline or know that you definitely want to fly with a certain company. A Which? survey of airlines found that Virgin was among the most highly rated, yet it currently has a code-share alliance with Continental, who came pretty near the bottom of the same report.

Kids stay free

Many operators offer this as an extra, but it is standard policy at many hotels to allow children to stay free in the same room as an adult. If you're NOT being offered this as an option, go elsewhere!

Length and type of visit

Fly-drive and tailor-made tours

Tailor-made tours are useful as there are so many options it would be daft for any tour company to force people into taking one particular tour. Fly-drives are popular and often combine LA and/or Phoenix with Las Vegas. Chapter 15 The Grand Canyon and Surroundings gives a good insight into great places to visit within easy striking distance of Las Vegas.

Coach and Tauck tours

If you don't want to worry about car hire, driving and all the other arrangements you will need to make, and you don't mind a coach-load of people crowding into an attraction at the same time as you, then this could be the way to go. Coach tours are not necessarily all-inclusive, though, and may not include meals so that you have the option of choosing where to eat.

Tauck tours are the posher version and usually include everything. They are run by an American company, and you will be greeted and treated as an individual, while the tours themselves tend to be shorter so you have more time to relax and explore sights by yourself. In addition, you are put up in first-class hotels with character.

Extras

Grand Canyon flights

One of the added bonuses of visiting Las Vegas is that you can experience the amazing scenery of Arizona's Canyonlands, plus other natural wonders Bryce Canyon and Zion Park, without the long drive. A whole host of scenic flight operators work out of Las Vegas (details in Chapter 11 Outdoor Adventure), but if you want to make sure of your seat or tie up all loose ends before you go, many of the tour operators are offering these flights. Again, ask even if they're not advertised as they may be able to arrange a scenic flight for you.

BRITTIP
Don't try to see too much in too short a space of time – you don't want to spend your whole holiday driving and you may even want to leave time for an adventure tour or ranch holiday.

13

© MGW

EFX show

Show tickets

You can buy these in advance to ensure you get a seat, but don't overdo it as you may miss out on cheap deals locally.

Hotel vouchers

The 3 basic kinds of hotel vouchers are the Liberty and TourAmerica Hotel Passes and the North American Guestcheque. In all cases you buy vouchers at a certain price in advance that are valid for one night at a participating hotel – usually a chain hotel.

You can book the hotel in advance and the room will accommodate up to 4 people. It can be a very good way of planning your holiday budget and pre-paying as far as possible. But one major drawback is that if you buy more than you need, there is usually a charge for redeeming any unused vouchers. Often it amounts to the value of one voucher and in some cases it can be one voucher plus an administrative charge of £25.

◀🇬🇧▶ BRITTIP

If you are flexible and don't mind waiting until the last minute, you can save lots of money on show tickets. There are many half-price ticket stands along the Strip and Fremont Street and shows that aren't overbooked will sell tickets through these dealers at cut rates to put bums on seats. You can often get tickets for shows at 50% off by buying a ticket on the day of performance from one of these shops. But this won't do for hard-to-find tickets, so Cirque extravaganzas are rarely available this way.

Another drawback is that you do not benefit from any promotions that participating hotels and motels may run locally. And do bear in mind that these chain hotels don't have much character and some may even seem a little soulless.

Mandalay Bay

© MGW

Hard Rock Café is the place for bike enthusiasts

- Purchasing the vouchers does not automatically give you the right of accommodation, so it is always best to book as far in advance as possible, especially if you intend to travel in the peak seasons.
- If you intend to arrive after 4pm, you will need a credit card to guarantee your reservation. If it is a hotel/motel in a particularly busy area, such as one of the major sights that is not near a big town or city, I'd recommend you ask them to send or fax the confirmation of your reservation.
- There are often many hotels of the same chain in the same town, so it is best to make a note of the full address so you go to the right one!

BRITTIP

To save money on everything from attractions to shows to wedding packages visit www.lasvegas-nv.com/las-vegas-coupons.htm.

The American way

Motorbike hire

Okay, so you fancy yourself as a modern-day cowboy enjoying the ultimate touring experience of travelling along those wide-open roads on anything from a Harley Davidson Electra Glide to a Fat Boy or Road King. You can do this from LA and

Vegas at night

Las Vegas, but it'll be a lot more expensive than a car. The few operators that offer this include American Holidays and Jetlife.

Amtrak and Greyhound

Greyhound's Discovery Pass (www. greyhound.com) allows you to go where you want, when you want, travelling by coach day or night. It costs $249 for 7 days, $356 for 15 days, $456 for 30 days and a bargain $556 for 60 days. Greyhound will take you from Los Angeles to Las Vegas, for around $60 each way. The trip takes 5–7 hours. Amtrak rail passes start from $389 adults, $194.50 children (2–15 years) for 15 days; $579 adults, $289.50 children for 30 days and $749 adults, $374.50 children for 45 days. Amtrak covers all the major destinations and sights in California. Few tour operators advertise Amtrak travel, but others may arrange it for you if you ask. Take a look at www.amtrak.com.

BRITTIP
Hotel prices in America are for accommodation only and do not include breakfast.

Other things you need to know

The seasons

There are 4: low or off-peak, low shoulder, high shoulder and peak. Basically, the most expensive times to travel are Christmas, July, August, Easter and during the American bank holidays: President's Day (George Washington's birthday) – the third Monday in February; Memorial Day – the last Monday in May and the official start of the summer season; Independence Day – 4 July (in the middle of the high season); Labor Day – the first Monday in September and last holiday of summer; and Thanksgiving – always the fourth Thursday in November.

Low or off-peak season tends to be November, then January to the end of March excluding the bank holidays and Easter. May, June and October are low shoulder and all other times are high shoulder.

Best times to travel

Without a doubt, Monday to Thursday flights are cheaper, airports less crowded for departure and arrival, and hotels in Las Vegas, in particular, are far less busy. The very best days to arrive in Las Vegas are Tuesday to Thursday morning.

A–Z of specialist tour operators

www.visitlasvegas.co.uk

American Holidays

0844 9940377, www.americanholidays.com
A Belfast-based operator with some excellent fly-drive packages.

American Sky

0844 3329 392, www.americansky.co.uk
Tailor-made luxury holidays – everything from fly-drive to adventure tours.

Archers Direct

0844 573 4806, www.archersdirect.co.uk
Packages to California and Las Vegas that are very busy indeed.

Bon Voyage

0800 316 3012, www.bon-voyage.co.uk
One of the bigger operators, but surprisingly, offers very few extras.

British Airways Holidays

0844 493 0787,
www.britishairwaysholidays.com
Following the launch of the BA flight in October 2009, this operator now also offers first class.

Expedia

0330 123 1235, www.expedia.co.uk
Popular online travel agent offering cheap flights, holidays, hotels and car hire.

Flight Centre

0844 800 8660, www.flightcentre.co.uk
With branches around the country, Flight Centre is a travel agent offering all aspects of a holiday at 'unbeatable prices'.

Funway Holidays

0844 557 3333,
www.funwayholidays.co.uk
Funway Holidays has bonus offers available at certain hotels: free meals and breakfasts for children, free children's clubs, free nights, free shuttle bus service. Plus with every booking: fun books, packed with money-saving deals on sightseeing

trips, attractions, shows, shopping and dining; free reduced rate phone card; free Rand McNally Travel Planner and VIP shopping discount card in conjunction with the Shop America Alliance. Funway's parent company has its own car rental and sightseeing options that can be reserved via its website.

Jetset
0845 0257 757, www.jetsetholidays.co.uk
Established operator offering tailor-made packages with free accommodation for children at certain hotels, Greyhound Ameripass and Air Passes.

Just America
08448 806 802, www.justamerica.co.uk
Has the best value, easiest-to-use arrangements for car hire. Also specialises in a highly personalised, tailor-made service.

Kuoni
0844 488 0625 (local rate call), www.kuoni.co.uk
One of the UK's best long-haul tour operators, Kuoni can offer extra nights free, room upgrades, free sports, meals and drinks and food discounts. There are also special deals for honeymooners and those celebrating silver or golden wedding anniversaries (though you'll have to take a copy of your marriage certificate with you!).

Lastminute.com
0800 072 1795 (toll free), www.lastminute.com
Still one of the most popular sites for those who looking for a last-minute bargain – offers everything from holidays to discount deals in restaurants.

North America Travel Service
020 7499 7299, www.northamericatravelservice.co.uk
Specialises in fly-drives but offers very little information about flights and availability of open-jaw and stopovers. Also offers some free night deals at certain hotels, and has separate brochures for coach, Tauck and adventure tours.

Premier Holidays
08444 937 531, www.premierholidays.co.uk
Premier Plus offers include extra nights

free at certain hotels, free transport to attractions, breakfasts, upgrades for honeymooners, tea and coffee and use of health clubs.

Thomas Cook Signature
0844 879 8025, www.tcsignature.com
This is the only company offering chartered flights direct to Las Vegas.

Trailfinders
020 7368 1200, www.trailfinders.com
The UK's largest independent travel agent, this is renowned for tailor-made itineraries and a good selection of discounted flights. One of the few tour operators still offering Amtrak passes.

United Vacations
0844 449 0033, www.unitedvacations.co.uk
No regional departures, unless you fly via Amsterdam, but free connecting flights from regional airports during off-peak times. Books of vouchers for cheaper dining and attraction entrance fees.

Virgin Holidays
0844 573 0088, www.virginholidays.co.uk
Virgin offer free kids' funpacks on flights, free breakfasts, free meals for children and extras for honeymoons and anniversaries at certain hotels. Don't forget to join the frequent-flyer programme if you qualify. Plus $50 discount at Virgin Megastores and better deals for single parents.

> **BRITTIP**
> To cut holiday planning call costs in the UK go to www.saynoto0870.com to check if companies have a cheaper alternative local number.

Escorted tour companies

Goldmedal
01772 251133 or 0800 014 7777, www.goldmedal.co.uk
Efficient and friendly large tour operator offering escorted and tailor-made holidays around the world.

Jetsave
0844 415 9880, www.jetsave.com
Jetsave give generous discounts for groups

13

The Venetian

of 15 or more, plus free places depending on the number travelling. No supplements for single travellers if prepared to share a room.

Page & Moy

0844 567 6633, www.pageandmoy.co.uk
Consistently rated highly by repeat-visit travellers.

Travelsphere

0844 567 9966, www.travelsphere.co.uk
National Express pick-ups to point of departure for £15–20; savings on hotel airports and regional departures.

Airports

McCarran International airport

5757 Wayne Newton Boulevard, 702 261 5211, www.mccarran.com
Just 1ml/1.6km from the Strip and 5mls/8km from downtown, McCarran International airport is one of the slickest, most modern and easy-to-use airports in America. In a passenger survey of 36 major airports – which looked at speed of baggage delivery, ease of reaching gates, ground transport, cleanliness, quality of restaurants, attractiveness, ease of parking and following signs – McCarran came sixth.

The casino at Paris Las Vegas

The lobby at the Luxor

The airport was ranked the 15th busiest airport in the world in 2008 and deals with over 800 flights a day and around 44 million passengers a year. The latest runway – opened recently at a cost of $80.5m – has given the airport the capacity to handle 60 million passengers a year. It has direct flights to 62 US airports and 9 international destinations and more than 5,000 cars a day use the parking facilities. It has more than 50 shops and nearly 30 restaurant, lounges and snack bars and more than 1,300 slot machines to start your gambling on arrival!

Like many other aspects of life in Las Vegas, the airport has the very latest technology. There is no need for departing passengers with tickets to go to ticket counters inside the terminals – they can check in their luggage at the ticketing/departure kerb. It is the first airport in America to use Common Use Terminal Equipment (CUTE). This allows airlines to use any gate as needed, which creates more efficient scheduling of gates and faster boarding for passengers. In addition, all facilities are accessible to the disabled and amplified phone sets are dotted throughout the terminal.

Los Angeles International airport

1 World Way, Los Angeles, CA 90045, 310 646 5252, www.airport-la.com
If you are planning a touring holiday or perhaps an open-jaw flight, you may want to come into or out of Los Angeles airport, the fourth busiest airport in the world with all the best facilities.

Independent booking

There may be many different reasons why you want to organise all or part of your trip independently. Some people (jammy dodgers, I call them!) fly to San Francisco or Los Angeles to visit friends and then decide to go off to Las Vegas and other parts of California or Arizona on trips. But by nature we Brits are an independent lot and one of the most appealing ideas for us is just to fly to the west coast of America and hit the open road. Whatever the reason, the following tips will help you to save money in all the right places so you have more to spend on enjoying the sights and buying those essential pairs of trainers!

Hoover Dam

Flights

Competition in the transatlantic flight market is fierce, which is good news for us the customers. It also means that it makes sense to shop around for the best deal you can get. I recommend that you read the tour operators section (see pages 222–23) first, so you can acquaint yourself with all the terms and deals available.

Once you have worked out what your priorities are, then you have a pretty good chance of beating the prices quoted in the brochures by phoning round the transatlantic flight bookers that advertise in the weekend newspapers – The *Sunday Times* is particularly good. Remember, too, that the tour operators specialising in the North American market also have access to deals being offered by the airlines, so can often beat their own published prices! Low and low-shoulder seasons (see page 222) are particularly good for brilliant deals, such as flights to Las Vegas or Los Angeles for around £300 or even 5-night packages from £399.

You can even go for a totally no-frills, mega-cheap flight with 'consolidated' fares. These are the old-style bucket-shop fares which have now been legalised. The travel agent negotiates deals on your part, so you get very cheap fares and they're happy, too, as they earn better commission rates. The main restriction with these fares is that you can only use one airline and sometimes it may involve flying via that airline's 'home' country, for instance, somewhere in Europe. Also you won't get free or extra stopovers, but you can get around this by buying air passes for internal flights (see page 219). These air passes are not available in the States so you need to buy them before you go.

Hotels

If you're happy touring around Nevada, Arizona and California staying in the rather soulless chains such as Days Inn, Ramada and so on, you could take advantage of many of the special deals that are advertised in local papers and find a room on an ad hoc basis. Generally this is no problem at all in cities and towns, but it may be worth booking a few days in advance for rooms at major sightseeing destinations, such as the Grand Canyon or Furnace Creek in Death Valley. Even if you'd prefer accommodation with a little more character, you can still find cheap deals through agents once you are in America (see opposite).

Las Vegas is one of the weirdest cities on earth for hotel prices. In most cities around the world, hotels tend to be busy during the week and offer incentives to fill their rooms at weekends. With Las Vegas, the reverse is true. So many Americans from Salt Lake City to Phoenix and Los Angeles use Las Vegas as a weekend destination that occupancy rates are a staggering 96% on Friday and Saturday nights (even with around 150,000 rooms to fill).

On top of that, the city hosts huge conventions and special events such as rodeos and prize fights that tie up hotels, restaurants, transportation, showrooms and traffic for a week at a time. For these reasons, although Las Vegas hotels have their rack (standard) room rates, prices vary wildly above or below that rate according to how busy it is and how much they think they can get away with! Having said that, the price of accommodation is probably cheaper than anywhere else in North America and given the class and quality of facilities on offer, you can live like a king or queen very cheaply at top resorts in Las Vegas.

◀▶ BRITTIP
Some of the best internet sources for booking Las Vegas Hotel rooms are www.lasvegasadvisor.com and www.hotels.com.

Cheap deals: If you happen to be in southern California in December or January and pick up a local paper, you may see promotional offers direct from Las Vegas hotels in which the rooms are practically being given away. On the basis that an empty room is a liability, they will be happy to do this just to get your foot in the door – and their casino! The deals often include not only incredibly cheap rooms, but also free shows and meals.

In addition, the travel sections of the Sunday papers just about anywhere in the States – and at just about any time of year – are good for picking up fantastic deals to Las Vegas.

By far the best places to buy good Las Vegas deals from are southern California (Los Angeles and San Diego), Phoenix, Denver or Chicago. The package usually includes room, transport and possibly rental car and shows. Even if you've already got your transportation sorted, you can still take advantage of the special deals by asking for the 'land only' part of the deal.

In almost all cases, you will get a better deal on Las Vegas hotels once you are in the States (with the possible exception of Funway Holidays, which has access to so many hotels at great prices), especially if you are travelling at low or shoulder seasons.

BRITTIP

A smart way to find the cheapest hotel rate? First, check online or with booking companies for hotels at a good rate. Then check the hotel's website – they often have internet deals that are lower than anything else available.

In the unlikely event that you can't find deals for Las Vegas in the *LA Times* or other local papers, contact airline tour companies such as American Airlines Vacations (www.aavacations.com) and Delta Dream Vacations (www.deltavacations.com) and ask if they have special deals at particular hotels.

Other Las Vegas agents that will help not just with the price of a room, but actually get you in at the inn, so to speak, include Las Vegas Hotels and Casinos, toll free on 1 800 992 3059, www.lasvegashotels-online.com.

BRITTIP

Most hotels in America work on a per-room price basis, though there may be a maximum number of adults allowed. In addition, the room usually consists of a double or 2 double beds – the latter can't be guaranteed, but can be requested. In some cases there may be a small extra charge if there are more than 2 adults, but this won't be much.

No room at the inn: It is also worth using one of the agents mentioned above if you're having trouble booking yourself into one of the top resort-hotels as they are more likely to have rooms. Once agents are given blocks of rooms to sell, as far as the reservations manager is concerned, those rooms are not available.

One word of warning: If booking a hotel yourself, always guarantee your first night with a credit card (even if you do not plan to arrive late). If you do, then sending a deposit is not needed. If you are booking by phone, make sure you are given a reservation or confirmation number so you can verify the reservation. With a confirmation number, no written confirmation is needed. I have had reservations cancelled by a mistake at the

Wonder websites

Check out the following for up-to-date prices, the best deals and to book.
www.hotelanywhere.co.uk: A British-owned website providing discounts on hotels anywhere in the world.

www.quikbook.com: A service providing discounts on hotels from coast to coast in America. It promises there are no hidden cancellation or change penalties, and pre-payment is not required.

www.hotels.com: A great internet discount reservation service.

www.laterooms.com: A good place for last-minute travellers to find a room.

hotel, but with the confirmation number, the hotel cannot turn you away. They must find you a room of at least the same standard or better than the one you reserved and at the same rate.

BRITTIP

Most hotels will allow children under a certain age to sleep for free if sharing a room paid for by one or more adults.

The internet

Take care when making bookings via the internet. As with all independent travel arrangements, you do not have a tour operator to complain to (and, possibly, get money back from) if things go wrong. Stick to bigger hotels and car-hire firms if you are booking some time in advance as you are not covered if the company goes bust before you arrive for your holiday.

Probably the biggest drawback to internet bookings, though, is that there have been concerns about the security of sending credit card details over the internet. Larger sites will use a secure server to process credit cards, and they are generally safe. If they do not, or for any reason you feel uncomfortable about giving the site your information, you can take details from the internet and make arrangements via the phone, fax or by letter. However, you are unlikely to get any special internet promotional rates by doing it this way.

The specialists

So you've seen the bright lights of the big cities, taken in the amazing natural wonders of the West and had a flutter in

Las Vegas – what more could you want?
Well, the truth is that we Brits not only
have an independent spirit, we also have
romantic notions of the rugged outdoors
and cowboy lifestyle. The chances are that
if you've gone all the way to the West,
you'll want to add on a ranch holiday
or 'soft' adventure tour such as rafting,
cycling, climbing and motorbiking or
perhaps go horse riding, bird watching,
play a little golf, do the jazz thing or get a
real taste of California wines. The following
companies offer those services. See
Chapter 11, Outdoor Adventure for further
companies and suggestions.

Adventure

Exodus: 020 8772 3936,
www.exodus.co.uk

Outlaw Trails: 0794 111 9785,
www.outlawtrails.com

Ranch America: 020 7666 1217,
www.wandotravel.com

Trailfinders: 020 7368 1200,
www.trailfinders.com

Trek America: 0844 576 1400,
www.trekamerica.com

Bird watching

Ornitholidays: 01794 519445,
www.ornitholidays.co.uk

Golf

The American Golf Holiday: 023 8046
5885, www.americangolfholiday.com

Destinations Golf & Leisure: 1-800 441
9329 or 212 757 5797 (US),
www.destinations-golf.com

Ranching

American Round-Up: 01798 865946,
www.americanroundup.com

Kuoni: 0844 488 0351, www.kuoni.co.uk

Ranch America: 020 7666 1217,
www.wandotravel.com

United Vacations: 0844 499 0033,
www.unitedvacations.co.uk

Virgin: 0844 573 0088,
www.virginholidays.co.uk

Wine

Arblaster and Clarke: 01730 263111,
www.winetours.co.uk

Winetrails: 01306 712111,
www.winetrails.co.uk

Cottonwood Ranch

How to get out and about on the open road

I t's the grand dream, isn't it – driving along the American highway, the only car on a stretch of road that goes on for so long you only lose it on the horizon, music blasting, shades on and not a care in the world? Believe me, it truly is an experience not to be missed. You cannot help but get a sense of being so much closer to nature when all around you is space, space, space on an unbelievable scale.

And while (thanks to the sheer size of America) you might on occasion feel as if you are driving through great swathes of nothingness, at least the skies are likely to provide some spectacular sights of their own, from multi-coloured sunsets to heavenly blue vistas and massive rainfalls that you can see from miles away. I once spent a whole day driving on a straight open road surrounded by Arizona desert landscape, with blue skies each side and a monumentally large downpour straight ahead – and not a drop fell on me until the night (when my tent almost got washed away!), which just gives you a feel for how vast the country is.

I tell you all this to help convey the scale of what you will encounter on a touring trip around the west of America, so be warned: unless you want to spend your entire time driving during your 2 weeks, don't try to tackle too much all in one hit.

The other point is that while you may have some reservations about your ability to drive on the wrong side of the road in a foreign country, it really is not a problem in America. The reality is that driving in America is both easier than driving in Britain and a great deal more fun, too. The whole system of getting on and off freeways and turning left and right is so much easier when driving on the right-hand side of the road.

Car rental

Now you must decide what type of car to hire and who to hire it from. Most of the tour operators have special deals going with Alamo, though one or two use Avis, Budget or Dollar. The prices have become pretty standardised since 2000, but the best deal can be found through the tour

operator Just America (see page 223), which offers many extras included in the price – and at a lower rate than any other operator.

Costs

Many of the tour operators give the price of hiring the car separately from what it will actually cost you to walk away from the rental desk with your car keys, though others do now show all-inclusive prices. This makes sense as there are charges you must pay in addition to the car hire fees: extended protection, collision damage waiver (CDW), airport user fee, local/state surcharges and taxes. Additional items are priced per item and are exclusive of local taxes and paid locally if selected. These include under-age driver fees and child/ infant seat, GPS and additional driver. In any case, when checking the price of hiring a car, make sure you look at the right area and right dates, as prices vary from place to place. Florida and California are cheaper than Western USA prices, which makes a big difference. Some rental companies consider Arizona and Nevada to be part of a region including California, while others consider them separate, and thus a higher rate.

✈ BRITTIP

Pre-renting can help you avoid hard-sell tactics by car hire staff wanting you to take out personal insurance. If you have extended protection and travel insurance (see Chapter 16) you'll be well covered.

Additional driver fees: This is rarely required by most car hire chains, but when it is, it is around $10 per driver per day.

Airport user fee: This will cost you up to 14% of the total charge.

Cash deposit: Very few places will even

Accidents and emergencies

If you have even a minor accident, the police must be contacted before the cars can be moved. The car-hire firm will also expect a full police report for the insurance paperwork. In the case of a breakdown, there should be an emergency number for the hire company among the paperwork they gave you. Always have your driving licence with you (remember an international driving licence is not valid) and your car-hire agreement forms in case you are stopped by the police at any time. If you are pulled over, keep your hands on the wheel and always be polite. If they find out you're British you might just get away with a ticking off for a minor offence (but not for speeding at 95mph/153kph!).

accept a cash deposit, much preferring a credit card to act as deposit. For places that do take cash deposits, be ready for delays as the counterperson has to go through rarely used forms. The deposit tends to be around $100 per week. In addition, you will often be asked to provide an additional credit card in the driver's name to cover any additional charges you may incur. If you want to leave a cash deposit, you'll be asked to show 2 forms of identification, for instance passport, driving licence or other government-issued photo card.

Child seat and deposit: Children up to the age of 5 must, by law, travel in a child seat in America, and you should book these in advance. The cost will be $5–8 per day plus $50 deposit (on a credit card).

Collision damage waiver (CDW): At $20.99 per day, this covers you for $10,000–50,000 worth of damage to your hire car regardless of the cause, plus theft or loss.

Environmental tax: A further $2 per day if car rental is arranged in the UK.

Extended protection: Many Americans do not have any or enough insurance and if they caused the accident, you would have no one to sue for damage to your property or for personal injury (the car is covered by CDW, see above). This type of insurance covers all liabilities and costs about $8–14 per day.

One-way drop-off fees: Most companies charge if you want to pick up your car in one location and drop it off in another, which can easily add $100–300 on to your rental costs. The exceptions tend to be

if you pick up and drop off in the same city, though always check.

Rental surcharges: During peak periods, you will be charged around a further £23 per week or £5 per day for your car rental. The peak seasons tend to be 15 July–31 August and 20–27 December.

State/local surcharges and taxes: 5–15% of the total cost depending on the exact location of rental and the rental company – some will include this in the overall fee.

Under-age driver fees: All the UK deals are for drivers with a minimum age of 25 and named drivers aged 21–25 will have to pay a further $20–25 per day.

Comprehensive Alamo rentals: The all-inclusive packages and comprehensive insurance cover schemes you take out in advance in the UK tend to cost £23–46 a day in Las Vegas/Nevada. They include extended protection, CDW, airport user fee and state/local surcharges and taxes, and generally work out cheaper than paying for all the above on arrival (which also saves a lot of time when you go to collect your car).

Documents and systems

Documents: You will need a UK driving licence or a driving licence (both paper and card) from your country of residence. An international driving licence is not acceptable.

Limits: You will not be allowed to drive your hire car in Mexico or off-road in America. Many Las Vegas car hire providers will further restrict your driving to Nevada, Arizona and California only.

Hiring cars locally: You may only wish to hire a car for a few days while you are on holiday, and this can easily be arranged when you arrive. You'll find phone numbers for all the major car-hire firms in a local phone directory, but remember that the prices they quote you will not include all the extras outlined above, so be sure to include those when you do your calculations. (For names and contact numbers of car-hire companies see page 15.)

Pre-rental: Some tour operators are now offering you the chance to fill out all the necessary paperwork before you leave home so when you arrive you can just pick up your car keys and go. Not only does this save you time, but it also means you can bypass efforts by the counter staff at American car-hire firms to give you the upgrade hard sell! In any case, you will generally get a better deal for bigger cars if you arrange this in advance. The possible exception is in Las Vegas where they

Six steps to safe driving

Know your route: Before leaving home, check websites for route planning and general advice. When you arrive to collect your rental vehicle, ask at the counter for specific directions to your destination, including motorway entrance and exit numbers.

Know your car: Familiarise yourself with your car before leaving the rental branch and make sure you know where everything is, including headlights, hazard lights, horn, door locks, automatic window controls and the spare tyre. Also ensure that you have the number for Roadside Assistance.

See the light: Should you become lost, suspect you have a problem with your vehicle or another motorist gestures to suggest you have a problem, drive to the nearest well lit, populated, public place such as a service station or restaurant. If you need to leave your vehicle – even briefly – be sure to lock it and take the keys with you.

Locked down and rolled up!: Keep your car doors locked, even while driving. Always be cautious when windows are open – particularly in residential areas where traffic is moving slowly or stationary – and keep items such as purses, wallets, cases and valuables hidden from plain view in the glove compartment or in the boot. Always remember to close windows fully before leaving your vehicle.

No free rides: No matter how innocent or needy they may appear, hitchhikers can mean bad news. Avoid them.

Ready, check, go!: Park in well lit areas and make sure you have your keys ready in your hand when approaching your vehicle. Re-lock your car doors once in the car. Always fasten your seat belt.

---

practically give away upgrades on a quiet week. But be warned, if you arrive in Las Vegas when the city is packed, it may be difficult to find the car of your choice.

Choosing the right car

Sorry, but size *is* an issue! If your flight includes car rental, it will normally be for a small, economy-size car, which probably won't be much good for a car even if there are only 2 of you. The biggest problem is the boot size – the boots of all American cars are much smaller than their European equivalents and you do have to take into account that you will need to accommodate your luggage.

This is what the different price brands will provide:

- **Economy:** Usually a Chevrolet Aveo or similar, equivalent to the UK's Vauxhall Corsa. Considered big enough for 2 adults.

- **Compact:** Usually a Chevrolet Cobalt or similar, equivalent to a UK Vauxhall Astra. Considered big enough for 3 adults.

- **Intermediate:** Usually a Pontiac G6, equivalent to the UK's Vauxhall Vectra. Considered big enough for 4 adults.

- **Full size:** Usually a Pontiac Grand Prix or similar, equivalent to the UK's Vauxhall Omega. Large enough for 4 adults.

- **Convertible:** Usually a Chrysler Sebring or similar, equivalent to the UK's Vauxhall Astra Convertible. Large enough for 3 adults.

- **Luxury van:** Usually a Cadillac Escalade or similar, equivalent to the UK's VW Sharan. Large enough for 7 people.

- **SUV (sport utility vehicle):** Usually a Chevy Trailblazer or similar, no UK equivalent. Large enough for 5 people.

◀▶ BRITTIP

Most accidents that Brits are involved in tend to take place on left turns, so take extra care here. Remember, too, there is no amber light from red to green, but there is one from green to red.

Automatics: All American hire cars will be automatics, unless you specifically get a high-performance car like a Maserati at a speciality car hire. Some things may confuse you at first if you are not familiar with automatics, for example you won't be able to drive until you put the car into D for drive and you probably won't be able to take the keys out of the ignition until you have put the car into P for park. D1 and D2 are extra gears, which you only need to use when going up or down very steep hills.

14

Most American cars have cruise control, which lets you set the speed at which you want to travel and then take your foot off the gas pedal (the accelerator). There are usually 2 buttons, either on the face of the steering wheel or on the switch that controls the car lights, for cruise control, one to switch it on and the other to set your speed. You take off cruise control by pressing the on button again or by simply accelerating or braking.

◀▶ **BRITTIP** ————————

During the summer in the desert, don't immediately enter your car. The temperature can be as high as 82°C/180°F. First open it and let the hot air escape. Better yet, reach in to turn on the motor and the fan or air conditioner (easy enough to do in an automatic, where there is no clutch to bother with and no need to be seated). Let the hot air blow out of the car before getting in.

Air conditioning: In the California/Nevada/Arizona area it would be rare for a car not to have air conditioning but you must keep the windows closed to make it work.

Fuel/gas: You've hit the highway and need to fill up, but just bear in mind that for the most part interstates (the main roads) do not have gas stations – you will have to get off, though they are not usually too far away. Practically all gas stations are self service.

On the road

Rules and regulations

Here are a few things you should know.

Alcohol limits: The legal limit for blood alcohol in America is lower than in Britain and the police are very hot on drink-drivers (drunk-drivers in American parlance). Generally a single drink can put you at or over the limit if you are a smaller person! It is also illegal to carry open containers of alcohol in the car itself.

Parking: It is illegal to park within 10ft/3m of a fire hydrant or a lowered kerb and you should never stop in front of a yellow-painted kerb – they are for emergency vehicles and you will get towed away! Never park on a kerb either.

School zone: Flashing orange lights suspended over the road indicate a school zone ahead, so go slowly.

School buses: These cannot be overtaken in either direction while they are unloading and have their hazard lights flashing.

Seat belts: These are compulsory for all passengers. Babies and small children are required to be secured in child safety seats (available through most car-hire agencies).

Signposts and junctions: One of the most confusing aspects of driving around towns in America is the way they hang up road names underneath the traffic lights at every junction. The road name given is not for the road you are actually on, but the one you are crossing. Another thing to be wary of is that there is very little advance notice of junctions, and road names can be hard to read as you approach them, especially at night. So keep your speed down if you think you are close to your turn-off so you can get into the right lane. If you do miss your turning, don't panic, as nearly all roads in American towns are arranged in a simple grid system so it will be relatively easy to work your way back.

Sometimes you will meet a crossroads where there is no obvious right of way. This is a '4-way stop' and the way it works is that priority goes in order of arrival. When it is your turn, pull out slowly. If 2 come together at the same time, the one on the farthest 'right' has priority. If 2 cars stop facing each other, the one going straight has priority over any car turning.

At red lights, it is possible to turn right providing there is no traffic coming from the left and no pedestrian is crossing, unless specified by a sign saying 'No turn on red'. A green arrow gives you the right of way when turning left, but when it is a solid green light, you must give way to traffic coming from the other direction.

Speed: No speeding, please! The speed limits on the main Interstates are well signposted and tend to be 55–70mph/86–113kph and up to 75mph/121kph on some lonely stretches in Nevada and Arizona – while the MINIMUM allowed is 40mph/64kph.

Be warned, the Americans take their speed limits very seriously. Most traffic police won't bother you if you are only 5–8mph/8–13kph over the posted limit, but 10mph/16kph or more and you are in danger of a fairly pricey fine. Go 20mph/32kph or more over the limit and you risk astronomical fines ($300 or more); 30mph/48kph over the limit and you might possibly enjoy a short term in gaol.

U-turns: These are forbidden in built-up areas and where a solid line runs down the middle of the road.

THE GRAND CANYON AND SURROUNDINGS

Must-see sights within easy reach of Sin City

Arizona and the Canyonlands

In California it's quite often the people and urban developments that make the state a truly remarkable experience. In Arizona it is the history and natural wonders that make it one of the most beautiful and thrilling of all of America's 50 states. This is the land of cowboys and Native Americans, of gold-mining and ghost towns, of movie-making and centuries-old history and of one of the 7 great natural wonders of the world: the Grand Canyon.

Without a shadow of a doubt it has some of the most spectacular landscapes ever crowded into such a compact area. On top of the Grand Canyon, there is the Petrified Forest, Walnut Canyon, Sunset Crater and Montezuma's Castle … and that's just for starters.

Arizona is a massive state, encompassing the cities of Phoenix (its capital) and Tucson. Travelling to these destinations would require a big investment in time. Getting to the Grand Canyon and the Canyonlands, however, is feasible within a matter of hours from Las Vegas.

In this chapter

Going native

Arizona has the largest Native American population and more land devoted to reservations than any other state. In addition, the prehistoric Native American tribes, such as the Hohokam of southern Arizona, the Sinagua of the central, and the cliff-dwelling Anasazi (ancient ones) of northern Arizona provide some extremely old historical ruins (rare in America). These are a monument to their high degree of sophistication in dry farming, water management, plus their far-flung trade routes and jewellery, pottery and textile-making.

Verde Valley

And let us not forget, of course, that Arizona was the birthplace of possibly the best known Native American of them all, Geronimo. The Apache warrior engaged nearly three-quarters of America's military ground troops in his pursuit after the Civil War and up to 1886 when he surrendered – having never been captured – at Skeleton Canyon in Southern Arizona!

Ranching

Peeples Valley and Yarnell: On the cowboy front, even today mining and ranching are the most important industries of the small communities of Peeples Valley and Yarnell on Route 89 north of Wickenburg. The lush grasslands are home to a thriving cattle industry that has cowboys still riding the plains. The whole area down to Wickenburg is known as the Dude Ranch Capital of the World because of all the ranches that allow you to visit and participate in the activities.

Prescott: The old capital of Arizona, surrounded by Prescott National Forest, the pine-covered Bradshaw Mountains and the Yavapai Indian Reservation, is known for its boulder-strewn granite dells and grasslands. Stately Victorian homes are a reminder of its heyday, while the rowdier side of frontier life is remembered on Whiskey Row, where 26 saloons once attracted cowboys from far and wide. The annual Frontier Days celebration is held here at the beginning of July, complete with fireworks, dancing, rodeo performances, a parade and cowboy golf tournament.

Jerome: Further north on State Route 89A is Jerome, which sprang up during the gold-mining boom on Cleopatra Hill overlooking the Verde Valley. Once the ore diminished, Jerome became known as America's largest ghost city and is now home to a colony of artists and visitors who walk the steep, winding streets to see the historic buildings and browse through shops and boutiques.

The best historic sites are the town's 'travelling jail', which has slid downhill 225ft/69m since a dynamite explosion dislodged it from its foundations during the 1920s, and Jerome State Historic Park, once the mansion of mining developer 'Rawhide' Jimmy Douglas.

Campe Verde: This is to the south-east (along Route 260), and was established in 1864 as a cavalry outpost to protect Verde River settlers from Indian raids. The old fort still stands in the middle of the town.

Montezuma Castle National Monument: Just north, along Interstate 17, are these well-preserved cliff dwellings, a 5-storey, 20-room dwelling built in and under a cliff overlooking Beaver Creek. It was misnamed by early settlers who thought it had been inhabited by Aztecs, but it was actually built by Sinagua Indians in the 12th and 13th centuries.

Clarkdale: Further north is Clarkdale, where you can see the 100-room pueblo that housed 250 people from the 13th century until they mysteriously disappeared some time in the 15th century. Clarkdale is home to the scenic Verde Canyon Railroad, a renovated New York Metro Line train that transports passengers along a 40ml/64km route through cottonwood forests and the base of a desert mesa (table). En route you'll see bald eagles, great blue herons, deer and javelina.

Flagstaff: This is just a little further north and considered to be the gateway to the Grand Canyon.

The Grand Canyon

Grand Canyon National Park, PO Box 129, Grand Canyon, AZ 86023, 928-638 7888, www.nps.gov/grca
Open: The park is open 24 hours a day. National Geographic Visitor Center, 928 638 2468, www.explorethecanyon.com in Canyon View Information Plaza open 8am–5pm.
Admission: $25 per vehicle, $12 per person arriving by other means. The speediest way to pay is by credit card at pay stations at the South and East entrances or at the Visitor Center. Admission is for 7 days but does not cover fees for use of overnight campsites, which are extra. Under-15s free. Free planning guides are available in advance from the National Park Service. Download a Trip Planner, North and South Rim guides, Park Maps or Accessibility Guide.

◀╢▶ BRITTIP

To avoid the crowds (5 million people visit each year) and searing heat, go in March, April, September or October either before 10am or after 2pm.

Two billion years in the making, the majestic spectacle stands from between 4,500ft/1,370m and 5,700ft/1,740m high and twists for an amazing 277mls/446km with an average width of 10mls/16km. To geologists, it is like an open book, as they can immediately see

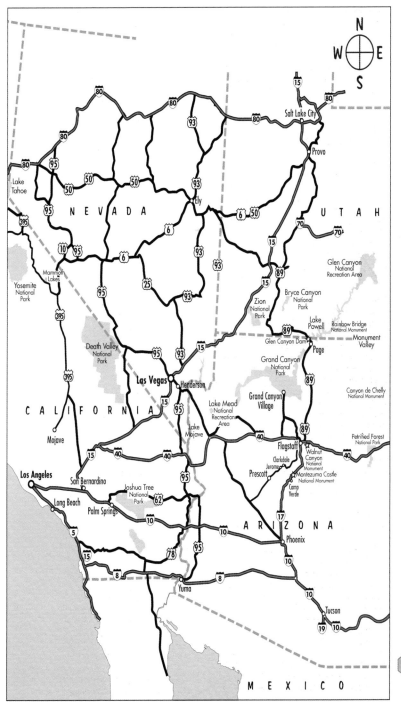

that the bottom layer is 2 billion years old while the top is a mere 200 million years old, with the geological ages in between represented in the Canyon's colourful stony strata.

Viewing it from one of the many vantage points on the South Rim, you will see the myriad rock formations change colour according to the sun's position throughout the day. The best times to see it (and the quietest) are at sunrise or sunset. You can also walk out over the Canyon on the Skywalk – a $30 million dollar horseshoe-shaped glass bridge suspended over the West Rim at Eagle Point. It juts out 230ft/70m at 4,000ft/1,219m above the canyon floor, but in some ways you can only get a feel for its awesome, breathtaking hugeness by descending into its depths by mule. If you don't have the 1–2 days to spare needed for the trip, you can stop at the IMAX theatre at Tusayan and watch the *Grand Canyon –The Hidden Secrets* film.

Seeing the Grand Canyon

More than 5 million people a year flock to the South Rim to view the Grand Canyon. Closer to the Colorado River than the North Rim, it also provides better views of the canyon.

You can either drive straight to the Grand Canyon Village or head for the Canyon View Information Plaza and the Visitor Center and bookstore – where you can pick up a copy of the park's newspaper for up-to-the-minute information on facilities, activities and transportation options, and a map, if you haven't downloaded them.

From here you can walk to Mather Point, which gives wonderful views of the Canyon, before making use of the free shuttle service to the Grand Canyon Village for further views.

The Grand Canyon

The film: The IMAX theatre, 928 638 2468, www.explorethecanyon.com, at the south entrance at Highway 64/US 180, Tusayan has shows at half past the hour 1 Mar–31 Oct 8.30am–8.30pm, 1 Nov–28 Feb 10.30am–6.30pm, daily, on a 70ft/21m screen with 6-track stereo sound. Adults $12.50, 5–10 $9.50, under-6s free. For 25% discount, buy online.

Grand Canyon Skywalk: 702 220 8372, www.grandcanyonskywalk.com Adults $29.95, children (3–11) $22.46, seniors $26.96, plus 7% tribal tax. Advance booking reduces wait times.

By train: The Grand Canyon Railway, 800 THE TRAIN or 928 773 1976 x2256, www.thetrain.com, runs a 1920s Harriman coach steam train from Williams to the South Rim, travelling through 65mls/105km of beautiful countryside, complete with an authentic style western shoot out.

By bus: Arizona Shuttle (800 888 2749 or 928 226 8060, www.arizonashuttle. com) operates between Flagstaff and Williams/Grand Canyon Village which costs $38 per person return trip. Guided coach tours are run by Xanterra Parks and Resorts (888 297 2757 or 303 297 2757, www.grandcanyonlodges.com) and include the Hermit's Rest Tour along the West Rim ($26), Desert View Tour travelling East ($45), Sunrise or Sunset Tour ($20.50) or a Combination Tour ($58) which can be taken in any order or on different days. Children 16 and under go free. The Trans-Canyon shuttle (928 638 2820, www. trans-canyonshuttle.com) is the only public transport between the South and North Rim. It runs once a day each way mid May–mid October, taking 4.5 hours and costing $80 per person one way, $150 round trip.

By mule: Xanterra Parks and Resorts (888 297 2757 or 303 297 2757, www. grandcanyonlodges.com) offer day-long and overnight mule trips from the South Rim year round – but these book up months in advance so book early. A 2.5 hour Abyss Overlook Mule Ride on the South Rim offered mid-May–mid-October costs $120.65 per person and an overnight ride to Phantom Ranch $497.89 for singles, $879.43 for 2 people and $394.46 each additional person.

On foot: Hiking into the canyon is one of the best ways to see it and rim trail hikes on both the South and North Rim, often on paved paths, offer spectacular views. Alternatively, if you are fit and healthy, you can hike down into the canyon. The free Hiker's Express shuttle from the Grand Canyon Visitor Center to the North Kaibab

A helicopter over the Grand Canyon

trailhead is available 3 times daily in the morning. As over 250 people are rescued from the canyon each year, it's a good idea to download a hike-smart podcast from www.nps.gov/grca or opt for one of the excellent ranger-led hikes on both rims (South Rim daily; North Rim, seasonally mid-May–mid October), a naturalist excursion from the National Geographic Visitor Center or one of 4 day hikes with Angel's Gate Tours (800 957 4557, www. angelsgatetours.com) for $159 adults, $139 children (aged 8–16).

Horseback rides: With the Apache Stables in Tusayan, adjacent to the park. Write to PO Box 158, Grand Canyon, AZ 86023, www.apachestables.com or call 928 638 2891. Rides for adults and children include 1-hour rail rides through the pines ($48.50) to evening rides ending up round the campfire ($58.50).

Jeep tours: Head off into the back roads in an open-air safari vehicle to learn about cowboys, early settlers, native wildlife and local legend with Grand Canyon Outback Jeep Tours, 800 320 5337 or 928 638 5337, www.grandcanyonjeeptours.com Choose from the Grand Sunset Tour, Grand Canyon Safari and Rim Walk departing at 9.30am (both tours adults $64, children 11 and under $49), Indian Paintings Tour at 3pm (adult $45, children $35) or one of 2 Deluxe Combo Tours, a 4.5-hour trip costing $104 for adults, $84 for children. You can even combine a jeep trip with a scenic helicopter flight (adults $232, children $212). Newer operator, Pink Jeep Tours, 888 900 4480 or 702 895 6777,

www.pinkjeep.com, also offer trips in the Grand Canyon.

Rafting the Colorado: Explore Indian ruins, discover waterfalls, spot wildlife, take side hikes or ride rapids on a rafting trip down the mighty Colorado. Trips include half-day floating excursions, motor boat trips and 18-day expeditions on rowing boats. Most trips begin at Lee's Ferry at the eastern end of the Canyon. You need to book at least 6 months in advance and companies include:

- **Arizona Raft Adventures:** 4050 East Huntington Drive, Flagstaff, AZ 86004, 800 786 7238/RAFT, www.azraft.com
- **Arizona River Runners:** PO Box 47788, Phoenix, AZ 85068, 800 477 7238, www.raftarizona.com
- **Canyon Explorations Expeditions:** PO Box 310, Flagstaff, AZ 86002, 800 654 0723 or 928 774 4559, www.canyonexplorations.com
- **Canyoneers:** PO Box 2997, Flagstaff, AZ 86003, 800 525 0924 or 928 526 0924, www.canyoneers.com
- **Grand Canyon Whitewater:** 916 Vista, PO Box 1300, Page, AZ 86040, 800 343 3121 or 928 645 8866, www.grandcanyonwhitewater.com
- **Hualapai Tribal River Runners:** 16500 East Route 66, Peach Springs, AZ 86434, 888 868 9378 or 928 769 2636, www.grandcanyonwest.com/rafting.php
- **Outdoors Unlimited:** 6900 Townsend Winona Road, Flagstaff, AZ 86004, 800 637 7238/RAFT or 928 526 4511, www.outdoorsunlimited.com

15

Watch the birdies!

You've seen them in cartoons, now you can see the birds of the Arizona deserts and mountains in real life. The south-eastern corner of the state is the most popular bird-watching area of North America and more than 400 species can be found here from migratory water fowl to native birds, nesting birds, grassland birds and mountain birds.

You can watch greater roadrunners chase lizards across the desert floors, black-chinned hummingbirds buzz around like bees, acorn woodpeckers drill holes in roadside telegraph poles and painted redstarts flit in the dappled light of oak woods with specialists such as **The Travelling Naturalist** (01305 267994, www.naturalist.co.uk) or **Sunbird** (01767 262522, www.sunbirdtours.co.uk). The Travelling Naturalist organises its 15-day trip in spring when the desert is comfortably cool and many birds are nesting while others are starting to migrate to their breeding grounds in the north. Sunbird's 2-week trip runs in September. Both offer spectacular views of the Grand Canyon.

Another favoured time of the year for birders to visit is August when the city of Sierra Vista has a birding festival complete with bat stalks and owl prowls.

- **Wilderness River Adventures:** PO Box 717, Page, AZ 86040, 0800 992 8022 or 928 645 3296, www.riveradventures.com

  Flightseeing: Flights by small aircraft or helicopter. Companies include:
- **Grand Canyon Airlines:** PO Box 3028, Grand Canyon, Arizona 86023, 866 235 9422 or 928 638 2359, www.grandcanyonairlines.com
- **Maverick Helicopters:** 6075 Las Vegas Boulevard South, Las Vegas, NV 89119, 888 261 4414 or 702 261 0007, www.maverickhelicopter.com
- **Heli USA Airways:** 245 E Tropicana Avenue, Suite 120, Las Vegas, AZ 89109. 01462 488227 (UK) or 702 736 8787 (Las Vegas), www.heliusa.com

◀██▶ BRITTIP

The canyon is 10mls/16km across, but the 1.6-ml/2.6-km deep Grand Canyon separates the North and South Rim, so make sure you allow for the 5 hours it takes to drive the 215 miles/346km from one side to the other.

- **Scenic Airlines:** 3900 Paradise Road, Suite 185, Las Vegas, NV 89169, 866 235 9422 or 702 638 3300, www.scenic.com
- **Papillon Grand Canyon Helicopters:** PO Box 455, Grand Canyon, AZ 86023, 928 638 2419. 0800 404 9767 (UK toll free) or 702 736 7243 (Las Vegas), www.papillon.com

  Lodging: For full and up-to-date details of lodges near the rim, contact Xanterra Parks & Resorts, 303 600 3400, www.xanterra.com.

  Staying on the floor of the Canyon: Phantom Ranch, the only place to stay

below the rim, offers separate-sex 10-bunk dorms with toilet and shower, plus 11 private rustic cabins. Book through Xanterra Parks & Resorts, 303 600 3400, www.xanterra.com.

North Rim

Through Jacob Lake on Highway 67, on the Utah side of the park, the North Rim is a lot quieter than the South Rim. It only receives 10% of the visitors to the Canyon and is open seasonally, from mid-May–mid-October. It is home to Canyon Trail Rides (435 679 8665, www.canyonrides.com), which runs 1-hour forest rides, half-day trips from the North Rim into the Canyon and full-day trips to Roaring Springs where you can frolic in the natural pools. Here you can stay at the Grand Canyon Lodge late May–mid-October. For reservations, contact Xanterra Parks & Resorts, 303 600 3400, www.xanterra.com. The Kaibab Lodge, 5mls/8km north of the park, is also open mid-May–early November. For reservations 928 638 2389, www.kaibablodge.com.

Howdy pardner!

Arizona is real cowboy country and if there is one way to see the stunning scenery, wide-open expanses and narrow gorges, it is on the back of a horse – as a cowboy. Nowadays, it is very easy to be a real 'city slicker' as a whole host of ranching options are available, depending on your riding abilities and need for luxury items, such as a bed. The types of ranches are:

  Guest ranch: This is where you live as a 'guest' of the ranch owners in an environment that is designed to entertain you while providing plenty of horse-riding opportunities and Western activities. It's the soft option that will give you a feel for the way of life but no hands-on experience.

Dude ranch: Holiday-based rather than the seriously business-like working ranches, you'll do a lot of riding, while Western activities from Wild West shows to rodeo visits, square dances, barbecues and sports provide plenty of fun.

Resort ranch: These offer the Western experience but also have golf, tennis and ballooning, and the whole environment is much more luxurious than dude or working ranches.

Working ranch: Still in business to raise livestock and grow crops, these are home to the real cowboys. Depending on the time of year and the work that is necessary on the ranch, you'll be able to learn to drive cattle, brand and rope steers, eat around a camp fire and sleep under the stars. Round-ups take place in spring and autumn when the ranchers prepare their cattle to be moved to summer and winter ranges. It's a high-activity time at the ranches so the hours are long and the work is physically demanding. On the cattle drives you are likely to travel 6–12mls/10–19km a day, but ride at least 3 times as far as you bring in strays from the flanks. Evenings spent around the campfire hark back to bygone days in what is a truly wonderful, friendship-forming experience. Horse drives are a much faster version as the horses like to travel at speed. These are only for very seasoned riders with lots of cross-country experience, but the long-distance gallops are a real thrill. The following UK specialist tour companies offer ranching holidays:

- **American Round-Up:** 01798 865946, www.americanroundup.com. Offers the full range.
- **Equitour:** 0800 043 7942, www.equitour.co.uk. This specialist riding holiday operator is excellent for working ranches all over America's West and even provides riding clinics to bring you up to speed!
- **Western & Oriental:** 020 7666 1217, www.wandotravel.com/what/ranch/. Also offers a range of holidays.

Trail rides with Outlaw Trails: 0794 111 9785, www.outlawtrails.com. For horse-riding vacations with a difference try Outlaw Trails, which runs specially tailored, fully researched trips to the old trails used by outlaws determined to avoid the long arm of the law. Closest to Arizona is the Robbers Roost trail in Utah on which you'll see the way stations and trail used by the Wild Bunch of Butch Cassidy and the Sundance Kid, the Hole in the Wall Gang and Robbers Roost Gang. Robbers Roost land is sprawled across 320mls2/830km2 of high desert and you'll ride through pinyon, sage and cedar flats, a maze of rock gorges and canyons, plus long mesas, arches, pinnacles and high-shouldered buttes. If you attempt any of the 'climbs' used by the outlaws, you'll get a pretty good idea of what brilliant horsemen they were! The seasons and numbers are limited because of the weather and nature of the trips, but the trails are perfect for lovers of the historical West who want a great big chunk of adventure.

Other Arizona marvels

Once you've been there, done that at the Grand Canyon, don't miss out on the many other natural and historical wonders Arizona has to offer.

Sunset Crater: 928 526 0502, www.nps.gov/sucr. Leave the South Rim on Highway 64 and take the 89 south to Sunset Crater Volcano National Monument. An active volcano more than 900 years ago, it now rises to 1,000ft/305m and rangers here offer geology, seismology and other tours while the Visitor Center can provide you with maps for self-guided trails.

Walnut Canyon: 928 526 3367, www.nps.gov/waca. Further south, join the Interstate 40 going east and take in Walnut Canyon National Monument for an awe-inspiring view of how Sinagua Indians lived in homes built out of the limestone cliffs. The Visitor Center Museum displays artefacts that make it possible to imagine how they existed.

Meteor Crater: 800 289 2362, www.meteorcrater.com. Nearby, this crater dates back 22,000 years when an enormous meteor travelling at 33,000mph/53,100kph plunged to Earth. Because of its resemblance to the lunar landscape, the 570ft/174m deep crater was used as a training site for Apollo astronauts and the museum displays a 1,406lb/638kg meteorite, the largest found in the area.

Petrified Forest: 928-524 6228, www.nps.gov/pefo. Further east is the Petrified Forest National Park and Painted Desert Visitor Center and Museum. There are more fossilised trees to be found here than anywhere else in the world with million-year-old agate logs lying in profusion on the ground.

Canyon de Chelly: 928 674 5500, www.nps.gov/cach. Further north on Route 191, you can view the Indian cliff-dwelling ruins at Canyon de Chelly National

15

Monument. At the base of sheer red cliffs and in canyon walls, the ruins date back to the 12th century and you can get to them on scenic rim drives, 4-wheel-drive vehicles, horseback or on foot. Phone the visitor center above for details. The area is rich with history, as the Anasazi Indians lived here until 1300 and the Navajo arrived in 1700, using it as a base to raid nearby Indian and Spanish settlements.

Monument Valley: 435 727 5874 or 928 871 6647, www.navajonationparks. org/htm/monumentvalley.htm. Take Highways 59 and 163 to see one of the best-used locations for filming Westerns such as John Wayne's Stagecoach. To the left of this area is the Navajo Nation, the largest of all the Indian reservations – extending across 25,000mls^2/64,750km^2, it is bigger than the state of West Virginia – which is home to around 175,000 Native Americans, who welcome visitors for sightseeing and shopping – buy silver and turquoise jewellery, exquisitely woven rugs, intricate kachinas and other crafts.

The land encompasses mile upon mile of desert and forest land, interrupted only by spectacular mesas, buttes and rock formations. The Navajos provide hiking, horseback and 4-wheel-drive tours through some of the most popular sites such as Canyon de Chelly and Monument Valley.

◀❚❱ BRITTIP
Did you know that more people have died of drowning in the desert than of thirst? It's all due to flash floods that are so violent and so sudden you have no time at all to react.

Lake Powell: 888 896 3829 or 928 645 2433, www.lakepowell.com. From this area, take Route 98 up to the shores of Lake Powell, a 25m acre/10m ha lake with more shoreline – 1,960mls/3,154km – than California, which was formed by

Monument Valley

the completion of the Glen Canyon Dam in 1963. Today it's a home for houseboats and pleasure craft that explore the 96 canyons discovered and mapped by intrepid, one-armed explorer John Wesley Powell in the 19th century.

Rainbow Bridge Natural Monument: 928 608 6200, www.nps.gov/rabr. A natural stone arch carved by the relentless forces of wind and water, the bridge only became easily accessible after the lake came into being. It is an amazing 290ft/88m high and 275ft/84m wide. Boat rentals, tours and accommodation are all available at the Wahweap Lodge and Marina on the lake's southern-most shore. For boat tour reservation to the bridge (marina is about 50m/65km away) phone 800 896 3829 or visit www.lakepowell.com.

Glen Canyon Dam: 928 608 6200, www.nps.gov/glca. Offers self-guided tours and day-long and half-day float trips along the Colorado river from the base of the dam, March–October. Phone for details. The town of Page, founded as a construction camp for crews building the dam, has plenty of restaurants and accommodation.

Cochise County: www.explorecochise. com (for a free visitors' guide). This southeast corner of Arizona is an 1800s Old West museum all by itself. This area is just a 1–2-hour drive from Tucson and includes such historical areas as Texas Canyon and Skeleton Canyon, where Geronimo waged war against the American Army with no more than 42 men. There is the old mining town of Tombstone, infamous for the gun battle between the Earps and the Clantons in the OK Corral. Finally, in Fort Huachuca lies the old museum and remains of Camp Huachuca, home to the famous Buffalo Soldiers, 2 regiments of freed African American slaves who battled Puma and Apache native tribes for decades.

Utah and the Wild West

Often overlooked thanks to the fame of the neighbouring Grand Canyon and Arizona, the south-western corner of Utah is home to an area known as the Grand Circle. Stunning national parks include Zion National Park, Kolob Canyons and Bryce Canyon. The Grand Circle also takes in Lake Powell and the Glen Canyon National Recreation Area, which straddles Utah and Arizona, and Nevada's Lake Mead National Recreational Area (see page 190).

Smith Valley

The beauty of Utah's natural wonders is matched by its sense of wilderness. Despite an increase in visitors, it is still an untamed environment with often only primitive facilities available, while the rich cowboy and outlaw history touches many sights and locations throughout the region.

Zion National Park

Within remarkably easy striking distance of Las Vegas, it takes just 2 hours to drive to the south-western end of the Grand Circle along Interstate 15 in the direction of St George. The entrance is on the south side just beyond the town of Springdale, where you will find the visitor center and 2 camping sites.

BRITTIP

Within Zion National Park is the Kolob Canyons area, which has its own Visitor Center.

Open: 435 772 3256, www.nps.gov/zion and zioncanyon.com. Park open daily. The Visitor Center is open year-round except Christmas Day, winter 8am–5pm, spring and autumn 8am–6pm and summer 8am–7.30pm, and provides everything from books, to information, maps, an introductory video and backcountry permits and even has a small museum.

Admission: 7-day pass $25 per car or $12 per person.

The natural rock sculptures and vividly coloured cliffs that tower above the floor of Zion Canyon pull in nearly 2.5 million visitors a year, making it one of the most popular sights in the region. To the Mormon pioneers who discovered it after the Paiute Indians had left, the beautiful rock structures so resembled natural temples they called it Little Zion. An early Methodist minister was so awe-struck that he gave many of the towers and cliffs that rise up 3,000ft/914m into the sky biblical names such as Three Patriarchs, Angels Landing and the Great White Throne.

Seeing the sights

Zion Canyon Scenic Drive: One of the easiest ways to appreciate its beauty is to take this 7ml/11km trek along the canyon floor – a narrow, deep gorge that is the centrepiece of the park, surrounded by wondrous monoliths that stand between 2,000ft/610m and 3,000ft/914m high. Along the bottom of the canyon flows the Virgin River. It may look small, yet it has the power of the once-mighty Colorado and is almost single-handedly responsible for carving the gorge – admittedly over a 13 million-year period! A round trip will take at least an hour and a half.

The Zion-Mount Carmel Highway: A 13ml/21km drive up steep switchbacks and through tunnels to Checkerboard Mesa. The road was considered an engineering marvel when it was completed in 1930 and cuts a swathe through rough up-and-down terrain to connect lower Zion Canyon with the high plateaux to the east.

Two narrow tunnels, including one over 1ml/1.6km long, were blasted through

15

the cliffs to complete the job. As you travel from one side of the tunnel to the other, the landscape changes dramatically. On one side are the massive cliff walls of Zion Canyon, on the other is an area known as Slickrock Country. Here rocks coloured in white and pastels of orange and red have been eroded into hundreds of fantastic shapes and etched through time with odd patterns of cracks and grooves. It is followed by the mountains of sandstone known as Checkerboard Mesa – one of the best examples of naturally sculptured rock art.

Ranger-led shuttle bus tour: These 2-hour trips run both morning and evening provide an intimate look at the Canyon – reservations are free, but must be made a day in advance at the visitor center.

Seasons in the sun

Each season provides a spectacular array of colours in Zion. Spring sees the waterfalls cascading into the Virgin River. Summer – easily the busiest time of year – is the time to enjoy the striking sight of the deep red cliffs peeking out above the lush green foliage. Come autumn those leaves turn brilliant red and gold, while in winter a layer of snow adds a pristine cleanliness to the rugged landscape.

BRITTIP
The best times to visit Zion National Park are May and September, when the weather is at its finest and the crowds are at their smallest.

Things to do

You can cycle, take a tram ride or go on a horse ride through the park, yet most people agree that the best way to experience the full majesty is to hike. Hiking and other relevant information is found in the Zion Map & Guide downloadable from the www.nps.gov/zion website. For adventurers with a bit more time, the backcountry (downloadable planner from the site) offers more opportunities for adventure in the form of canyoneering and climbing as well as backcountry hiking trails.

Guided walks: These are offered along fairly easy trails – some of which are accessible by wheelchair. A huge range of other hikes, from moderate to strenuous and one day or more are available, although all only accessed by shuttle bus,

so plan ahead. True adventurers, though, will want to do the 16ml/26km hike through The Narrows, in the backcountry, which involves wading through the Virgin River. Be aware, though, that advance preparation and a permit are necessary to do this.

Guided horse rides are available from early March to the end of October. Call 435 772 3810 for information or book a trip with Canyon Trail Rides (www.canyonrides.com) who offer 1.5-hour rides here.

BRITTIP
It is not advisable to drink untreated water from streams or springs. Water can be bought at the visitor center, campgrounds, Zion Lodge, Grotto Picnic Area and the Temple of Sinawa.

Bicycles: These are only permitted on established roads and the Pa'rus Trail, which leads from the campgrounds to the Scenic Drive junction.

Camping: This is allowed only in the campgrounds or in designated backcountry sites with a permit. The 3 campgrounds in Zion Canyon are South and Watchman, and Lava Point, which is about an hour's drive from the others. If visiting June–August, make sure you have a reservation.

Climbing: Information is available at the visitor center. But many of Zion's cliffs are sandstone with much loose or 'rotten' rock and climbing tools and techniques used for granite are often less effective here.

BRITTIP
Kolob Canyons may be lesser known than Zion Canyon but is just as spectacular, and uncrowded.

Kolob Canyons

In the north-western reaches of Zion National Park, just off Interstate 15 at Exit 40 about 45mls/72km from the entrance to Zion.

Open: Visitor Center: 435 586 9548, www.nps.gov/zion open 8am–4.30-6pm (depending on season) daily, apart from 26 November and Christmas Day.

Admission: $25 per vehicle for 7 days.

Kolob Canyons Road is one of 2 scenic routes, which provides stunning views of the spectacular finger canyons, carved out by springs along the edge of Kolob Terrace. It will take you 5mls/8km into the red rock, running perpendicular to the walled Finger

Canyons and providing a high viewpoint at the end.

The Kolob Terrace Road overlooks the white and salmon-coloured cliffs at the left and right forks of North Creek. Both routes climb into forests of pinyon and juniper, ponderosa pine and fir, while aspen trees are found at Lava Point. In early spring the Kolob is still buried under thick snow, and in summer there is still a feel of mountain coolness to the air. Hikes and ranger-led activities are also available here, visit www.utah.com/nationalparks/zion/kolob_canyons.htm for ideas.

BRITTIP

Did you know **127 Hours** was filmed in Utah's stunning Blue John's Canyon? If you fancy an adventure, with a happy ending, get in touch with Zion Adventures 435 772 1001, www.zionadventures.com

Lodging in Zion National Park

Zion Lodge, 303-297 2757, www.zionlodge.com
Open year-round and provides a choice of motel rooms, cabins and suites. It is the only lodge in the park and the only restaurant. There is also a gift shop and post office and access to hiking trails and horse riding.

Lodging in Springdale: The Zion Park City

Conveniently, the Zion shuttle leaves from Springdale where these lodgings are all located.

Bumbleberry Inn: 97 Bumbleberry Lane, Springdale. 800 828 1534 or 435 772 3224, www.bumbleberry.com. Large, spacious rooms with private balconies or patios overlooking wonderful scenery in a quiet, off-road location. Facilities include a heated pool, indoor Jacuzzi, indoor racquetball, games room, restaurant and gift shop.

Canyon Ranch Motel: 668 Zion Park Boulevard, Springdale 866 946 6276 or 435 772 3357, www.canyonranchmotel. com. Recently-built and remodelled cottages, some with kitchens, around a quiet, shady lawn with panoramic views of Zion characterise this motel just 0.5ml/800m from the park entrance. Amenities include a pool and Jacuzzi.

Cliffrose Lodge & Gardens: 281 Zion Park Boulevard, Springdale. 800 243 8824 or 435 772 3234, www.cliffroselodge.com. At the entrance to Zion National Park along the Virgin River. All rooms have excellent views, while there is also a large pool and 5acres/2ha of lawns, trees and flower gardens.

Lodging in Rockville

Hummingbird Inn B&B: 37 West Main, Rockville, 800 964 BIRD or 435 772 3632, www.sites.infowest.com/hummingbird, on Highway 9, just 3mls/5km from the entrance to Zion National Park. All 4 guestrooms have private baths and a large country breakfast is included. The inn has a Jacuzzi plus an upstairs deck and a library/games room loft. Outside activities include croquet, horseshoes and badminton.

Lodging in Hurricane

Half-way between Zion National Park and St George. Visitor info 435 635 3402.

Pah Tempe Hot Springs: 825 North 800 East, 35–4 Hurricane, 888 726 8367 or 435 635 2879, www.site.infowest.com/business/g/gentle/springs.html. A tiny retreat where no smoking or alcohol is allowed, but where massage and therapy programmes are available, plus a relaxing hot mineral pool along the Virgin River.

Park Villa Motel 6: 650 West State Street, 435 635 2164. Luxury units with fridge and microwave, just 1ml/1.6km from mineral hot springs. Facilities include heated pool and spa, laundry, kitchen and cable TV.

Bryce Canyon

1 888 467 2757, www.nps.gov/brca and www.nationalparks.org
72mls/116km from Zion National Park. Follow Highway 89 towards Hatch, then turn into Highway 12 to Bryce village and the Visitor Center is just inside the entrance on Highway 63.

Open: Visitor center 435 834 5322. Open 8am–8pm May–Sept, 8am–6pm Oct, 8am–4.30pm Nov–Mar, 8am–6pm April except Thanksgiving, Christmas and New Year's Day. Provides information, books and backcountry permits. The park is open 24 hours daily except as above.

A short introductory video on the park is shown on the hour and the half hour and short geology talks are given in the visitor center museum.

Admission: 7-day pass $25 per vehicle, $12 per person. You can buy a National Parks Pass by phone or from the website.

15

BRITTIP

The best times to see large mammals in Bryce Canyon are summer mornings and evenings in roadside meadows.

Hoodoos and other formations

Bryce Canyon National Park consists of 37,277acres/15,085ha of scenic, colourful rock formations and wonderful desert and has been home to Indian tribes – including the Anasazi and Fremont – for about 12,000 years. The most recent tribe to inhabit the region was the Paiute, who were still here when explorers John Wesley Powell and Captain Clarence E Dutton 'discovered' the area in the 1870s.

In 1875, Ebenezer Bryce settled in the Paria Valley to harvest timber from the plateau and neighbours called the nearby canyon Bryce's Canyon – a name that stuck!

The canyon is a geological wonder – home to a series of horseshoe-shaped amphitheatres carved from the eastern edge of the Paunsugunt Plateau. Erosion has shaped colourful Calron limestones, sandstones and mudstones into thousands of spires, pinnacles and fins that together provide unique formations known as hoodoos.

The Paiutes called the hoodoos Legend People who had been turned to stone by coyote because of their evil ways. In fact, they are fantastically shaped and incredibly tall pillars of rock that have been created by a series of massive land movements and river erosions.

Thor's Hammer

The result is a geological paradise filled as it is with wonderful examples of the effects of sedimentation from both fresh and sea water, erosion through wind, water and ice and earthquake and volcanic action over a period of millions and millions of years. The plateaux, staggering vertical columns, gullies and canyons are a joy to behold, while the high elevations – between 6,000ft/1,830m and 9,000ft/2,740m – provide panoramic views of 3 states and a perfect spot for stargazers.

Sights to look out for: The monoliths of Thor's Hammer, Deformation, Uplift and the Grand Staircase.

Nature's way

The differing and diverse soil and moisture conditions throughout Bryce Canyon have allowed more than 400 species of wild flower to grow including rare gentian, bellflower, yarrow, gilia, sego lily and manzanita.

The meadows and forests are also home to many animals from foxes to deer, coyote, mountain lions and black bears. Elk and pronghorn antelope, reintroduced nearby, can also sometimes be spotted in the park.

On top of that there are more than 160 bird species who visit the park every year. Most migrate to warmer climates in the winter, but those that stay include jays, nuthatches, ravens, eagles and owls.

Scenic drives

A scenic drive along the 18mls/30km of the main park road affords outstanding views of the park and southern Utah scenery. From many overlooks you can see further than 100mls/160km on clear days.

Rainbow or Yovimpa Points: On crisp winter days, views from Rainbow or Yovimpa Points are restricted only by the curvature of the Earth. Driving south from the Visitor Center to Rainbow Point, you gradually climb 1,100ft/335m. En route you will notice how the pines change to spruce, fir and aspen. Both points provide magnificent views of a large chunk of southern Utah. On most days you can see Navajo Mountain and the Kaibab Plateau, which is 90mls/145km away in Arizona. On the clearest day you can even see as far as New Mexico. In the foreground are the colours of the long-eroded slopes and remnant hoodoos. While you are here, search out The Poodle to the north west of Rainbow Point, and the Pink Cliffs behind it.

The park road ends at Rainbow Point with a road loop that turns you back

Arches National Park

towards the park entrance. In 2009, a free guided roundtrip shuttle bus tour was introduced along this route, 11am–3pm, 22 May–13 Sep.

Agua Canyon: This displays some of the best contrasts of light and colour in the park. Look for small trees atop a hoodoo known as the Hunter, while in the distance you will also be able to see the rims of southern plateaux and canyons.

BRITTIP

Picnic tables, water and WCs are available at Sunset Point, Yovimpa Point and the south end of the north campsites. There are also picnic tables along the road to Rainbow Point, but no amenities.

Fairyland Canyon/Point: This offers stunning views of the Fairyland Amphitheater and its fanciful shapes, the Sinking Ship, Aquarius Plateau and Navajo Mountain in the distance. Because Fairyland Canyon lies between the entrance station and the park boundary, and 1ml/1.6km off the main road, many visitors miss this viewpoint, yet it has some of the most spectacular views in the park.

Farview Point: This provides a panoramic view of the neighbouring plateaux and mountains and far to the south-east even the Kaibab Plateau of the Grand Canyon's North Rim. The Natural Bridge is actually

an arch that was formed by the combined forces of rain and frost erosion rather than the work of a stream.

Paria View: This looks out across hoodoos in an amphitheatre carved by Yellow Creek. The Paria River valley and Table Cliffs Plateau form the backdrop. To the south, the White Cliffs, weathered out of Navajo sandstone, can also be seen.

Ponderosa Canyon: This area reveals a series of multi-coloured hoodoos that are framed by pine-covered foothills and the Table Cliffs Plateau to the north.

Bryce Amphitheatre: The Sunrise, Sunset, Inspiration and Bryce Points ring Bryce Amphitheatre, the largest natural amphitheatre in the park. The Queen's Garden Trail begins at Sunrise Point. From Sunset Point, you can hike to Thor's Hammer and Wall Street. Inspiration Point offers the best view of the Silent City. The Under-the-Rim Trail begins at Bryce Point. From each point you can see as far as the Black Mountains in the north-east and Navajo Mountain in the south.

Things to do

You can avoid driving round the park by using the shuttle bus system, which has 3 different shuttle lines and leaves every 13–30 minutes depending on the time of day 6th May–9th Oct in 2011. The Visitor Center provides details of birding, camping, hiking, photography, star gazing,

15

wildlife watching and trail rides. At the Visitor Center, you can see a film about the park and also get a schedule to join a National Park Service ranger to explore the Canyon's natural and cultural history and learn about the forces that shaped the landscape.

Cycling is only allowed on paved roads and there are no mountain biking trails.

Guided horse rides are available in the morning and afternoon April–Oct. For details contact The Lodge at Bryce Canyon (877 386 4383, www.brycecanyonforever.com) or Canyon Trail Rides (435 679 8665, www.canyonrides.com). Easy to strenuous hikes and backcountry hiking (for which a permit is required) are detailed on the website. One of the most adventurous, and spectacular, is the 23-ml/37km Under-the Rim-Trail, with camping en route, from Bryce Point to Rainbow Point. In winter, snowshoes or cross-country skis can be rented outside the park to tackle the plateau top.

Lodging in Bryce Canyon and Bryce

The Lodge at Bryce Canyon (877 386 4383, www.brycecanyonforever.com). The only hotel accommodation inside the canyon, Bryce Canyon Lodge has 114 rooms including suites, motel rooms and cabins. The lodge also has a restaurant, gift shop and post office. There are also 2 campsites in the canyon itself, while backcountry camping is possible for a fee of $5.

Best Western Ruby's Inn: 26 South Main, Highway 63, Bryce Canyon City, 866 866 6616 or 435 834 5341, www.rubysinn.com. Has 370 rooms including 2 suites and handicapped rooms. All rooms are non-smoking. Facilities include in-room spa, cable TV, indoor swimming pool, spa, hot tub, restaurants, general store, gallery, internet access and gift shops. Also offers trail rides, scenic flights, mountain biking, chuckwagon cookouts, rodeo, ATV rides and cross-country skiing.

Bryce Canyon Pines Motel: Highway 12 Milepost 10, Bryce, 800 892 7923, www.brycecanyonmotel.com. Has 51 rooms including cottages, 2 rooms with kitchenette and a room for the disabled. Facilities include a restaurant, swimming pool and spa, gift shop, campsite and day-long horse riding trips with real cowboys.

Bryce Pioneer Village: 89 South Main Street, Tropic, Bryce, 435 679 8546, www.brycepioneervillage.com. This wooden western-style hotel open seasonally offers rooms, cabins - some with kitchenette – and tent sites for wannabe cowboys. In 13 acres, outdoor activities can be arranged from here and amenities include an on-site dinner theatre and outdoor fire pit.

Death Valley National Park

From Las Vegas you can reach the park's southern end via Highway 95, which takes you to Amargosa Valley and Death Valley Junction. You can also get there by heading to Pahrump and then following the State Line Road to Death Valley Junction.

◄✚► **BRITTIP**
Death Valley tours are not cheap but they do offer a great first-hand experience if you want to see it close up!

Furnace Creek Information Center

Furnace Creek Resort Area on California Highway 190, CA, 760 786 3200, www.nps.gov/deva
Open: daily 8am–5pm

Death Valley is the largest of all America's national parks outside of Alaska and covers more than 5,156mls^2/13,354km^2. At the bottom of the 300-ml/483-km long Sierra Nevada mountain range that stretches to Lake Tahoe in the north, it is the hottest place on Earth. In summer the average temperature is 45°C/113°F and the rocks almost reach water-boiling point. The lowest point – 282ft/86m below sea level – in all of America is in the heart of the Valley.

Wimps can visit in March and April when it is just 18°C/64°F and admire the desert spring blooms that shoot out of the sculpted rocks. But let's face it, the whole point of going to Death Valley is to drive through it at the hottest time of year! I would, however, advise giving yourself – and your car – an even chance of making it across in one piece by setting off early in the morning and making sure both your car radiator – and you – have plenty of water.

The National Parks of California warn you not to stop your car in the heat of the day (it'll probably not restart until nighttime) and don't drive too quickly, again to prevent overheating. Always ensure you have enough petrol as stations are thin on the ground, but can be found at Furnace Creek, Stovepipe Wells, Scotty's Castle and Panamint Springs.

Just bear in mind that if you do break down you'll be on your own for some time as there is no public transport in the Valley and not many Americans are daft enough (mad dogs and Englishmen and all that) to go through in the summer. However, if you're sensible you will survive and will be amazed by the breathtaking beauty of the miles and miles of sand and rocks that have been hardened into a sea-like landscape by the melting sun.

◀▶ BRITTIP

Death Valley may be the extreme when it comes to heat, but summer in all the regions surrounding Las Vegas is very hot, so always ensure you have plenty of water with you – dehydration is a real danger.

The main sights include Furnace Creek, the ruins of Harmony Borax Works, Zabriskie Point with its gorgeously golden hills that are best seen at sunrise or sunset, Badwater and the amazing heights of Dante's View where you get precisely that – a spectacular vista of the white salt lakes that stretch to the Panamint Mountains.

Other sights include Scotty's Castle, an incongruous mansion retreat built for American millionaire Albert Johnson in the 1920s, Ubehebe Crater, a 500ft/152m deep hole, which is all that remains of a volcano, the 700-ft/213-m high Eureka sand dunes and Racetrack Valley, so named because it is a dry mud flat covered in wind-blown boulders.

If you're mad enough to go hiking, try the 14ml/22.5km round trip to the top of Telescope Peak, which does at least get cooler as you get higher!

Some people opt to stay at Furnace Creek, though I can't see the point of being boiled alive for quite so long! However, if you do wish to stay, head for the rustic **Furnace Creek Ranch** (800 236 7916 or 760 786 2345, www.furnacecreekresort. com) which has 224 rooms and a pool, stables, restaurant, bar, shop, tennis courts and even an 18-hole golf course – the lowest anywhere on Earth!

Mammoth Lakes

Mammoth Lakes Visitors Bureau: toll free in the US 888-466 2666, from elsewhere 760 934 2712, www.visitmammoth.com

A short 1.5-hour drive north of Big Pine in Death Valley National Park on Highways 190 and 136 is the majestic world of Mammoth Lakes. At the gateway to Yosemite, it is one of the best places in the Sierra Nevada for outdoor activities and is second only to Tahoe as a ski resort in winter. The magical setting and 50ml/80km trail make it popular with mountain bikers, while expert guides offer climbing, kayaking and hang-gliding. The Mammoth Shuttle on 760 934 2571 ext 9238 is good for getting around.

The whole area is also good for golf, canoeing, swimming and searching out wildlife, gold mines and ghost towns. Recent investment in Mammoth Mountain mean there is now an 18-hole championship golf course and a pedestrian resort, Gondola Village, with shops, restaurants, a skating pond and gondola, which connects the centre of town to the heart of the mountain for unmissable views.

Lodgings include: Shilo Inn Mammoth Lakes (2963 Main Street, 0800 222 2244 or 760 934 4500, www.shilo-inn-mammoth-lakes.com); Mammoth Mountain Inn (1 Minaret Road, 800 626 6684 or 760 934 2581, www.mammothmountain.com) and Sierra Nevada Lodge (164 Old Mammoth Road, 800 824 5132 or 760 934 2515, www.sierranevadalodge.com). Or write to the Mammoth Lakes Visitor Bureau at PO Box 48, Mammoth Lakes, CA 93546 (760 934 2712, www.visitmammoth.com) for a free vacation planner.

Other useful contacts: Devil's Postpile National Monument (760 934 2289, www.nps.gov/depo); Mammoth Museum (5489 Sherwin Creek Road, 760 934 6918); Mammoth Mountain Bike Park and Adventure Challenge Course (800 626 6684 or 760 934 2571, www. mammothmountain.com); Mammoth Mountain Ski Resort (760 934 2571, www.mammothmountain.com) and Tamarack Cross-Country Ski Area at Mammoth Lakes (760 934 2442, www.tamaracklodge.com/Ski_Center).

Yosemite National Park

This has to be one of the most stunning natural sights in America. Mile-high cliffs gouged out by glaciers thousands of years ago are topped with pinnacles and domes from which waterfalls cascade. Coyotes and black bears roam the valley floor, which is never more than 1ml/1.6km wide. In winter, roads in the park get blocked by snow and in summer by the thousands of visitors who flock to the area. It takes at least half a day to tour the Yosemite Valley, but would take 2 days to see all the sites and areas.

15

Open: The Park is open all day, every day during daylight hours although some areas are closed due to snow Nov–May. The Valley Visitor Center 209 372 0200, www.nps.gov/yose is the only visitor center open year round, 9am–5pm daily. It can give you all the latest information on park and surrounding road conditions (essential at all times except summer), transport, recreation, lodging, camping and dining options.

Admission: $20 per car or $10 per person, for 7-day pass

More info: www.yosemite.national-park.com; www.yosemite.com

Yosemite Sierra Visitors Bureau: 41969 Highway 41, Oakhurst 93644, 559 683 4636, www.yosemitethisyear.com.

Open: 8.30am–5pm Mon–Sat; 9am–1pm Sun.

Full details of mountain biking, fishing, boating at Bass Lake, steam train, the historic park and Native American museums are available here. Write to them for a visitors' guide. Guided tours, including trips around the valley and into the mountains, are bookable through most of the hotels in the area.

BRITTIP
Fill up with petrol on your way into Yosemite as there are no petrol stations in the park.

Yosemite View Lodge: Yosemite Motels, 11136 Highway 140, El Portal, CA 95338, 888 742 4371 or 209 379 2861, www.yosemiteresortsus.com. Adjacent to the wild and scenic Merced River, Camp Grizzly opened early in 1999. Based on a theme of a 1950s summer camp, it provides educational nature trails, barbecue-style dining, country line dancing and other special events. Contact them to book and get more information on motels in the area.

BRITTIP
Some roads close from late autumn to early summer – check in advance and have tyre chains at the ready for sudden falls of snow if driving in winter.

Other useful numbers: Yosemite Mountain Sugar Pine Railroad (559 683 7273, www.ymsprr.com) which runs steam trains through the Sierra National Forest near Yosemite Park; Yosemite Sightseeing Tours (559 642 4400 or toll free 800 585 0565, www.yosemitetours.com); All-Outdoors Whitewater Trips (800 247 2387, aorafting.com) for half, 1-, 2- and 3-day rafting trips April–Nov; and Whitewater Voyages (800 400 7238, www.whitewatervoyages.com) for wonderful runs down the Merced with guides, food and equipment.

Deer Springs

SAFETY FIRST

Safety, insurance, hints and tips on making the best of your holiday

No one wants to think about anything going wrong with their dream holiday, but it is worth thinking about a few commonsense aspects of safety and security so that you can avoid any preventable problems.

General hints and tips

Don't allow your dream trip to Las Vegas and beyond to be spoilt by not taking the right kind of precautions, be they for personal safety or of a medical nature.

In the sun

Let's face it, most Brits tend to travel to America at the hottest time of the year – the summer – and most are unprepared for the sheer intensity of the sun. Before you even think about going out for the day, apply a high-factor sunblock, as it is very easy to get sunburnt when you are walking around, sightseeing or shopping. Reapply regularly throughout the day. It is also a good idea to wear a hat or scarf to protect your head from the sun, especially at the hottest time of the day, 11am–3pm, so you do not get sunstroke. If it is windy, you may be lulled into thinking that it is not as hot, but this is a dangerous illusion – especially in the desert valley of Las Vegas! If you are spending

Rio Las Vegas

the day by the pool, it is advisable to use a sunshade at the hottest time of the day, and apply waterproof sunblock regularly, even when you are in the pool, as the UV rays travel through water. Always make sure you have plenty of fluids with you when travelling. Water is best. Try to avoid alcohol during the day, as this will have an additional dehydrating effect.

Paris Las Vegas

At your hotel

In America, your hotel room number is your main source of security. It is often your passport to eating and collecting messages, so keep the number safe and secure. When checking in, make sure none of the hotel staff mentions your room number out loud. If they do, give them back the key and ask them to give you a new room and to write down the new room number instead of announcing it (most hotels follow this practice in any case). When you need to give someone your room number – for instance when charging a dinner or any other bill to your room – write it down or show them your room card rather than calling it out.

When in your hotel room, always use the deadlocks and security chains and use the door peephole before opening the door to strangers. If someone knocks on the door and cannot give any identification, phone down to the hotel reception desk.

When you go out, make sure you lock the windows and door properly. Even if you leave your room just for a few seconds, lock the door.

◀▶ **BRITTIP**
Use a business address rather than your home address on all your luggage.

Cash and documents

Most hotels in tourist areas have safety deposit boxes, so use these to store important documents such as airline tickets and passports. When you go out, do not take all your cash and credit cards with you – always have at least one credit card in the safe as an emergency back-up and only take enough cash with you for the day. Using a money belt is also a good idea. Keep a separate record of your travellers' cheque numbers. If your room does not have its own safe, leave your valuables in the main hotel safe.

Emergencies

For the police, fire department or ambulance, dial 911 (9-911 from your hotel room).

If you need medical help in Las Vegas, there are 3 main options, all of which are open 24 hours a day, 7 days a week: **Harmon Medical Center**, 150 East Harmon Avenue (702 796 1116, www. harmonmedicalcenter.com); **Fremont**

Medical Center, 4880 South Wynn Road (on the corner of Tropicana and Wynn, 702 871 5005, www.fmcnv.com); and **University Medical Center (UMC) Hospital**, 1800 W Charleston Boulevard (702 383 2000, www.umcsn.com).

Cars

Most of the advice is obvious, but when we go on holiday we sometimes relax to the point of not using our basic common sense. Never leave your car unlocked and never leave any valuable items on the car seats or anywhere else where they can be seen.

Travel insurance

When travelling anywhere around America the one thing you should not forget is travel insurance. Medical cover is very expensive and if you are involved in any kind of an accident you could be sued, which is very costly indeed in America.

If you do want to make savings in this area, don't avoid getting insurance cover, but do avoid buying it from tour operators, as they are notoriously expensive.

The alternative, particularly if you plan to make more than one trip in any given year, is to go for an annual worldwide policy directly from insurers. The worldwide annual policies can make even more sense if you're travelling as a family.

In all cases, you need to ensure that the policy gives you the following cover:

- **Actual coverage of the United States** – not all plans include America

- **Medical** cover of at least £2m in America

- **Personal liability** cover of at least £2m in America

- **Cancellation and curtailment** cover of around £3,000 in case you are forced to call off your holiday

- **Lost baggage and belongings** cover at around £1,500 – most premiums only offer cover for individual items up to around £250, so you will need additional cover for expensive cameras or camcorders

- **Cash cover** (usually around £200) and documents including your air tickets, passport and currency

- **24-hour helpline** to make it easy for you to get advice and instructions on what to do

- **Membership of the Financial Ombudsman Service** in case you are unhappy with the outcome of a claim.

Check and check again

Shop around: You do not have to buy your policy from your tour operator, so don't let them include it as a matter of course. You will almost certainly be able to get a better deal elsewhere.

Read the policy: Always ask for a copy of the policy document before you go and if you are not happy with the cover offered, cancel and demand your premium back – in some cases you will only have 7 days in which to do this.

Don't double up on cover: If you have an 'all risks' policy on your home contents, this will cover your property outside the home and may even cover lost money and credit cards. Check if this covers you abroad – and covers your property when in transit – before buying personal possessions cover.

Look at gold card cover: Some bank gold cards provide you with insurance cover if you buy your air ticket with the gold card, so it is worth checking, although there will be terms and conditions.

BRITTIP

Put away maps and brochures in the glove compartment, as these will be obvious signs that yours is a tourist's car.

Check dangerous sports cover: In almost all cases mountaineering, racing and hazardous pursuits such as bungee jumping, skydiving, horse riding, windsurfing, trekking and even cycling are not included in normal policies. There are so many opportunities to do all of these activities that you really should ensure you are covered before you go. Backpackers and dangerous sports enthusiasts can try Insure & Go (0844 888 2787, www.insureandgo.com). Direct Travel Insurance (0845 605 2700, www. direct-travel.co.uk) is also an excellent place to look for travel insurance. It specialises in insurance for backpackers aged 18–35 and the cover includes walking holidays, sports and activities, skiing and scuba diving, bungee jumping and abseiling; as does Leading Edge (01892 836622, www. leadedge.co.uk).

Make sure you qualify: For instance, if you have been treated in hospital in the 6 months prior to travelling or are waiting for hospital treatment, you may need medical evidence that you are fit to travel. Ask your doctor for a report giving you the all-clear (you will have to pay for this) and if the insurance company still says your condition is not covered, shop around.

Insurance policies

This is a competitive market, so it pays to shop around to find the best policy for you. Some companies offer discounts if you already have another policy with them. These companies are worth checking out for annual-cover or single-trip travel insurance.

To compare deals, visit www. moneysupermarket.com or phone 0845 345 5708. It has cheap deals from more than 450 policies to compare online, with links directly through for purchasing. You can also compare leading providers of the most comprehensive deals at www.top4deals.com.

- **Atlas Direct** 0844 482 3400, www.atlasdirect.net.
- **Citybond Travel** 0845 618 0345, www.citybond.co.uk.
- **Clydesdale Bank** 0845 602 6917, www.cbonline.co.uk
- **CostOut** 0844 980 0271, www.costout.co.uk.
- **Direct Travel** 0845 605 2700, www.direct-travel.co.uk.
- **Flexicover Direct** 0800 093 9495, www.flexicover.co.uk
- **Giles Insurance Brokers** 01332 693 200, www.gilesinsurance.co.uk
- **Leading Edge** 01892 836622, www.leadedge.co.uk
- **Marks & Spencer Financial Services** 0800 068 3918, www.money.marksandspencer.com
- **More Than** 0800 980 5573, www.morethan.com
- **MRL Insurance Direct** 0845 676 0691, www.mrlinsurance.co.uk
- **Nationwide BS** 08456 40 59 30, www.nationwide.co.uk
- **TravelPlan Direct** 0870 412 3110, www.travelplandirectinsurance.com
- **Worldwide Insure** 01892 833338, www.worldwideinsure.com
- **Zurich** 08000 966 233, www.zurich.co.uk

Other useful contacts

- **Association of British Insurers (ABI):** 020 7600 3333, www.abi.org.uk
- **Financial Ombudsman Service:** 0800 023 4567, www.financial-ombudsman.org.uk

16

INDEX

Major page references are in **bold** - A=Attraction
H=Hotel S=Show